Edinburgh University Library

Books may be recalled for return earlier than due date;
if so you will be contacted by e-mail or letter.

D1758622

Due Date	Due Date	Due Date
2 2 DEC 2008		

Edinburgh University Library

Books may be recalled for return earlier than due date;
if so you will be contacted by e-mail or letter.

30150 023820993

The Later Prehistory of the
Western Isles of Scotland

The Later Prehistory of the
Western Isles of Scotland

Ian Armit

EDINBURGH UNIVERSITY LIBRARY
WITHDRAWN

TEMPVS REPARATVM

BAR British Series 221
1992

B.A.R.

All volumes available from:
BAR, 122 Banbury Road, Oxford OX2 7BP, England

The current BAR catalogue, with details of all titles in print, post-free prices and means of payment, is available free from the above address.

All volumes are distributed by BAR.

BAR−221

Armit I 1992

The Later Prehistory of the Western Isles of Scotland

© I Armit 1992

ISBN 0 86054 731 0

Tempvs Reparatvm Volume Editor: John W Hedges

British Archaeological Reports are published by

TEMPVS REPARATVM
Archaeological and Historical Associates Limited

All enquiries regarding the submission of manuscripts for future publication should be addressed to:

David P Davison MA MPhil DPhil
General Editor BAR
Tempvs Reparatvm
29 Beaumont Street   Tel: 0865 311046
Oxford OX1 2NP   Fax: 0865 311047

Acknowledgements

The research which forms the basis of this monograph could not have been carried out without the help of a number of individuals and institutions. Prof. Dennis W Harding, who supervised my original thesis research, provided help and encouragement at all stages. I am also indebted to the following:

Prof L Alcock, John Barber, Gordon Barker, Alan Braby, Dr Joanna Close-Brooks, Trevor Cowie, Prof B Cunliffe, Steve Dockrill, Bill Finlayson, Andy Foxon, Elizabeth Fraser, Lord and Lady Granville, John Hedges, Heather James, Dr. Alan Lane, Dr Euan MacKie, Dr Ann Morton, Dr Ian Ralston, Jack Scott, David Shaughnessy, Beverley Smith, Pat Storey, Gordon Thomas, Dr Patrick Topping, Dr T Watkins and the staff of the NMRS and NMAS.

I am grateful to the Society of Antiquaries of Scotland, the Prehistoric Society and Glasgow Archaeological Journal for permission to reproduce illustrations from their respective journals, and to Chris Tabraham and Historic Scotland for permission to reproduce the plan of the excavations at Dun Carloway.

Final thanks must go to Diane Nelson for her tireless assistance with the preparation of the illustrations and for proof-reading the text.

The research was carried out during the tenure of a Major Scottish Studentship awarded by the Scottish Education Department.

Abstract

This study aims to establish an understanding of the nature of settlement development in the Western Isles in the period from c.1000 BC - 800 AD. A new classification of the sites is formulated to deal with the specific Hebridean context and with the restrictions of the available evidence. This provides a framework for analysis and replaces previous schemes, imported from elsewhere in Scotland, which have tended to confuse the settlement patterns and the settlement development of the area.

The large number of older excavations are reassessed in the light of both new approaches to classification and interpretation, and the evidence of recent survey and excavation. A coherent settlement sequence can be seen to emerge, showing a development of monumental architecture in the mid-1st millennium BC from a background of non-monumental domestic settlement: this monumentality persists for several centuries in the form of the atlantic roundhouses and wheelhouses before being gradually replaced by non-monumental, cellular and linear structures in the 1st millennium AD.

Structural, locational and spatial analyses combine to demonstrate patterns of settlement development which show the progressive adaptation of Hebridean populations to the changing socio-economic context. The development of architecture is linked to social and economic processes. The environmental context of settlement development appears to shape broad trends of settlement development, while the specific responses of human groups indicate the importance of social factors.

The final part of the study proposes models for the interpretation of settlement change. Material culture, including architecture, can be seen to be used actively in the negotiation of social relationships, both within the islands and between the islanders and the emerging states of Scotland in the 1st millennium AD.

Note

This monograph is based on research originally undertaken for a PhD thesis at Edinburgh University on <u>Later Prehistoric Settlement in the Western Isles of Scotland</u> (1990). The text has undergone significant alterations in the transition from thesis to monograph. Some of the work from the thesis has since been published elsewhere - for example, the analysis of the chronology of the Atlantic Scottish Iron Age now published in Armit 1991. Such material has been removed from the present study. Perhaps the main alteration has been the removal of much of the negative evidence in the later chapters on structural, locational and spatial analysis.

iii

Contents

List of Illustrations

Chapter One - Introduction

General

The later prehistoric settlement sites of the Western Isles form part of one of the richest archaeological landscapes in north-west Europe. The quantity of preserved sites and the quality of individual site preservation are outstanding even in the context of Highland Britain. The richness of the artefactual record, relative to the rest of Scotland, in association with this settlement record, further enhances the research potential of the area. The islands share these features with much of Atlantic Scotland but here the degree of landscape preservation, the absence of later agricultural damage, and the relative lack of exploitation by early antiquarians, increase the archaeological potential. The lack of modern syntheses and the absence of credible models for settlement development in the islands have prevented the full realisation of the area's potential.

Definition of terms

Later prehistory

I have taken later prehistory in the Western Isles to comprise the 1st millennium BC and the 1st millennium AD prior to 800 AD, the conventional beginning of the Norse period. This definition requires some defence. There is no settlement evidence securely dated to the late 2nd millennium BC or to the early 1st millennium BC and this period forms a notable gap in the settlement record of the islands. The Beaker settlements at Northton (Simpson 1966) and the Udal (Crawford 1985), dated to c. 1700 - 1500bc, are not succeeded by any known, full Bronze Age settlement sites in the Western Isles. The next settlement which can be reasonably securely dated comes from the pre-roundhouse occupation on the islet in Loch Bharabhat, Valtos, Lewis in the mid-1st millennium BC, with a C-14 date of 600 ± 50bc (App. 1). While there is some evidence for the construction and use of funerary monuments in the intervening period, the evidence is sparse.

This settlement break isolates the early part of Hebridean prehistory, the Neolithic and Beaker periods (in the absence of known Palaeolithic and Mesolithic occupation), from the later part. The character of the archaeological record for the later part of the prehistoric period in the islands is entirely different from that of the earlier; from the mid-1st millennium onwards settlement archaeology is dominant, in sharp contrast to the funerary bias of the earlier periods. A notional date of 1000 BC can be set for the start of the present study and as a convenient, though not in itself significant, date for the beginning of the later prehistoric period. Later prehistory in this sense comprises the periods often referred to in the literature as the Late Bronze Age, the Iron Age and the Dark Age, Early Christian, Early Historic or Pictish periods.

Recent excavations have hinted at links between the settlement patterns of the earlier and later prehistoric periods in the islands (e.g. Armit 1988b) and the settlement break may well be the result of research priorities in the past. I will examine aspects of this problem later. Nonetheless the definition of the Hebridean Late Bronze Age, Iron Age and Dark Ages as a relatively coherent later prehistoric period is a useful analytical device.

The date of 800 AD for the end of the study marks the conventional approximate date of Norse incursions and settlement. The evidence from the Western Isles themselves for the nature of these incursions is very slight. Norse material culture and settlement forms are sufficiently distinct to prevent confusion with late pre-Norse settlement (Lane 1983) and discussion of the Norse material will be restricted to the nature of its impact on native societies.

Western Isles

The Western Isles are defined as the modern political and administrative unit of that name comprising the Long Island, from Lewis in the north to the smaller islands to the south of Barra i.e. the Outer Hebrides (Ill. 1.1). The islands of this group are closely linked to each other by short sea crossings and form a coherent geographical unit. The islands of the St. Kilda group have not been included.

Aims of the study

The later prehistoric archaeology of the Western Isles is essentially an archaeology of settlements. The great majority of known later prehsitoric sites are settlement sites, often centred on structures of monumental character. Other types of site undoubtedly exist but are currently undateable. Land divisions, for example, fall into this category, as do many midden sites and possibly many undated burials. The most useful approach to the period at present is through the study of settlement sites and the material derived from them.

A central aim of this study is to disentangle the mass of settlement evidence for the Western Isles in the later prehistoric period which has been subject in the past to classification systems imported from other areas. I will argue that these systems have prevented an unbiased evaluation of settlement types and patterns in the area and have led to a stagnated prehistory. Inappropriate frameworks for the evidence have hindered the design of appropriate research programmes and appropriate targeting of rescue priorities.

The first task is to structure a classification system designed for utility within the area, which is sufficiently flexible to avoid stifling future interpretation. From there, we can approach a relative chronology and examination of the functional, chronological and structural relationships between settlements. A provisional chronology of associated material culture can also be attempted.

The second task is to formulate models which deal with developing settlement patterns in the area and which can provide a starting point for future research designs in the absence of current serious or credible models. The achievment of the first aim is a prerequisite for this.

Ill. 1.1 Western Isles: Location Map

A Hebridean approach

The approach taken to the material in this study is to examine monuments in relation to their context; this includes environmental context, the context of past archaeological interpretation, and particularly the context of inter-site relationships. It is a specifically Hebridean approach. The relationships with monuments outwith the Western Isles have formed almost the sole classificatory and analytical tool in the past. It is a deliberate decision, within this study, to bring in outside comparisons at a secondary stage in analysis rather than at the primary stage of site classification and the attribution of function and chronology. I will discuss the reasons for this decision in Chapter Four.

This approach can usefully be contrasted with that described by Iain Crawford for his work at the Udal, North Uist, most specifically stated in his pamphlet of 1985. Crawford explicitly set out, at the Udal in 1963, to initiate a long-term excavation which would provide an archaeological sequence of structures and artefacts, analogous to a pollen core through the whole prehistoric sequence, giving a sample of the cultural development of the area from the earliest occupation until c.1700 AD. In his 1985 publication Crawford claims to have achieved the aim of setting up a sequence of material culture by reference to which other sites can be dated and assessed when the Udal is published. The statement that "almost all significant new archaeological information .... is produced by excavation" (Crawford 1985, 17) underlies Crawford's approach. Crawford's view of the archaeological record is that it forms in a continuous and unchanging way akin

to the uniform deposition of types of environmental evidence; the only valid archaeological objective, as seen by Crawford, is sequencing material culture as ammunition for the historian to construct an unspecified form of regional history. Archaeology in this view is purely descriptive and it is far from clear what useful contribution it can make to any form of relevant and interpretative history.

Such a simplistic and essentially unarchaeological treatment of excavated evidence has distorted the settlement record of the islands and led to a number of unwarranted assumptions which have tended to obscure the potential value of the results of the excavations at the Udal. For example, a change in artefactual evidence at around 100 - 300 AD was interpreted by Crawford as entailing an invasion by Scotto-Picts (Crawford 1974); in retrospect, after excavations at Eilean Olabhat, North Uist (Armit 1988b) and Cnip, Lewis (Armit 1988a), this artefactual 'break' is seen to be the result simply of a gap in the Udal stratigraphy. This case will be discussed in detail in later chapters but it is cited here as being symptomatic of an over-reliance on the situation at one site, outwith even its local settlement context. Changes in the use of the site relative to wider settlement patterns between different periods, as well as differences between periods of intensive settlement and periods of abandonment or sporadic use, mean that the simplistic approach which sees the cultural remains or the lack of them at any given period at the Udal, as typical of the whole of the Western Isles, will inevitably distort and prejudice the evidence.

In this study I want to approach the development of an understanding of the period through the relationships between sites, making use of the great archaeological advantages of the Western Isles. The large numbers of extant field monuments, and the rich body of excavated data, have been largely ignored in the course of the interpretations of the results of the Udal project. In the present study, excavation will be treated as one of a range of ways in which 'new' archaeological information can be generated; it will be argued that the pursuit of excavation, as at the Udal, without the initial construction of settlement development models and in a random, core-sampling way, is of very limited use in the area. That the Udal remains entirely unpublished some twenty-five years after the start of the project indicates the problems involved in becoming committed to an open-ended large-scale excavation without specific research direction.

The Udal sequence shows the development of the land use on one patch of machair over several millennia with no indication of how any of the various settlements of various periods which were sited there related to their surrounding landscapes, and with no information on the location of sites of intervening periods. The importance of the eventual published artefactual and structural sequence is not in question, although much of its value has inevitably been superseded in the 1980s, but the formulation of a research strategy for the whole of Hebridean archaeology based on the Udal approach, proposed by Crawford, denies the richness and potential of the region and squanders the limited resources available to research. The Udal has been the sole long-term research project in the Western Isles prior to the establishment of the Edinburgh University's Callanish Archaeological Research Project and the Loch Olabhat Research Project in North Uist. It is in this context that the present study begins.

Report structure

This monograph is divided into four parts. Part One provides an introduction to the aims of the study and sets the context, both of previous research in the area and of the environmental background. Part Two re-evaluates the evidence of the excavated sites in the light of recent work,

both excavation and survey, organised according to the preliminary classification system formulated in Chapter Four. This system provides a framework for analysis by classification at several levels, including construction method, morphology and spatial organisation, without the imposition of assumptions of functional, chronological or cultural relatedness between classified types. The abandonment of certain preconceptions drawn from outside of the Western Isles allows for a more coherent picture of many of the excavated sites to emerge. Each of the defined classes are examined, on the basis of the re-evaluated excavated evidence and the available data from field survey, in terms of their structure, chronology and function. The validity of the defined classes of settlement site is assessed at this stage and the utility of further subdivisions is discussed.

Part Three deals with the application of a number of techniques to elucidate the Western Isles settlement sites. These are discussed under the headings of structural, locational and spatial analysis. Each has been used extensively in areas of Atlantic Scotland but here the applicability and utility of a range of analytical techniques will be examined in relation to the problems of the single area under study.

In conclusion, Part Four discusses the results of the re-evaluation and analysis and goes on to propose models for settlement patterns throughout the period. The results of the study are set within the context of current theoretical approaches and its implications for the prehistory of areas outwith the Western Isles will be discussed.

In the chapters which follow, individual sites will be cross-referenced to the catalogue (App. 3). This will take the form of the catalogue reference code in brackets after the name of the site. Where sites with multiple, distinct structural forms (which have more than one catalogue entry) are referred to, the entry most relevant to the particular discussion will be used.

Chapter Two - Environment and Archaeology in the Western Isles

It is impossible to consider the settlement patterns of any period in any area without developing an understanding of the environmental background. Whilst environmental factors are not the only forces affecting prehistoric society and economy, the environmental background of the Western Isles provides its own set of economic possibilities and restrictions, establishing a context, changing over time, within which societies of all periods must operate. As well as defining the available range of economic and settlement potential, the environment of the Western Isles has had a great part to play in determining the archaeological visibility of the various site types. Differential destruction has prejudiced the development of archaeological interpretation, particularly through the effects of deposition and erosion of soils in different areas, and through coastal change.

Great changes are known to have taken place in the Western Isles since they were first occupied by human populations, in terms of climatic deterioration, sea-level change, peat growth and machair formation. The rate and chronology of change, however, and their effects upon human settlement are not fully understood. In later chapters I will stress the role of environmental factors as important influences on later prehistoric settlement patterns and settlement changes, so it is as well to discuss the environmental evidence in some detail.

For the purposes of this discussion it is convenient to divide the environmental features of the Western Isles into two groups. Firstly there are those features which on our archaeological timescale can be regarded as constant; features of location, solid geology and topography which were the same in later prehistory as they are today. Secondly there are the changing features which are of central importance in the study of prehistoric settlement patterns and which will necessarily take up most of this discussion: these include climate, soils and vegetation, and coastal change. I will first describe the 'constant' environmental factors and their influence on human settlement, and then assess the evidence for the changing features in an attempt to present an approximate picture of the environment as it was in later prehistory. Finally I will consider the effects of environmental forces on archaeological perceptions of prehistoric settlement.

Location

The Western Isles form a distinct geographical and geological unit lying off the west coast of the Scottish mainland separated from the Inner Hebrides by the Minch (Ill. 1.1). The chain of islands is some 210km long from the Butt of Lewis to Barra Head and the main islands are separated only by narrow straits, which have always made sea-communication relatively easy.

The Western Isles belong to the Atlantic Province, linked to other areas of western Britain and Ireland by the western seaways and to the Orkneys and Shetlands in the north. It is important not to see the islands as a peripheral part of Scotland which, as a political or cultural unit, is wholly irrelevant to the later prehistoric period, depending as it does on the vagaries of relatively recent history. The Western Isles are geographically and geologically

unrelated to the central belt of Scotland and, from the Neolithic onwards, the cultural unity of the Atlantic West is a recurrent theme. On this view the Western Isles need not be peripheral. It can be argued that it is their essential unrelatedness to central and eastern Scotland which has led to their misuse by Scottish mainland authorities over several centuries resulting in their being seen as wholly peripheral today.

Geology

Geologically the Western Isles are extremely homogeneous, consisting almost entirely of Lewisian gneiss, one of the oldest rock formations of Europe. The long island chain is the surface expression of a ridge of Lewisian rock which stretches as far as the west of Shetland. The weathering of this rock has produced an undulating landscape and has yielded thin acid soils. The rock contains no appreciable metal deposits and is not outstanding as a building stone. It is notable that one of the first areas settled in the Neolithic was the only substantial area of non-Lewisian rock in the island chain i.e. the area around modern Stornoway (Henshall 1972, 118). The undulating inland areas containing large numbers of small, shallow lochs are characteristic of the islands, often fringed on the West by strips of machair, grass-covered shell sands separated from the sea by modern dune systems. The east coast by contrast is much rockier, with bare hills rising sharply from the sea, and these eastern areas have generally been avoided by settlement in recent centuries.

Climate

The climate of the Western Isles is mild in comparison with the Scottish mainland due to their location and topography. Precipitation is high although spread very evenly throughout the year. Mean air temperature varies little, with snow and frost rare. Perhaps the most obvious climatic feature of the islands are the extremely high winds which persist throughout most of the year. The climate, as elsewhere in Britain, has clearly been subject to major change since prehistoric times, but an analysis of prehistoric climate can only be approached through a study of indirect evidence such as soil, pollen and faunal history. For the purposes of this discussion the changes in the prehistoric climate will be examined in the context of the evidence from soil and pollen studies.

Soils and vegetation

The central feature of the Hebridean landscape today is the marked division between the white and black lands, i.e. the heavily settled coastal strips and patches of machair and the much more extensive inland peat-covered areas. Both of these soils are of relatively recent formation and their rate and chronology of appearance and dominance are central to any understanding of past settlement patterns. Illustration 2.1 shows the distribution of modern soil types on Barra and South Uist, simplified from data made available by the Macaulay Institute in Aberdeen. This indicates the extent of the main soil types divided principally between the shelly sands of the machair and the peaty soils and blanket peats.

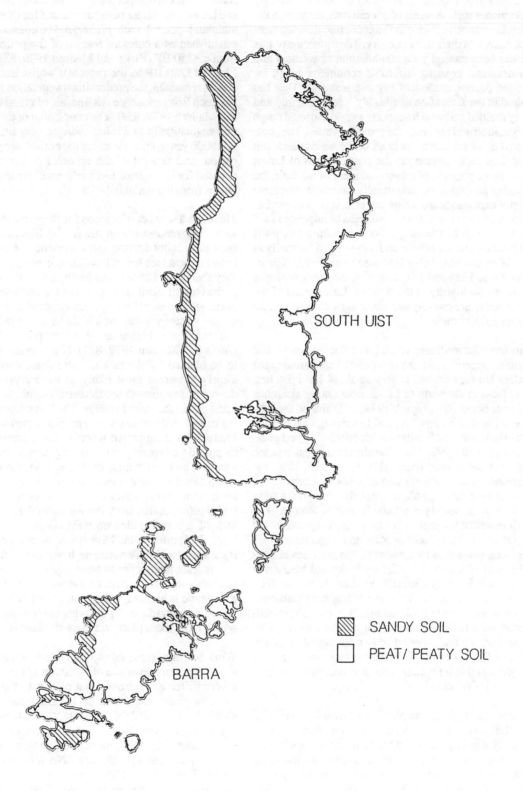

SOUTH UIST

BARRA

⧄ SANDY SOIL
☐ PEAT/ PEATY SOIL

Ill. 2.1 Soils in South Uist and Barra

The blanket peat and peaty gley soils which cover much of the inland areas of the islands, and are overwhelmingly the dominant soils in terms of overall area, have been the principal restrictive factor in the economic development of the islands in their recent history. The formation of this peat has been caused by a combination of wetness and poor drainage, creating anaerobic conditions which inhibit the decomposition of organic material. This has resulted in the formation of a highly infertile, acidic and poorly drained soil which supports a very restricted range of vegetation and prevents the growth of trees. The peat-covered areas are extensive in all of the main islands but are at their most extreme in the northern part of Lewis where, in the absence of substantial areas of machair, the blanket of peat has covered virtually the whole land area: the only exceptions are where the efforts of post-medieval farmers have carved out small areas of improved land around individual townships. For agriculture today the peat is an extremely hostile soil, being rated normally at 6 or 7W on the MacAulay land assessment scale (Glentworth 1979, 132) and 5W at best on the shallow slopes which can be slightly better drained. Large areas of the islands today are entirely useless to agriculture or viable only for rough grazing.

Apart from the machair, which I will discuss below, and the anthropogenic soils, the non-peat covered areas in the Western Isles are limited to very small, isolated patches, e.g. at Ness in the north of Lewis where non-calcareous gley soils occur (Glentworth 1979, 132) and on the hillslopes of southern Harris around Leverburgh and Rodel, where the brown earth soils provide relatively good grazing (Glentworth 1979, 132). The absence of peat beneath excavated chambered tombs (Henshall 1972, 506), the occurrence of submerged wood deposits, and tree stumps found in peat cuttings all confirm that the present-day dominance of peat is a relatively recent feature. The development of the peat and its associated vegetation and the nature of the preceding soils and vegetation types have been studied in two recent pollen analyses at sites in the west of Lewis (Ill. 2.2); by Birks and Madsen at Little Loch Roag (Birks and Madsen 1979), and by Bohnke and Cowie at Tob nan Leobag near Callanish (Bohncke and Cowie forthcoming, Bohncke 1988). Additional information derives from work on mollusc remains from the multi-period settlement site of Northton in Harris (Evans 1971). Perhaps the most important recent work is that on macroscopic sub-peat plant remains from Lewis (Wilkins 1984).

The analysis of pollen samples from the Little Loch Roag mire (NB 142 248) near Miabhaig in the west of Lewis was carried out by Birks and Madsen, two botanists from Cambridge University, in an effort to establish the vegetation history of Lewis in the Flandrian period. The site was chosen because of its proximity to the standing stones of Callanish, some 11km distant, and because of the absence of peat cutting in the immediate vicinity. The main finding of their work relevant to this study was the absence of arboreal pollen, of any period, sufficient to suggest that there had been woodland in the area. The 18% of arboreal pollen recorded as the highest for any zone of the Flandrian is dismissed by the authors as the result of windblown mainland pollen (Birks and Madsen 1979, 836). In zone LLR-2, from 9140 BP to 4450 - 3250 BP, the Loch Roag pollen study indicates an open grass-

land vegetation, with stands of willow and tall herb communities in damper areas and isolated stands of birch and hazel scrub (alder being accounted for by windblown mainland pollen) with *plantago lanceolata* becoming established as a constant feature of the pollen diagram from c.3350 BP (Birks and Madsen 1979, 839). In zone LLR-3 (3250 BP to the present), whilst isolated birch copses remained, the predominant vegetation reflected in the Loch Roag sequence is a 'mosaic of grassland' (Birks and Madsen 1979, 839). The conclusion of the authors is that vegetation in Lewis has changed very little over the last 5000 years, encompassing the entire later prehistoric period, and that all of the arboreal pollen can be accounted for by isolated birch and hazel scrub and pollen blown from the mainland of Scotland.

There are a number of reasons for disputing this point of view. The reconstruction offered by Birks and Madsen fails to account for the clear evidence of tree stumps found in peat (see below) and submerged in some areas: they themselves accept that birch, alder and hazel occur at the base of blanket peats at Bragar and Barvas on the north-west coast of Lewis, areas exposed to the full force of the westerly gales which Birks and Madsen claim prevented any Flandrian afforestation of the islands (Birks and Madsen 1979, 827). If the westerly gales are to be blamed for the lack of Hebridean woodland then clearly the areas most likely to have supported some degree of tree growth are the areas on the sheltered east coast and in the inland valleys. The Little Loch Roag site is situated on the west coast in precisely the location least likely to have supported woodland and cannot be taken to provide a typical picture of vegetation conditions in Lewis. The contribution of pollen from the east coast, when faced by the extreme westerly winds, is likely to have been minimal and the absence of any land mass contributing pollen from the west could account for the lack of arboreal pollen on west coast sites. The Little Loch Roag mire would have collected what was primarily a very local pollen sample from one of the areas of Lewis least likely ever to have supported woodland. Its relevance to other areas of Lewis and to the Western Isles as a whole is highly questionable. The Loch Roag study is further contradicted by the other environmental studies which have taken place in Lewis and Harris.

Work by John Evans on the land snail remains from the multi-period machair site of Northton in Harris suggests a very different environmental picture to that proposed from the pollen analysis at Little Loch Roag. Species of shade-dwelling mollusc dominate, particularly in the earlier neolithic levels. Evans postulates an initially forested environment becoming more open, presumably through human interference, in the Later Neolithic and Beaker 1 phase (Evans 1971, 58). Evans sees actual woodland regeneration in the ensuing Beaker 2 phase prior to Iron Age clearance. This Northton work, though not based directly on soils or vegetation but on the study of mollusc species and their modern habitats, is clearly at variance with the treeless Flandrian moorland envisaged by Birks and Madsen. The results from this site are supported by the results from the other major site upon which recent environmental work has been carried out, at Tob nan Leobag in Lewis.

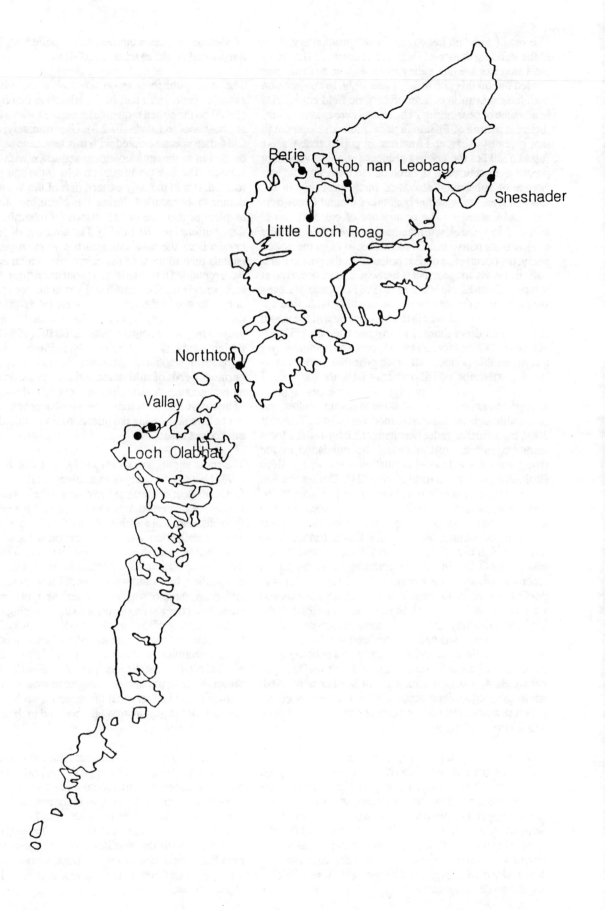

Ill. 2.2 Principal Environmental Sites Discussed in the Text

The site of Tob nan Leobag is a small promontory close to the standing stones of Callanish and some 11km from the Little Loch Roag valley mire. Pollen analysis was carried out on this site in 1978 and 1979, in conjunction with the excavation of later prehistoric field boundaries in advance of peat cutting. The results here present a very different picture of Flandrian vegetation development to that given by Birks and Madsen. In pollen zone CaN-1 (up to 5320 bc) the Leobag sequence shows a very high percentage occurrence of birch pollen reflecting the existence of substantial stands of birch, probably in the low-lying and now submerged areas around Great Bernera and Callanish. The occurrence of oak and elm is ascribed to windblown mainland pollen and while the evidence for native pine is inconclusive from the pollen study, the occurrence of pine boles under the peat in other parts of Lewis suggest that it too would have occurred at this period (Birks and Madsen 1979, 827). Areas of Lewis wooded certainly with birch and possibly with pine appear to have existed even in the exposed west of the island in early Flandrian times. In sub-zone CaN-2a (5320+/-100 bc to 5000 bc) forest fires appear to be common over a considerable period, indicating probable human activity. An expansion of willow occurred at the expense of birch, followed in sub-zone CaN-2b by the first appearance of cereal pollen and a decline in rowan, willow and birch, although the latter remained above 14%. Towards 2000 bc a further reduction in birch may reflect local anthropogenic use of timber and the inundation by the rising sea of the low-lying sheltered wooded valleys (Bohncke and Cowie forthcoming, 21). During the last two millennia bc indicators of pasture, e.g. white clover, occur along with cereal pollen and herbs associated with agriculture and the pollen record as a whole suggests heavy use of the area (Bohncke and Cowie forthcoming, 24). Significantly, these indicators decrease towards the end of zone CaN-3 in the latter centuries bc and the pollen record is witness to a regeneration of birch. If it was possible for birch to recolonise an area on the exposed west coast of Lewis even in the last centuries bc, the implication is that in the easterly areas and more sheltered parts of inland Lewis natural woodland would have been entirely capable of surviving at least to this period despite the effects of climatic deterioration. From 0-800 ad, in zone CaN-4, a regional increase in heather is marked, while local conditions become wetter, although cereal pollen persists until near the end of this zone (Bohncke and Cowie, forthcoming, 24).

The results from the Leobag peninsula present a very different picture of vegetation history to that given by the Little Loch Roag study. Leobag is perhaps the more reliable site for several reasons: the sample site itself lies in a more open area with less chance of a purely local and atypical sample; it is in an area known archaeologically to have been settled throughout prehistory; and its results accord with the observed sub-peat, macro-vegetation evidence which are inexplicable by the Loch Roag model of vegetation development.

Leobag is still far from an ideal site from which to derive information on the vegetation history of Lewis. The strength of the prevailing westerly winds make it unlikely that Leobag can provide any information on the conditions on the east side of the island and the problems of differential spread and differential production of pollen

of various species, common to all pollen analysis, are heightened by the extreme conditions.

The only published environmental work which does examine the eastern half of the islands is that by Newell (1988) on the pollen sequence associated with a field wall at Sheshader in Lewis (Ill 2.3). Unfortunately, only one C-14 date was associated with this sequence so it cannot be tied in to the archaeological sequence with any confidence. The Eye peninsula, on which the sample site is located, lies in the only eastern part of the Western Isles demonstrably settled during the Neolithic and is thus atypical of this side of the islands (cf. chambered tomb distributions Henshall 1972). The intensity of settlement here relates the area more to the western part of the islands than to most of the east coast, which appears to have remained unsettled throughout prehistory. Nonetheless periods of birch and hazel wood and/or scrub were demonstrated in the sample (Newell 1988, 88) and from the available date, Newell suggested that blanket peat growth may have begun around 2200 BC (1988, 88). The pollen study showed intensive anthropogenic interference in woodland clearance including episodes of burning, weeds of cultivation and species associated with animal grazing. Although of interest in its demonstration of intensive human activity, the Sheshader sequence does not help in addressing the question of woodland survival on the east coast.

The most significant recent analysis is that by Wilkins (1984) based on a study of macroscopic arboreal remains from sub-peat contexts at forty sites in Lewis and Harris. A number of tree stumps were collected for study from these sites, all from within 50cm of the base of the peats. Sample collection was dependant on suitable depth of peat-cutting in each area and the gaps on Wilkins' distribution of sites need not relate to an absence of forest cover. Pine, birch and willow were found at several sites and each sample was interpreted as representing the woodland cover at its site prior to the covering of the site by peat. Dating of the samples produced markedly different concentrations for the samples of each species, with willow samples concentrating from 7190 - 6600 BC, birch at 6030 - 3080 BC and pine at 2920 - 1960 BC. The preservation of the samples suggested relatively fast peat growth and it is likely that the dates for each sample are reliable for the termination of woodland in their immediate environment.

The distribution map of Wilkins' sites indicate a striking pattern of peat encroachment on the Hebridean Flandrian woodland. The early encroachment on willow and birch woodland occurs at the margins of the area of the distribution and does not affect the pine sample sites, concentrated in areas more remote from expected human settlement, until the Neolithic. This suggests that while pine forest developed from the birch woodland in some areas, in others peat encroachment was already halting all tree growth.

Importantly for the later prehistoric period it indicates that pine forest persisted in many areas of Lewis into the 2nd millennium BC and presumably, in well-drained areas of the Harris Hills or sheltered areas of Harris itself, for some time after that. The Harris Hill valleys would not be exploited for timber while easily accessible woodland remained in Lewis and Harris, and better drainage would prevent natural peat encroachment, so it is probable that substantial woodland resources remained into the late 2nd millennium at least.

From the end of the Neolithic timber was becoming, if not a scarce resource, then at least one which required increasing effort to obtain. This factor may contribute to an understanding of some aspects of the archaeology of our period.

Reviewing Birks and Madsen in the light of the incontrovertible and substantial presence of pine forest in the islands, it becomes clear that their dismissal of the local pollen contribution to their *spectra*, and to the arboreal component in particular, must itself be dismissed. Their arboreal *maxima* correspond with Wilkins' findings of the woodland composition through the Flandrian as peat encroached at the forest margins. The occurrence of willow prior to c.5000 BC, the dominance of birch from c.5000 BC to 3000 BC and then the first appearance of pine at 3350 BC, all correspond to the woodland pattern suggested by the macroscopic remains. The occurrence of hazel in the Flandrian woodland is thus also to be expected on the basis of the pollen results, although this species did not survive macroscopically. The problem in the pollen studies is the very low absolute values, corroborated by Wilkins in his study of pollen from his site 13 yielding macroscopic remains of pine boles. The most probable explanation for the low absolute values is the action of prevailing winds from the Atlantic over long periods, displacing much of the local pollen and preventing westward pollen movement on any scale (Wilkins 1984, 258).

More analyses are required, particularly from the east coast and the upland areas and sheltered valleys of the North Harris Hills, to settle the rate and chronology of woodland decline on prehistoric Lewis, although a broad outline may now be discerned, for Lewis and Harris at least. Various other factors do point to the existence of woodland areas even on the exposed west coast during the later prehistoric period; wild cat and blackbird were identified from an iron age site in 1936 (Barber 1985, 19) while on the east coast the North Tolsta crannog (M.3) in the drained Loch Osabhat was described as an artificial island formed of wooden stakes (Blundell 1913, 298), as was the site in Loch Airidh na Lic (RCAHMS 1928, No.51; M.6).

Work in the Uists has set out to study the environmental history of the islands through the analysis of pollen cores from machair lochs and infilled lochs on the peat/machair interface (Hirons 1986). The preliminary results from the machair loch site of Askernish in South Uist and the bog at Balemore in North Uist indicate a complex and varied number of local environmental situations with strong indications of anthropogenic interference at an early stage in the Neolithic or Mesolithic. Such early human interference in the natural vegetation pattern of the Uists may help to explain the lack of recorded arboreal vegetation on the west side of the islands. The dating of the Uist cores and the expansion of the project should eventually enable a far fuller picture of vegetation development in the Uists to emerge. Further work on a range of environmental material underway at Sheffield University, and the study of waterlogged macroscopic environmental material, insects and pollen from the Loch Olabhat excavations will also greatly increase our knowledge of the developing prehistoric environment (Armit 1988b).

The development of the present inland peat soils and vegetation would appear to have occurred fairly recently, although it is clearly difficult to date directly. Woodland can be traced, even in the least conducive areas, until the latest centuries BC at least, on the basis of the Leobag results, interpreted in the light of Wilkins' findings; birch regeneration took place in these areas even at a very late stage. Initial peat growth would have begun in ill-drained areas and hollows and would have expanded at the expense of woodland in a progressively wetter and cooler climate, with the likelihood of a strong anthropogenic dimension from the Neolithic at least. The peoples of the later prehistoric period in the Western Isles would have been living at a time of woodland retreat and peat growth; this process is central to an understanding of later prehistoric settlement patterns.

The machair lands upon which agriculture in the islands has been centred for many centuries are spread over some 8% of the Uists and Barra with smaller patches in Lewis and Harris. This machair land, consisting of white shell sands, contrasts sharply with the black peat covered inland areas. The machair is characteristically low-lying and formed of gently undulating sand hills consolidated by a vegetation of grasses fringed on the shore side by modern unvegetated sand dunes. In terms of agricultural potential the wealth of the machair is only relative to the adjacent, barren peatlands. The machair is highly unstable and prone to wind erosion when devoid of vegetation, as when ploughed. Drainage too is a problem with summer drought, due to rapid drainage through the sand, alternating with winter flood as the water table rises. The winter machair landscape is studded with temporary machair lochs which add to the problems of erosion by undercutting the sand hills. The alkalinity of the sand further reduces the machair's agricultural value to an overall value of LUC3 (Glentworth 1979, 136). Cultivation has largely depended on the mixing of the sand with peat, seaweed or dung, both to reduce the alkalinity and to reduce the susceptibility to erosion.

Although the machair is a geologically recent formation it has played a part throughout its development in the environmental background to human settlement of the Western Isles. The history of machair development is one of constant erosion and redeposition of material throughout the greater part of the Flandrian period. The machair consists of glacial sands, marine shell and other skeletal material which appear to derive principally from the now submerged shallow areas off the west coast of the islands, where from 13-18 miles out into the Atlantic, the sea-bed has been stripped of glacial sand. This theory assumes a rising sea-level and the evidence to support this assumption is discussed below. It is not probable that any other sources could account for the material which forms the machair as no sizable rivers drain into the Atlantic from the islands, and erosion of the Lewisian rock is not rapid enough to account for a substantial amount of the material. Much of the development of the machair landscapes is accounted for by the instability of the shell sands in an extremely windy climatic regime. The sub-machair relief appears continuous with the black lands further inland and the machair appears to have been deposited over a relatively uniform area by wave action scouring the sea-bed as sea-levels rose (Ritchie 1979, 112). This sea level change is confirmed by the lack of the raised beaches common on the Scottish mainland and in the Inner Isles, by the intertidal deposits of organic material including birch stumps at sites like Vallay, Pabbay and Berneray (Ritchie 1966, 81) and by the historical accounts of land lost to the sea in relatively recent times e.g. at Baleshare and Udal (Barber 1985, 82), which show that the process is still continuing. Deposits of soft glacial drift at HWM at sites in South Uist, e.g. Orasay and Vorran Island (Ritchie 1966, 80), demonstrate that sea level is now at its highest Flandrian level and is still advancing, albeit very slowly.

From the study of inter-tidal and submerged organic deposits it is estimated that the relative sea-level in the Western Isles has risen by some 4 - 5m. since 3100 BC, producing the characteristic Hebridean coastal pattern of tidal strands, fords and off-shore islands (Ritchie 1985). The action of this rising sea level, as well as greatly reducing the area of the islands, has thrown material from the submerged land surface up onto the shore creating, and continually pushing back, the machair. Ritchie estimates that 75 - 80m of sea level rise has taken place in the Flandrian (Ritchie 1979, 112) although the great majority of this occurred prior to the later prehistoric period. Even a relatively small rise in sea level could cause enormous changes in the machair landscape and slow but steady change was in progress throughout prehistory. The possibility exists of land bridges between many of the islands even into the later prehistoric period: the Uists and Benbecula in particular may have formed one large island. The shallow sloping west coasts appear to have been far more vulnerable to land loss than those of the east, which show no sign of significant change in later prehistory.

Two key archaeological areas can shed light on the effects of the forces of coastal change both during and since the later prehistoric period. These are the areas of Vallay Strand in North Uist and the Valtos Peninsula in the west of Lewis. The locations of many of the archaeological sites in and around Vallay Strand (see Ill. 12.4), many of which were excavated by Erskine Beveridge in the early C20th, show that the local landscape has been subject to great change since the later prehistoric period. Sites like Garry Iochdrach (W.7) and Foshigarry (W.4) lie too near the present HWM to be practical for settlement and are regularly flooded, and the floor levels of excavated sites such as A Cheardach Bheag (W.16), in South Uist, lay below the present water table. The great concentration of sites on and around the large expanse of inter-tidal sand which is Vallay Strand strongly suggest that when the sites were occupied the area was a large machair plain drained by the two streams which still exist at low tide on either side of Vallay itself. The drowning of Vallay Strand would not have required any appreciable rise in sea level (although a rise of some magnitude is probable), but could have been accomplished by the forces of erosion and redeposition acting upon the local machair which, as the Udal stratigraphy shows, was extremely unstable in the later prehistoric period. The

breaching of coastal sand dunes on either side of Vallay would have led to wholesale flooding of the low-lying machair plain, creating the inter-tidal expanse of Vallay Strand and casting up new sand dunes over the sites on higher ground around the present HWM. A change related to only a minimal rise in sea level could by this means have a catastrophic effect on the human settlement potential of a sizable area of land, of relatively high fertility, over a very short period of time.

The Valtos peninsula in West Lewis highlights another of the ways in which the processes of machair development can distort the prehistoric settlement pattern. The wide beach of Traigh na Berie shows all of the signs of continuing erosion which conform to Ritchie's model B of machair development, suggested for sites in South Uist (Ritchie 1966, 112). The occurrence of steep hills immediately behind the machair has led to the piling up of sand, forming machair slopes rising up to these hills at their nearest points to the beach and to the infilling of two lochs, Loch na Berie and Loch na Cuilc, which lie between the machair and the high ground. The retreat of the coastal dunes continues today both at Berie, where the coastal sites recorded by the RCAHMS in 1928 (RCAHMS 1928, Nos. 84 and 98) have disappeared, and at the neighbouring beach of Cnip where the rate of erosion was of the order of 1m per year until the recent construction of a sea-wall. The eroded material is continually redeposited further inland but the local topography prevents the development of a true machair plain. Probing of Loch na Berie has revealed that the Berie broch (A.L19) lies on a rocky island in what originally was a much more extensive loch, now reduced to a reed filled marsh, lying behind a machair plain stretching considerably further seawards (Harding and Topping 1986, 34). Sand has accumulated in the loch from the side nearest the coast, filling it to the extent that the broch is now joined to the shore for most of the year. When the Berie site was occupied the sea would have been at a somewhat lower level and the dunes would have extended several hundred metres further away from the site. Alternating bands of sand and peat formed in the flooded periods have, since the later prehistoric period, virtually obliterated a loch which acted as a settlement focus. The site's classification as a broch tower had to await excavation in 1985.

The landscapes of the Berie beach area and the other beaches of the Valtos peninsula have changed dramatically over the past 2000 years. Large areas of former machair have been lost and with them have gone the recorded traces of a number of settlement sites and doubtless many which were never recorded; the sand redeposited from those eroded areas now covers and therefore obscures the sites which survive on the remaining machair and similarly distorts the landscape which would have existed in prehistory. The form and size of the two surviving lochs have been altered beyond recognition and any lochs which may have existed further towards the sea will have been entirely obliterated. The processes which can be seen to have drastically affected the Berie settlement picture were also at work in many other less well-studied areas and must be taken into account in a study of prehistoric settlement in coastal areas of the islands as a whole.

Archaeological visibility

The environmental changes discussed in this chapter have greatly affected the development of settlement studies in the islands. The instability of the machair has led to the erosion of much of the iron age coastline, and coastal sites, while the consequent redeposition of the eroded material has further hampered study by obscuring sites further inland. Peat on the black lands has covered vast inland areas making the identification of sites extremely difficult and often impossible by conventional means. The acidity of the peat and the alkalinity of the machair means that preservation on the sites of different areas favours different materials, making comparison difficult.

Despite these problems the Western Isles do have advantages in terms of site identification and classification which make this study not only possible but well-suited to the area. The use of stone for building combined with the lack of particularly destructive later agriculture have meant that the state of preservation of many structures of the later prehistoric period is remarkably good. The limitations of the evidence, occasioned mainly by the forces of environmental change, must be taken into consideration to prevent too great a reliance on the completeness of the survey data, which may result from a superficial examination of the high degree of preservation and clarity of the preserved and recorded structures. Distributions are clearly and inevitably distorted for machair sites and for low-lying sites in areas of blanket peat. The completeness or otherwise of distributions of the various site types will be discussed in the individual chapters concerned with those sites.

The later prehistoric environment - an approximation

During the later prehistoric period, the environment of both the coastal and inland areas of the Western Isles was undergoing complex processes of change which are still in operation. The two major processes of deforestation and peat growth on the one hand, and machair development on the other, being largely independent, cannot be co-ordinated justifiably on the basis of the evidence currently available: both, however, were central forces in the economic and settlement activities of communities throughout the later prehistoric period.

The evidence for woodland, particularly on the east side of the islands, persisting into this period is strong. During our period the tree cover on the west was probably becoming exhausted, perhaps through overuse as well as through the effects of a wetter climate, encouraging peat growth and making woodland regeneration increasingly difficult.

Throughout the later prehistoric period the environmental processes which shaped the historic environment of the islands were in progress, and settlement patterns and economic patterns over this period would have had to continually adjust to the varying restrictions imposed by these forces. It is impossible to isolate one chronological section of prehistory and compare directly the settlement situation and the corresponding stage of coastal and inland vegetation and soil development: in subsequent chapters I will attempt to identify the trends and patterns observable from the settlement record and to examine those patterns in the light of the environmental processes discussed here.

Models based on environmental determinism cannot in themselves explain the detail of material culture change as recent post-processualist critiques have pointed out (e.g. Hodder 1986), but this should not be allowed to deny the importance of environmental factors in restricting the range of available economic strategies. A society pursuing a set of social and economic strategies within the context of one environmental regime may well be forced into radical changes by environmental change of the magnitude demonstrated in the Western Isles. Settlement patterns can only develop if they are adaptive (by definition since if they were not adaptive they would not survive to develop). The environmental background remains a vital factor in the interpretation of settlement change. The specific response, in terms of specific forms of material culture, will depend on many factors beyond those which are purely environmentally adaptive. Part Four of this monograph will discuss the role and value of processual, and particularly environmentally based, forms of interpretation, and of post-processual modes of explanation in the contexts of this period and area.

Chapter Three - A Critical History of Research

The present confusion in the archaeology of the Western Isles is a legacy of the way in which the history of archaeological research in the islands has progressed. Specific excavations have often been undertaken on the basis of non-archaeological factors and systems of classification of the Hebridean monuments have long been dependant on classifications of monuments in other areas where more recent work has taken place. In much the same way as environmental features, such as peat or machair, distort the evidence and reveal false concentrations, so the vagaries of research patterns over the past century have had a substantial effect on the received archaeological picture. The literature, mostly over 40 years old, cannot be taken to reveal a representative sample of Hebridean sites or even a random one. To understand how our present archaeological record has accumulated we must consider the reasons and motives behind past research and to identify the biases which have been introduced into the archaeological record.

In the Western Isles, until recent years, individual projects have never been related to overall research strategies. The archaeology of the islands has evolved gradually and sporadically through the interest and work of a number of individuals over more than a century, each working within the context of different archaeological approaches, and with diverse techniques drawn from the mainstream of British archaeology. In this chapter I will divide the history of archaeological research in the Western Isles into four phases which, although not strictly chronological, represent the main stages in the evolution of the present archaeological situation.

Phase 1 - Initial fieldwork

The first serious work on the prehistory of the Western Isles was published in 1890 by Captain F.W.L. Thomas, a serving naval officer and amateur antiquarian, based on his extensive travels to archaeological sites in Lewis and Harris. Thomas' surveys were highly selective but relatively well recorded and provided valuable and detailed descriptions, particularly of structures which have since deteriorated. It is unfortunate that he concentrates virtually exclusively on the most obvious structures, the brochs and duns, includes few plans and ignores the context of the central structures within the sites as a whole.

Some years after Thomas' publication the antiquary Erskine Beveridge built a house on the island of Vallay, which is joined at low tide to the mainland of North Uist. Beveridge, who had already published material on the archaeology of Coll and Tiree (Beveridge 1905), went on, in the years from 1897 until his death in 1920, to excavate a very large number of sites on North Uist, concentrating on the area around Vallay Strand, and to carry out an extensive survey of the island. The results of his most prolific period of work were published in 1911 in his lavishly illustrated book, North Uist (Beveridge 1911), which contained over 150 black and white photographs of sites of all types on the island. Excavations carried out after this publication, at Dun Thomaidh, Foshigarry, Garry Iochdrach and Bac Mhic Connain, were published after his death by Graham Callander (Beveridge 1930 and 1931). These excavations and surveys still provide the main database for the archaeology of North Uist. An unparalleled concentration of sites was excavated in the Vallay area, albeit to a very rudimentary standard of recording, providing a huge body of data which has never been properly assessed, perhaps due to its volume and the idiosyncrasies of the excavations which vary in quality and thoroughness between sites.

Beveridge concentrated his work on the machair wheelhouse sites and over a period of some fifteen years excavated 19 sites in North Uist. This campaign on North Uist, and particularly on Vallay Strand, has resulted in a great distributional bias towards that area. Most of the sites were visible only as grassed-over machair hills which Beveridge excavated initially to determine their nature, and continued to excavate fully if he found them productive or interesting. Without this trial and error approach which Beveridge had the time to adopt, it is most unlikely that a number of his sites would have yet been located. This is the situation which undoubtedly exists in a number of other machair areas throughout the Western Isles, e.g. in the closely comparable area of Uig Sands. The archaeology of Vallay cannot be compared to any other area without stressing the importance of this distributional bias.

The RCAHMS survey of the Outer Hebrides published in 1928 was based on survey work carried out between 1914 and 1925 at what was clearly a far from ideal time for an orderly and organised field survey. The purpose of the RCAHMS volume was to catalogue and classify the archaeological monuments of the Western Isles. The fieldwork, however, was carried out in a piecemeal fashion over many years and in several areas was very quick and erratic. Barra and its surrounding islands were surveyed in only ten days (including two Sundays when presumably no work was possible). Given that 38 sites were recorded in that area there can have been very little time to spare for more than cursory field-walking in the vicinity of known sites. The lack of a boat meant that many island duns could not be visited, other than by viewing from the shore:

"In some cases a partially submerged causeway could be used though only at the cost of a wetting; very rarely a boat was available; more often the remains were inaccessible without special provision and observations consequently had to be made from the shore." (RCAHMS 1928, v)

When these sites were visited the descriptions concentrated on the central structures to the virtual exclusion of the other features of the sites.

Apart from the efforts of Thomas, Beveridge and the RCAHMS survey, archaeological research in the Western Isles prior to the 1940s was very limited. Excavations were carried out at Galson (Edwards 1923) and at the North Tolsta crannog, reported by the Rev. Odo Blundell (Blundell 1913). Blundell recorded a number of other artificial islands in the Western Isles as crannogs and it appears to be as a result of this that the RCAHMS included crannogs as a term in their classification system covering island sites which lacked classifiable central structures and which appeared to be partly or wholly artificial. They did not account for the relationship of these sites to the other forms of island structure which also appear to be sited on artificial islands.

The initial period of archaeological fieldwork in the Western Isles was one of data collection. Excavation and survey were often dependant on the whims of individuals. These were principally visitors to the islands like Thomas and Blundell, and Beveridge operating in the area around his own home. The RCAHMS collected further reports on known sites but could not afford the time for extensive survey to correct the distributional biases already inherent in the data. The basic site distribution preserves the activities of the early workers and places undue emphasis on particular areas and types of site.

It was during this early period that the greatest number of excavations took place and the majority of the Hebridean later prehistoric assemblage was collected. Very little was done to classify this material or the sites from which it came. Beveridge, who dominates this early phase of research, was not apparently interested in classification or in the wider comparisons of his sites. The initial formulation of the classification of Atlantic Iron Age sites and material was left to those like Joseph Anderson and his contemporaries, whose main research interests lay in the Northern Isles and particularly in the Orkneys. This initial use of sites in the north as type sites for monument classes, which were then extended to cover the Western Isles, has continued to plague Hebridean archaeology throughout its development.

Phase 2 - Interpretation and data gathering

The initial phase of data gathering and antiquarianism ended with the publication of the RCAHMS report in 1928 which laid the foundation for all later work. A gap in terms of original fieldwork in the later prehistory of the Isles lasted from 1925 until 1946 when Sir Lindsay Scott began excavations on the aisled roundhouse at Clettraval in North Uist. Scott's work marked a new phase of research, based on the excavation of specific sites to attempt to answer specific problems in the prehistory of Atlantic Scotland. Scott had been greatly influenced by Childe's Prehistory of Scotland (Childe 1935) in which he had defined the 'castle complex' of Atlantic Scotland, encompassing brochs and duns, and had put forward the hypothesis that they and their associated material culture derived from diffusion from south-west England.

In his paper 'The Problem of the Brochs' (Scott 1947) Scott had sought to trace the development of brochs from a wider tradition involving wheelhouses and other structures, deriving ultimately from south-west England. Using a brief survey of the brochs of Barra and Harris, Scott devised a developmental sequence which he then attempted to test by the excavation of Clettraval. This latter site produced quantities of decorated pottery which formed the basis for a general typological series which Scott was to apply to the Western Isles as a whole. Scott had progressed from the days of Thomas and Beveridge by developing a more planned approach to his research. He treated all of the later prehistoric sites of the islands

together, recognising basic similarities in the structure and the material which lay behind the typological division of brochs, duns, wheelhouses etc., and was dismissive of the approach which segregated 'broch towers' from other types of site. This approach of Scott's was a valuable contribution which has been largely ignored by later workers until recently (cf. Barrett 1981). By placing the much vaunted uniqueness of brochs into perspective and arguing for brochs as one element of a wider settlement tradition with most brochs as relatively low defended farmhouses, his contribution was considerable, although his enthusiasm was perhaps carried too far in his refusal to recognise any chronological basis to the division of brochs and wheelhouses in general.

The great problem of the legacy left by Scott to the prehistory of the Western Isles was that, by his use of the Hebridean brochs to argue for brochs as a varied, dun-related group of structures of various heights and forms, he led later workers, mainly working in other areas, to believe that it was the Hebridean brochs specifically which were somehow degenerate or untypical. The Western Isles were the only major broch area not to be visited by Euan MacKie in the course of his thesis research in the early 1960s because of his belief that the brochs there were atypical and dun-like (MacKie 1965, 94).

By Scott's time the main concerns of broch studies were the typological classification and structural development of the monuments and the analysis of the minutiae of their diffusion from the south-west of England, which had become a very strongly held dogma by the 1940s. Shortly after Scott's work at Clettraval, a further major wheelhouse excavation was carried out by T.C. Lethbridge at Kilpheder on the South Uist machair. Lethbridge used his excavation report to launch an attack on Scott's interpretation of the structural reconstruction of wheelhouses and to put forward the unusual idea that the wheelhouse was an elaborate windbreak for an internal tent used by the Iron Age colonists (Lethbridge 1952, 180). More importantly, Lethbridge was the first to claim that wheelhouses were chronologically successive to brochs in the Western Isles, even if for very subjective reasons; he saw the brochs as the initial strongholds of invaders with the wheelhouses developing from them at a later, more settled stage.

More influential was Alison Young, Scott's immediate successor in the Western Isles, who developed his ideas and carried out excavations at the wheelhouse of Tigh Talamhanta in Barra (Young 1952) and at the nearby site of Dun Cuier (Young 1955), which she classified as a galleried dun. Young followed the accepted tradition of the time in regarding brochs as a special category of site which demanded rigourous definition, and even proposed her own classification system (Young 1961). This proposed the division of the brochs into Classes I and II of which only Class II, with their relatively small internal diameters and defensive locations, occur in the Western Isles. The galleried duns were supposed to represent a degeneration of this type of broch (Young 1961, 176) with a greater diversity of form. Young took a step backwards from Scott by divorcing brochs from the context of the hundreds of dun sites, with which they are geographically and structurally associated, basing this division principally on the results of her excavations at

Dun Cuier which produced late material of the C6th and C7th (Young 1955, 304). As we shall see below, this material derives from secondary occupation of the site and Dun Cuier was originally a broch in the traditional terminology. The interpretation of Dun Cuier is of central importance in the discussion of the relationship between brochs and duns and will be dealt with fully in a Chapter Five.

Young's view, that the Hebridean brochs were built by recently arrived colonists who proceeded to build wheelhouses when conditions became more stable and then resorted to the use of duns in the face of later incursions by the Dalriadic Scots, went unchallenged at the time and became firmly established in the literature. Young retained Scott's views on the ultimate southern English origin of brochs but replaced his theories on the integrity of the Hebridean Iron Age drystone building tradition with a view of successive structural forms built in response to inferred historical situations. The late date of Dun Cuier was used to separate the broch tradition from that of the galleried and, by implication, the island duns. Since Phase 2 the emphasis in Atlantic Scottish prehistory has shifted to the Northern Isles with the result that, for the Hebrides, the structural sequence proposed by Alison Young and Scott's Clettraval sequence have become fixed in the general literature.

The work of Young, Lethbridge and Scott represents the main theoretical and interpretative progress of the 1940s, 1950s and early 1960s, but a number of other excavations also took place during this period. Most notable among these were the excavations carried out as a result of the building of a rocket range in South Uist and Benbecula by the MoD. Several machair sites were excavated including a number of wheelhouses.

The main aim in this second phase of archaeological research was to relate the archaeological record of the islands to events and developments in England, supposedly nearer to the centre of the prehistoric world. The assumption was that the north was, in prehistory as now, a peripheral and dependant area where sophisticated structural and material forms introduced from southern England soon degenerated into less accomplished forms. Scott envisaged a rapid colonisation over a century or less, followed by a slow, painful decline into land congestion, cultural degeneration and raiding, giving rise to the development of broch towers. The development of the whole Iron Age drystone building tradition within Atlantic Scotland was not considered as a serious possibility at this stage.

Phase 3 - the 1960s and '70s

After the 1950s the attention in Atlantic Scottish studies was focused away from the Western Isles. The dominant figures in this third phase were Euan MacKie, working mainly in the Inner Hebrides and publishing widely on the origins and culture of the broch builders, and J.R.C. Hamilton working in the Northern Isles, notably at Clickhimin and Jarlshof. As MacKie, who dominated broch studies in the West, failed even to visit the Western Isles in the course of his thesis research (MacKie 1965, 94) and Hamilton's fieldwork was based in the North, the resulting interpretations and hypotheses on brochs, duns

and wheelhouses tended to identify the Inner Hebrides and the Northern Isles as the core areas.

The main preoccupations of this period were with the structural typology of the brochs and their architectural evolution. Their south-western origin and their function as defensive structures were affirmed by most workers at this time. Unlike Scott, who considered brochs as one element in a wider structural range, MacKie abstracted brochs from their context as part of prehistoric landscapes and treated them as a uniform phenomenon which could be meaningfully studied in isolation throughout Atlantic Scotland. Brochs were defined by very rigourous criteria based on architectural detail; landscape study was largely ignored. The most extreme manifestation of this is in the treatment, by MacKie, of the brochs in Glen Beag on the mainland opposite Skye; sites which were evenly spaced along a narrow glen represent, according to MacKie, the beginning and end of the broch-building tradition, with Dun Grugaig as an alleged semi-broch and Duns Troddan and Telve as solid-based broch towers at the end of the broch sequence (MacKie 1965, 109). That MacKie does not consider the implications of this theory in terms of landscape study is indicative of the general lack of concern for site context in this phase of broch studies. The purpose of the present study is not to set out to challenge the various interpretations of brochs on a national basis but to examine brochs as elements within the settlement patterns of one area. The approach adopted by MacKie may be usefully cited as the antithesis of the present work and serves to illustrate how architectural typology has dominated all other aspects of the Atlantic Scottish Iron Age.

Throughout the period very little fieldwork was carried out on the later prehistory of the Western Isles where excavation tended to concentrate on earlier periods (e.g. Northton, Rosinish, parts of the Udal). Small scale excavations at Toe Head (Simpson 1966), Dun Carloway (Tabraham 1976), and parts of the Udal sequence represent the main work done in the 1960s and 1970s. The typological site sequence proposed by Alison Young went unchallenged and, with increasing age, settled into the archaeological literature. MacKie's work placed wheelhouses later than brochs, mainly on the basis of the evidence from the Northern Isles, but he accepted Young's views on the late date of duns which enabled him to avoid dealing with the problem of the structural parallels between the brochs and duns of the Western Isles. This period was one of stagnation for the archaeology of the Outer Isles during which little fieldwork was undertaken and even less work attempted on interpretation and synthesis.

Phase 4 - Recent work

In recent years the field of broch studies has again attracted attention with the excavation of sites, such as Bu and Howe in the Orkneys, which have tended to cast doubt on the previously held theories concerning brochs. Work over the past few years in the Western Isles has again begun to tackle the problems of Hebridean prehistory through specific research projects. Work by Cowie and Bohncke at Tob nan Leobag sought to provide a picture of the environmental history of the region linked to the archaeological monuments on the peninsula

(Cowie and Bohncke forthcoming). Iain Crawford's work at the Udal in North Uist has been in progress since the early 1960s and seeks to trace the settlement history of one small and well-defined area. This site, when finally published, will be of considerable value in terms of the succession of structural forms and material culture. Unfortunately by the nature of the single-site or single-area approach the settlement patterns of any period are not reflected and we are presented with a chronological section demonstrating activity at one small location without any indication of its place in the wider settlement system. In terms of the Iron Age settlement patterns the evidence from the Udal has not affected the traditional model simply because it fails to tackle the basic problems of the relationships between site forms and between inland and coastal settlement.

Since 1985 a research project has been underway centered on the Edinburgh University Archaeological Field Centre at Callanish Farm in Lewis. This has involved land and air survey, land and underwater excavation and the setting up of an experimental farm, all designed to investigate the later prehistory of the region. Initial field survey demonstrated that there were many features in common between the various sites classified as island duns, brochs and crannogs in Lewis and Harris (Armit 1985). Excavation at the site of Dun Bharabhat in West Lewis (A.L18), combining land and underwater techniques, has begun to indicate that island duns and brochs may be very difficult to separate typologically and chronologically (Harding and Armit 1990). Excavations at this site, at the nearby Berie broch (Harding and Armit 1990; A.L19) and at the iron age settlement complex at Cnip (Armit 1988a; C.1), together with field survey, are aimed at producing a settlement study of an area which combines a large number of recorded settlement sites of various types.

Patrick Topping's doctoral thesis on later prehistoric pottery in the Hebrides broke down Scott's Clettraval sequence, by examining the stratigraphic evidence from the excavated sites which produced large amounts of pottery. This revealed that the numerical analysis which produced the sequence was flawed, being based on too few sherds in certain cases and on unproven stratigraphic connections between spatially unconnected parts of the site (Topping 1985). The removal of the support of this pottery sequence eliminated the last justification of Alison Young's structural typology. Another doctoral thesis, by Alan Lane, has set out a convincing sequence for the late pre-Norse and Norse pottery of the region, based on the material from the Udal (Lane 1983; 1990), and this has clarified the chronological position of a number of sites.

Recent work in North Uist at the sites on Loch Olabhat, carried out by the writer since 1986, has revealed a further complication in the classification of later prehistoric settlement types (Armit 1986, 1987, 1988b and 1990b): the site of Eilean Domhnuill a Spionnaidh (M.13), previously classified as an island dun of the later prehistoric period, has shown on excavation only early neolithic occupation material. The implications of this site for settlement study and classification will be discussed below in Chapter Ten. The settlement at Eilean Olabhat (C.19) has also produced material datable to the later prehistoric period (Armit 1988b).

A number of rescue excavations carried out by SDD/HBM on sand-dune erosion sites in the Uists has continued to add to the corpus of excavated material. The site of Hornish Point in South Uist (W.14), with its succession of wheelhouses, is particularly important in terms of its chronology as will be discussed in Chapter Six. Survey work both by Sheffield University, in Barra, and by the Loch Olabhat project, in North Uist, has begun to show a previously undemonstrated density of sites in the areas under study.

Summary

The mistrust of the old hypotheses and the lack of any convincing model of prehistoric settlement is reflected in the confusion of the most recent book on the archaeology of the Western Isles: this suggests that brochs, duns and wheelhouses may all be constituents of one hierarchical settlement pattern as the abodes of, respectively, chiefs, sub-chiefs and ordinary farmers. This view ignores not only the wealth of chronological material but also the distributions and numbers of the sites concerned. It is in this context that the present study begins. The lack of a convincing and testable model of later prehistoric settlement, involving all of the settlement forms, is a serious handicap to the planning of any research project. In the following chapters the structural and material evidence from the many early excavations will be reassessed without the restrictions imposed by the initial assumption of south-western origin or of any subjective assessment of varying architectural 'worth' between structural types. This re-examination will be aided by evidence from field survey, the recent excavations and by the application of structural, locational and spatial analysis, where applicable, to the site distributions. The history of research shows that the value of past work in the islands lies primarily in the wealth of structural and material remains. Previous syntheses have been hampered by the belief in diffusion from the south and by the geographical extension of inappropriate typological schemes from other areas. It is essential to return to the original material and to reconsider it in the light of present, more flexible approaches to Atlantic Scottish prehistory.

Chapter Four - Classification

The Western Isles are particularly rich in prehistoric field monuments: the long traditions of drystone building, which persisted from the earliest prehistoric settlement of the islands until as recently as the end of the nineteenth century, have resulted in the formation of landscapes covered by the grassed-over remains of abandoned settlement and burial sites. To attempt any analysis of settlement sites and their distribution over particular, archaeologically defined, periods we must first define the criteria of selection.

Euan MacKie has written, in reference to brochs specifically, that "unless the term is defined exactly any discussion becomes too diffuse to be constructive" (MacKie 1984, 108). I will argue below that rigid adherence to typological classification can often lead to the discussion becoming too specific to be constructive, with classifications introduced to rationalise interpretations rather than as tools for study. The analysis of artificially segregated groups can lead to a form of tunnel-vision when the validity of the classification system in defining exclusive groups is too readily assumed. The relationships between the types of site which our classification systems define are at least equal in importance to relationships between sites belonging to any one type.

Nonetheless MacKie is correct in that we must have a classification system in order to define our groups of data and to give concrete form to our interpretations. It must be stressed, in relation to the classification of brochs and duns in particular, that classification systems are tools to be used during archaeological analysis and not facts inherent to the data.

Systems of classification are not, in themselves, the problem; rather it is the use made of such systems in the analysis and interpretation of data which can become obstructive to an objective understanding of that data. In the case of the brochs it has long been the practice to define the type by a rigourous classification system; sites which are adjudged to fit the required criteria (often on the basis of good preservation) are then removed from the context of the other monuments with which they are associated, to compare them with sites from widely different local contexts which also happen to fit the same prescribed criteria. From analyses of this artificial distribution, conclusions are drawn, largely without reference to the associated monuments. The perceived nature of the problem of the brochs, involving questions of architectural typology, has dictated the way in which data have been gathered and the classification of the sites themselves. The classification which will be developed in this chapter will attempt to group the sites without assuming that there need be any special treatment of the sites which have been previously thought to belong to the category of brochs, and have been thus divorced from the context of the other sites. Classification will be on the basis of observed features from field survey and the limited excavation evidence, prior to a detailed consideration in subsequent chapters of the nature of the settlement systems of which these sites were a part.

This classification is concerned with sites which can be reasonably securely interpreted as having been used for human habitation. It excludes therefore, in the primary consideration of the evidence, sites which may have been stock or field enclosures, find scatters and isolated middens. These sites represent settlement evidence in a wider sense but the evidence from these types of site in the Western Isles is not sufficiently clear as to date or function on any one site, or sufficiently coherent in terms of site distribution, to enable any detailed analysis. The sites discussed here are those which have structural evidence of later prehistoric settlement.

The dating of sites to the later prehistoric period, or indeed to any archaeological or historical period, on the basis of surface traces is inherently problematic especially in an area as poorly understood as the Western Isles. It is not necessarily the case that structural or morphological features need relate to a specific archaeological period. In the case of the many occupied island sites in the Western Isles this problem is particularly acute, as it is clear from excavations, such as that at Eilean Domhnuill, Loch Olabhat in North Uist (Armit 1990b; 1992; M.13), that these locations were a favoured settlement focus from at least the third millennium bc. The problems in classification vary in detail between the various site types and will be discussed more fully below. It is important here again to take note of the numerous sites without extant structural remains, which may nonetheless have originally formed part of the same settlement systems as their more obvious neighbours. It will be important to assess the nature and distribution of such sites in relation to the settlement distribution patterns examined in the following chapters.

Before defining the classification system I will first review the way in which the material has been classified in the past. The first attempt at classification was by the RCAHMS and was formulated to accommodate the results of their Hebridean survey. This was based on the state of knowledge at the end of the long period of antiquarianism in the area. The next important classification of brochs and duns was MacKie's, from his paper of 1965. Although it did not devote much attention to the Western Isles, this classification was central to later work. The classification of the monuments of the Western Isles apart from the brochs and, to a lesser extent the duns, has not been reassessed since 1928 and is in need of updating in the light of large amounts of new data from the islands and from related monuments in other areas.

The RCAHMS survey recognised the basic unity of the structures classified as brochs, duns and promontory forts (RCAHMS 1928, xxxv). The group of Defensive Constructions into which these monuments were placed was used interchangeably with the term 'dun' so that, in effect, brochs are being classified as a specialised form of dun (RCAHMS 1928, xxxv). The other main group of relevance here is the group classed as 'earth-houses' which was taken to include such variants as the wheelhouses. No precise criteria were given for these two wide groupings other than that earth-houses were drystone buildings constructed just under ground level. Presumably the term 'Defensive Constructions' was thought to be self-evident. The two main groups were thus defined on the one hand by assumed function and on the other by construction technique. The earth-house category had no real subdivision but the division of the Defensive Constructions is of interest as it has to some extent survived.

The first subdivision of the Defensive Constructions was the group of Galleried Duns. These were defined as drystone forts with galleries and/or cells within the thickness of their walls but with irregular or oval plans which prevented them from identification with the brochs. The brochs themselves were defined by the combination of a series of specialised architectural features including circularity, galleries and cells within the walls, long narrow entrances and guard chambers. 'Forts in Lochs' represent the class which came to be known as island duns; there are no set criteria given for their definition except that 'Late Duns', a sub-class, are separated by virtue of rectilinear central structures, outer walls with boat noosts and occasional use of lime-mortar (RCAHMS 1928, xl). The other two groups of Defensive Constructions were the Seashore Forts and Promontory Forts; the Promontory Forts were simple walls across the landward side of promontories while the Seashore Forts had walls surrounding a whole promontory.

This early stage in the classification of the monuments was generally imprecise and unsystematic, based variously on location, structural typology and assumed function, combined in an intuitive fashion to group the inventory of surveyed sites. A prime example of this is the use of the term 'crannog' to designate, as if as a separate site type, any artificial island with collapsed stone but insufficient preserved structure to be classified as an island dun. It has, however, been the only attempt to deal specifically with all of the later prehistoric monument types of the Western Isles.

Subsequent work in the Western Isles did not attempt a full-scale re-evaluation of the classification, although Scott did define wheelhouses more specifically as a separate class and subdivided them into wheelhouses and aisled roundhouses (Scott 1948). MacKie's study of the brochs of Atlantic Scotland (MacKie 1965) was the next major work affecting the classification of the Hebridean sites and the way in which they were perceived by archaeologists.

MacKie's work dealt with brochs at a national level. Inheriting a long tradition of broch studies, MacKie's initial preoccupations were with the definition of brochs on architectural grounds as a means of defining a distribution which could then be used to construct hypotheses on the origin and spread of the type. These were basically the aims of several preceding generations of broch scholars of a school represented most forcibly by Joseph Anderson, who pioneered work on the interpretation of the brochs (1883). The basic requirement for this study, as MacKie saw it, was a strict definition of what does and does not constitute a broch (MacKie 1965). MacKie's work was initially set out in 1965 and pursued in a series of subsequent papers (e.g. MacKie 1971, 1974, 1975, 1980). In his most recent restatement of his case (1984) he refers back to his original classification of 1965. In this earliest paper, MacKie divides the 'small stone forts' of Scotland into two groups on the basis of the presence or absence of specialised architectural features (MacKie 1965, 100). Those lacking the defining characteristics of

brochs are described as duns, which can contain galleries within their walls but which lack the supposed regularity and homogeneity of the brochs. MacKie assumed that these 'duns' varied widely in age and in their cultural context (MacKie 1965, 100) and they are not subject to any internal classification; from that point the duns play no further major part in MacKie's hypothesis, except as a reservoir to contain sites, such as Crosskirk in Caithness (Fairhurst 1984), which on excavation fail to fulfil the stringent criteria for structure and dating which MacKie requires for acceptance as a broch (MacKie 1984, 125).

MacKie followed the long archaeological tradition of seeing the brochs as a distinct, highly specialised group of tower-like structures, their height made possible by their main defining characteristic, the technique of hollow-wall building. By the use of this technique two concentric walls tied together at intervals by rows of lintels, forming super-imposed intramural galleries, enabled the structure to be built to a great height whilst retaining considerable structural stability. The further elaborations and subdivisions on the basis of architectural typology are not of particular relevance to the Western Isles and need not be discussed here: the implications of the Western Isles data, and the interpretations put forward in this study for the wider field of broch and broch-related studies, including MacKie's ideas, will be discussed in later chapters. For any given structure in the field to fit MacKie's definition as a broch it must display a number of architectural features. Central to the definition is the requirement that structures must show positive evidence of having had at least one upper intramural gallery (MacKie 1972, 59). In practice this means that a site must have preservation up to a level above the floor of the upper gallery for some part of its circuit as even the presence of intramural stairs may simply mean that there was access to a relatively low wallhead.

This definition in itself, as with any definition, is not objectionable, although its utility is open to question. It defines a group of sites on the basis of clearly set out criteria. It is in the use to which this and other classifications of the monuments of Atlantic Scotland have been put that the problems arise. From his work on the architectural typology and distribution of the sites defined as brochs by this means, and on the basis of further subdivisions within the group on architectural grounds, MacKie feels justified in invoking "the facts of structural detail and geographical distribution" to help defend his hypotheses (MacKie 1984, 120). Clearly the definition of sites described above and their analysis reflects only assumptions of the relevance of structural and architectural detail and geographical distribution, since the initial definition of the sample of sites used reflects pre-existing ideas on the nature and number of brochs and on their homogeneity. If the definition of brochs was widened, or indeed further restricted, these 'facts' would quickly change.

There are several ways in which, in the Western Isles, we may feel that the MacKie definition of brochs distorts the perceived settlement pattern, and why we may wish to adopt a different approach to the study and classification of the 'small stone forts' in the area. The first and most obvious objection to MacKie's definition is that it is not applicable in the field. Factors of preservation dictate that although relative to elsewhere in Britain the preservation of later prehistoric monuments is extremely good in Atlantic Scotland, it is rare for a drystone structure to survive to any great height for almost two millennia in an area where drystone building has been virtually continuous. An abandoned structure soon becomes a quarry for stone for later constructions. Within living memory, archaeological sites in the islands have been systematically robbed of their building stone. Under these circumstances it is only occasionally that a broch will have been allowed to survive up to its first floor level. As well as stone robbing, the collapse of a massive structure like a broch will inevitably obscure the galleries and other defining characteristics. Even if one accepts that the brochs were a distinct and homogeneous type separate from the other types of 'dun', one must concede that employing MacKie's criteria will drastically under-represent the numbers of brochs in any area. A denuded or collapsed broch will almost inevitably be indistinguishable from an ungalleried drystone structure in a similar state of disrepair. If one accepts that this inability to distinguish between such sites will occur then one cannot speak in terms of 'facts' of geographical distribution.

The second main difficulty with the traditional school of broch studies, of which MacKie has been the most authoritative representative, is that the classification systems in practice have employed a qualitative judgement on the architectural merit of sites and the relationship of this to site function. It has often been assumed that brochs represent the dwellings of an elite or else the periodic refuge of a wider community, or indeed both. In this context there has been a marked reluctance to allow too many brochs to 'exist'. In the Western Isles any site which cannot be shown to have possessed those architectural features characteristic of the brochs has been assumed to be a dun, which, as we have seen in the discussion of the history of research in the islands, has meant that it has been interpreted as belonging to a later and degenerate manifestation of the tradition which produced the brochs. Thus the number of duns has swollen while the number of brochs has been kept at its lowest possible level. The view that duns are heterogeneous and unclassifiable at a detailed level has helped this situation to develop. This problem will assume primary importance in Chapter Five, which will show that there is no archaeological evidence to suggest that a distinct class of drystone ungalleried duns existed in the Western Isles in the mid-1st millennium AD, or indeed at any other time.

In the Western Isles, MacKie accepted 9 sites as definite brochs, with 2 further probable sites and 17 further possible sites. This maximum total of 28 brochs fitting MacKie's criteria leaves well over 100 sites as 'duns', so it becomes imperative that one understand this class of site and its relationship with the brochs to determine whether or not it really is a distinct grouping.

MacKie's scheme is intrinsically likely to underestimate the number of brochs in any area due to factors of preservation, and does not attempt to deal with the classification of duns. Instead it employs the concept of a large class of undifferentiated duns to accommodate sites which, for architectural reasons, fail to qualify for the broch class. The validity of any discussion of brochs at a wider level must depend to a great extent on the relationship between this wider class of site and the brochs themselves. This central problem has not been addressed in the broch-orientated literature. In formulating a classification system for the present study it is essential to deal with this problem and to avoid pre-judging the relationship between sites in a subjective evaluation of architectural features.

A broader classification has been proposed for the roundhouses of Atlantic Scotland as a whole (Armit 1991) using the term 'atlantic roundhouse' to cover the range of roofed structures known variously as brochs, semi-brochs, duns and galleried duns. This system allows for greater variety of construction and makes no initial assumptions of origins or function: it includes any free-standing, thick-walled drystone roundhouse in Atlantic Scotland. Within this class one can recognise 'complex atlantic roundhouses' by the presence of the architectural traits of hollow-walled construction ('broch architecture') and within this the 'broch towers', MacKie's 'brochs', where the techniques of broch architecture are combined to create a tower-like multi-storey roundhouse. This is the terminology used in the following discussion.

The classification system presented in Ill. 4.1 has been formulated to divide the structures of the later prehistoric period in the islands on the initial basis of structural form, and then on the basis of the arrangement and partition of space within the structure. I have not assumed that brochs, or any other type of monument, need represent a distinct and specialised class. The system is designed to give flexibility of classification and to avoid qualitative labelling of sites whilst allowing enough division to make the data manageable. I have not set out to define types of site such as brochs at an initial stage. The purpose of the classification is not to give defined form to site types already assumed to exist on the basis of archaeological tradition but simply to provide a framework within which the monuments of the Western Isles can be meaningfully discussed. In subsequent chapters I will assess whether or not the divisions made on the basis of structure and space have meaning in terms of function, chronology and other archaeological concerns. Later chapters will deal with the validity of more specific subdivisions within the broad categories of site defined here.

The present system is designed purely as a research tool. It is not assumed that these categories have meaning other than as a convenient means of defining structurally-related monument forms. It is designed to deal only with the monuments of this one area and it is accepted that classification on the basis of alternative criteria such as location or size could be equally valid in studies related to different aspects of the archaeological record. There is nothing definitive about the classification.

The first step in the classification of Ill. 4.1 is the defining of that group of structures in the Western Isles characterised by the use of coursed drystone walling, which would appear to include all of the known structures of the later prehistoric period as well as of many subsequent periods. It does not include the structures noted at earlier prehistoric sites such as Eilean an Tighe (Scott 1950), or Eilean Domhnuill, Loch Olabhat (Armit 1988b), where structures appear to have been based on boulder settings which seem unlikely to have supported coursed walling.

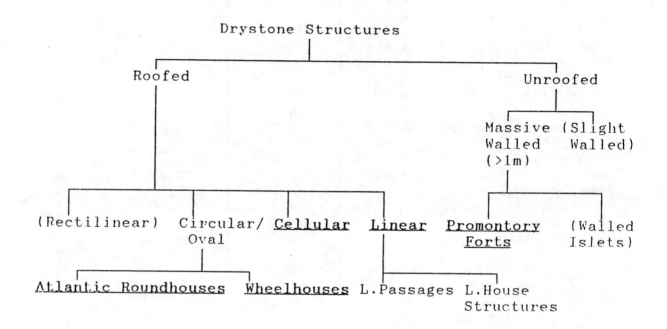

(Underlined classes represent chapter headings)

Ill. 4.1 Preliminary Classification of Western Isles Drystone Field Monuments

	Atlantic Roundhouse	Wheelhouse	Cellular	Linear
Dun Carloway	A.L12			
Dun Bharabhat	A.L18		C.4	
Loch na Berie	A.L19		C.5	
Rudh an Duin	A.NU3			
Dun a Ghallain	A.NU4		C.14	
Eilean a Ghallain	A.NU6		C.15	
Dun Thomaidh	A.NU7		C.16	
Garry Iochdrach	A.NU13	W.7		
Cnoc a Comhdhalach	A.NU14	W.8		
Eilean Maleit	A.NU17	W.10		
Buaile Risary	A.NU20			
Dun Ban, Grimsay	A.NU51		C.23	
Dun Cuier	A.B4		C.28	
Cnip		W.1	C.3	L.1
The Udal		W.3	C.10	L.7
Foshigarry		W.4	C.11	L.8
Bac Mhic Connain		W.5		
Sollas		W.6		
Clettraval		W.11		
Bruach Ban		W.12		
Bruthach a Tuath		W.13		L.12
Hornish Point		W.14		
A Cheardach Mhor		W.15	C.24	
A Cheardach Bheag		W.16		
Usinish		W.19		
Kilpheder		W.22		
Tigh Talamhanta		W.25		
Galson			C.2	
Sithean an Altair			C.12	
Eilean Olabhat			C.19	
Unival			C.22	
Gress Lodge				L.3
Vallay				L.9
Drimore				L.13

Ill. 4.2 Presence and Absence of Defined Types on Excavated Sites
(Codes Refer to Catalogue Entries)

These related structures will be discussed in Chapter Ten. It also omits structures constructed of stone-faced turf banks although some of these, e.g. at Druim nan Dearcag, North Uist (Armit 1988b), may belong in the very latest pre-Norse period. The numerous hut circles recorded in the islands are also ruled out for this reason. There have been no excavations of hut circles in the Western Isles so there is no secure dating evidence. Site associations often suggest, however, that many of these sites may be of medieval or later date while excavations of such sites elsewhere may produce early prehistoric dates. In the absence of any basic morphological or survey data to distinguish examples of the later prehistoric period it would be premature to attempt to bring these sites into the present study.

The second level of classification is the division of this very broad range of structures into two principal types: those which can reasonably be interpreted as roofed or potentially roofed structures, and those which, through size and/or irregularity, could not be other than unroofed enclosures.

The roofed structures can be further subdivided into four basic structural forms; rectilinear, circular or oval, linear or passage-like, and cellular. No rectilinear structures are known to belonging to the prehistoric period of the Western Isles as yet, and this group is dominated by the many hundreds of blackhouse settlements which are a dominant feature of the Western Isles landscape. For the basis of this study this rectilinear group is not further subdivided.

The linear/passage form of structure is restricted to the types generally referred to in the literature as souterrains and earth-houses. These are divided into two classes on the basis of dimensions. Those which are less than 1m wide and roofed with lintels are classed as linear passages. Those which are greater than 2m in width, and too wide to be roofed with lintels, have been classed as linear house structures. The reasons for this subdivision will become clear in Chapter Eight. The linear house structures could equally be classed as rectilinear structures by their proportions, but their subterranean construction and relationship to longer linear structures elsewhere create an argument for them to be kept distinct from the vast numbers of above-ground rectilinear structures of all periods in the Western Isles.

The circular and oval drystone structures account for the bulk of the sites which have been interpreted as being of later prehistoric date. These require further subdivision to organise the subsequent discussion effectively. This level of classification is based on the internal organisation of space; sites with a radially partitioned internal area, based on the construction of regularly spaced drystone piers, appear to constitute a well-defined subdivision separate from sites with open central areas. This radially partitioned group can be manageably discussed at this level of classification. In the Western Isles radially partitioned sites have previously been classified as wheelhouses and aisled roundhouses, although in other areas, notably the Orkneys, many sites classed as brochs would fall into this group. This subdivision on the basis of spatial organisation is a purely organisational device at this stage of analysis. For convenience and consistency

of terminology these sites will be referred to as wheelhouses throughout this thesis.

The group with open interiors encompass the sites variously known in the literature as brochs, duns, island duns, galleried duns etc. These are the atlantic roundhouses in the terminology described above and they will be classified as such here. This organisational division will be examined in later chapters to assess its meaning for later prehistoric settlement analysis in the islands. It must be stressed at this stage that the descriptive classification proposed here cuts across previous classifications which have tended to combine several levels of classification e.g. architecture, preservation, chronology and dimensions. The present classification divides the monuments according to those morphological and other features which are most often visible through field survey: it is recognised that alternative classifications with alternative criteria (e.g. on the basis of access analysis or internal spatial patterning) may be equally valid in other analyses. It is important to avoid confusing the levels and criteria of classification.

The fourth subdivision of the drystone roofed structures are the 'cellular' structures. These are defined as being formed of one or more cells enclosed by a wall which follows the shape of the internal spatial arrangements. Unlike atlantic roundhouses, where the main cell is central to the structure and where its position is dictated by the nature of the walling, the cellular structures may form irregular agglomerations of cells within regular or irregular walling.

The other group of structures which come into consideration for the later prehistoric period are the drystone enclosures. Within this extensive category it is possible to recognise two recurring forms which may be linked to settlement of this period. The promontory forts and walled islets are defined by their location and relatively massive construction. Both types are formed of walls which follow the course of the promontory or island on which they are built, normally resulting in an irregular shape; both types may also consist of discontinuous lengths of walling rather than simple circuits. By analogy with sites in other areas and by the comparison of structural features with other forms of later prehistoric settlement, the promontory forts, defined by location, can be studied along with the monuments classified above. In the absence of any dating material and of any closely comparable sites elsewhere, the walled islets will be discussed in Chapter Ten along with other 'miscellaneous structures'.

I will apply the term 'monumental' to certain types of structure in the following chapters. In the context of the present study, this term will be taken to describe any structure in which the investment of skill and labour in construction greatly exceeds the requirements of structural stability. It can also describe, but is not exclusive to, structures which are so constructed or located as to be highly visible in the landscape.

Chapter Five - Atlantic Roundhouses

The majority of the known later prehistoric structures of the Western Isles are atlantic roundhouses - free-standing, circular and oval, drystone roofed structures known variously in the literature as *brochs*, *galleried duns*, *island duns* and *forts*. 140 of these sites are presently recorded (Ill. 5.1). The division between the atlantic roundhouses and wheelhouses is problematic, especially for those monuments known only through field survey where radial partitions may be difficult to detect. Atlantic roundhouses in the Northern Isles commonly contain radial partitions. An additional complicating factor is the possibility of unrecognised timber radial partitions in the 'open' interior roundhouses. The division is organisational rather than archaeological at this stage: the relationships between the various types will be discussed in the Parts Three and Four.

This discussion begins with reviews of the thirteen excavated sites and goes on to examine additional data derived from field survey. Much of our information on the atlantic roundhouse sites of the Western Isles derives from excavations carried out in the early part of this century and the quality of the evidence is highly variable. Of the relatively recent excavations of the 1970s and '80s, two, Dun Bharabhat and Loch na Berie, are not yet complete and the third was conducted on a very limited scale in one cell of Dun Carloway. The discussion presented here is hampered by the lack of recently excavated sites as the older excavations were seldom recorded in sufficient detail to support extensive reinterpretation.

The excavated sites will be examined individually from north to south through the island chain. They will be discussed in terms of their overall site structure, their internal structure, material culture and chronology. The codes in each site heading relate to the site's catalogue entry in Appendix 3.

Excavated sites

A.L12 Dun Carloway, Lewis NB 1901 4122 (Tabraham 1976)

Introduction - Dun Carloway is the best known and most completely preserved of the Hebridean atlantic roundhouses. It has long been regarded as one of the archetypal *brochs* and is one of the tallest surviving prehistoric structures in Scotland. Excavation in 1971 was restricted to one intra-mural chamber at risk from the effects of masonry consolidation.

The site stands on a rocky hillside at c.50m OD. The present wallhead, at some 9m in height, commands an extensive view across much of the coast of West Lewis, although the structure itself is obscured from view by the dark hillside. Although imposing from the immediate vicinity the site is not obvious from any great distance.

Site structure - There are no signs of multi-period construction at this site and it is perhaps for this reason that it has survived so well. The massive-walled roundhouse was built using characteristic hollow-wall construction and is, by MacKie's typology, a *transitional broch*, i.e. it has galleries and cells for only part of its basal circuit (Ill.

5.2). The overall diameter is 14.3m at the base and the central cell has a diameter of 7.4m (RCAHMS 1928, no. 68, 18-20). The wall thickness varies from 2.9 - 3.8m overall at the base.

The original height of the structure was probably little in excess of the surviving height as the gallery narrows to an almost inaccessible width towards the wallhead.

Internal structure - The interior of the roundhouse was dominated by an open central cell containing an outcrop of rock in its north-eastern sector. This cell gave access into five cells or galleries. Gallery B gave access to an upper floor by means of a staircase running up over Gallery C. Galleries A and C were self contained with access only through the central cell. Gallery D on the ground floor was entered only from the south wall of the entrance passage and formed a 'guard cell'. A fifth gallery is represented by a blocked entrance between Gallery A and the main entrance but its extent is unknown. Blocking appears to be relatively recent and is not indicated on the RCAHMS plan of the site. Details of the first and upper floors are less well known as the surviving walling at that height occupies only a third of the circuit.

Only Gallery A was excavated and it is only here that there is any evidence for function although, as will be seen from the artefactual material and the C-14 dates, there is no evidence that this represents its original function. The excavator interpreted Gallery A as a pottery kiln because of the association of the position of the hearths with wall-voids and the absence of metal-working debris and domestic refuse. Doubt has been cast on this interpretation by Alan Lane who cited the lack of wasters, the small size of the sherds (indicating disturbance and redeposition) and the mixed nature of the pottery assemblage as evidence of the use of the chamber as a rubbish tip (Lane 1983, 265).

There seems to be no reason why, over the long duration of the use of the chamber, both of these interpretations should not have applied. Lane's hypothesis does not account for the presence of coherent hearths and the correlation of ash spread with the wall void, while the rubbish deposit idea is more plausible in accounting for the remainder of the material. None of the stratified deposits contains any material which can reliably dated before the mid-1st millennium AD, although the structural evidence demonstrates beyond reasonable doubt that Dun Carloway was built many centuries earlier (Armit 1991). It is not therefore possible to demonstrate the primary function of the chamber: although the wall-voids appear almost certainly to be original, their primary function may well have been for storage and only one (no. 1 in Tabraham 1976, Fig. 3) had any demonstrable link with the supposed pottery kiln.

Material culture and chronology - The excavated material does not appear to relate to the original occupation of the site. Clearly a structure of this sort would have been a focus for settlement until relatively recent times and the periodic clearing out of the cells and galleries and displacement of deposits would render it unlikely that any primary material would survive. Given also the small

Ill. 5.1 Distribution of Atlantic Roundhouses in the Western Isles

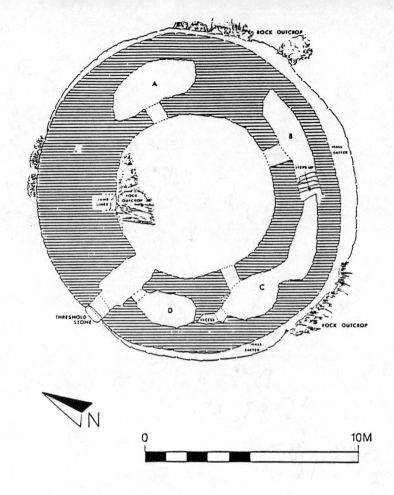

Ill. 5.2 Dun Carloway (after Tabraham 1976)

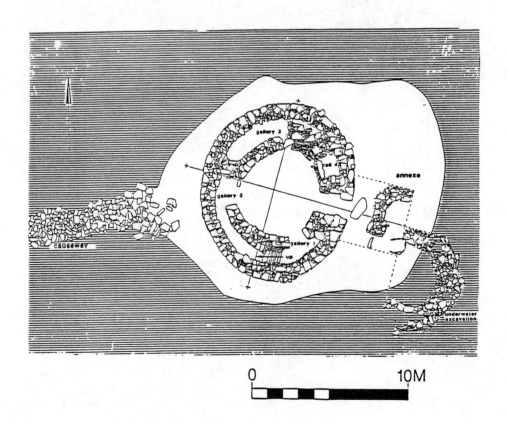

Ill. 5.3 Dun Bharabhat, Cnip

scale of the excavation it is not possible to conclude much from the material.

The pottery from the site is of a type commonly associated with the mid-late 1st millennium AD (App. 2). The assemblage is characterised by round-shouldered jars with flaring rims but notably includes shorter everted rims (e.g. Close-Brooks 1976, Nos. 5 and 57). Lane also noted the presence of a diagnostic Viking-Age platter sherd (Lane 1983, 265, Close-Brooks 1976, no. 43) in a layer stratified below a double cordoned globular jar of late Iron Age or Dark Age type. This double cordoned vessel (Close-Brooks 1976, no. 49) is closely paralleled in contexts dated AD 124 - 273 (GU 2327), at the 68% confidence limits, at Eilean Olabhat (Armit 1986, Fig. 5) and at Dun Cuier (Young 1955, 308, Fig. 10 no. 92). The mixture of types, in view of the likely use of the chamber at some stages for depositing rubbish, suggests that the assemblage derives from periodic cleaning of the interior. The only other find from the site was part of a disc-shaped rotary quern from context AG of the excavated chamber.

A C-14 date was obtained from a deposit of mollusc shell towards the top of the chamber deposits. The medieval date of 1300+/-150 ad (GX 3428) has no relevance to the original occupation of the site, serving only to reinforce the mixed nature of the material. None of the material from the excavations can justifiably be used to date the construction of the structure.

A.L18 Dun Bharabhat, Cnip, Lewis NB 0988 3531 (Harding and Topping 1986, Harding and Armit 1990)

Introduction - Dun Bharabhat in Uig parish in West Lewis is one of three sites on which excavations have been carried out so far through the Callanish Archaeological Research Centre. The excavations began in 1985, running parallel to the excavations at Loch na Berie some 500m distant.

The site lies on an islet in a small loch set among the hills behind the broad beach, Traigh na Berie. The site is not easily accessible from the beach, involving a steep, although short, ascent of a ravine in the hills, down which runs the outflow from the loch. The causeway from the islet reaches the shore directly opposite this access from the beach. Clearly the site has not been designed with convenient access to the machair and the sea as its main consideration. All other approaches to the site must be made through the surrounding hills, presently a maze of ill-drained peat-filled hollows. Although the site lies close to potential agricultural land it has been sited in such a way as to render access from that land more time-consuming than is necessary. Its siting gives a view out to sea, although only to a restricted area of the Traigh na Berie.

Site structure - The site consists of a small islet some 18 x 14m in extent, upon which sit the remains of an atlantic roundhouse recorded initially as a *dun* (RCAHMS 1928 no. 72, 21): its wall galleries and intra-mural staircase show it to be a complex atlantic roundhouse (Ill. 5.3). A causeway some 20m long connects this islet to the shore. Both the structure and the causeway had suffered through extensive stone-robbing, in the construction of an ad-

jacent sheep fank, but large quantities of stone remained both inside the structure and in the water around its perimeter, indicating an originally massive superstructure.

The structural evidence excavated at the site, so far, can be divided into three principal phases: pre-dun occupation, the roundhouse itself and secondary modifications in the interior of this roundhouse, post-dating its collapse. The main structure at Dun Bharabhat is central to the arguments presented later in this chapter and must be discussed in some detail. The secondary modifications, forming a cellular structure, will be discussed in Chapter Seven.

Perhaps the most significant feature of the excavation of Dun Bharabhat is the difference between its observed surface traces and its revealed structure. Prior to excavation the site appeared to be a typical ungalleried *island dun*; it was small in size; it had no visible traces of any cells or galleries; it had no tradition or local knowledge of having had any such feature, despite its use as a quarry; and its unimpressive remains consisted of a large heap of collapsed stone with occasional facing stones visible amid the rubble. In short the structure appeared to be an archetypal *dun* of the sort found widely throughout the islands. It was partly for this reason that the site was selected for excavation as an initial part of a project examining the various forms of structure of the region.

The site was taken to be an *island dun* of a form distinct from the *brochs* and of a type therefore which had not been subject to modern excavation. That this site, deliberately selected for its unimposing state, its non-monumentality and its apparent representativeness of the *island dun* class of structures, should be shown on excavation to contain extensive intra-mural galleries and cells, is potentially of great significance for the classification and archaeological interpretation of this class of field monument.

The central structure on the site shares a number of features with the *brochs* as defined by MacKie and others, but combines other features which would deny such an interpretation. It is of small overall size; only 11m in external diameter and 5.5m internally, significantly smaller than the traditional *broch* in the Mousa mould. The building technique is of the *broch* type: its two concentric drystone walls each averaging 1m in thickness, separated by intra-mural galleries of the same width around virtually the whole of the circuit at ground level, are tied by drystone walling at the entrance, by an intra-mural staircase and, on the pattern of other sites with such features, by capstones roofing the galleries (although those have not survived *in situ* on this site).

This pattern of construction reflects the traditional model for a ground-galleried *broch* as defined by MacKie (MacKie 1965) in a somewhat scaled-down version. The technique argues for an original multi-floored construction giving a combination of stability and height through a minimisation of the mass of stone used and an effective channelling of the weight. The presence of the intra-mural stair of seven steps again strongly suggests upper levels of occupation, although it could, on the pattern of many larger *galleried duns* in Ireland and south-west

Scotland, simply provide access to the wallhead. Other *broch* features at Dun Bharabhat include the low entrance passage with a rebate for the door, bar-holes and a pivot-stone indicating the original position of a wooden door at the inner edge of the outer wall.

Apart from its small size, Dun Bharabhat displays features which would make its interpretation as a *broch* difficult. The width of the entrance to the structure is 1m, extending to 1.4m inwards from the rebates. This is relatively wide but the opposite entrance to Gallery 2 is exceptionally so, measuring from 1.6m to 2m in width, although narrowed by an orthostat at a secondary stage in the site's occupation. This entrance seems to present unnecessary difficulties in roofing with a lintel and must have been occasioned by some functional factor in the need for access to Gallery 2. It is possible that the widening of this gallery entrance relates to the secondary modification of the site which occurred after the collapse of parts of the original structure: this possibility will be explored further in Chapter Seven. The entrance to Gallery 1, at 0.7 - 1.2m in width, is much more in the range which one would expect to enable easy human access whilst not placing an unreasonable strain on the lintel.

The atlantic roundhouse which dominates the islet lies between the causeway and an 'annexe' or extension. The entrance to the roundhouse leads onto this 'annexe' and some form of walk-way must have existed to enable access from the causeway to the rear of the roundhouse. Excavation of this area has been carried out both on land and underwater, and the latter work especially has begun to show indications of a long structural sequence underlying the level of the main roundhouse with well-preserved organic remains. Fragments of walling and a hearth on land behind the roundhouse entrance may be connected with the primary use of the main structure, but at the present stage of excavation this relationship is not clear and the nature of these structures remains uncertain.

Structurally Dun Bharabhat is an anomalous site which possesses virtually all of the requirements necessary to define it as a *broch* but which combines these features with exceptionally small size, a distinctly non-monumental siting and structural features which, if original, would have restricted possible height and stability. In the atlantic roundhouse terminology the structure is a complex roundhouse. This structure would appear to represent only the most archaeologically visible stage in a lengthy settlement sequence of which it was neither the first nor the last representative. This re-use of a single settlement focus over long time periods is a theme which is relevant to almost all of the excavated sites discussed in this study. Its importance in the context of the early excavations where such sequences were not expected or recognised is of crucial importance in the consideration of chronology.

Internal structure - The interpretation of the internal features of Dun Bharabhat is made especially hazardous by the displacement of stratigraphy caused by the collapse of the walls prior to the deposition of the latest occupation levels. These latest levels appear to be associated with secondary modifications to a number of structural features and clearly do not relate to the same structural form as is under discussion here. These later levels will be examined in Chapter Seven.

The only feature which can so far be recognised as original to the construction of the roundhouse is a central clay hearth defined by edge-set stones. This hearth was rebuilt many times throughout the use of the structure. The spatial organisation of the structure is based around a dominant central cell, some 5.5m in diameter and with an area of 23.7m^2, seemingly unpartitioned and with a central hearth. This cell gave access into 3 intra-mural chambers: Gallery 3, running for approximately a third of the circuit in the north-east, was the longest; Gallery 2, only slightly shorter ran along the south and west; Gallery 1 was in effect only a small cell slightly over 2m in length giving access to the stairs. Each of these peripheral chambers or galleries had only one entrance into the interior and none were interconnecting.

Material culture and chronology - Three C-14 dates have been obtained from the roundhouse deposits (App. 1). These are the first C-14 dates relating directly to the occupation of an atlantic roundhouse in the Western Isles and provide far earlier dating evidence than the conventional picture of *island dun* or *galleried dun* chronology would suggest. The dates give a *terminus post quem* for construction and *terminus ante quem* for the collapse of the structure. GU 2436 calibrating to 807 - 671BC, at the 68% confidence limit, and with a centroid of 733BC provides the *terminus post quem*: this derives from pre-roundhouse occupation material directly under the roundhouse floors. GU 2434 and 2435 with centroids at 31BC and 143BC respectively date the post-collapse occupation. The construction and occupation of the atlantic roundhouse is likely to date to the period from the C7th - C3rd BC (given that substantial primary occupation debris accumulated before the C-14 dated secondary deposits).

The ceramic assemblage from Dun Bharabhat includes a wide range of decorative motifs familiar from other Hebridean later prehistoric sites. These have recently been shown to have little positive dating value at present, without substantial well-stratified assemblages (Topping 1985 and App. 2). Motifs include applied cordons, ring bosses, chevron and other linear incision but lack ring-headed pin impressions and arcaded 'Clettraval Ware', as defined by MacKie at Dun Mor Vaul in Tiree (MacKie 1974, 159).

Apart from pottery the site has yielded glass beads of Guido's types 8 and 13. The small yellow bead of class 8 from Gallery 3 is of a widely recognised but poorly dated type (Armit 1991): Scottish parallels include examples from Dun Mor Vaul (MacKie 1974, 147) and Clickhimin (Hamilton 1968, Fig 41). Crucibles of the ubiquitous triangular type have also been recovered but again their distribution is wide, both chronologically and geographically.

A.L19 Loch na Berie, Lewis NB 1035 3525 (Harding and Armit 1987; 1988; 1990)

Introduction - The remains of a suspected *broch* were recorded by the Royal Commission (RCAHMS 1928 no. 69, 20) in Loch na Berie at the foot of the hills which surround the machair of the Traigh na Berie. Excavations by the Callanish Archaeological Research Project began in 1985 and work is still in progress.

The area and its reconstructed environmental history have been discussed in Chapter Two: the loch in its present form is little more than a peaty marsh for most of the year, although with the rise of the water table in winter it assumes the character of a shallow machair loch. Coring of the area suggests that the loch was formerly of much greater extent. This hypothesis fits with the expected picture formed on the basis of Ritchie's theories on the mechanisms of machair development (cf Chapter Two). The original loch would have been filled up by the retreating machair blocked by the surrounding hills. This process would have occurred over a very long period, and indeed is still continuing, with periods of sand movement alternating with periods of relative stability, resulting in the observed pattern of alternating bands of windblown sand and peat in the loch cores.

The excavated structures lie on what would have been an islet in the original, much larger, Loch na Berie. The siting is therefore superficially similar to that of the nearby Dun Bharabhat as both are structures built on islets in relatively small lochs. The siting at Berie is in fact considerably different: the Loch na Berie site lies only a few metres above present sea level and would always have commanded an extensive view over much of the Traigh na Berie. The position of the Berie causeway, leading westwards to the foot of the adjacent hills, may however have entailed a relatively extended walk around the loch to reach the flat machair plain and it is, in this respect, similar to that of Dun Bharabhat, sharing an apparent disregard for convenience of access to potential agricultural land as a factor in siting. It is important to note that the causeway in its present form cannot be original to the construction of the original roundhouse on the site. It lies at a level at least 1m above that of the foundations of this structure and must relate to the intrusive cellular structures. From the position of the islet relative to the probable original extent of the loch, it seems likely that this would also have been the only viable route for a causeway in the earlier period.

Site structure - The site as revealed by surface traces prior to excavation was an extremely unimposing one although, unlike Bharabhat, local knowledge of its original character had been preserved through the Royal Commission Inventory. The identification as a *broch* was originally doubtful, primarily because of the small size of the inner diameter and the width of the entrance (Armit 1985, 15). Excavation revealed these features to be the result of secondary modification in the construction of a series of cellular structures within the original roundhouse. These cellular structures are discussed separately in Chapter Seven.

The main roundhouse, which by its monumental construction enabled the site to remain archaeologically visible above the infilling loch, fits the definition of a *broch* even in its strictest application although excavation has not yet progressed to primary occupation of the interior. It is a *transitional broch* in MacKie's terminology with an overall diameter of c. 18m, with outer and inner concentric walls both 1m in thickness and an inter-

vening gallery of similar width. It is a broch tower with the whole range of the features of broch architecture in evidence (Ill. 5.4 and 5.5).

The structure has been extensively robbed but the rising peat and sand around it have preserved it to a probable height of over 3m in places: excavation has, therefore, begun at first floor level (Ill. 5.4). Gallery capstones of the first floor gallery level have been revealed *in situ* around almost the whole of the circuit. The ground floor plan contains a remarkable 7 separate cells and galleries linked by a staircase to the first floor. This staircase continues upwards to a (now destroyed) second floor level. A scarcement ledge of 35cm width has been uncovered at present ground level, continuous around the interior. The position of the 1st floor gallery entrances relative to the stairs show that the 1st floor must have been at the level of this scarcement.

This incontrovertible evidence of the existence of an upper level indicates that the structure is clearly a transitional *broch* by MacKie's definition and a broch tower in the terminology used here.

Internal structure - Any description of the internal structure of the Loch na Berie roundhouse must recognise the importance of the multiple floor-levels as a constraint on interpretation. The first floor has disappeared and leaves only two entrances, one to the intra-mural gallery which surrounds it and one to the stairs leading up and down. The second floor is entirely lost. The ground floor has seven cells or galleries leading off the main cell, which can be split into three groups. The first is the 'guard-cell', different from the rest in appearing to be accessible from the entrance passage. Secondly there is the elongated gallery segment, entered at a point opposite the main entrance, which gives access to the stairs to the first and second floors. The remaining five cells are of various sizes and do not appear to interconnect. The sketch plan of the ground floor (Ill. 5.5) is based on the upper parts of the cells which are visible below the 1st floor capstones.

Subdivisions of the large internal central cell will not become clear until after substantially more excavation. This central cell of 10 x 11m in diameter is exceptionally large compared to the central cell at Dun Bharabhat which is only 5.5m in diameter. The Berie roundhouse, with an interior area of 86.5m^2 compared to 23.7m^2 at Bharabhat, was more than three times as large in terms of enclosed space. Such massive differences of scale must clearly be accounted for in any interpretative model and will be examined in Part Three.

Material culture and chronology - The majority of the material recovered from the site in the excavations carried out prior to the end of 1988 relates to the secondary, cellular structures and will be dealt with in Chapter Seven. Only the deposits excavated in the first floor gallery constitute material older than these structures but even this material need not relate to the primary occupation of the massive roundhouse: any number of intervening levels may separate the two structural horizons.

The putatively primary material consists of pottery of a very different character from that of the interior of the

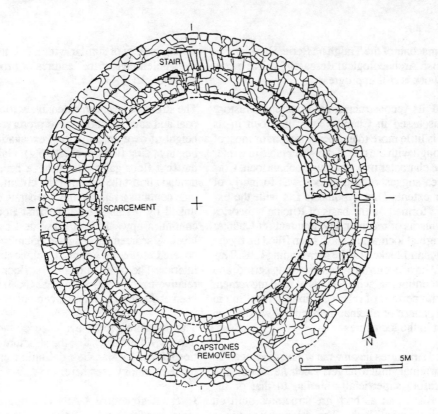

Ill. 5.4 Loch na Berie First Floor Plan

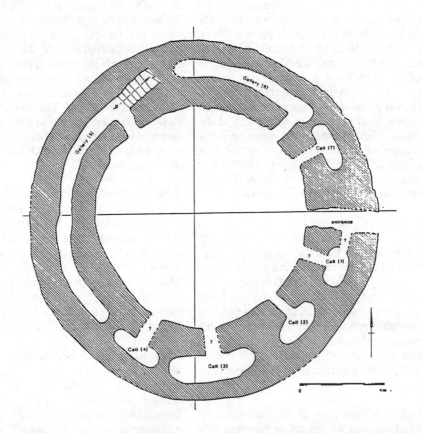

Ill. 5.5 Loch na Berie Ground Floor Sketch Plan

cellular structure: in contrast to the total absence of decoration on the later assemblage the gallery pottery is profusely decorated and made in a harder fired ware. The motifs represented include a wide range similar to those of Dun Bharabhat and characteristic of the traditionally Hebridean Iron Age assemblages (App. 2).

A.NU3 Rudh an Duin, Vallay, North Uist NF 7857 7617 (Beveridge 1911)

Introduction - The site of Rudh an Duin, lying on a low rocky promontory on the south-east side of the island of Vallay, was excavated by Erskine Beveridge prior to 1911. Beveridge describes the site as a "*broch* or *broch-like* structure" (1911, 216, [my italics]). Very little information is given and it appears that the site did not capture Beveridge's imagination sufficiently to provoke full excavation. The site was not excavated to bedrock and it is likely that occupation layers continued below the level to which Beveridge excavated. The site remained obscure in subsequent studies (classed as a *dun* in RCAHMS 1928 no. 184, 57, and accepted as such by MacKie 1972, 129).

Rudh an Duin has been subjected to severe tidal erosion prior to and since its excavation. High tides flooded the interior at the time of the excavation to a depth of 0.5m. The roundhouse lies on a small rocky promontory jutting into Vallay Strand, joined to Vallay itself. The local geomorphology has been discussed above (Chapter Two): Rudh an Duin would have been situated, prior to the drowning of the Strand, on either a rocky eminence above the machair plain or, perhaps more likely, on an islet in a loch behind the coastal ridge which the present island of Vallay would have formed. It would have been sheltered from the sea by Vallay, commanding an extensive view across the machair plain.

Site structure - The sole recorded structure from Rudh an Duin is the atlantic roundhouse. This structure was very badly dilapidated: part of its circuit had disappeared even on the interior, on its south-east side, and all but the north-west part of its external wall-face had been lost through erosion.

As at Dun Bharabhat and Loch na Berie, the surface traces of the site gave little indication of its structural character: Beveridge recalled that the site had "a rather unpromising aspect" (1911, 215). Excavation revealed the remains of a massive circular drystone roundhouse of exceptionally large dimensions (an external diameter of c. 24m and an internal diameter of c. 14m) preserved to a maximum of 1m in height on its inner face. Beveridge noted the presence of two concentric walls on the east side of the circuit and although his plan appears to confuse the course of the two, it is clear that on this part of the circuit at least there was a ground level intra-mural gallery. The plan hints at a continuation around the south and south-west but in the absence of clearer recording it is only possible to say that a ground gallery existed for part of the circuit.

Rudh an Duin is a complex atlantic roundhouse with the characteristic low narrow entrance passage, apparently roofed by lintels, which Beveridge found only slightly displaced. Clearly the presence of upper levels could not be demonstrated in such a badly damaged structure. In

the traditional terminology Rudh an Duin would be a transitional or ground-galleried *broch*, of exceptionally large size.

The site is unusual in having no evidence of later occupation. Beveridge habitually recorded such structures on his many other excavations even if he did not attempt to unravel their sequence or relationship to each other: this suggests that at Rudh an Duin there was no secondary rebuilding.

Internal structure - Apart from a covered drain there are no internal features which can be related to the occupation of Rudh an Duin. The large central cell, some 14m in diameter, is not divided by any stone partitions and contains no hearth, at least in the excavated levels. It is not clear how much damage the tidal submersion of the site will have done to the more fragile internal structures but it is likely that if any internal stone partitions had existed Beveridge would have noted them.

The means of access to the gallery was not recorded and it would appear that no gallery entrances were traced in the surviving internal circuit.

Material culture and chronology - The material from the site has no recorded contexts. The ceramic assemblage included sherds with incised and applied decoration belonging to conventional Hebridean Iron Age types. One sherd, GT7 in the Royal Scottish Museum, is considered by MacKie to be from a carinated vessel of Iron Age 'A' type, dating from the period after 400BC (MacKie, 1972, 129).

The only find which distinguishes the assemblage is the 'two-edged longsword' of which fragments were found, in the remains of a wooden scabbard, close to the northern wall in the interior of the structure (Beveridge 1911, 217). The few details available relating to this find do not enable detailed reconstruction: the greatest blade width appears to have been 59mm with a 25mm wide flat tang in a rounded cross-piece or guard.

A.NU4 Dun a Ghallain, North Uist NF 7479 7598 (Beveridge 1911)

Introduction - This site was one of two islets in Loch an Eilean incompletely excavated by Beveridge prior to 1911. The sites were briefly described, though without plans, in his book North Uist (Beveridge 1911, RCAHMS 1928 no. 191, 60). The islet is the westmost of the two in Loch an Eilean, on undulating ground less than 1km from the present north coast of North Uist. The loch is now a marsh, inaccessible both by foot and by boat. It has not therefore been possible to make any independent observation to supplement Beveridge's account.

Site structure - The natural islet upon which the structures lie appears to have had a causeway to the shore, now just traceable in the marsh: Beveridge mentions that it may have had a causeway to Eilean a Ghallain, some 70m distant, although he is not clear about the evidence either for this or for the apparent doubt which he expresses (1911, 196). The irregular plan and construction which

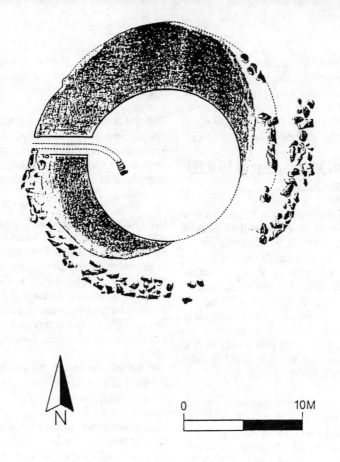

Ill. 5.6 Rudh an Duin (after Beveridge 1911)

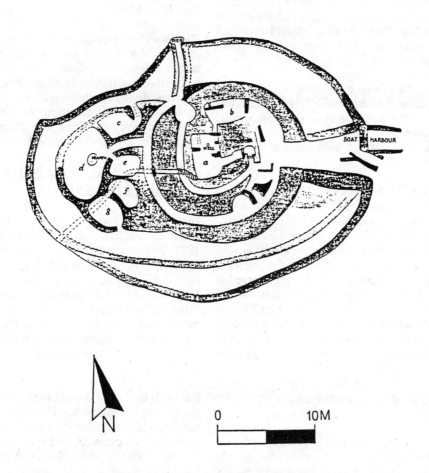

Ill. 5.7 Dun Thomaidh (after Beveridge 1930)

Beveridge describes appears to refer only to the internal described as being probably a "secondary lining inserted within an older and more substantial structure" (1911, 197). Such details as are recorded of this intrusive structure are discussed below in Chapter Seven.

The excavation of Dun a Ghallain tells us nothing of the form of the original structure other than that there existed, on this islet, a massive-walled drystone structure which formed a focus for secondary settlement.

Internal structure - There are no recorded details of the site's internal structure.

Material culture and chronology - There is no full description of the material from the site and no context for the material which is recorded. The report mentions only 'lozenge-shaped' iron rivets, a decorated 'dirk' and a curved knife (which presumably derive from the secondary levels), cetacean vertebrae and part of a large quern or mill-stone.

A.NU6 Eilean a Ghallain, North Uist NF 7483 7589 (Beveridge 1911)

Introduction - This islet lies in the same loch as Dun a Ghallain, to the eastern side of the latter site, and was partially excavated by Beveridge in the same period prior to 1911. The same locational factors and constraints on the interpretation of the site apply as to the neighbouring site (RCAHMS 1928 no. 192, 61).

Site structure - According to Beveridge (1911, 197) the islet has a 40m causeway. The site was dominated by a circular drystone structure some 12.75m in external diameter and with walls of from 2.3 - 3.3m in thickness. No further information is available except that the interior contained "several minor erections", of which no details are recorded (Beveridge 1911, 197), and a paved entrance on the east side, facing the causeway. The excavation appears to have been on a very small scale and it is unlikely that the nature of the walling was investigated. On present evidence the structure can only be regarded as massive-walled roundhouse of unknown specific structural type.

Internal structure - No details of the internal structure of the site are recorded.

Material culture and chronology - The only recorded finds from the site are pottery of unknown form, an unknown quantity of bone, hammerstones and a whetstone.

A.NU7 Dun Thomaidh, North Uist NF 7564 7562 (Beveridge 1930)

Introduction - Our information on Dun Thomaidh is the result of a fortnight's excavation by Erskine Beveridge in the summer of 1914, the results of which were collated and published after the excavator's death by J. Graham Callander. The original imprecision of excavation and recording was thus compounded by being published, from notes, by someone with only second-hand knowledge of the site.

Dun Thomaidh lies in a location similar to that of Rudh an Duin in relation to its local topography, on a tidal islet on the opposite, south-west end of the island of Vallay. Like Rudh an Duin, this would have been an islet in a loch or a rocky outcrop on the machair plain. This symmetrical siting of Dun Thomaidh and Rudh an Duin in relation to Vallay and the original machair plain is striking. Again like Rudh an Duin, the islet on which Dun Thomaidh sits is subject to tidal submersion.

Site structure - The only feature which is clear from Beveridge's plan is that the excavated structures were the result of a number of periods of construction and occupation (Ill. 5.7). The site is a mass of wall fragments and passages which Beveridge was unable to disentangle, a fact which is scarcely surprising given the scale of the site and the duration of the excavation. Clearly such a maze of structures, built at various levels and inadequately recorded, can be open to multiple interpretations and it is not possible to define phases or a sequence in the site structure. It is possible only to point out some regularities which are relevant to the wider study of the Hebridean sites. The mass of small cells on the west side of the large roundhouse will be considered in Chapter Seven with the other Hebridean cellular structures. Discussion here will be restricted to the central roundhouse and the surrounding walls.

The plan of Dun Thomaidh suggests that an original roundhouse with evidence of intra-mural galleries, built on an islet enclosed by a drystone wall, has been re-used for the construction of secondary cells both within and around it. The roundhouse would have been some 14.6m in external diameter but the plan gives no useful indication of its internal diameter. The passage from the southeast to north-west of the circuit suggests an original intra-mural gallery. Beveridge records that the remainder of the circuit, on the north-east, was the most extensively damaged due to quarrying (1931, 317). The other recorded cells and passages do not seem to form any coherent structure and appear to confuse secondary phases of construction.

The original entrance may have been on the west as indicated on the plan, although it is impossible to be sure that this is not a secondary feature. The entrance at the north is also a possibility and this is diametrically opposite the causeway (not shown on the plan) on the pattern of many other island dun and broch sites.

The surrounding wall of the islet was poorly preserved but may be taken to define the original extent of the islet on which the structure was situated. The substantial causeway which linked the site to the shore reportedly had a regularly squared end some 4m from the islet itself: this is a feature which will be discussed again in relation to other atlantic roundhouse sites.

Internal structure - The published plan and description give insufficient information with which to attribute any of the interior features to the roundhouse phase of occupation.

Material culture and chronology - No material is specifically attributable to the atlantic roundhouse. The most significant finds from the site were the querns: two saddle querns and fragments of a rotary quern came from unknown contexts. These finds may indicate that activity on the site began relatively early in the Iron Age, prior to the local quern replacement.

A.NU13 Garry Iochdrach, North Uist NF 7724 7427 (Beveridge 1931)

Introduction - This site was excavated by Beveridge in 1912 and 1913. It consists of a wheelhouse which appears to be intrusive into an atlantic roundhouse (Ill. 5.8). The wheelhouse is discussed in Chapter Six.

Site structure - The plan of Garry Iochdrach defies detailed interpretation but the surrounding gallery does suggest the presence of an original complex roundhouse. It appears to make no sense in relation to the wheelhouse. The gallery on the plan makes little sense as an atlantic roundhouse gallery and the question must remain unresolved at present. Examination of the site on the ground does not clarify the situation.

Internal structure - The internal structure of the original roundhouse was never excavated.

Material culture and chronology - No material is attributable to the atlantic roundhouse.

A.NU14 Cnoc a Comhdhalach, North Uist NF 7708 7413 (Beveridge 1911)

Introduction - The radially partitioned structure at Cnoc a Comhdhalach is discussed in Chapter Six. It appears that this structure may have been inserted into a pre-existing atlantic roundhouse. Cnoc a Comhdhalach was excavated by Beveridge in the first decade of the C20th and is reported briefly in his book North Uist (1911, 200-7). Beveridge believed the radially partitioned structure to be intrusive into a pre-existing 'broch-like structure' (1911, 202, [my italics]).

The site lies on a knoll 30m from the west shore of Vallay Strand. It lies on undulating ground and would have commanded an extensive view over what is now the Strand.

Site structure - The radial piers, if secondary, were inserted into a massive-walled drystone structure which, from its surviving north-west circuit and indications in other parts of the wall, was constructed by building two concentric walls separated by an extensive intra-mural gallery and possibly a 'guard' cell at the south-east (Ill. 5.9). This hypothesis is strengthened by the fact that these cells and galleries do not have access into the central chamber and are seemingly irrelevant to the use of the radially partitioned structure.

Internal structure - The internal structure of the possible early phase of occupation on this site is not known.

Material culture and chronology - None of the excavated material can be attributed to specific occupation phases.

A.NU17 Eilean Maleit, North Uist NF 7748 7388 (Beveridge 1911)

Introduction - This site was excavated by Beveridge prior to 1911. The main structure on the site as shown by the plan was a radially partitioned roundhouse described in the next chapter: it is included here because the plan indicates a construction involving regular intra-mural cells arranged around parts of the circuit which are not apparently linked to the interior during the phase of radial partitioning which Beveridge investigated (Ill. 5.10). Beveridge himself, as at Cnoc a Comhdhalach, without explicitly stating his grounds, believed the piers to be secondary features (1911, 202).

Site structure - Where the wall is complete, on the south-western quarter of its circuit, the dimensions and position of the cells suggest that an original galleried wall has been modified or re-occupied. The site records do not enable any more detailed investigation of this possibility. It can therefore only be suggested that a complex atlantic roundhouse with an open interior may have pre-dated the radially partitioned structure at Eilean Maleit.

Internal structure - There is no evidence for the internal spatial organisation of a pre-radial phase at Eilean Maleit.

Material culture and chronology - The material from the site was not assigned to contexts.

A.NU20 Buaile Risary, North Uist NF 7665 7278 (Beveridge 1911)

Introduction - The structures at Buaile Risary are unusually poorly understood even by the standards of Beveridge's excavations. The site is included here only to indicate the possibility that it may have contained an atlantic roundhouse.

The site lies on the slopes of Beinn Risary facing north across Vallay Strand. The structures are on a large mound which gives an extensive view across the north coast of the island.

Site structure - The main roundhouse was of drystone construction and some 11m in overall diameter. No plans exist and the details of the internal structures are not sufficiently clear to permit reconstruction. Beveridge's measurements of the inner cells entail that at least one of the rectangular cells was in the walling of the main roundhouse (Beveridge 1911, 210), but in the absence of a plan it is not justifiable to claim this as evidence of hollow-walled construction or an original intra-mural cell. The description given of rectangular and square chambers suggests intrusive, and perhaps relatively recent, reoccupation of the structure. The Royal Commission reported that the walls of the main circular structure were 2m wide (RCAHMS 1928 no. 193, 61) but present surface traces give no indication.

Internal structure - The published report gives insufficient information upon which to base any interpretation of the interior organisation of the structure.

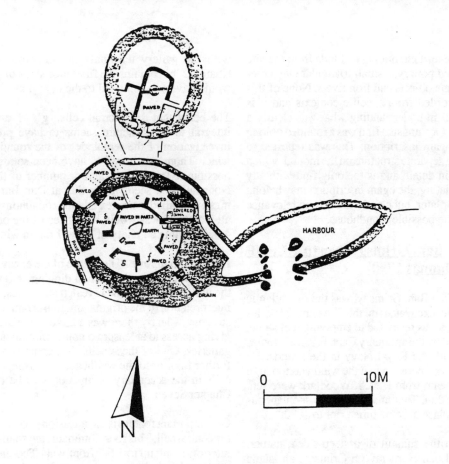

Ill. 5.8 Garry Iochdrach (after Beveridge 1930)

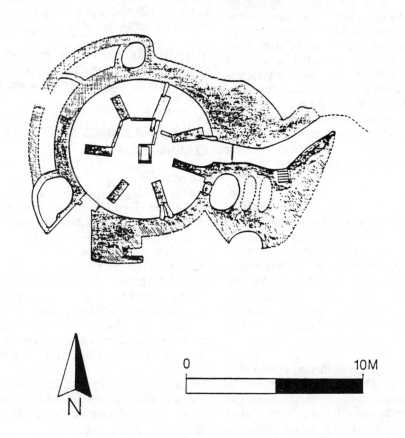

Ill. 5.9 Cnoc a Comhdhalach (after Beveridge 1911)

Material culture and chronology - Finds from the site included decorated pottery, a small triangular clay crucible, flint and stone objects and iron rivets. None of this material was recorded from specific contexts and it is entirely unhelpful in understanding what was clearly a multi-period site. One unusual find was a rounded oblong pebble with an ogam inscription. This was reported to have come from a separate structure on the mound, which is not described in detail, and is the only find with any significance for dating: the ogam inscription may belong to the C6th AD or later, but clearly this has no relevance to the dating of the possible roundhouse.

A.NU51 Dun Ban, Grimsay, North Uist NF 8699 5695 (Thomas 1890)

Introduction - Dun Ban, Grimsay, was the first atlantic roundhouse to be excavated in the Western Isles, although excavation was restricted to emptying it of stone. The site was noted by the antiquary Capt. F.W.L. Thomas whilst serving with the Royal Navy in the islands. He records that, during a period when the wind was too high for surveying, a team from H.M.S. Woodlark were sent to investigate the dun. This small-scale and spontaneous excavation took place at some time prior to 1890.

Dun Ban lies on the summit of a steep-sided, natural outcrop islet in Loch Horneray on Grimsay, an island connected to North Uist at low tide. The loch is surrounded by hills from beyond which it is not visible.

The small hill adjacent to the shore, immediately to the south of the site, overlooks the roundhouse structure and gives a view of the substantial stone causeway, capped with massive flagstones, which links the site to the shore. This causeway is now submerged by up to 1m, indicating a substantial loch level change since the occupation of the site. The entrance to the roundhouse faces this causeway directly, in contrast to the arrangement at sites like Dun Bharabhat and Loch na Berie: the nature of the islet in this case would have prevented access around the structure to a rear entrance. The location of the site does not appear to add to the defensive qualities inherent in the structure itself.

Site structure - Prior to excavation the site was described by Thomas as a "huge cairn, covered with brambles and sweet herbage" (1890, 400). It was excavated because of its convenience rather than any intrinsic interest in this particular site. From surface traces the site appeared as an unimposing mound, with no indication of structural complexity, but was shown on excavation to have possessed a range of architectural features which led to its acceptance as a probable *broch* by MacKie (1972, 172, Ill. 5.11).

The massive-walled complex roundhouse, which dominates the island, is some 15m in external diameter. Its interior is filled with structures which can, with hindsight, be interpreted as secondary modifications to an original hollow-walled roundhouse. Thomas did not recognise the multi-period nature of the site. Chambers 'h' and 'f' on the original plan appear to represent, from their size and position relative to the enclosing walls, the butt ends of two ground level, intra-mural galleries. Thomas records that they were corbelled and this would be consistent

with the gallery terminals on numerous other sites. Chamber 'h' contains the first three steps of stairs which would have originally led to the next floor.

The belief that the internal cells, 'g', 'd' and 'e', were integral to the structure seems to have prevented the investigation of the remainder of the roundhouse wall, which Thomas believed to have been solid, so it is not possible to know the extent or number of the galleries. Nonetheless it seems clear that at Dun Ban we have a massive-walled, complex atlantic roundhouse. The overall wall thickness would have been of the order of 3.5 - 4m, including a gallery of some 1.6m in width.

Internal structure - The nature of the excavation, clearing of stone rather than actual digging, and the belief in the unitary nature of the revealed structures, prevent any interpretation of the original internal arrangements of the structure. Clearly there was a large, circular, central cell giving access to at least two non-communicating cells or galleries. One of these cells, 'h', contained access to a further floor or to the wallhead. The arrangement of the cells in the secondary occupation will be discussed in Chapter Seven.

One important feature is the intrusion of outcrop rock into the central cell. This rock dominates the south-west of the interior, rising up to 1.6m from what Thomas took to be the floor level. A sloping rock shelf in the north-west of the interior formed natural 'steps' and may have formed a part of the internal division of the site. Such outcrops are common on the Hebridean sites, most notably at Dun Carloway where a large outcrop emerges from the interior on the north-west of the structure, and at Dun Cuier.

Material culture and chronology - Finds from the site comprised an unknown number of pot sherds, which were apparently coarse and undecorated, and a few waterworn pebbles.

A.B4 Dun Cuier, Barra NF 6708 0345 (Young 1955)

Introduction - Dun Cuier was excavated by Alison Young, initially as an adjunct to the excavation of the wheelhouse, Tigh Talamhanta, in Allasdale. The site is of central importance in this study as its interpretation by Young led to the formulation of the hypothesis that the *duns* of the Western Isles represent a mid-1st millennium AD return to fortified settlement long after the abandonment of the *brochs*. If the date of the occupation at Dun Cuier is as the excavator suggests, in the C7th AD, then the case for a separation of *duns* and *brochs* into two chronologically distinct settlement systems would seem to be justified. It is of great importance to examine in detail the excavator's interpretation of the site.

The problem rests with the question of whether the structure is a single-period construction or represents the re-use in the mid-1st millennium AD of a much earlier site.

The site is located on a steep rocky knoll above the valley of Allasdale commanding an extensive view of the surrounding land and an long stretch of the Barra coast. The roundhouse is consequently visible from most of the

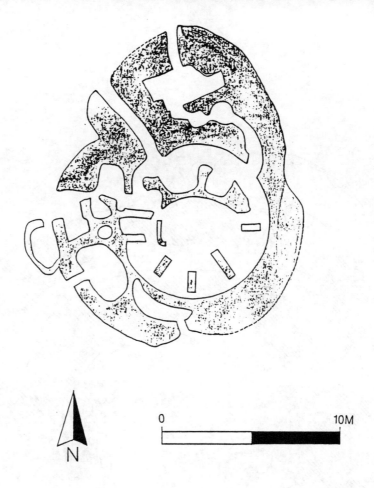

Ill. 5.10 Eilean Maleit (after Beveridge 1911)

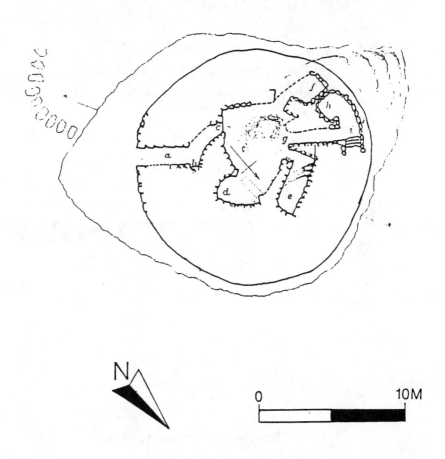

Ill. 5.11 Dun Ban, Grimsay (after Thomas 1890)

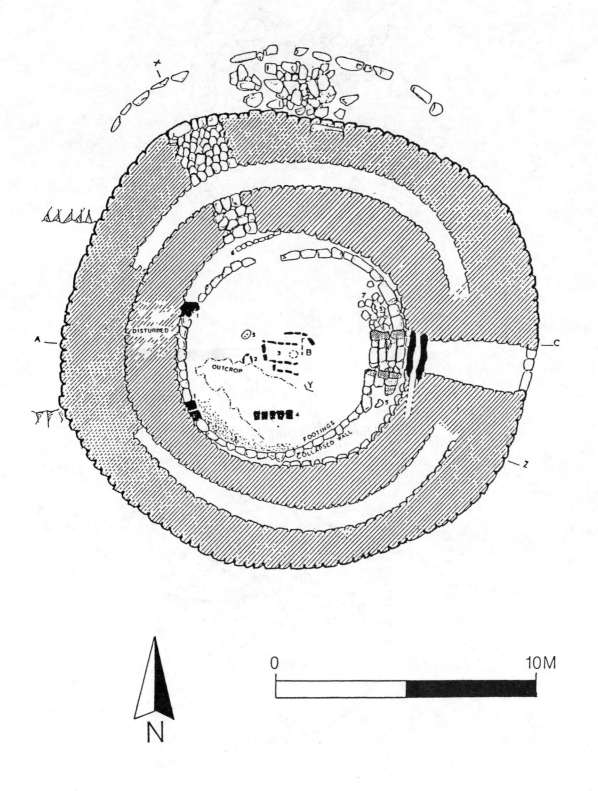

Ill. 5.12 Dun Cuier (after Young 1955)

surrounding area. The rock rises in terraces towards the site and anyone approaching would be visible from some distance.

Site structure - An examination of the published plan and the site on the ground suggests that the site is a massive-walled roundhouse built with two concentric walls and an intervening gallery, with many of the features characteristic of broch architecture (Ill. 5.12). The site is 19.5m in mean external diameter with an overall wall thickness of c. 5.25m containing a gallery 0.8m in width. The width of the gallery appears from the surface evidence to have been underestimated due to the instability and partial collapse of the inner of the two main walls, which has begun to lean outwards into the gallery. The internal diameter, excluding the slighter innermost wall, averages 9m. It contains a scarcement ledge and a low, narrow entrance passage. It is important then to consider the arguments used by Young, and later by MacKie, to classify the site as a *galleried dun* bearing no direct relationship to the *broch* class.

Young claimed that the gallery contained no stairs and so could not have given access to an upper level: this is without foundation as only one small slit trench was excavated through the gallery and it could not have been known what lay under the grassed-over rubble around the remainder of the circuit. Young stated that the scarcement was flimsy and not able to support an upper floor: the scarcement is 32-35cm in width and securely bonded into the wall. This is an important point since the scarcement of Dun Carloway, one of the 'archetypal' *brochs* and certainly the most widely accepted representative of the class in the Western Isles, is far narrower and less substantial (RCAHMS 1928, 19). On examination of the site itself in 1987 (pers. obs.) it was seen that many of the first floor gallery capstones are still in position and are eroding out of the side of the mound as the outer wall falls away. This is particularly marked to the south of the entrance. Dun Cuier appears to have had at least one upper level and the size and solidity of the scarcement, despite Young's comments, only serve to reinforce this interpretation.

Young attempted to explain the double-walling of the structure by maintaining that the outermost wall was a retaining device: it does not touch the innermost of the two main walls, except at the entrance, and it is difficult to see how it could have served such a function. In this connection it is important to note that the section ABC in Fig. 6b of the Dun Cuier report does not accord with the plan in Fig. 6a, nor indeed with the present surface evidence. On this section it appears that the inner of the two main walls is substantially wider than the outer wall, leaving no space for the intervening gallery, creating the misleading impression that the outer wall may indeed be a retaining wall. There is no evidence that the two main walls served any different function on this site than similar concentric walls on any other complex roundhouse. Young maintains further that there was no access to the gallery from the interior of the structure. As the slight, innermost wall of the structure, which rose to the level of the scarcement, was not removed during the excavation, it is not justifiable to claim that there was no access through the inner of the two main structural walls.

Without access to the gallery it is difficult to support the idea that the third, innermost wall formed part of the same design as the outer walls. The different character of the construction and the scale of the wall suggest that it was a secondary modification, most probably revetted into pre-existing material: its flimsiness of construction seems unlikely to have enabled it to stand unsupported. Young's assumption that this slight, inner wall was integral to the original structure led to the misclassification of a structure which appears to have been a complex roundhouse, or even a broch tower, re-used in the building of an intrusive cellular construction.

A re-examination of the excavation report, and of the site on the ground, suggests that it is closely similar to the structure at Loch na Berie, where a secondary thin skin of walling has been inserted into a pre-existing roundhouse to create a smaller cellular structure. Additional evidence for the link in building form and general site context between the two sites emerges from the re-examination of a reference made to the nature of the material found between the innermost wall and the inner roundhouse wall. Young stated that the space formed between these two walls on the south side appeared initially to have been entered by steps (Young 1955, 301): this idea was discounted when it became apparent that the steps were founded on the greasy earth which was assumed to represent the occupation material of the 'chamber'. On the pattern of the construction at Berie (see Chapter Seven) this would seem to suggest that the cellular structure was backed into pre-existing material: this would account for the irregular backing of the cellular wall and explain how the steps came to be founded on occupation material.

The re-interpretation proposed here suggests that the bulk of the material from the excavation, now to be regarded as a mixed assemblage, would derive from this later cellular structure. From the misclassification of the structural character of a *broch* came the attribution of a late date to the whole class of *duns* in the Western Isles. The readiness to accept a quick solution to the dating of the site without thorough excavation, the method of excavation by digging a central hole without exploring the gallery fully, and the failure to remove the secondary walling, all contributed to a misunderstanding of the site and a consequent mis-dating of a whole class of monument.

The revetted internal structure will be further discussed in Chapter Seven now that it can be seen to be intrusive into the main roundhouse or broch.

Internal structure - Very little can be said about the interior organisation of the Dun Cuier roundhouse prior to its secondary modification: as has been indicated above, the entrances to the galleries and the subdivisions of those galleries are not known since the intrusive inner wall was left in place throughout the excavation. There was a large central cell, with an area of 67.9m^2, leading into extensive intra-mural chambers. There is no evidence for radial partitioning of this original roundhouse interior. The scarcement and the scale and construction of the structure would suggest at least one upper storey.

One feature which would have affected ground-floor spatial organisation is the protrusion of outcrop rock into the interior, as at Dun Ban, Grimsay, Dun Carloway and other sites.

Material culture and chronology - The bulk of the diagnostic material on the site relates to the secondary occupation and will be discussed in Chapter Seven. The material was not divided by structural phase so it is only from parallels elsewhere that some finds can be suggested as belonging to the primary occupation. The extent of the excavation of the interior is unclear. It is possible that excavation did not progress to the primary deposits in all parts of the interior, especially where these may have lain substantially below the foundations of the intrusive walling.

The nature of the flooring, certainly natural outcrop for large areas of the interior, would have made the periodic clearing out of the structure easy and it is unlikely that much primary material would survive under these conditions. The galleries, to which the intrusive structure gave no access, would seem the most likely part of the site to yield material relating to the primary occupation of the roundhouse.

The pottery from Dun Cuier has been examined and re-evaluated repeatedly since its original publication. Young expressed three differing interpretations (Young 1955, 1959, 1976), Close-Brooks considered it in reference to the material from Dun Carloway and Lane and Topping both attempted to re-interpret the assemblage with regard to its importance for the Hebridean Dark Age and Iron Age respectively (Lane 1983, 253-7, Topping 1985, 151-7).

The re-interpretation of the structural evidence presented here accommodates the inconsistencies in the assemblage. Young initially regarded the pottery as a unified assemblage of the C7th AD, characterised by large vessels with weak flaring rims and long flaring rims, with occasional decoration in the form of applied wavy cordons. The pottery was of an apparently uniform fabric, ring-built of reddish paste from local sources, with a small element in a greyish fabric. Inconsistencies were apparent in the form of a few small incised sherds (106-8) and one clear example of ring-headed pin stamped decoration (sherd 109), as well as a number of sherds with inturned rims (sherds 66-81).

In the excavation report for A Cheardach Bheag, Young widened the date of the assemblage to encompass the C5th - C7th AD (Young 1959), and in a general account of Hebridean Iron Age pottery (Young and Richardson 1966, 47) she divided the Dun Cuier assemblage into two chronological phases: the first with long flaring rims and occasional applied decoration, and the second with weakened rims and an absence of decoration. It appears that Young was unsure of the stratigraphy of the site to the extent that the retrospective division of the pottery into two chronological phases was considered permissible, although no stratigraphic information is included in the pottery report.

Lane saw the assemblage as thoroughly mixed, incorporating Dark Age and earlier elements (Lane 1983, 255).

The nature of the Dark Age pottery will be discussed in Chapter Seven. Elements which are alien to that tradition (App. 2) appear to be represented by the very small sherds with incised decoration and ring-headed pin stamping (sherds 106-9).

The lack of contextual information prevents any real correlation of the potentially early sherds with the structural sequence, but the small size of the sherds may be indicative of redeposition and disturbance of primary layers. The decoration of pottery with ring-headed pin impressions is parallelled at a number of sites and may cover a wide chronological period. Early examples of this motif occur in the Phase 1A deposits at Dun Mor Vaul, dated to the C5th - 6th BC (MacKie 1974, 128).

Of the non-ceramic assemblage only a few finds can be attributed to the pre-cellular phase. A saddle quern, found amid tumbled stone outside the structure, may indicate some activity on the site prior to c. 200BC (Armit 1991) but need not relate to primary occupation of the roundhouse itself.

While we cannot date the atlantic roundhouse at Dun Cuier due to the absence of contextual information, it is clear that none of the later finds are likely to relate to the period of primary occupation. This later assemblage is discussed in Chapter Seven.

Survey evidence

The evidence from field survey gives additional information on the atlantic roundhouses but this is largely restricted to site structure and location. Information on internal structure is slight and material culture and dating evidence are generally absent. This survey evidence will provide much of the data for Chapters 11-13. The discussion which follows here deals with more general points, particularly of site structure.

Distribution

Atlantic roundhouses are widely distributed throughout the Western Isles with examples known on each of the main islands (Ill. 5.1). Their size and distinctive plan (round or oval rather than the rectilinear shape of the mass of later field monuments) have made them relatively easy to locate. Their locations, characteristically small islets in lochs or rock outcrops, have also aided discovery. All of these factors have resulted in a large corpus of sites with fewer of the inherent research biases which afflict the distributions of other field monuments. Nonetheless concentrations in some areas do appear to reflect patterns of research. For example, the distribution of 52 sites in North Uist compared to only 22 in South Uist, despite roughly similar land mass and quality of land appears to reflect the activities of Erskine Beveridge in North Uist. Barra and Benbecula also appear to be relatively well-explored archaeologically. South Uist has always been under-researched and the situation in Lewis and Harris is similar: recent fieldwork in Lewis has located a number of previously unrecorded sites. It is likely that the corpus is considerably below the original number of sites in several of the islands but it will be argued in Chapter Twelve that the North Uist and Barra distributions may approach the original distributions.

Site structure

The sheer number of extant sites provides a great deal of information on site structure but this inevitably creates difficulties of interpretation given the widely variable states of preservation of the sites and the problem of assessing contemporaneity of features. The atlantic roundhouses will be treated here as one group: the recurrent site features will be discussed to give an indication of the range and regularity of these features and assess their significance for site function.

Intensive field survey in Lewis in 1984 demonstrated a site-complexity previously unrecorded (Armit 1985). It has not been possible to repeat this degree of survey coverage throughout the islands: therefore the site features recorded have a bias towards Lewis. This does not indicate that these features do not exist elsewhere but rather demonstrates the range of features which intensive field survey might be expected to yield in the other islands. The additional details on the outer walls, cross-causeway walls etc. of the North Uist sites, for example, have come largely from the more sporadic fieldwork which has been possible on that island.

Galleries/cells, stairs and scarcements: Of the 140 atlantic roundhouses recorded, 38 have visible evidence of having contained intra-mural cells and/or galleries. Of these 11 have been excavated. Every excavated site where the wall has been examined has been shown to contain galleries or cells. The numbers of sites with these features must therefore be far greater than the 27% indicated by surface traces.

Intra-mural features, as has been discussed in Chapter Four, are always difficult to trace by field survey. They can be hidden by collapse, grassed-over and indistinct, removed by stone-robbing, exist only at robbed-out upper levels, hidden by later structures etc. In this context the 27% figure appears to be relatively high and must reflect a considerably higher presence of the complex roundhouse form.

Intra-mural stairs are subject to the same problems of discovery as intra-mural cells, with the added problem of being confined to a restricted part of the circuit. Nonetheless, several unexcavated sites can be seen to contain intra-mural stairs. In Lewis for example, Dun Bharabhat, Great Bernera (Ill. 5.13; A.L17), Dun Cromore (Ill. 5.14; A.L26 and Dun Borve (Ill. 5.15; A.L8), all contain this feature.

Scarcement ledges are visible only where structures survive to first floor level. Even then they can be obscured by rubble or be grassed-over. They are present at a number of unexcavated sites including Dun Loch an Duna, Bragar (Ill. 5.16; A.L11), Dun Bharabhat, Great Bernera (Ill. 5.13; A.L17) and Dun Borve (Ill. 5.15; A.L8), all in Lewis.

Enclosing walls and/or annexes: These are very common features on atlantic roundhouse sites. 35 sites have either a walled or open annexe area at the rear of, or around, the main structure. These annexes do not contain any of the clustered structures common on northern atlantic roundhouse sites.

These annexes vary widely in size and are characteristically located to the rear of island sites, away from the causeway e.g. Dun Bharabhat, Cnip (Ill. 5.3), Dun Loch and Duna, Bragar (Ill. 5.16) and Dun Loch an Duin Carloway (Ill. 5.17; A.L15). In these cases it appears that the annexe is being deliberately shielded from the main access to the site: any approach to the annexe would entail passing below the roundhouse walls.

The original size of these annexes is difficult to gauge due to fluctuations in loch levels, which have submerged structural features in some cases. The only excavated annexe is at Dun Bharabhat, Cnip (the annexe of Dun Thomaidh was not examined below the cluster of late cellular structures): this revealed the presence of slight structures of indeterminate function and date, possibly earlier than the roundhouse itself. In the case of Dun Cromore the annexe in front of the roundhouse appears to represent an earlier structure (see below). In some cases the existence of annexes, particularly those restricted in size, may indicate the presence of a sequence of earlier structures stratified under the roundhouse. In other cases such as Dun Loch an Duna, Bragar, and particularly where they are walled, the annexes appear to be associated with the function of the site in its roundhouse phase. At Bragar in particular the overall plan suggests contemporaneity as the enclosure walls adjoin the roundhouse and the overall size and position of the annexe suggest a separate functional area demarcated behind the roundhouse.

Several atlantic roundhouses on non-islet locations also have walled annexes, e.g. St. Clement's Dun, Rodel (Ill. 5.18; A.H10) and Dun Bhuirgh, Borve (Ill. 5.19; A.H4), both in Harris, and Dun Mara in Lewis (Ill. 5.20; A.L2). There may be a local dimension to these enclosed areas since it appears that none of the Barra roundhouses were associated with an enclosed annexe (with the possible exception of Dun Scurrival, A.B1, where early reports indicate a possible outer wall).

The problem of the function of the annexes is complicated and obscured by the occurrence of much later structures which utilise the building stone from the roundhouse and the level building area of the annexe. In cases such as Dun Loch an Duna, Bragar, and Dun an Sticer, North Uist (A.NU1), large rectilinear structures occupy the extensive, flat, rear annexes. Nonetheless there appears to be no evidence of contemporary settlement within the annexes on the Orcadian model. The most likely function at present appears to be for storage structures or for livestock.

Harbours/boat noosts: The access to almost all of the islet-sited atlantic roundhouses was by substantial stone-built causeways. Only two such sites are known with no trace of a causeway: Dun Shiavat (A.L7) and Dun Bharabhat, Croulista (A.L20), both in Lewis. In the former case it appears that raised loch levels, due to drastically altered drainage, may have submerged any causeway: the water level now rises above the wall foundations. A similar situation may apply at Croulista but it is less easy there to account for the raising of the loch level. Overall, the access to the islet-sited atlantic roundhouses is overwhelmingly by causeway.

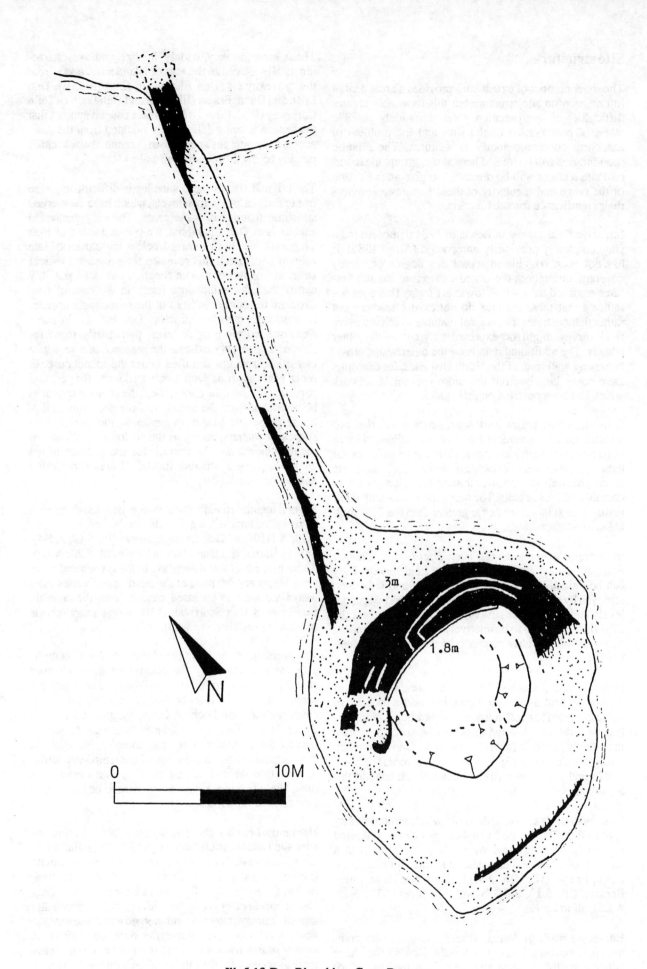

3m

1.8m

N

0   10M

Ill. 5.13 Dun Bharabhat, Great Bernera

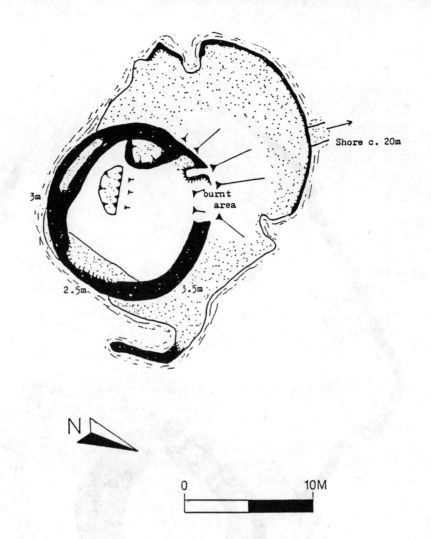

N

0   10M

Ill. 5.14 Dun Cromore, Lewis

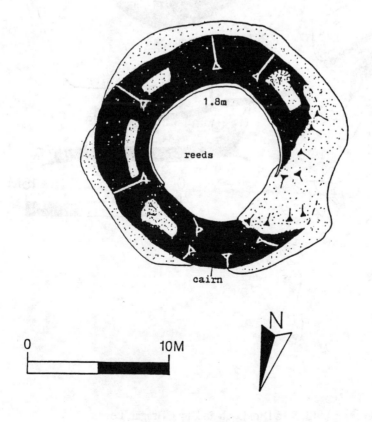

0   10M

N

Ill. 5.15 Dun Borve, Lewis

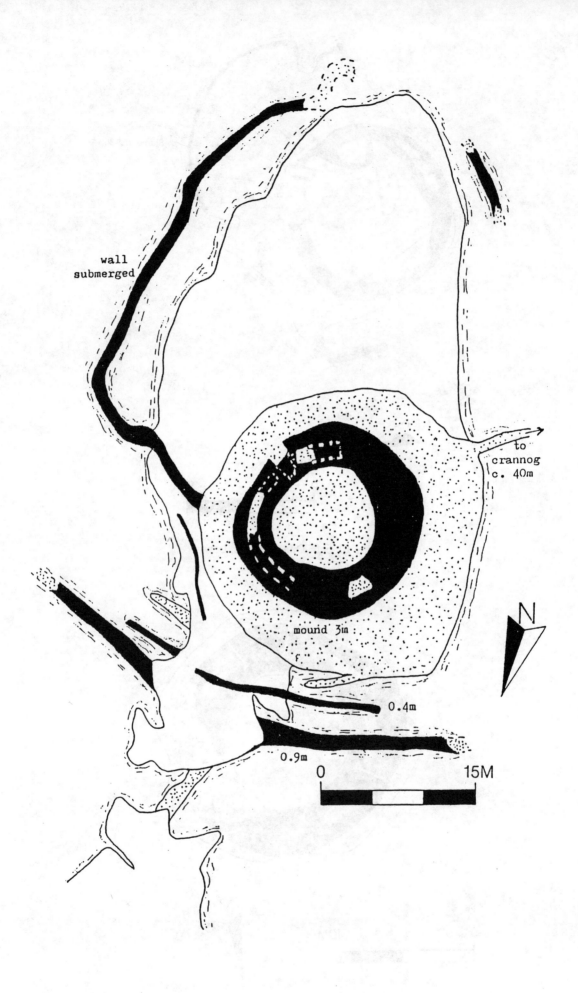

wall
submerged

to
crannog
c. 40m

N

mound 3in

0.4m

0.9m

0 15M

Ill. 5.16 Dun Loch an Duna, Bragar, Lewis

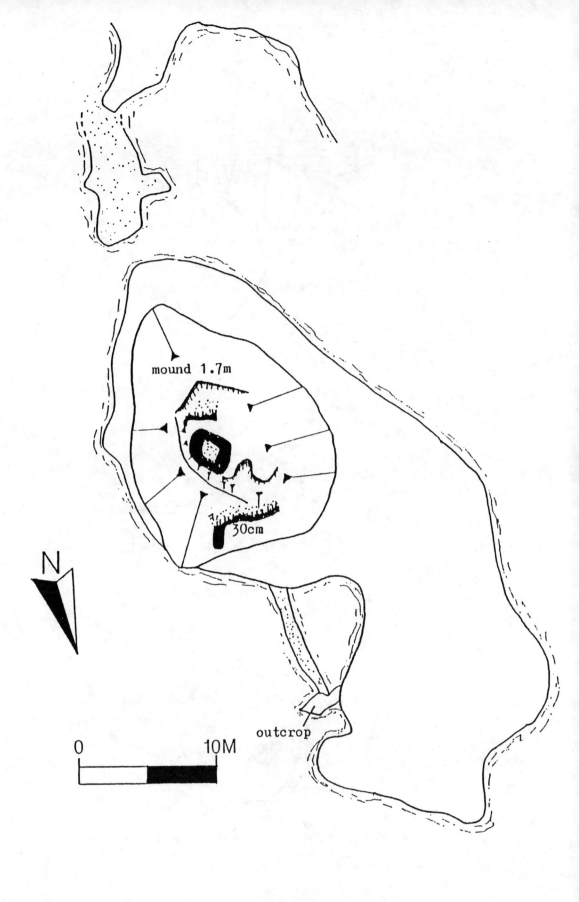

mound 1.7m

30cm

N

outcrop

0   10M

Ill. 5.17 Dun Loch an Duin, Carloway, Lewis

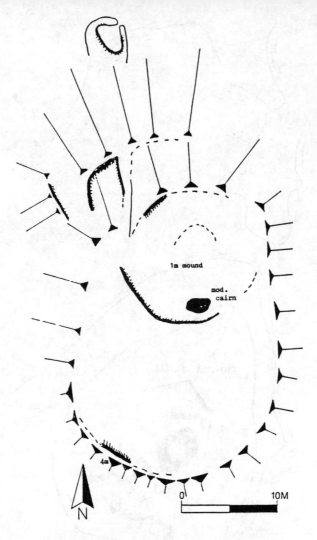

Ill. 5.18 St. Clement's Dun, Rodel, Harris

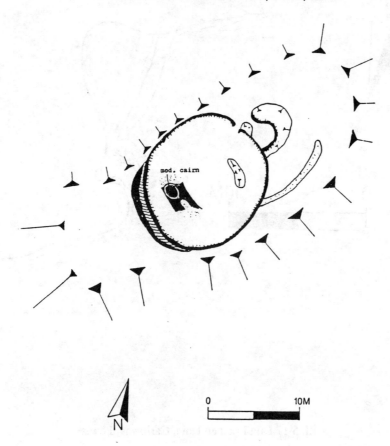

Ill. 5.19 Dun Bhuirgh, Harris

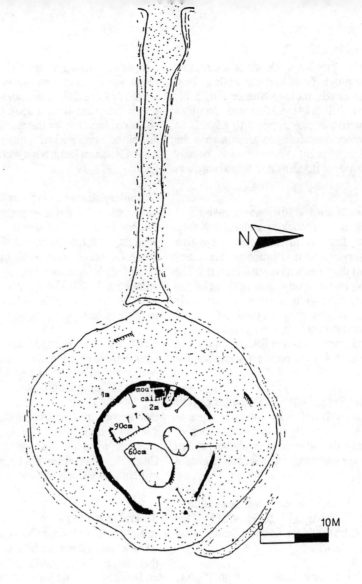

Ill. 5.20 Dun Mara, Lewis

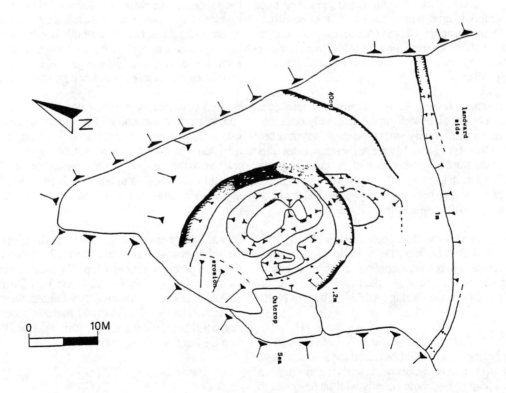

Ill. 5.21 Dun Loch an Duin, Shader, Lewis

Nonetheless many sites provide evidence of alternative access by boat in the provision of harbour walls or boat noosts. Examples in Lewis include Shader (Ill. 5.21; A.L9), Dun Cromore (Ill. 5.14; A.L26) and Croulista (A.L20). This alternative access appears to have been simply to enable immediate access to areas across the loch other than the area adjacent to the causeway, or may have been used in periods of flooding if the causeway was inaccessible.

Cross-causeway walls and additional causeways: Seven sites have evidence for blocking walls across their causeways. Of these, four are in Lewis and were first noted in the 1984 survey and it is probable that many more sites throughout the islands have such features. The common submerging of causeways and robbing of the walls has meant that most such features are presently submerged. This type of feature is not confined to later prehistoric sites: similar cross causeway defences, in timber, were replaced several times at Eilean Domhnuill, Loch Olabhat, in the Early Neolithic (Armit 1988b; 1990b).

Dun Loch an Duna, Bragar (Ill. 5.16), has the most imposing array of causeway defences with three separate cross-walls. These three are all in different states of preservation and only the outermost is above present water level so they may well represent successive phases of rebuilding.

Much less well-preserved cross-walls are detectable at Dun Loch an Duin, Carloway (Ill. 5.17; A.L15), Dun Bharabhat, Galson (A.L5) and Dun Loch an Duin, Lower Bayble (A.L25), all in Lewis.

Two sites in Lewis have extra causeways in addition to the main access causeway. At Dun Borranish (A.L24) a residual causeway, parallel to the better preserved one, appears simply to represent an earlier phase of construction. At Dun Bharabhat, Galson (A.L5), three additional causeways radiate out from the islet below present water level. These have no recorded parallels and their function is entirely unknown.

Causeway gaps: A second form of causeway defence is represented by the sites with gaps deliberately built into their causeways, normally where the causeway reaches the islet. Only four sites have clear evidence for this feature: in the state of preservation of the great majority of causeways such gaps would not generally be noticed. In other cases the gap between causeway and islet will be overgrown or infilled with collapsed masonry.

The feature survives at Dun Loch an Duin, Shader (Ill. 5.21; L9) and Dun Loch an Duin, Carloway (Ill. 5.17; L15), in Lewis, where the causeways end abruptly before reaching the islets, and was noted at Dun Thomaidh (A.NU7) and Dun nan Gealag (A.NU48), both in North Uist.

It is probable that the gaps would have been crossed by a timber bridge which could be raised to prevent access. This, as with the cross-causeway walls, need not be a defensive feature but could equally well be designed to keep livestock on or off the islet.

Secondary occupation: The great majority of atlantic roundhouses have some form of secondary occupation within or around the roundhouses themselves. The roundhouse provided both a source of building stone and a sheltered location for the insertion of slighter structures. All of the excavated structures, with the probable exception of Rudh an Duin, have secondary occupation of some form.

Secondary structures include the wheelhouses and cellular structures of the later prehistoric period and the rectilinear structures of the medieval and post-medieval periods. In some cases, e.g. Dun Barraglom A.L21), a medieval 'baile' or township may be sited over the roundhouse, while sites such as Dun an Sticer, North Uist, Dun Aonghais, North Uist (A.NU18), and possibly Bragar, have substantial medieval tacksmen's houses built over their remains.

Contemporary occupation: In no case in the Western Isles is there any unambiguous evidence for the contemporaneous existence of any other domestic structure on an atlantic roundhouse site.

Earlier occupation: As indicated above a number of the sites have indications of earlier occupation. The clearest example from the excavated sites is Dun Bharabhat, Cnip. The suggestion of a long sequence through the 1st millennium BC is supported by evidence from field survey.

Several islet-sited atlantic roundhouses lie in lochs which contain smaller residual islets, often artificial in construction, which appear to be earlier than the roundhouses themselves. In Lewis this situation occurs at Dun Loch an Duin, Shader, where a residual islet of collapsed stone lies just below the water surface some 50m from the roundhouse. The residual islet is of similar size to the roundhouse and has a parallel causeway to the same shore of the loch. An earlier stone-built islet structure of unknown form was robbed out to construct the surviving roundhouse. A similar submerged rubble islet lies some 40m from the shore of Dun Loch an Duna, Bragar.

At Dun Cromore the walled frontal annexe is of similar construction to the wall of the roundhouse and projects into a circle of similar dimensions. It also appears to have a residual entrance which makes no structural sense relative to the surviving roundhouse structure. It appears that the surviving complex roundhouse was built over and quarried from an earlier structure of similar construction.

In many other cases, as noted above, the islets on which the structures are sited may be formed substantially of the debris of preceding occupation. The excavation of Eilean Domhnuill, Loch Olabhat, in North Uist (Armit 1988b; 1990b) has shown that similar locations were used for settlement in the Neolithic and there is no evidence to suggest that they did not persist in use from that period into the later prehistoric period.

Discussion

Construction method

The basic construction methods of the atlantic round-houses of Scotland are well understood and the Hebridean examples employ the same range of structural techniques. The definition of the atlantic roundhouses, based primarily on constructional information, has been discussed in Chapter Four. The atlantic roundhouses are thick-walled, free-standing, drystone roundhouses. The complex atlantic roundhouses and broch towers incorporate features of broch architecture which combine to provide stability with height: the construction of two concentric walls, tied together at vertical intervals by lintels forming galleries, creates a structure in which the overall mass is minimised while still achieving considerable potential height. Outward battering of the walls channels weight stresses effectively, adding stability.

A range of secondary architectural features spring from this basic technique. Multiple floor levels can be inserted with access from intra-mural stairs and with relatively narrow gallery entrances piercing the inner wall. Wall-voids above the entrances spread the weight and avoid placing too much stress on the lintels. Internal scarcement ledges provide support for upper floors and possibly for roofing. Main entrances tend to be single, low and narrow to avoid creating a major weak point in the structure.

The whole design of a broch tower such as Dun Carloway or Berie suggests the existence of a considerable body of expertise in the Hebridean communities, as elsewhere in Atlantic Scotland, concerning drystone construction. The restrictions on architecture imposed by the basic hollow-wall building technique created a degree of uniformity throughout Atlantic Scotland and produced a range of recurring features across the area. Considerable variation occurs in the internal design and combination of architectural features employed: the existence and arrangement of cells and galleries on the basal levels of the structures, for example, vary greatly throughout the Atlantic province, as MacKie noted in his search for typological and chronological variation amongst *broch* sites (MacKie 1965).

Broch architecture only makes structural sense in the context of structures of more than one floor level: all of the excavated atlantic roundhouses of the Western Isles, where data is available, appear to be complex round-houses i.e. they employ features of broch architecture. Most of these structures therefore are likely to have been multistory. The inferred existence of upper floors implies the existence of a timber architectural component used in parallel with the archaeologically visible stone architecture on the majority of the excavated sites. At Loch na Berie, for example, the position of the 1st floor gallery entrances relative to the stairs demonstrates that an internal timber floor at scarcement level would have been necessary to enable access into the 1st floor gallery. The number of upper floors cannot be reliably estimated at any site since weight-relieving wall-voids cannot always be distinguished structurally from gallery entrances.

Timber roofs as well as timber floors would have been used in the atlantic roundhouses and at the height which these structures could achieve it would probably have been necessary to protect the lower parts of these roofs from the wind by a stone parapet. It is probable that the outer walls were slightly higher than the inner walls and protected the roofs from the wind. The pitched timber-framed roof would have drained into the outer wall or gallery.

A number of significant issues are raised by the construction of the atlantic roundhouses. The mass of stone used indicates a great investment of labour in construction: this has led to the suggestion that the structures were built by elite groups commanding a large workforce (cf Chapters Twelve and Thirteen). The skill involved in construction has invited suggestions of a class of professional builders (MacKie 1965), although the emergence of the extended chronology has weakened this case (Armit 1991). Above all the question is raised of why the Hebridean communities of the later prehistoric period, and their northern neighbours, should invest so much time and effort in the construction of monumental structures so removed from their traditional building forms. The questions of monumentality and its function will be addressed in Chapter Fourteen.

The atlantic roundhouses stand out from the other prehistoric building traditions of Atlantic Scotland, which tend to be semi-subterranean, to save heat, and cellular, to save timber in roofing. In terms of use within the natural environment the atlantic roundhouses cannot be regarded as well-adapted.

Some examples from the Western Isles undermine the traditional concepts of the mastery of broch architecture. Dun Bharabhat, Cnip, collapsed relatively soon after completion due to being built on too soft a foundation (consisting of older midden and structural deposits). The perception of the success of broch architecture in terms of its stability should not be conditioned by the impact of the few standing examples: the failures of the type will, by definition, be the least visible to archaeologists. Dun Carloway, an archetypal broch tower, exemplifies another point which should make us cautious in our admiration for the broch builders. Although regarded as a tower, Dun Carloway is 9m high (and was probably never much higher) and c. 15m in diameter. It is therefore considerably wider than it is high and its tower-like appearance is produced by the inward battering of its upper walls. This produces and exaggerated visual impression of height. Whilst not denying the skill in construction, the visual impact which so impresses many observers of broch towers may be exactly the impression which the builders intended the structures to have. In terms of actual proportions none of the surviving broch towers, including Mousa, is taller than it is in external diameter.

The construction of the atlantic roundhouses and particularly of the broch towers was designed to produce height and stability and was a fully-fledged architectural tradition with the potential to produce truly monumental structures. This potential was achieved at the expense of other considerations such as insulation and ease of roofing.

Chronology

The absolute chronology of the atlantic roundhouses of the Western Isles is poorly defined at present. Only from Dun Bharabhat, Cnip has produced C-14 dates. These dates suggest a construction and primary occupation prior to the C2nd BC with collapse of the structure in the C2nd or perhaps somewhat earlier. The structure therefore fits within the period of complex roundhouse construction for the north (Armit 1991) which appears to commence around the C4th or C5th BC.

None of the atlantic roundhouses has yielded querns with reliable contexts or any Roman material from primary occupation. It is worth noting that saddle querns, without reliable site contexts, have been found at Dun Thomaidh and Dun Cuier and may be associated with pre-quern transition activity on these sites.

Ceramic assemblages which can be reliably associated with atlantic roundhouse primary occupation are only available from Dun Bharabhat and possibly the galleries at Loch na Berie. All of the other assemblages have been shown to comprise material from later occupations along with any primary material, except perhaps the material Rudh an Duin where no details are available.

Despite the existence of 140 known sites and despite thirteen excavations of atlantic roundhouses in the Western Isles, the Bharabhat and Berie assemblages are our only indication of the ceramics associated with primary occupation of these monuments. The material from these sites falls within the largely undifferentiated group of later prehistoric pottery with a high percentage of decorated vessels and everted rims, characteristic of the later centuries BC (App. 2). This poorly defined picture at least provides some support for the early dating of Dun Bharabhat.

It is unfortunate that we have to rely so much on structural typology (the least reliable dating level defined in Armit 1991) to provide a chronological framework for the atlantic roundhouses of the Western Isles. The excavated sites all appear to be complex roundhouses or broch towers wherever evidence is available (as it is for all excavated sites except Dun a Ghallain and Eilean a Ghallain) and conceivably all may have been broch towers. Given the relative frequency with which simple atlantic roundhouses have recently been found in excavations in the north (e.g. Bu, Pierowall, Quanterness, Tofts Ness) it is significant that no such structure has been found in the west. This suggests that the Hebridean sites all date from the period of c. 400BC onwards after the initial development of the elements of broch architecture (Armit 1991). Unfortunately no further chronological resolution is possible unless the growth of clustered village settlements around certain broch towers is seen as a chronological phenomenon: this development manifestly does not occur in the west. There is however insufficient evidence in the north to claim that the single roundhouse settlements cease to be occupied in the last centuries BC and even if there were this would have no necessary validity in the Western Isles.

The atlantic roundhouses appear to pre-date wheelhouses on the few sites where the two forms occur. Unfortunately there is still in each case a measure of doubt regarding the relationship between the forms and the possibility remains that they may represent unitary structures. Nonetheless at Garry Iochdrach, Cnoc a Comhdhalach and Eilean Maleit the sequence of atlantic roundhouse followed by wheelhouse does seem likely. At several of the sites cellular structures are constructed in the abandoned atlantic roundhouses. It is probable that the atlantic roundhouses are occupied prior to the cellular structures, which will be argued to date from the C1st BC onwards in Chapter Seven. The relationship with the wheelhouses is less clear. On the present evidence the Hebridean atlantic roundhouses appear to inhabit a chronological range from c. 400 BC until perhaps the C1st BC, but the weakness of the chronological evidence is obvious.

Function

The function of atlantic roundhouses, and in particular the *brochs* however defined, has occupied the attention of archaeologists and antiquarians for well over a century. Originally the dispute centred on whether they functioned as forts, wholly defensive in intent, or as farmsteads occupied on a day-to-day basis (whether by an elite or by the wider population). The use of atlantic roundhouses as domestic with a defensive component is now generally accepted especially since Fojut's work in Shetland, which demonstrated the siting of atlantic roundhouses with regard to available agricultural land (Fojut 1982).

Only one primary floor plan is available for any of the Hebridean atlantic roundhouses, from Dun Bharabhat, Cnip. The structure is dominated internally by a central hearth, and the quantities of broken pottery and midden debris are suggestive of normal domestic use. In the absence of other floor plans and detailed excavated evidence the survey record can provide limited evidence for function from a combination of architectural features and aspects of site structure.

Defense as a primary function is immediately suggested by the visual impact of tall, externally featureless stone towers with their small narrow single entrance. The visual correspondence with medieval defensive architecture provoked interpretation in terms of defence from the early antiquaries. It is not clear, however, what kind of defence the atlantic roundhouses are intended to provide or against what threat they were established.

MacKie was never specific as to the form of the threat with which his *brochs* were intended to deal but seemed to imply a form of siege warfare (1974, 98). The defensive capacities of the atlantic roundhouses, however, are purely passive. Once locked into a roundhouse one could only wait until the attackers had pillaged the surrounding land and stolen one's livestock. The narrow broch entrances could not easily have enabled the accommodation of stock inside. Determined attackers could presumably starve or smoke out the inhabitants relatively easily: blocking up the single entrance from the outside would be a simple means of achieving this and even the tallest broch towers could not have been far out of the range of fire-brands.

The location of many of the atlantic roundhouses on islets linked to the shore by stone causeways may have been a much more effective defensive mechanism than the architecture of the roundhouses. While the architecture of hilltop-sited roundhouses such as Dun Cuier and Dun Scurrival in Barra clearly adds to their defensive capability, these structures are no more defensive than a simple wall around the hilltop would have been. Nothing in the architecture of these sites seems necessary to improve on the natural defensive capability of the site. The simpler architecture of contour forts, utilising the natural defensive capabilities of their locations to the full, or the control of access and concentration of defense shown by the promontory forts, would have been considerably more efficient for purely defensive purposes.

Causeway cross-walls and gaps would have greatly impeded attack and enabled defence to be highly concentrated. The annexes would have provided space for storage and for stock. Surprise attack or night raids would have been easily detected by the simple expedient of guarding the causeway or lifting the bridges from the causeway gaps. The architecture of the roundhouses appears to be a device of limited defensive application in the face of these more practical measures. We must draw on further explanations for its existence other than the purely defensive.

The density of atlantic roundhouse sites and the locational factors in their siting will be discussed in Part Three. In general terms both factors indicate that the structures were a common settlement form in the later centuries BC and were situated with the requirements of a farming economy in mind. Their density precludes their interpretation as strongholds of an elite. Nonetheless the construction methods described above show that they were not simple, utilitarian, domestic structures.

The atlantic roundhouses of the Western Isles cannot be interpreted as either simple farmsteads or as simple defensive structures. They were used as a standard settlement form but with a variable defensive capacity and in the context of a monumental architecture which removed them from the purely utilitarian sphere.

Subdivision

The conventional division of the atlantic roundhouses into *brochs*, *galleried duns*, *island duns* etc. has been rejected above as unhelpful and misleading in the context of the Western Isles. The excavated atlantic roundhouses, where classifiable, are all complex roundhouses, and three at least, Berie, Dun Carloway and Dun Cuier are broch towers. These three sites are all *brochs* by Mac-Kie's criteria and all of the remaining ten could be *brochs* given their state of preservation. The utility of the conventional division of *brochs* and *duns* is therefore highly questionable in this context.

No architectural division has been shown in the class of atlantic roundhouses other than differences in apparent complexity, all of which are accommodated within the atlantic roundhouse architectural form as defined elsewhere (Armit 1991). If a class of solid-walled *dun* ever existed in the Western Isles, in the mid-1st millennium AD or at any other time, it has yet to be demonstrated by

excavation. Of thirteen excavations every one has turned out to contain a complex roundhouse, despite the deliberate selection of Dun Bharabhat for its lack of complex architectural features visible prior to excavation, and despite the work of Erskine Beveridge who excavated sites almost randomly, based on proximity to his house on Vallay. Thomas too, excavated Dun Ban, Grimsay, not expecting it to be a complex roundhouse or broch tower and Young, even after excavating Dun Cuier, believed it not to be a broch tower. Only Dun Carloway was excavated in the knowledge that it was a broch tower while Loch na Berie had only the evidence of oral tradition. The lack of a solid-walled *dun* is therefore not the result of a history of broch-orientated research but the result of widespread excavation, often without any real research strategy: it is the nearest we are likely to achieve to a random sample of excavation. That no solid-walled *dun* has been found despite this pattern of research strongly suggests that the type does not exist in the Western Isles. No structural or architectural division is suggested by the examination of excavated or surveyed sites.

The chronological information on the atlantic roundhouses is too slight to provide any basis for subdivision. On the basis of structural typology the sites could all date to the same broad period of c. 400BC or earlier to c. 100BC or later. At present there is no evidence to subdivide them or narrow this range. The conventional division between *brochs* and *duns*, which was the basis of the study of the later prehistory of the islands, does not stand up to the evidence of field survey and excavation. The use of the terminology of the atlantic roundhouse assimilates both of these structural classes and shows their overwhelming unity in comparison to other types of structure. This structural and architectural unity appears to extend to site function on the basis of the survey data.

Parallels outwith the Western Isles

The atlantic roundhouses of the Western Isles share a range of features with similar structures in the Northern Isles and north mainland, and with the west coast of Scotland. Atlantic roundhouse forms are also found sporadically in Lowland Scotland but the wider issues of the distribution of the type are outwith the scope of this study. The wider issues of the development of atlantic roundhouses in Scotland as a whole have been recently discussed elsewhere (Armit 1990d)

The main difference between the atlantic roundhouse sites in the Western Isles and those of the north, or at least of the Orkneys, is the total absence of clustered village settlements around the western roundhouses. In all cases the western roundhouses are single structures and in no case can any contemporary building be cited. Elements characteristic of broch architecture are also found on non-atlantic roundhouse sites including the *duns* of Argyll and a number of Irish Late Iron Age or Early Christian forts (e.g. Warner 1983). The atlantic roundhouses of the Western Isles lie on an axis of communication which was capable of carrying cultural information, by whatever mechanism, over wide areas throughout the later prehistoric period.

Summary

The atlantic roundhouses appear to represent a standard settlement type of the later centuries BC in the Western Isles. Their architecture raises questions on the meaning of monumentality in the domestic context and its relationship to otherwise utilitarian farming settlements. Their nature as defended monumental settlements is relatively easily described but difficult to explain, as is their relationship, chronological and functional, with the wheelhouses. The widespread parallels of the atlantic roundhouses and in particular the different distributions of atlantic roundhouses and wheelhouses on the inter-regional scale further complicate the formulation of explanatory models. Further discussion in Part Three will attempt to clarify the structural, locational and spatial relationships within the class and explore the relationships of the atlantic roundhouses with other structural forms.

Chapter Six - Wheelhouses

The radially partitioned roundhouses of the Western Isles have been classified in the past as wheelhouses, earth-houses and aisled roundhouses. The term wheelhouse will be used here to refer to all of these types. The wheelhouses of the Western Isles conform to a uniform construction: their circular interiors contain a number of radial drystone piers regularly spaced around the whole circuit. These radial piers appear similar on plan to the spokes of a wheel and if projected would converge on the centre of the structure. The regularity of the plans and uniformity of proportions appear to result from a specific construction method.

Seventeen definite wheelhouse sites have been excavated in the Western Isles. Many of these are relatively poorly recorded early excavations. The additional evidence from field survey is slight for this class, providing only nine more examples of which few are definite (Ill. 6.1). The following discussion examines the excavated sites from north to south through the islands.

Excavated Sites

W.1 Cnip, Lewis NB 0980 3665 (Armit 1988a)

Introduction - The complex of structures at Cnip included two wheelhouses, several cellular structures (Chapter Seven) and a substantial linear house structure (Chapter Eight). The site was excavated in 1988 in advance of the construction of a sea wall and sewerage system. The site lay on the eroding beach front of the Traigh Cnip sands in an area of formerly consolidated machair.

Site Structure - Phase 1 on the site comprised two adjoining wheelhouses of which one was never completed (Ill. 6.2). This incomplete structure, Structure 2, was left with construction material stacked in its interior and entrance. It was used as an outbuilding or annexe to the occupied wheelhouse, Structure 1 (Armit 1988a, 15-17). The dismantling of this incomplete structure enabled a detailed reconstruction of building methods while the survival to roof level of parts of Structure 1 provided complementary information on superstructure and roofing.

Both structures were sand-revetted and their upper parts were packed with midden material. Structure 1 was some 7m in internal diameter and contained eight aisled piers. Structure 2 appears to have been planned as a structure of similar dimensions. The bays of Structure 1 were individually corbelled, forming a ring of roofed cells around the open central area. This central area would have had a timber-framed roof resting on the ring of masonry provided by the circle of bay roofs. The building and roofing methods are discussed in more detail later in this chapter along with evidence from other excavated sites.

Internal Structure - Only Structure 1 was occupied as a domestic structure in this earliest phase on the site. Few internal features can be linked with the primary occupation since excavations of the primary floor were limited in scale. A large central hearth seems to have been the dominant feature. No primary blocking of access to the bays was noted and no internal features were noted in the bays. At this earliest period access was possible through the aisles between each of the bays.

Material Culture and Chronology - Initial observation of the pottery shows that the assemblage contains a wide variety of both incised and applied decorative motifs and is dominated by incurving and sharply everted rim forms. Vessels are generally small and globular in form; all were flat-based. The assemblage belongs to the highly decorated typological stage which is so far undifferentiated for the last few centuries BC and possibly extends into the C1st AD (App. 2). A series of C-14 dates is currently being processed.

Other finds from the site were generally unhelpful in dating. Several rotary quern fragments were found built into walling which suggests a construction date after the local quern transition (App. 1). A date between approximately 200BC - 100AD may be suggested for the construction of the Phase 1 structures.

W.3 The Udal, North Uist NF 824 783 (Crawford 1967/78, 1975, 1977, nd)

Introduction - The Udal is a multi-period machair site which has been under excavation since the early 1960s (having been previously excavated by Beveridge). The wheelhouse lies on a sand-hill on an eroding headland in the north of North Uist. Details of the material remain unpublished and no archaeological plans are available. The excavator declined to make the material available for the present study.

Site Structure - The main wheelhouse at the Udal lies amid a lengthy sequence which includes pre-Norse cellular structures as well as Norse and later structures. None are stratigraphically associated with the wheelhouse as far as can be ascertained from the interim excavation reports.

The main wheelhouse on the site appears to have been a large, sand-revetted structure with 11 free-standing piers. Although sand-revetted for much of the circuit, parts of the wall on the west were double-faced and free-standing. This structure was associated with a small contemporary adjoining cell with three stone piers projecting from one wall (although the two appear to have been linked only at an early phase in the use of the wheelhouse). Another wheelhouse is indicated on some plans as lying adjacent to this structure.

Internal Structure - No information is available on the internal features of the structure.

Material Culture and Chronology - No detailed information is available on the material associated with the wheelhouse, although Lane indicates that the wheelhouse levels contained pottery with everted rims and a range of decorative motifs in contrast to the later assemblage with which he was concerned (Lane 1983).

EX BIBL. UNIV. EDINBURGH

EDINBURGH UNIVERSITY LIBRARY

WITHDRAWN

Ill. 6.1 Distribution of Wheelhouses in the Western Isles

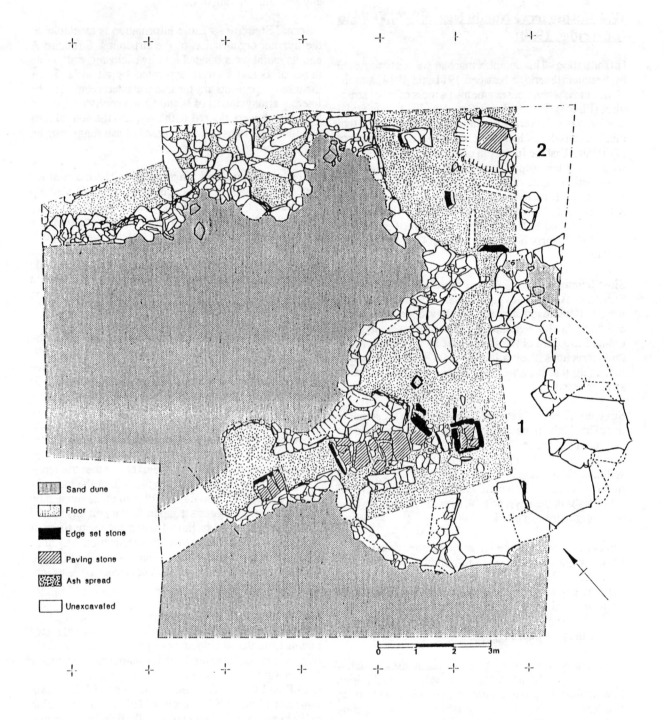

Sand dune

Floor

Edge set stone

Paving stone

Ash spread

Unexcavated

0 1 2 3m

Ill. 6.2 Cnip Phase One Structures

C-14 dates from the wheelhouse have not been published. Dates from the post-wheelhouse cellular structures have been claimed to centre on the C1st AD, but again the data is not fully published (App. 1).

W.4 Foshigarry, North Uist NF 7430 7636 (Beveridge 1930)

Introduction - This complex machair site was excavated by Erskine Beveridge between 1911 and 1914, and includes three wheelhouses amongst a mass of other structures (Ill. 6.3). The site has suffered greatly through tidal erosion since Beveridge's day and it is probable that much material was lost to the sea prior to his discovery of the site. That the full depth of the sand hills can still be seen to contain super-imposed structures of drystone construction (pers. obs. 1987) shows that Beveridge's excavations revealed only a small part of a far more extensive site. The prehistoric occupation lies towards the base of sand-hills capped by the post-medieval township of Foshigarry on the north coast of North Uist near Vallay.

Site Structure - There are three wheelhouses on the site, Structures A-C on the original plan. Structures B and C were half removed by later building operations while Structure A, although undamaged by later activity, was reduced to a third of its original size by tidal erosion. All three structures share a flimsiness of wall construction indicating that they were never free-standing but were sand-revetted.

Structure A is the best preserved of the three, standing over 2m high in its southern arc, and gave the only indications of the form of roofing of any structure on the site. Beveridge reported a considerable degree of over-sailing in the upper course slabs of Structure A, especially in bays A1 and A2, which, along with the quantity of fallen slabs in the bays, he took as evidence that the bays were originally corbelled.

Structures B and C were far less well preserved than A, being caught up in a maze of re-building and stone-robbing which Beveridge was unable to disentangle. The northern parts of the two wheelhouses were disturbed by post-medieval buildings associated with the overlying township. The degree of confusion is therefore even greater than the plan suggests.

The drain system linking the two wheelhouses would, if original, suggest that Structure C is the earlier as the drain leading from Structure B appears to be a later addition to that leading from C. Given the lack of proper recording and the structural similarities between the two, the succession is of little relevance, save to note that the two could not have co-existed in their original forms. Both structures have a confusion of piers which are unlikely all to be original, but all of the true radials (i.e. those which lead towards the centre of the structure) are free-standing, slight structures, only 0.3m to 0.35m in thickness. The relationship between B and C and the structures which surround and overlie them is problematic and probably unresolvable in the light of Beveridge's methods of recording. It is unlikely that Scott was correct in his belief that Structure H (the linear passage discussed in Chapter Eight) pre-dated the wheelhouses; although its

level is generally below C, it rises up through the floor level of C and would have made C unusable unless it was built after the abandonment of the wheelhouse and dug down into the mound. Structure H at no point underlies any standing walling of C.

Internal Structure - Little information is available on the internal organisation of the structures. Structure A had its radial piers bonded into its enclosing wall while those of B and C were separated by an aisle. Later disturbance prevents any meaningful interpretation of the internal arrangements of B and C: the surviving bays of Structure A were floored with clay, and the central area would appear to have held a spread of ash suggesting an original central hearth.

Material Culture and Chronology - The material recovered from the site, although plentiful, is of little help in establishing the site sequence due to the rudimentary standard of the recording. The problem is exacerbated by the fact that the publication of the material was compiled only after the death of the excavator. The pottery covers a wide range of later prehistoric forms (App. 2); a wide variety of incised and stabbed motifs occur along with applied wavy cordon decoration while rim forms include everted and flaring forms.

It is possible to discern a relative chronology for the wheelhouses at Foshigarry. It is unlikely that Structure A could have preceded the other two, since its high degree of preservation shows that it was never robbed. It is therefore likely that A was the last of the wheelhouses to be used although it cannot be shown that B and C were necessarily out of use by the time A was built. The spatial separation of the structures in contrast to the over-building common on other wheelhouse sites suggests a degree of contemporaneity between at least two of the structures. The position of A - lower down the side of the mound - supports this view. The survival of A uncontaminated by later occupation suggests a gap in activity on this part of the site over a period sufficient to obscure the position of so much good building stone. Re-occupation on top of the mound then initiated the partial destruction of B and C; their re-use is shown by the occurrence of later material such as composite combs.

The absolute date of the structures is difficult to gauge but the recovery of a saddle quern as well as several rotary querns from the wheelhouses suggests a relatively early date, at least for Structure C, and perhaps provides further slender support for the inferred on-site succession from C to B and then to A at around the time of local quern transition (Armit 1991). This would represent a transition at Foshigarry from wheelhouses with slight free-standing piers to one with more massive bonded piers at around the time of this artefactually defined horizon, perhaps c. 200BC.

W.5 Bac Mhic Connain, North Uist NF 7695 7620 (Beveridge 1931)

Introduction - This site was excavated by Beveridge in 1919 and published after his death from his incomplete notes: the account thus suffers from the same lack of precision as the Foshigarry report, although the site itself was less complex (Ill. 6.4). Extensive quarrying was

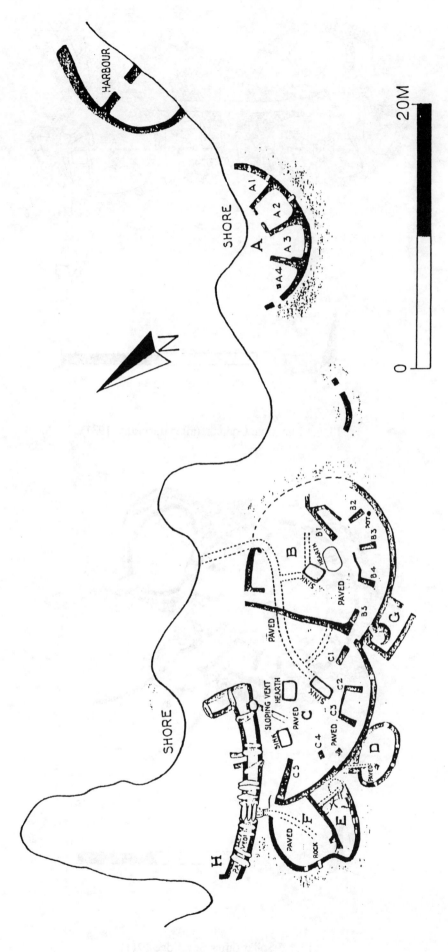

Ill. 6.3 Foshigarry (after Beveridge 1930)

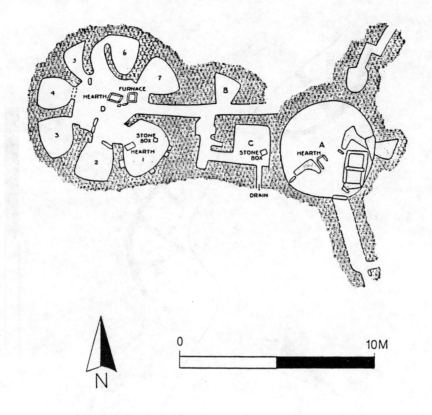

Ill. 6.4 Bac Mhic Connain (after Beveridge 1931)

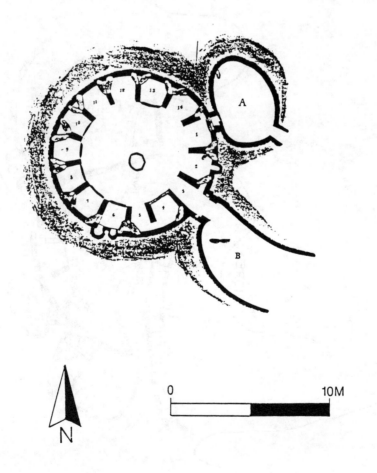

Ill. 6.5 Sollas (after Beveridge 1911)

carried out, especially on chamber A, during the building of Vallay House and the plan of that structure in particular must be regarded, as Scott observed, as 'tentative' (1948, 75).

The site lies on the island of Vallay itself, some 200m from the western shore, on the machair plain. It is likely to have overlooked the now drowned machair plain of Vallay Strand.

Site Structure - Structure D is the only definite wheelhouse on the site and it was also the best preserved, standing over 2.5m high in places. A series of outer cells appear to be associated with part of the occupation. Like the structures at Cnip, the Udal and Foshigarry, the Bac Mhic Connain complex was dug into existing machair hills and revetted against the sand.

The 8 piers preserved in Structure D are bonded into the surrounding wall and Beveridge noted that the upper courses indicated corbelling of the bays. The wheelhouse had been subject to extensive reconstruction, with modifications to the upper parts of the piers apparently providing a more solid base for the corbelling. This strengthening of the structure may have been carried out at any point in the use of the wheelhouse which clearly extended over a considerable period. In excess of 1m of deposits filled the chamber and, at a late stage, a furnace had been dug down into the centre.

Structure D does not represent the earliest activity on the site as Beveridge records finding midden material under the floor level. The finds, which are unstratified, could in part derive from these underlying levels. Structure D is demonstrably earlier than any of the other structures which Beveridge recorded at Bac Mhic Connain. Three superimposed drains were traced from the entrance passage of D and it is the uppermost (well above the original floor of D) which leads in to A, B and C. Chambers B and C may indicate progressive extension of the entrance of D to avoid the build-up of sand blocking the entrance. It is not possible to determine the true structure of A, which was quarried and used as a rubbish tip prior to excavation, but there are vague indications of possible radial piers (Ill. 6.4). When this building was in use it is unlikely that D was habitable due to the accumulation of material inside. It is probable that, as the furnace indicates, D was used only as a sheltered hollow for a workshop. We may then be seeing at Bac Mhic Connain the successive use of a number of wheelhouse structures on the same site over a long period.

Internal Structure - The internal organisation of the wheelhouse focuses on the central area from which all access to the bays was controlled. The piers, by the nature of their construction, allowed no access between bays. It is therefore relatively easy to demonstrate the patterns of access within the structure. No information is available on the possible differences in use between bays. None of the recorded internal features can be shown to relate to a specific phase of occupation. It is apparent that access to some of the bays, which were bridged by lintels, would have been impossible after the accumulation of substantial occupation debris (the lintel of Bay 4 was only 0.5m above the 'original' floor level).

Material Culture and Chronology - A saddle quern was found in the filling of Structure A. This appeared to have fallen in from the walling and it is likely that the activity on the site began prior to the local quern transition (the only other quern stones found were of the rotary variety). A number of clay and stone moulds, as well as confirming on-site metal-working, indicate a possible date in the Roman period for the post-domestic occupation. Bac Mhic Connain also produced one fragment of the rim of a Samian bowl.

A whalebone mirror handle from the site has parallels to bronze items in Ireland (Raftery 1984, 209) and an almost identical bronze version at Lochlee (MacGregor 1976, No. 272), and falls into the early part of Warner's EIA2 style (Warner 1983, 164) perhaps in the C1st or C2nd AD. The Ogham inscribed bone knife handle and perhaps the bone die indicate later activity and it is not possible to link the Roman period material to any phase of the site's use, save to note that the metal-working material may be contemporary with the furnace and thus later than the initial use of Structure D, perhaps in the C1st or C2nd AD. None of the artefacts has any secure connection with the construction or primary domestic use of the wheelhouse.

W.6 Sollas (Machair Leathann), North Uist NF 8035 7577 (Beveridge 1911)

Introduction - The Sollas wheelhouse lies on the broad machair plain, the Machair Leathann, overlooking Vallay Strand. It was excavated initially by Beveridge, after its discovery by a local shepherd, and re-excavated by Atkinson in the 1950s; this later work still awaits publication. A number of discrepancies between Beveridge's plan and that of Atkinson must make us wary of the reliability of Beveridge's plans on other sites as well as at Sollas, but nonetheless it is only from his work that published material is available (Ill. 6.5 is Beveridge's plan).

Site Structure - The main structure on the site is a wheelhouse, c. 12m in internal diameter, with 12 unbonded piers linked to the surrounding wall, and to each other, by paired lintels. This leaves a central area with axes of 7-8m. The lintels, where preserved, showed a consistent height of 1.3 - 1.5m and no sign of corbelling was noticed in the outer wall.

The wheelhouse had an extended entrance passage and an adjoining smaller cell which appeared to be of secondary construction, its entrance passage being founded on midden material.

Internal Structure - Beveridge notes that 7 of the bays were blocked by walling at their inside edge and, although Scott takes this to indicate a simple kerb, Beveridge is quite clear that it was a total blocking, and access to several of the cells could only be achieved through the narrow aisle between the piers and the outer wall. The central area did not therefore channel all access to each bay individually. A more complex pattern of access can be postulated than for sites with bonded piers, e.g. Bac Mhic Connain and Foshigarry A.

The main importance of Atkinson's re-excavation lay in the discovery of a large number of pits dug into the floor of both the central area and the bays. These ranged in size from 1m to only a few cm in depth, and many were found intercutting and with a variety of contents, ranging from deposits of burnt bone and pot, to one containing a vessel full of mouse skeletons (Topping 1985, 224). The pits demonstrate a strong ritual element in the occupation of the wheelhouse.

Material Culture and Chronology - Rotary querns were in use throughout the occupation. One fragment (not illustrated by Beveridge) was said to be incised with a 'rude Latin Cross'; the dating significance of this, and its relevance to the structure, is unknown. Insufficient information is available to assess the chronological value of the ceramic assemblage.

W.7 Garry Iochdrach, North Uist NF 7724 7427 (Beveridge 1931)

Introduction - Garry Iochdrach was excavated by Beveridge in 1912 and 1913 and published posthumously. The wheelhouse lies on the west side of Vallay Strand partly below the present high water mark. It lies on an eroding rocky coastline overlooking the drowned machair of the Strand. The possible atlantic roundhouse which it occupies has been discussed in Chapter Five.

Site Structure - The main prehistoric element of the site is a substantial wheelhouse (Ill. 5.8). An outer enclosure wall, noted by Scott (1948, 73), is as likely to belong with the associated later structures as with the wheelhouse. The wheelhouse appears to be partly free-standing and partly built into the hillside. Parts of the outer wall survived to a height of around 1.6m and the best preserved piers were of a similar height.

The plan and description of the outer wall at Garry Iochdrach defy interpretation; the thin surrounding wall appears to serve no structural purpose and does not appear to be a separate settlement structure. It is possible that in this, as in other cases, Beveridge excavated by means of a central hole and did not explore the outer of the two walls fully; an underlying atlantic roundhouse has been postulated (Chapter Five). Sadly the quality of the recording makes it impossible to put forward a convincing structural sequence for this site, except to say that the wheelhouse is clearly not the only structure present.

Internal Structure - Internally the structure contains 7 short radial piers separated by an aisle from the enclosing wall (except for one bonded pier on the east side). These leave a central area some 7.9m in diameter containing a central hearth. The majority of the bays were blocked by kerbs of uncertain height built of slabs placed on end.

Material Culture and Chronology - Finds from Garry Iochdrach cover a lengthy period. The latest occupation may be shown by a coin of Constantius II, dating from the C4th AD, found in the passage. None of the finds can be related to the primary occupation of the wheelhouse.

W.8 Cnoc a Comhdhalach, North Uist NF 7708 7415 (Beveridge 1911)

Introduction - Cnoc a Comhdhalach was excavated by Beveridge between 1905 and 1907 and published briefly in 1911. The atlantic roundhouse in which the wheelhouse is revetted is discussed in Chapter Five.

Site Structure - The central wheelhouse, enclosing an area of 7m, appeared to have been inserted into a pre-existing free-standing structure which incorporated hollow wall construction (Chapter Five, Ill. 5.9). The wheelhouse contained 7 unbonded radial piers linked by paired lintels to the surrounding wall; all of the structural elements survived to a height of 1.3 - 1.5m. A long low entrance passage extended out from the entrance through secondary modifications of the walling, containing cells and steps, to a raised wall area. Almost 2m of debris inside the structure testified to a lengthy occupation which again reduces the archaeological value of the poorly recorded material remains.

Internal Structure - The wheelhouse contained a central hearth and a kerbed perimeter at the inner ends of the bays. No other internal features were noted.

Material Culture and Chronology - No artefactual material can be attributed to any phase of the site's occupation.

W.10 Eilean Maleit, North Uist NF 7748 7388 (Beveridge 1911)

Introduction - Beveridge excavated the summit of the central stony mound of Eilean Maleit after the site was quarried for stone to build a nearby bridge. A very brief account of the work appeared in his book North Uist (1911). Eilean Maleit is a rocky tidal islet in Vallay Strand connected to the shore by a substantial stone causeway. It is probable that, prior to the drowning of the Strand, the islet would have lain in a machair loch. The atlantic roundhouse on the site has been discussed in Chapter Five.

Site Structure - A free-standing wheelhouse, 8m in internal diameter and with 9 piers, dominated the islet (Ill. 5.10). The probable presence of an underlying galleried structure is discussed in Chapter Five. This structure contained a number of free-standing piers with 3 bays blocked off from the central area on the north side. The form of roofing is unknown, due to the structure's state of preservation, and similarly the relationship of the numerous surrounding cells to the wheelhouse remains unresolved: some appear to be galleries of the atlantic roundhouse while others may be associated with the wheelhouse.

Internal Structure - No details were recorded of the internal features of the structure but the patterns of access are important in their contrast with most other wheelhouse sites. Three of the bays appear to be entirely walled off from the central area while the two by the entrance are bonded and the remaining four aisled. Access patterns were therefore not all channelled through the central area.

Material Culture and Chronology - No information is available on the artefactual material or dating of the site.

Clettraval, North Uist NF 7489 7136 (Scott 1948)

Introduction - This site was excavated by Scott in 1946 and 1948. The publication was the first major wheelhouse excavation report to make a serious attempt at reconstruction and interpretation. The wheelhouse lies on a hillside location a few km south of Vallay Strand, built over a chambered tomb.

Site Structure - The wheelhouse lies amid a complex of other structures with which the excavator believed it to be contemporary, forming a farmyard with outbuildings and an enclosure wall (Ill. 6.6). There is however no evidence that these structures were all contemporary, and the site seems to have been a focus for activity from the Neolithic through to post-medieval times.

The central structure was a free-standing wheelhouse with aisled piers joined by lintels to the main surrounding wall (Ill. 6.7). This left an aisle 0.6m wide and a central area 4.3m in diameter. Traces were found in the collapse pattern which Scott took to be evidence of a collapsed stone architrave between certain of the piers.

The site underwent four identifiable phases of use of which the first two involved the use of the wheelhouse in its original form. Phase 1 was the initial construction and occupation followed by partial rebuilding and reduction of the roofed area in Phase 2. The surrounding farm buildings and wall appear to represent a continuation of the periodic reuse of the site of phases 3 and 4 and have no demonstrable chronological connection with the occupation of the wheelhouse in its original form.

Internal Structure - The central area of the wheelhouse contained a central hearth which appears to have been replaced several times. Several of the bays were wholly or partially paved and most were kerbed.

Material Culture and Chronology - Pottery from the site, which was used to construct the traditional Hebridean Iron Age sequence, has recently been subject to stringent review (Topping 1985). The problems of poor recording and inadequate sample size have been highlighted to the extent that it is not possible to recognise any trends in the pottery throughout this site's occupation. The ceramic assemblage comprises a range of the decorated and everted rim forms of the later centuries BC (App. 2).

The initial construction of the site may be related to the loss of a broken globular bead of translucent green glass found under the floor of bay 9. This type, rare in Scotland, is Guido's Class 7, group ii or iii, which she dates to the Roman or early post-Roman period (but see discussion of bead dating in Armit 1991).

W.12 Bruach Ban, Benbecula NF 787 567 (Scott pers.comm.)

Introduction - The wheelhouse site of Bruach Ban was destroyed in the construction of the airport at Balivanich in Benbecula in 1956. Prior to this the site was excavated by Mr. JG Scott, who kindly supplied the information from which this account is compiled. The site lay on the machair plain behind the coastal sand dunes on Benbecula and was revetted into a pre-existing machair hill.

Site Structure - The structures on the site comprised the main wheelhouse, some fragmentary subsidiary walling and the remains of what may have been an adjoining wheelhouse. The main structure was a wheelhouse some 10m in internal diameter divided by radial drystone piers, some of which were aisled. Apart from the main northern entrance, an entrance led from the west bay into a further, unexcavated roundhouse structure which had indications of at least one radial pier and a curving outer wall. This entrance had been blocked. The situation provides a close parallel to the first phase wheelhouses at Cnip. A third entrance, to the east, was not investigated.

Internal Structure - No internal features were found apart from a hearth at a high level in one of the bays, interpreted by the excavator as indicating late squatter activity. It is probable that the primary floor levels of the wheelhouse were not reached during the brief excavations.

Material Culture and Chronology - Finds from the excavation are lodged in Glasgow's Kelvingrove Museum and an inspection of these provided a limited amount of information on chronology. In general the material represents a standard but undiagnostic assemblage of later prehistoric bonework and pottery. A rotary quern upperstone found *in situ* dates the latter part of the occupation to the period after the local quern transition (Armit 1991).

The pottery includes vessels decorated with applied cordons and bosses, fingernail impressions and impressed finger-prints. The rim forms are characteristically weakly everted. The incised decoration of the last centuries BC is absent and the assemblage finds its closest parallels for decoration in the Phase Three pottery from Cnip, though the rim forms might suggest a slightly later development. This would indicate that the earliest floor levels were not excavated. The pottery typology would favour a date in the C1st or C2nd AD for this secondary assemblage.

W.13 Bruthach a Tuath, Benbecula NF 787 566 (compiled from excavator's notes)

Introduction - This site was excavated by Mr J.C. Wallace over a period of less than two weeks in 1956. The brief and incomplete excavation was carried out in advance of destruction to make way for the Balivanich airfield. The site lies within a few hundred metres of Bruach Ban and prior to excavation was a low machair mound on the plain behind the coastal sand dunes. Mr Wallace's notes for publication were donated to the Na-

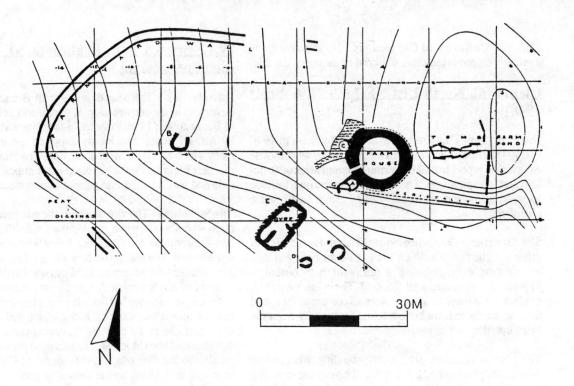

Ill. 6.6 Clettraval Site Plan (after Scott 1948)

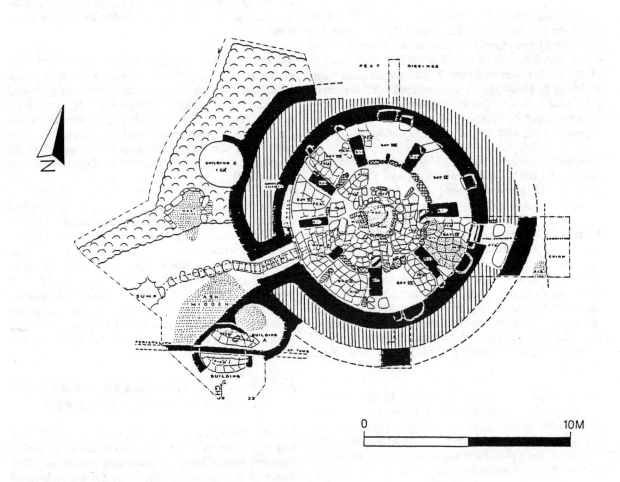

Ill. 6.7 Clettraval Wheelhouse (after Scott 1948)

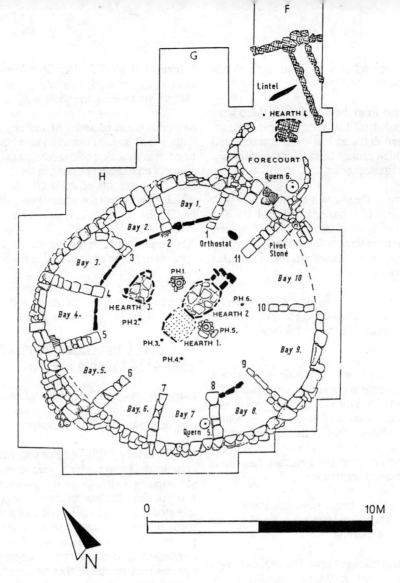

Ill. 6.8 A Cheardach Mhor (after Young and Richardson 1959)

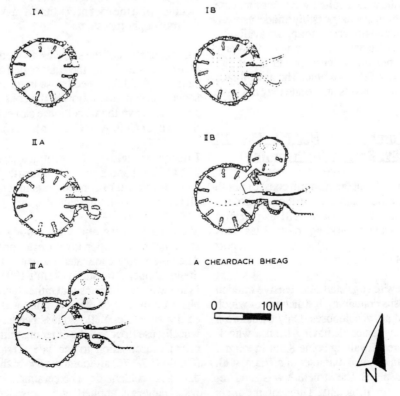

Ill. 6.9 A Cheardach Bheag (after Fairhurst 1971)

-tional Museum of Scotland after his death and provide the basis for this account.

Site Structure - Apart from the wheelhouse there were two structures recorded on the site, a linear passage discussed in Chapter Eight and a small unexcavated boulder structure which cannot be stratigraphically tied in to any part of the site sequence.

The primary structure on the site was a wheelhouse with 7 surviving aisled piers of a probable original 10. The wall was sand-revetted and c. 8.8m in internal diameter, surviving to a maximum of three or four courses in height. The SE entrance appears to have led out into a complex extended entrance passage.

The piers survived up to c. 0.7m in height. At least one aisle had been deliberately blocked in antiquity, as was the case on a number of other sites, best demonstrated at Cnip.

Internal Structure - Like many of the older excavations it is not clear that the primary levels of the Bruthach a Tuath wheelhouse were excavated. No central hearth was found but a major concentration of peat ash in the centre may indicate a hearth below. Two of the bays contained hearths which appear to have been secondary and possibly belong to a period after the structure had been abandoned as a permanent settlement.

At least two, and probably three, bays contained postholes in a central position, indicating the use of timber posts to prop up the bay roofing.

Material Culture and Chronology - The decoration on the ceramic assemblage was restricted to applied wavy cordons, bosses and fingernail impressions on rims. No incised decoration is recorded apart from one sherd with a horizontal groove above an applied wavy cordon. One sherd has circular impressions possibly made using a ring-headed pin. No details on vessel forms are available. Typologically the assemblage may date from the early 1st millennium AD but the absence of sufficient rim sherds makes closer dating impossible. The assemblage does indicate that primary levels on the site may not have been excavated.

W.14 Hornish Point, South Uist NF 758 470 (Barber et al 1989, Barber forthcoming)

Introduction - Hornish Point on the north coast of South Uist was excavated by the Central Excavation Unit of the Scottish Development Department in 1981 as part of a wider programme of work on eroding coastal sites. This discussion is based on a preliminary stratigraphic report made available by Mr. John Barber.

Site Structure - The site consisted of extensive midden and cultivation deposits containing 8 structures of which 3 may be interpreted as wheelhouses. Only Structure 5 had clear structural evidence of having been a wheelhouse; this was an arc of walling some 8.5m in length, possibly indicating an original diameter of c. 7.5m, with four surviving radial piers. The structure was sand revetted and stood to 1m in height. Three of the piers abutted the wall while one was aisled.

Internal Structure - The floor levels of the structures were not excavated, so nothing can be said about the internal structure of the wheelhouse.

Material Culture and Chronology - A group of C-14 dates were obtained from Hornish Point (App. 2). Structure 5 was stratified below contexts yielding a consistent series of dates concentrating in the period from 400 - 200 BC. The centroids of dates GU 2015, 2024 and 2025, which directly seal the wheelhouse, were 253BC, 241BC and 353BC respectively. A *terminus post quem* is provided by GU 2027 dating from 474 - 402 BC at 68% confidence limits. A date in the C4th or early C3rd BC appears to be the most probable for Structure 5.

The ceramic assemblage from the site appears to comprise a wide range of decorated and plain forms characteristic of the later centuries BC.

W.15 A' Cheardach Mhor, South Uist NF 7571 4128 (Young and Richardson 1959)

Introduction - A' Cheardach Mhor, situated on the Drimore machair of South Uist, was excavated in 1956 in advance of the MoD rocket range development.

Site Structure - This wheelhouse was sand-revetted and contained 11 piers which were unusual in abutting the surrounding wall without being bonded into it (Ill. 6.8). It is possible that the structure was originally aisled but adjusted to provide additional roof support, although the method does not result in as stable a structure as a properly bonded wheelhouse. The upper courses are oversailed up to the preserved height of 1.3m with some clay used as mortar, either as an additional stabilising influence on the wall or to keep out water. A large stone embedded in clay in the middle of the entrance, and two internal whalebone post supports, may confirm that difficulties with the roof necessitated makeshift additions to the roof support system.

The occupation of the site was divided into 5 successive phases of which only the first, sealed by a layer of clean sand, involved the wheelhouse in its primary form. Subsequent occupation followed the construction of smaller structures from the wheelhouse stone, and extended into the C5th or C6th AD (Chapter Seven).

Internal Structure - The central area of the wheelhouse had a central and a peripheral hearth. The abutted piers were equivalent to bonded piers in terms of channelling all access through this central area.

Material Culture and Chronology - A rotary quernstone below the floor level of the primary wheelhouse dates the whole excavated sequence to the period after the local quern transition (Armit 1991). A saddle quern in the walling indicates that either there was a preceding phase on the site or else the stone was quarried from an earlier structure. Yellow glass beads, one found on the wheelhouse floor and the other unstratified, may date the primary occupation to the late C1st BC or C1st AD (Guido 1978, 76) although the use of these bead types for dating is problematic. The ceramic assemblage shows a wide range of applied and incised decorative motifs characteristic of the later centuries BC (App. 2).

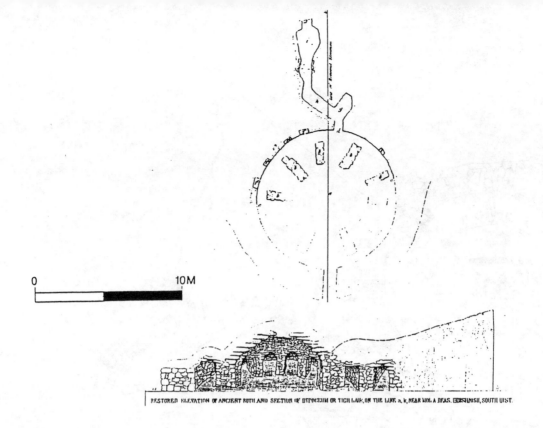

RESTORED ELEVATION OF ANCIENT BOTH AND SECTION OF DUNGEON OR TIGH LAIR, ON THE LINE a, b, NEAR MOL A BEAS. USSINISH, SOUTH UIST.

Ill. 6.10 Usinish (after Thomas 1870)

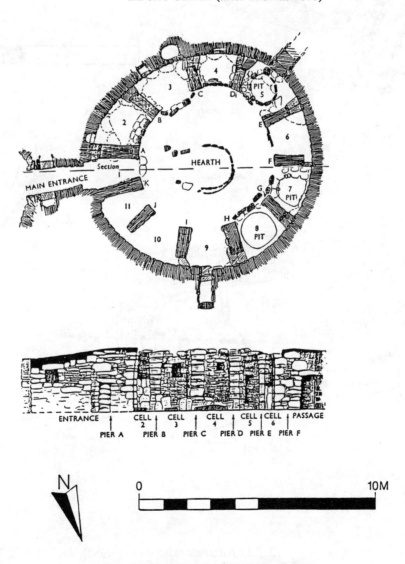

Ill. 6.11 Kilpheder (after Lethbridge 1952)

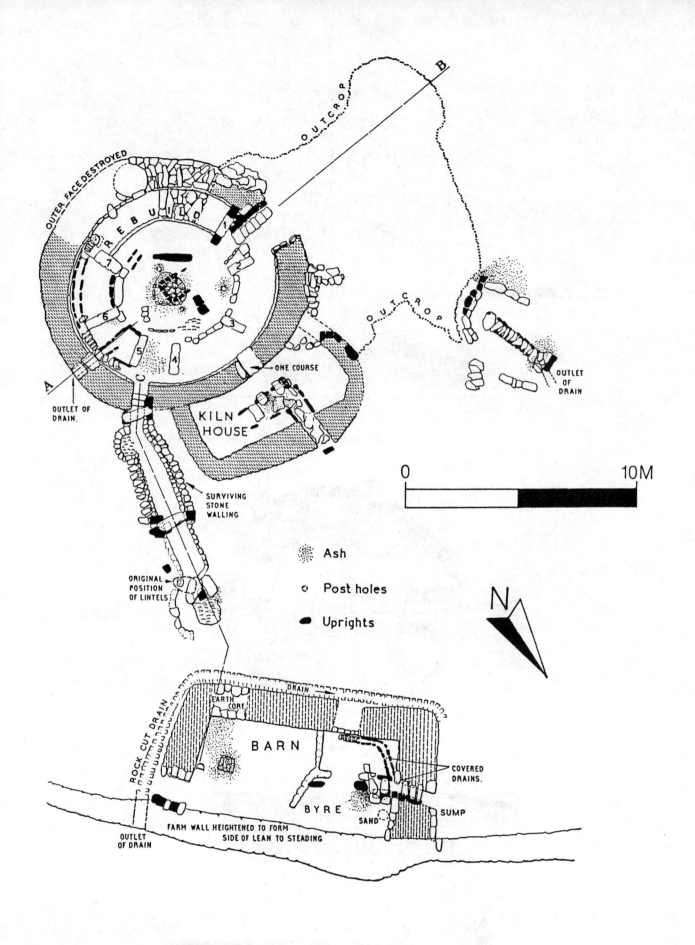

OUTER FACE DESTROYED

OUTCROP

B

REBUILD

7

2

6

3

5

4

A

C

ONE COURSE

OUTCROP

OUTLET OF DRAIN.

KILN HOUSE

OUTLET OF DRAIN

SURVIVING STONE WALLING

0   10M

ORIGINAL POSITION OF LINTELS

Ash

Post holes

Uprights

N

ROCK CUT DRAIN

DRAIN

EARTH CORE

BARN

COVERED DRAINS.

OUTLET OF DRAIN

BYRE

SAND

SUMP

FARM WALL HEIGHTENED TO FORM SIDE OF LEAN TO STEADING

Ill. 6.12 Allasdale (after Young 1952)

W.16 A' Cheardach Bheag, South Uist NF 7577 4037 (Fairhurst 1971)

Introduction - A' Cheardach Bheag, situated on the Drimore machair some 500m south of A' Cheardach Mhor, was excavated by Horace Fairhurst in similar circumstances and in the same year as the latter site.

Site Structure - The site consisted of one major wheelhouse and one adjoining subsidiary piered structure, built over earlier occupation debris (Ill. 6.9). The excavation of this early occupation along with the lowest occupation levels of the wheelhouses was hampered by the high water table, which made stratigraphic excavation virtually impossible.

The main wheelhouse was a sand-revetted structure with 12 bays separated by unbonded radials surviving up to 1.3m in height, the upper courses over-sailing by some 120mm. Fallen slabs indicate a considerable degree of corbelling in the bays in contrast to the lack of fallen slabs in the central area.

This first building was occupied through phases 1A-2B with progressive lengthening of the entrance passage into a forecourt with a cell, presumably in response to sand build-up. In phase 2B a small adjoining cell was built, to which access was obtained through the main wheelhouse. This secondary structure was a smaller, less well-built wheelhouse only 6m in internal diameter, probably with five bays with lintels linking the piers to the wall at a height of 1.3m.

Internal Structure - The central area was c. 5.5m in diameter and contained a central hearth and the unusual feature of a 'kerb' of unburnt, red deer mandibles placed overlapping, teeth downwards, into the floor.

Material Culture and Chronology - The assemblage from the primary deposits includes vessels decorated by incision, stabbing, and the ubiquitous applied wavy cordons. The assemblage lacks channelled decoration, applied bosses, ring-headed pin stamps and applied cordons under the rim. The secondary assemblage appears to contain less decoration and a reduction in the number of everted rims which characterise the early assemblage. The early assemblage would appear to date to the last century BC or C1st AD, immediately prior to the appearance of the less decorated assemblages of the early centuries AD (App. 2).

A worked bone pommel from the secondary wheelhouse may be attributed to the C2nd or C3rd AD (Topping 1985), for the secondary occupation of the site. The querns from the site were exclusively of rotary type.

W.19 Usinish, South Uist NF 8433 3326 (Thomas 1870)

Introduction - The site of Usinish lies on the east side of South Uist in an area otherwise largely barren of recorded field monuments; the site is one of a group of structures recorded by Thomas.

Site Structure - The wheelhouse was partly free-standing, with a wall some 2m wide, and partly cut into the hillside; it was already half destroyed when Thomas visited the site. Five piers remained of an estimated ten, and these were unbonded, standing to a height of c. 1.5m, leaving a central area 5m in diameter (Ill. 6.10). An adjoining passage or cell appears to have been excavated into the hillside, leading out from the wheelhouse.

The principal difficulty with this is the interpretation of Thomas's restored elevation, which shows corbelling as the roofing method over the central area as well as over the individual bays. Scott accepted this reconstruction, pointing out that Thomas was an experienced surveyor and hardly likely to invent such features, but it is unlikely for several reasons. The state of preservation was such that corbelling, if it ever existed, could not have been standing when Thomas arrived; Thomas was used to recording the beehive houses of the Hebrides and therefore in a reconstruction would be likely to invoke the roofing method which he was accustomed to seeing, especially as he had no idea of the relative age of his prehistoric structures. The remains of corbelling in the bays may have encouraged his reconstruction. In any event it is not possible that Thomas could have seen corbelling over the central area and it is unlikely that unbonded piers only 0.5m in thickness could have supported the enormous weight of stone required to corbel the central span. It is preferable to see Usinish as a structure similar to other wheelhouses, with corbelled bays and a timber-roofed central area.

Internal Structure - No details of the internal structure of the wheelhouse are known.

Material Culture and Chronology - No material was recovered from the site.

W.22 Kilpheder, South Uist NF 7327 2026 (Lethbridge 1952)

Introduction - Kilpheder was one of three adjacent wheelhouse sites noted by Lethbridge in the South Uist machair. Lethbridge also noted a number of other wheelhouses on the island but provided insufficient information to enable relocation.

Site Structure - The excavated structure was a sand-revetted aisled wheelhouse (although Lethbridge believed it was built on an old land surface, it is probable that a level surface was created with midden material as at other sites e.g. A' Cheardach Bheag) with a clear central area 5.5m in diameter (Ill. 6.11). The piers rose to 2.5m in height oversailing in the upper courses and linked to the surrounding wall by paired lintels. The inner faces of the piers were dressed and concave, the latter presumably a feature designed to channel the lateral thrust of the roof into the piers. A number of entrances into probable cells or passages were noted but not excavated.

Internal Structure - The central area of the wheelhouse contained a substantial hearth. The bays were generally kerbed and three contained substantial pits.

Material Culture and Chronology - A *terminus ante quem* for the occupation of the structure is provided by a

Romano-British brooch on the ledge in an aumbrey in Bay 3. This brooch has a close parallel at Newstead where it was dated by Collingwood to the mid-C2nd AD (Collingwood 1953, 225). The Kilpheder example had been repaired prior to its abandonment so it may have been deposited towards the end of the C2nd or later. The initial construction is shown to be relatively late by the occurrence of a broken rotary quern in the walling of the wheelhouse. The pottery from the site was not given proper contexts during the excavation, so this potentially valuable assemblage is of no use in establishing a stratified pottery sequence.

W.25 Tigh Talhamanta, Allasdale, Barra NF 6768 0220 (Young 1952)

Introduction - The Allasdale wheelhouse in Barra was initially excavated by Sir Lindsay Scott and completed by Alison Young after Scott's death. The site lies on a terrace at 130m above sea-level.

Site Structure - The site was surrounded by an enclosure wall and associated with a variety of less substantial structures. There is no indication that any of these are contemporary with the wheelhouse. The wheelhouse itself is a free-standing structure, 8m in overall diameter, with 7 aisled piers connected by lintels to the outer wall, and with signs of corbelling in the upper courses (Ill. 6.12). Several of the piers exhibit signs of rebuilding and the occupation material was divided into an earlier and a later phase separated by a thick layer of ash, interpreted as collapsed roofing material, over the beaten clay floor of the interior.

The chronological association of the wheelhouse with the other structures on the site is unclear; the 'souterrain' is the only clearly-linked structure, leading down from the interior of the wheelhouse into a semi-subterranean passage 9m in length. The entrance to the adjacent 'kilnhouse' appears to have smashed through the wheelhouse wall; this structure may well represent part of a much later farm complex focused on the site due to the availability of good building stone.

Internal Structure - The interior of the wheelhouse was dominated by the large central hearth. All of the bays were kerbed except for those which led into the main entrance and into the linear passage entrance.

Material Culture and Chronology - Three small yellow annular beads, one from the ash in the rebuild wall so presumably in use in the early period, may place the site's primary occupation in the late C1st BC or C1st AD (Guido 1978, 76) although severe reservations about this form of dating have been advanced elsewhere (Armit 1991). The ceramic assemblage includes a variety of decorated forms.

Survey Evidence

Wheelhouses are difficult positively to identify in the field since their definition depends upon the recognition of slight and generally subterranean internal features. The survey evidence does not therefore greatly extend the number of known sites. Some, such as Calum MacLeod's wheelhouse (W.2) and A' Cheardach Ruadh (W.12), have been partially examined by excavation in the past and are more or less positively identified, but the majority are represented by circular mounds of the appropriate size often associated with midden deposits and later prehistoric pottery.

Distribution - All but four of the twenty-six excavated and unexcavated wheelhouses are situated on the machair and, even allowing for the possible increased occurrence of the type on unexcavated upland sites, the weight of excavation evidence suggests that the machair was the prefered siting for these structures. The construction of the type, examined below, was ideal for the machair but problematic for above-ground upland sites.

There are two great concentrations of sites which are related to non-archaeological factors; the Vallay area of North Uist was the centre of Beveridge's excavation activities and the Drimore machair of South Uist was the area of the MoD Rocket Range development of the 1950s. The recorded distribution of sites is unlikely to reflect directly the original distribution.

Site Structure - No information on site structure is provided by the survey evidence from the wheelhouse sites.

Discussion

Construction Method

The clearest evidence of the processes of wheelhouse construction come from Structures 1 and 2 at Cnip. From the dismantling of the unfinished wheelhouse and an examination of the superstructure and roofing of Structure 1 most of the construction phases can be described. The reconstructed Structure 1 is shown in Ill. 6.13 using the evidence of the surviving roofed cells to project the complete circuit of the superstructure. The process can be broken down into a number of stages:

1. The first stage in the construction of the wheelhouses was the excavation of a large circular pit which was to form the interior of Structure 1 (the pit for Structure 2 was not excavated until Structure 1 was completed). This pit was cut into a pre-existing sand-hill of naturally accumulated windblown sand. A linear trench was also excavated from the main pit to the side of the sand-hill to form the entrance.

2. The construction material for the lower parts of the walls was placed in the pit and stacked in the interior. This was how the stone was found during the excavation of Structure 2. Stone was similarly stacked in the entrance passage.

3. The sides of the main circular pit and the entrance passage were lined with a stone revetment wall only one stone in thickness. These stones were graded with the smaller stones at the bottom. This building phase was carried out from inside the excavated pit with stone from the stacks. These walls were footed directly on the sand with no foundation trench; no packing was used behind this lower part of the wheelhouse wall, which was backed directly into sand. During this stage, in Structure 2 at Cnip, a complete pot, the skull of a great auk and two

Ill. 6.13 Cnip Structure 1 Reconstruction (by Alan Braby)

cattle vertebrae were placed behind the wall, packed against the sand.

4. When these lower parts of the wheelhouse wall were completed the piers were set out and built up to the same level. This level was immediately below the level at which the piers were to be bonded into the outer wall with lintels. A small orthostat in place of one of the piers at Cnip suggests that the piers may all have been marked out in advance of this phase of building. The piers were founded directly onto the clean sand, as were the walls. The stones of the piers were graded in width and narrowed towards the bottom. They widened as they rose, enabling a lintel to bridge each bay at a height of c. 3.5 - 4m above floor level.

Both piers and walls were entirely drystone built. At other sites the occasional use of clay is reported but it appears to be a superficial 'plaster' to hold back water seepage, rather than a 'mortar'.

5. At a level of c. 1.5m above floor level (although each pier varied), paired lintels were used to bridge the aisle between piers and outer wall. This formed the base for progressive corbelling of each individual bay. The space between the corbelling stones was filled with irregular rubble, while relatively flat slabs (though by no means ideal building stone) were used to reduce the corbelling span level by level.

This part of the construction process was the most difficult to accomplish and would have entailed building up the piers and outer wall at the same rate. Corbelling has to be weighed down to remain stable, so the wall packing of midden material used to pack the upper parts of the Structure 1 wall must have been added at this stage. It is also probable that some form of scaffolding, and internal structural supports, may have been required. Only actual experiment will determine how easily the process of corbelling could be accomplished.

6. With each cell individually corbelled a self-supporting ring of cells would have been created, packed in its upper parts with midden material. The open central area would then require roofing in timber (Ill. 6.13). A pitched roof is the most likely reconstruction, as this would allow water to drain down over the cell roofs into the sand-hill. The timber roof would have to cover only the limited span of the central area, some 4m in the case of Cnip. The bays could have been capped with turf at a lesser pitch, which could have allowed gradual drainage into the sand.

The Cnip reconstruction highlights a number of features of wheelhouse construction which combine monumentality with utility. The structural is monumental in a number of ways. The height of the structure from floor to apex of roof, assuming a 45° pitch, is some 6m or more, clearly far more than is necessary for utilitarian purposes, especially since the construction technique will not easily allow multiple floors. The construction of the wall and piers appears deliberately to create difficulties in the grading of the stones with the smallest at the base. Although visually imposing this is extremely difficult to construct in a stable fashion, as the ubiquity of secondary buttresses and insertions of posts demonstrates. The construction of cellular structures (Chapter Seven) amply

demonstrates that far simpler means of construction in the machair environment were available.

The use of unbonded piers, leaving an aisle around the outer wall, appears to be a de-stabilising influence. Many wheelhouses, including Cnip Structure 1, show signs of lintel cracking or collapse over the aisle and on most sites at least some of the aisles appear to have been blocked at a secondary stage. All of the excavated aisles at Cnip had been filled in apart from those under the surviving roofing. The bonded pier wheelhouses appear to be more stable. It is possible that the bonded pier structures were built late in the period of wheelhouse construction as structurally more stable forms. This question will be discussed below.

As well as these monumental features the wheelhouses at Cnip and elsewhere exhibit more utilitarian aspects of construction. They are semi-subterranean, thus providing good insulation, and the individual roofing of bays enables a considerable saving of timber when compared with the roofing of atlantic roundhouses.

The Cnip structures appear to be typical of the less well-preserved Hebridean machair wheelhouses. Where sufficiently preserved, these all show indications of corbelling. This begins above the bonding of the piers to the wall with paired lintels at the aisled sites and is also demonstrated at Bac Mhic Connain D and Foshigarry A, which have bonded piers. There is no evidence for any other roofing technique among the Hebridean wheelhouses, although at Jarlshof in Shetland a wheelhouse with a radically different roofing method was built. This latter site is discussed below.

In the free-standing wheelhouses at Clettraval and Allasdale, as well as the wheelhouses revetted into atlantic roundhouses, the construction appears to have been similar, with the massive outer wall acting in place of the sand-hill for structural support and drainage.

Chronology

C-14 dates from wheelhouses are so far restricted to the dates from Hornish Point and the Udal (App. 1). The Hornish Point dates are particularly important as this relatively large group derives from contexts deposited before and after the construction and use of the wheelhouse. As has been suggested above, a date in the C4th or C3rd BC seems probable for Structure 5. This date contradicts the traditional mid-1st millennium AD dates for the wheelhouses proposed on the basis of artefactual evidence. Two dates were obtained for immediately post-wheelhouse occupation at the Udal and these are briefly mentioned by Crawford (1986, 9): the dates suggested a C1st AD date for this 'squatter' occupation.

Future C-14 dates from other excavated sites, especially from the sequence at Cnip, will be needed to confirm this earlier dating of wheelhouses and clarify their chronological range. The only C-14 dates so far available clearly suggest that the type was in use prior to the last century BC and possibly several centuries earlier.

Additional evidence of potential chronological significance comes from the occurrence of querns on wheelhouse sites. This pertains to the second level of dating evidence defined in Armit 1991. In the Hebrides the rotary quern is the common form associated with wheelhouses, with examples being found on the majority of sites, but there are contexts in which saddle querns have been found. At Foshigarry a saddle quern was recovered from Structure C, which has been argued to be the earliest wheelhouse on the site. At Bac Mhic Connain a saddle quern was recovered from a high level in the fill of the wheelhouse, a position consistent with the hypothesis that it had constituted part of the wheelhouse wall which had collapsed at a late stage in the site's history. At A' Cheardach Mhor a broken saddle quern was found built into one of the wheelhouse piers.

The quern evidence would suggest that Foshigarry C was the earliest of the excavated examples to be constructed. This would place the construction of Foshigarry C prior to c. 200BC (Armit 1991), a dating broadly consistent with that of Hornish Point. The sites of Kilpheder and A' Cheardach Mhor, with unbonded and abutted piers respectively, were constructed after the local quern replacement, as both incorporate rotary querns in their construction material, in the walling at Kilpheder and under the floor at A' Cheardach Mhor. The quern evidence suggests a similar picture to the C-14 dates with construction of wheelhouses both before and after the transition period. The two forms of dating combined suggest construction from the C4th or C3rd BC and abandonment of some sites (e.g. the Udal) by the C1st AD.

A fragment of Samian Ware with no clear context from Bac Mhic Connain is the only Roman-associated find yielded by the Hebridean wheelhouse sites.

The traditionally late date given to wheelhouses has its origins in the 1955 paper by R.B.K. Stevenson on metalwork , and in particular pins, from Atlantic Scottish sites. Stevenson argued that a number of finds from wheelhouses could be used to provide a date in the C3rd to the C7th AD (Stevenson 1955, 294). This evidence applies to several sites and it is worth examining each piece of evidence in turn.

Native pins of mid-1st millennium AD date with Irish parallels, including hipped pins, were found at Foshigarry and Sithean a Phiobaire. Unfortunately the Sithean a Phiobaire material has no context at all and in all probability derives from a site with a long and complex sequence of occupation, as is the case with almost all wheelhouse sites. At Foshigarry the late pins could come from any part of a sequence covering many centuries and as many structural forms. The material from Kilpheder, which was fully excavated, lacked secondary occupation and also lacked late pins. There is no reason to link any of the Hebridean hipped pins to the wheelhouse structural form. The same problem of context applies to the devolved bone comb from Foshigarry and ascribed to a late 1st millennium AD date (Stevenson 1955, 287).

The case of the projecting ring-headed pins from Hebridean contexts is different. Stevenson accepted that this form had its origins in the early 1st millennium AD but argued that the Hebridean examples, whether as pins or indirectly as pin-stamping on pottery, develop after the

Lowland Scottish series (which evolves for some three centuries) due to inferred time lag. It is argued that they persist for a further two centuries in the Hebrides. This allows Stevenson to date the Hebridean wheelhouse, projecting ring-headed pins some five centuries later than their Lowland Scottish parallels at sites like Traprain, in order to bring them forward into a period in which they could be contemporary with the late hipped pins allegedly associated with the same wheelhouse sites (Stevenson 1955, 288). There is no justification for assuming any time lag and the proposal of up to five centuries seems particularly pessimistic. The evidence for a late date rests solely with the late hipped pins with no clear context and no demonstrable or likely association with the period of wheelhouse construction. Nonetheless these ideas seem to be at the root of the persistent late dating of wheelhouses which has been conventionally used ever since (e.g. Ritchie and Ritchie 1981, 117).

The earliest typologically dated artefacts from Hebridean wheelhouses are three yellow glass beads of Guido's Class 8 from Allasdale and two similar examples from A' Cheardach Mhor, which Guido dates from the late C1st BC to the C1st AD (Guido 1978, 181). The beads appear to come from the primary occupation at both sites. Similar beads come from Dun Troddan and the excavated Skye *brochs* as well as *dun* and *crannog* sites, which may be of importance for the dating of wheelhouses relative to the broch and dun sites further south, although a similar bead, not seen by Guido, was reported in the pre-*broch* levels at Clickhimin. A typologically slightly later green glass bead, of Guido's Group 7 iii, occurs at Clettraval in an unclear context, either on the primary floor or under the paving, and has been dated to the Roman or early post Roman period, although it is the only representative of this type in Scotland (Guido 1978, 169).

The problem with the dating of such beads in an Atlantic Scottish context is the tendency still to assume diffusion and time-lag. The mere fact of being found in Scotland is sufficient to add a century on to the date, as if any individual bead moved up the west coast at a constant rate from its source in Southern England. The lack of a clear source of such beads and their low incidence suggests that many of our assumptions concerning their dating are unwarranted. It is as easy to suggest from their context and distribution that these particular bead types were of Scottish origin and that we should invoke a time-lag on the English examples. Such a proposal would be entirely unsupportable but is no less valid than the current dating practice. It is unfortunate that we must still depend on allegedly exotic artefact types to provide the basis of our chronology: clearly it would be desirable to have a broader base of non-artefactual dating.

At Bac Mhic Connain a whalebone mirror handle was found and dated to the Early Irish 2 phase of Warner's typology of Irish metalwork, which lies in the C1st or C2nd AD (Warner 1983, 168), but unfortunately the piece has no precise context from the site sequence. Most of the very rich bonework found on Hebridean wheelhouse sites has remained unstudied due to the lack of proper archaeological contexts. It is hoped that future excavations can do more to clarify the chronological value of this material.

None of this artefactual material can be shown to have direct relevance to the problems of wheelhouse dating. The earlier dating suggested by the C-14 and quern evidence is in no way contradicted. The ceramic assemblages from the wheelhouse sites can provide a further source of chronological information (App. 2). Where ceramic assemblages can be reliably associated with primary wheelhouse occupation they are exclusively of the undifferentiated type characteristic of the later centuries BC, with everted rims and a relatively high frequency of decoration. At Cnip this type of assemblage is also associated with the post-wheelhouse cellular structures, suggesting that the wheelhouse here was out of use prior to the latter part of the currency of this pottery type. This may suggest abandonment of the wheelhouse form (though not the site) in the C1st AD. A similar situation seems to apply at the Udal (Lane 1983) where C-14 dates discussed above may indicate abandonment in the same period. Similar assemblages are associated with wheelhouse occupation at Clettraval, Hornish Point, A' Cheardach Mhor, A' Cheardach Bheag, Kilpheder and Allasdale. The weight of this ceramic evidence suggests that the main period of wheelhouse construction and use ended in the C1st AD or earlier.

A combination of the C-14, quern and ceramic evidence indicates a chronological currency for wheelhouses from the C4th or C3rd BC until the C1st BC or C1st AD. None of this evidence supports the traditional late dating of Stevenson and others, which is founded on unreliable artefactual associations from poorly recorded excavations. Nonetheless the chronology of these structures remains insecure, dependant on the combination of a large number of individually slight elements. Further C-14 sequences, including the sequence from Cnip, should clarify the situation.

Function

All of the excavated sites where reliable evidence is available suggest a domestic function for the wheelhouses. The widespread occurrence of central hearths suggests that the central area represents the domestic focal point of the structure, with the surrounding bays serving other related functions. Outbuildings and adjoining cells again appear to be linked to the domestic function of the structures. The generally large ceramic assemblages are suggestive of casual domestic breakage. The relative ubiquity of the type within confined areas such as Drimore and the Vallay Strand also suggests that the wheelhouses were a standard domestic settlement form of their period.

No wheelhouse site has produced evidence of a specialised or non-domestic function in its primary phase of use, although Bac Mhic Connain had been used for metalworking at a late stage in its occupation. The ritual deposits of deer jawbones at A' Cheardach Bheag, pits at Sollas and a complete decorated pot and bones behind the wall at Cnip Structure 2 all suggest that ritual or religious practices could also be focused on the wheelhouse settlement and construction. Nonetheless each of these deposits occur on sites where the remainder of the excavated material indicated standard domestic use.

The function of the structures will be examined in more detail in Part Three when structural, locational and spatial relationships between sites are considered.

Subdivision

The internal classification of wheelhouses can be based on two main variables: free-standing or revetted enclosing walls and unbonded or bonded piers. The first of these divisions appears to be determined by location rather than any other factors. The Hebridean machair sites are invariably revetted into sand-hills and the two clearly free-standing examples, at Clettraval and Allasdale, are both situated on hillside locations far from the machair. The sites at Cnoc a Comhdhalach, Eilean Maleit and Garry Iochdrach are also free-standing, but in these cases the wheelhouse does not appear to be the original structure on the sites and the structural effect is equivalent to revetting a new construction into a sand-hill.

The structural and material similarities between the sites far outweigh the one locational difference of revetted or free-standing walls. Revetting was the favoured technique where suitable sand-hills or disused structures were available, but the builders of wheelhouses did not allow themselves to be limited to this narrow range of locations.

The variation between bonded and unbonded piers cannot depend simply on location, and may be more significant in developing a meaningful typology. The occurrence of both variants at different points in the sequence at Foshigarry indicates that we may be able to discern a developmental sequence. At present there is only relative chronological evidence for the division: in terms of absolute chronology we cannot differentiate between the two forms. The development of bonded piers would seem to be a logical progression from a structural point of view, giving more stability by channelling weight stresses more effectively from the roof into the outer wall or revetment. This relatively straightforward structural alteration need not imply anything more than a refinement of building techniques at different sites at different periods in response to structural deficiencies in pre-existing wheelhouses. It would be dangerous to postulate a chronological range over which the change occurred. Nonetheless the Foshigarry sequence is matched by that at Jarlshof in Shetland (see below), and may indicate that the progression from unbonded to bonded pier construction was a widespread occurrence. Clearly, however, not all unbonded pier wheelhouses were succeeded by bonded pier versions.

It is in the use of space that the major changes must have taken place between wheelhouses with bonded and unbonded piers. To attempt to understand these changes we must consider why wheelhouses were ever built with unbonded piers. The technique could have resulted from the derivation of the wheelhouse ground plan from timber roundhouses with the piers taking the place of wooden posts: this is the explanation assumed by past workers. This interpretation would see the development of bonded piers as a purely structural innovation as the weaknesses of a straightforward translation from timber to stone became apparent. The problem with this superficially attractive idea is that wheelhouses were developed in areas with a long tradition of drystone construction stretching back to the early Neolithic and with no developed tradition of timber building. Unless we postulate the arrival and sudden dominance of a wholly new and alien population with no background of drystone building, this idea cannot be sustained.

The skill of building at sites like Kilpheder and Cnip denies us this interpretation of a people struggling to build stable structures in an unfamiliar medium, and the clear connection of the wheelhouses with the atlantic roundhouses in aspects of their material culture precludes any dramatic change of population. The only structural evidence cited for the alleged derivation of piers from wooden posts was for the aisled house at Jarlshof but, as will be discussed below, the excavated evidence does not support Hamilton's conclusions. It would appear that the builders of the early wheelhouses accepted the loss of stability necessitated by the use of unbonded piers deliberately and adapted to the use of bonded piers at a later stage.

This leads us to a consideration of the use of space inside the wheelhouses, and to the principal difference which would have distinguished the internal organisation of a bonded pier wheelhouse from one with unbonded piers, i.e. the lack of access between the bays. It is clear from a number of sites, notably Sollas and Eilean Maleit, that several bays would have been inaccessible from the central area with access possible only through the narrow aisles. In this way space would have been divided into units of various sizes arranged around a central area containing the hearth. This spatial organisation could divide areas of differing function, segregating some from the central area and allowing varying amounts of space for distinct units in much the same way as the interior of a broch could be divided between central space, galleries and cells. By contrast, the bonded pier wheelhouses made available a central area surrounded by small discrete cells of equal size necessarily all leading out from the centre. This would necessitate a considerable change in the organisation of the internal space of the wheelhouse and this may explain the reluctance of the original wheelhouse builders to adopt a technique which, although structurally more sound, did not allow the internal spatial divisions by which they were accustomed to organising their dwellings. The spatial differences between the two forms will be explored further in Chapter Twelve.

The typologically transitional site of A' Cheardach Mhor has piers which abut the surrounding wall of the structure without being bonded into the walling. It is probable that this would have given an added measure of stability over unbonded piers, but it cannot have been as secure as bonded piers. It is not clear whether the pier design is a secondary feature of the site (although this would certainly account for the odd arrangement and provide some evidence to suggest a chronological dimension to variations in pier construction) or whether a recognition of the structural advantages of bonded piers became apparent during construction. At other sites there is evidence of secondary blocking of some of the aisles, between the piers and the walls, which would have resulted in a structure similar to A' Cheardach Mhor. The clearest examples of this are at Cnip and Sollas and similar alterations are apparent at A' Cheardach Bheag. The sum of this individually slight evidence supports the idea that

a gradual realisation of the limitations of the unbonded pier building technique led to its replacement by pier bonding in later wheelhouses and to the alteration of existing buildings.

Parallels Outwith the Western Isles

The closest parallels to the Hebridean wheelhouses are the structures from two sites in Shetland, Jarlshof (Hamilton 1956) and Ward Hill (Smith pers. comm.). Both of these sites contain structures almost identical in construction, scale and structural detail to the Hebridean examples. As well as these Shetland wheelhouses there are a number of radially partitioned atlantic roundhouses from the Northern Isles and Caithness. These share elements of spatial patterning with the wheelhouses but the specific construction techniques and the architectural repertoire of the wheelhouse are absent.

The Jarlshof sequence for the period in question comprises a series of three successive wheelhouses, in turn successive to a complex atlantic roundhouse. The chronology of the site sequence is discussed elsewhere (Armit 1991). The chronological evidence suggests similar dating to that discussed above for the Hebridean wheelhouses. Wheelhouses 1 and 2 at Jarlshof have evidence of the same construction and roofing technique found at Cnip. The bays of Wheelhouse 2 survive with roofing intact and are corbelled, leaving a small central span. Both of these wheelhouses have bonded piers and may be relatively late in the wheelhouse building period if a chronological dimension to the structural typology is accepted.

The 'aisled house' at Jarlshof was claimed by the excavator to be a transitional structure in the evolution from brochs to wheelhouses and ancestral to the common wheelhouse form. Hamilton believed that the drystone piers replaced original timber posts which had held a timber gallery around the open central area (this was derived from Hamilton's similar reconstruction of broch interiors). The argument was supported by the existence of a scarcement ledge, one of the characteristic traits of broch architecture, around the inner face of the 'aisled house' wall. Hamilton, however, had not removed the piers and so could not have known if they had replaced timber posts: the post-holes cited to support his case occur in a seemingly random spread with only one on the arc of the proposed timber gallery. Nonetheless the existence of the scarcement ledge rules out the corbelling of the bays on the Hebridean model. The paired lintels linking the piers to the surrounding wall are at scarcement height and it appears that the effect was to create a level foundation for a second storey or for roofing. The structure does show that we cannot assume that all of the Hebridean wheelhouses will be roofed in the same way and structural variation may be more common than their very uniform ground plan suggests. Had the 'aisled house' been less well-preserved it would have appeared identical to the Hebridean series.

The only other definite wheelhouse in the north is at Ward Hill, Shetland, found by Beverley Smith in 1988 after its partial destruction (pers. comm.). This site was not excavated but photographs of the exposed sections record a structure of similar form to the Jarlshof wheelhouses.

The absence of wheelhouses in areas such as the Orkneys is potentially as significant as their presence in Shetland. Given the numbers of excavations in the Orkneys it seems unlikely that wheelhouses could have altogether escaped detection if they had ever been built in the islands. This is particularly significant in view of the regularity of their discovery in the Western Isles. It does appear, albeit from this negative evidence, that wheelhouse construction was restricted to the Western Isles and the Shetlands.

Summary

The wheelhouses of the Western Isles appear to have been a characteristic domestic settlement form in the period from the C4th or C3rd BC until the C1st AD. Most appear to have been sited on previously unoccupied locations (although most have considerable post-wheelhouse occupation), generally in the machair with a scatter of inland examples known. The structures were monumental in scale and construction but showed a respect for the cold and wind of the Hebridean climate and a concern with timber conservation. Like the atlantic roundhouses they appear to represent a monumental do-mestic architecture too ubiquitous to be associated with an elite group. Again, like the atlantic roundhouses, they generally represent single-structure settlements, although often with associated smaller cells.

The major difference from the atlantic roundhouses was that wheelhouse architecture abandoned all semblance of defence. Island locations appear to have been avoided with only Eilean Maleit occupying a location of this type. Wheelhouses were generally unenclosed and their roofs projected at ground level. No protection from aggression is offered by the wheelhouse structural form and their monumentality is entirely inwardly projected.

Direct evidence of contact with areas outside the Western Isles is restricted to the Shetland wheelhouses but the striking structural parallels here show close links. These links do not appear to have been restricted to one isolated episode, since the change from unbonded to bonded piers occurs in both areas. The Orcadian links demonstrated by the atlantic roundhouses are noticeable by their absence among the wheelhouses.

Chapter Seven - Cellular Structures

Cellular structures are known from twenty-eight sites in the Western Isles, of which fifteen have been excavated (Ill. 7.1). In the older literature they have tended to be referred to as 'earth-houses' or simply dismissed as squatter structures in abandoned wheelhouses or atlantic roundhouses. The group have never been discussed in detail. No excavation has actively sought to examine a cellular structure, and the excavations have generally been by-products of work on structures of other types.

Excavated Sites

C.2 Galson, Lewis NB 44 59 (Edwards 1923)

Introduction - The extensive middens on the west coast of Lewis by the township of Galson contain the remains of structures of many periods. The middens continue to yield material after every storm and a depth of several metres of deposits is visible (pers. obs. 1987). The structures described here, excavated by A.J.H. Edwards in 1923, were adjacent to the cultivated machair between the sea and the wall of the 'Sand Park' field. These do not represent the totality of this site. The cellular structures had disappeared by 1969 when only deposits of midden were reported in the vicinity (NMR).

Site Structure - Four sites, A-D, were examined by Edwards but of these only Site C revealed substantial structural evidence of occupation. The excavated area of Site C contained a small complex of cellular structures, all roofless when found and with walls of c. 0.5m in thickness (Ill. 7.2). The excavator believed that the structures were free-standing and formed one larger overall building, but the excavation does not appear to have explored the outer wall. Once the walls were located only the interior was excavated so it is equally possible that the structures were sand-revetted. All of the cells were small, the largest being c. 2.3m in diameter internally (Chamber 1). All had low lintelled entrances to the south.

Adjacent to this complex was a long narrow lintelled passage-like construction some 7m in length and with a maximum width of only 0.5m. Its height, to the lintelled roof, was only some 0.75m: it appears to be likely from these dimensions that the structure was a drain or linear sump underneath another structure which was not recognised by the excavator.

Internal Structure - Few internal features are reported from the structures, but it is important that Chamber 3 is reported as having two possible 'seats' in the wall. This would be a close parallel for architectural features at cellular structures at Loch na Berie, Cnip and Dun Cuier (see below). Each of the cells were partially paved.

Material Culture and Chronology - Slag, bones, charcoal and pottery are reported from the midden and structures. The pottery is described in some detail. The assemblage has no precise contexts but is split into a group from the structures and one from the midden. The pottery from the structures comprises a range of flat-based globular jars with everted rims, and straighter sided vessels with upright flat or rounded rims. Decoration included applied wavy and plain cordons and one piece of classic 'Clettraval Ware' with incised arches above a wavy cordon (Edwards 1924 Fig. 8; 19). Other vessels had finger-nail impressions and incised decoration. A range of later prehistoric material was found in the midden around the site. This included several bone combs, querns and a ring-headed pin.

Only the pottery is of any help in dating the structures. The presence of everted rims and varied motifs suggests a relatively early date prior to the mid-1st millennium AD (App. 2). The flaring rims characteristic of pottery from the C2nd AD onwards are absent and the quantity of decorated sherds would suggest an earlier date. This assemblage is similar to that of Phase 3 at Cnip, and typologically earlier than assemblages from Berie, the Udal and Eilean Olabhat, all discussed in this chapter.

C.3 Cnip, Lewis NB 0980 3665 (Armit 1988a)

Introduction - The cellular structures at Cnip occupy Phase 2 of the site sequence. The wheelhouses and a linear house structure from the site are discussed in Chapters Six and Eight respectively.

Site Structure - The cellular structures comprise six separate structures built after the main wheelhouse had fallen into disrepair (Ill. 7.3). They were sealed by the construction of Structure 8, the linear house structure described in Chapter Eight. All were sand-revetted and all, with the exception of the re-used wheelhouse, utilised a lower course of vertical slab-revetting surmounted by conventional coursing. Roofing of Structure 3 was by lintels, while the other structures appear to have had timber roofs resting on the sand surface at the top of their revetted walls.

The two main structures of this phase were the re-used wheelhouse, Structure 1, and the newly constructed Structure 4 which overlay the wheelhouse entrance cell. Structures 3, 5, 6 and 7 were small storage units dispersed around the site, all of which were too small for occupation but which reinforce the cellular arrangement of the settlement in this period.

The extent of occupation in Structure 1 at this phase is unclear due to the restricted area available for excavation. It appears that several of the bays were blocked off and occupation was probably concentrated in the central area. Structure 4 was constructed during Phase 2 as a second domestic focus. It was a relatively substantial structure measuring 4 x 3m internally.

Internal Structure - The two domestic *foci*, Structures 1 and 4, were dominated by central hearths. Structure 4 had a succession of three hearths and had been rigorously cleared of debris on a number of occasions.

Structure 4 had a number of significant internal features. The vertical slab walling was graded so that the largest slabs were across the hearth from the entrance, focusing attention on this area. Built into the wall on the east side was a small box-like shelf, possibly one of a pair, which is paralleled at Berie and Dun Cuier.

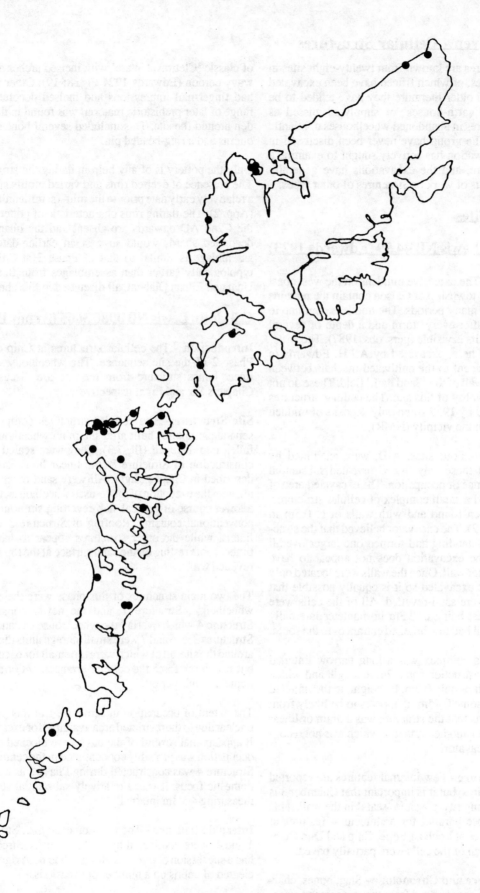

Ill. 7.1 Distribution of Cellular Structures in the Western Isles

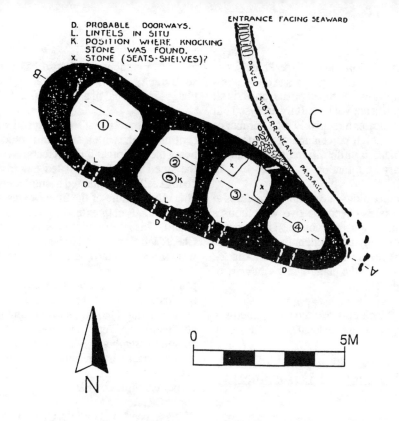

D. PROBABLE DOORWAYS.
L. LINTELS IN SITU
K. POSITION WHERE KNOCKING
   STONE WAS FOUND.
X. STONE (SEATS-SHELVES)?

ENTRANCE FACING SEAWARD

PAVED SUBTERRANEAN PASSAGE

C

N

0   5M

Ill. 7.2 Galson (after Edwards 1923)

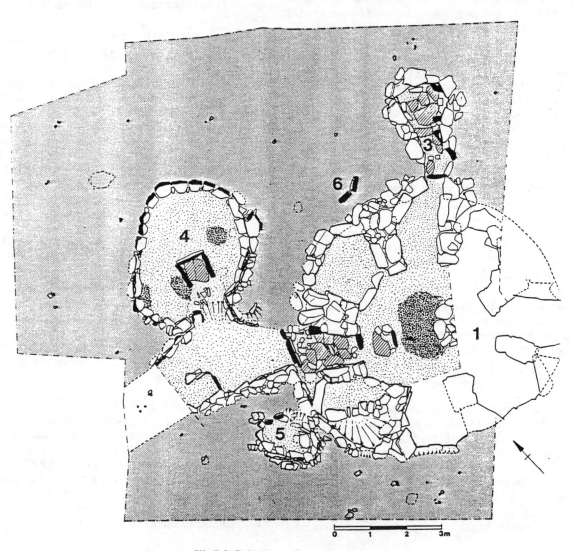

0   1   2   3m

Ill. 7.3 Cnip Phase Two Structures

Material Culture and Chronology - The Phase 2 deposits contained a large ceramic assemblage and a number of bone and antler-working deposits and small artefacts. The pottery has not yet been fully analysed but a preliminary study indicates a relatively high number of decorated sherds and a high percentage of everted rim vessels. The assemblage is little different from that of Phase 1 on preliminary examination.

In terms of relative chronology the cellular structures at Cnip occupy the period between the two wheelhouses and the Phase 3 linear house structure. The ceramic assemblage is typologically earlier than the Eilean Olabhat assemblage, dated to the C2nd or C3rd AD (App. 2), which is in turn earlier than the plain flaring-rim ware of sites like Berie and the Udal.

The cellular structures include discarded rotary querns in their walling and thus post-date the local quern transition.

C.4 Dun Bharabhat, Lewis NB 0988 3531 (Harding and Topping 1986, Harding and Armit 1990)

Introduction - The sequence of occupation at Dun Bharabhat terminates with a period of modification of the atlantic roundhouse after it had ceased to be viable in its original form. The excavations of parts of the site are still in progress and conclusions are provisional.

Site Structure - A phase of occupation within the roundhouse was recognised as having occurred after the partial collapse of the walls (Harding and Topping 1986, 28) and was probably contemporary with the reconstruction of part of one of the galleries, forming a small cell. The structural evidence for this cellular phase is slight and comprises this latter cell and the roundhouse interior (Ill. 5.3).

The central cell of this cellular structure was the roundhouse interior and it does not appear to have been re-faced (it was already only c. 5m in internal diameter). The collapse of the walling would have entailed that the structure could not have achieved any great height. Rafters could have been bedded in the roundhouse gallery, forming a low roof.

It is unclear how much of the periphery of the roundhouse was used in this phase. Gallery 1 was blocked by a slab feature in the secondary floor and Gallery 3 appears to have been full of collapsed rubble (except where cleared to build the small cell). The status of Gallery 2 is unclear but there is no evidence for its reuse.

Entrance to the cellular structure may have been through the reduced walling of the south-western sector, facing the causeway. This may explain the unusual width of the Gallery 2 entrance which may have been deliberately extended at this secondary stage. An orthostat set within the doorway appears to form part of a secondary entrance construction. If this were the case the newly constructed small cell, with its internal niche, would be visible directly across the hearth from the entrance in the same way as features at the cellular structures at Berie, Dun Cuier and Structure 4 at Cnip. Nonetheless the evidence is ambiguous and largely circumstantial. The disturbance caused by structural collapse has greatly confused the stratigraphy at Dun Bharabhat and reconstructing the plan of individual phases is difficult.

Internal Structure - The main cell was dominated by a central hearth, with a slab-built 'box' on the south wall being the only other internal feature. As mentioned above the small secondary cell led out from the east of this central cell and contained a small niche in its south wall. One other feature of the interior was an arc of disarticulated animal teeth extending for 0.6 - 0.7m around the hearth. This is paralleled closely in the wheelhouse at A' Cheardach Bheag (W.16) where a line of deer jaw-bones were set around the hearth (Fairhurst 1971, 80).

Material Culture and Chronology - The secondary occupation is dated by two C-14 determinations (full details in App.1) to the final two centuries BC. The latest occupation on Dun Bharabhat is represented by a large ceramic assemblage which has not yet been subject to detailed analysis. Preliminary accounts suggest that it contains decorated vessels indistinguishable from the earlier examples on the site.

A glass bead of Guido's Class 13 (Guido 1978) was associated with the secondary floor levels but this cannot be precisely dated (the C-14 dates from this site in fact provide the most secure dating for the type).

C.5 Loch na Berie, Lewis NB 1035 3525 (Harding and Armit 1987 and 1988)

Introduction - A sequence of cellular structures were constructed inside the remains of the atlantic roundhouse at Loch na Berie, described in Chapter Five. The final two of these structures have so far been excavated (Structures 1 and 2 here) and it is apparent that further structures remain stratified below these inside the roundhouse. This account is therefore incomplete, describing only the latter part of the sequence of cellular structures.

Site Structure - Structures 1 and 2 share a number of constructional features, although Structure 1 was far better preserved (Ill. 7.4). Structure 2 appeared to have been deliberately levelled to enable the construction of Structure 1, leaving only those elements which were to be incorporated in the walling and internal features of the latter structure. The construction of Structure 1 should be viewed as only the most complete phase of rebuilding in a sequence where reconstruction was perennial. Both structures show indications of refacing and replacement of walls and the incorporation of different cells during the use of the building.

Both structures were built of vertical slab walls, surmounted by conventional coursing, revetted into the remains of the roundhouse and earlier, unexcavated, cellular structures. Structure 1, which survived virtually intact, also incorporated a conventional coursed wall for part of its circuit to enable the construction of two niches (see below). The slab walling is a recurrent feature visible in a number of Hebridean cellular structures, including the nearby site of Cnip.

Structure 1 comprised one large principal cell some 6.5m in diameter and a smaller curving cell around its northern

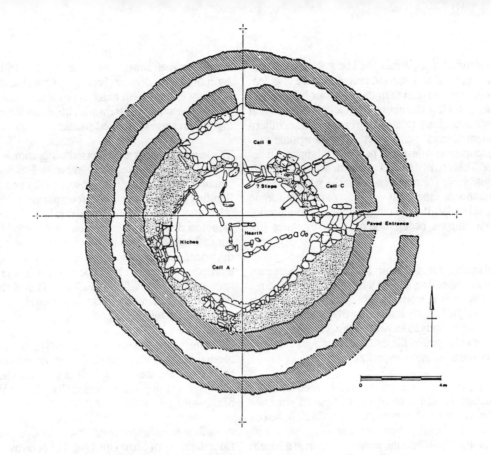

Ill. 7.4 Berie Structure 1

Ill. 7.5 Berie Structure 1 Reconstruction (by Alan Braby)

and north-eastern arc. Several rebuilding phases had progressively modified this second cell. Structure 2 is less easy to reconstruct in plan than its successor but appears to have had a similar arrangement of a central oval cell with a linear subsidiary cell leading out from its northern wall. Both structures' walls were revetted against pre-existing occupation debris and packed with upcast from the interior. This created a level platform behind the walls which would have formed a base for the roof. The surviving roundhouse inner wall would have provided some shelter for this roof. It does not appear that the galleries were used during the occupation of these structures (Ill. 7.5).

The cellular structures appear to have been occupied when the site was still an islet in the original, larger, Loch na Berie. The visible stone causeway to the west shore lies at a level significantly higher than the original roundhouse base and is likely to have been progressively raised as the loch level rose and the cellular structures replaced the primary roundhouse occupation.

Internal Structure - Structure 1 could be reconstructed in some detail. It was entered by a re-paved entrance through the original roundhouse entrance. Straight across the large central hearth, from the entrance, were two niches or shelves built into the western circuit at a height of c. 0.8m above the primary floor. These niches form a detailed architectural parallel with Structure 4 at Cnip and with the secondary structure at Dun Cuier (below). Kerbing around part of the southern interior may have revetted some form of bedding as has been suggested for other sites including the Udal. A small box-like slab construction on the north-west may have formed some similar kerbing and certainly was protruding above the primary floor, but its primary function was as part of the lower Structure 2 wall. This central cell of Structure 1 was the domestic focus of the site and the peripheral cell to the north contained no surviving internal features.

The central cell of Structure 2 was also entered by the original roundhouse entrance and contained a large central hearth. It also contained a further hearth to the south-west and may conceivably have been subdivided at a constriction in the wall. To the north of the main hearth was a line of kicked-over kerbstones defining an area of less compact earth; probably some form of bedding as suggested for Structure 1. Two wall recesses may have had a function parallel to the niches of Structure 1. The peripheral northern cell, as for Structure 1, had no internal features.

The two structures were constructed to the same general plan and using the same structural technique. It is probable that they fulfilled identical functions for successive generations.

Material Culture and Chronology - A number of finds of chronological significance have been recovered from the cellular structures along with a substantial ceramic assemblage. No C-14 dates have yet been obtained.

A bronze penannular brooch from Structure 2 floor deposits has no precise parallels, but some general observations by Conor Newman (pers. comm.) help to set it in context. The brooch, missing its pin, is completely flat but otherwise similar in form to the wider class of zoomorphic penannular brooches. One side of the brooch is finely incised with hatching in a series of curvilinear panels: the expanded terminals have incised cross-hatching within lozenge-shaped panels.

The lozenge panels with incised decoration and the small size of the piece are comparable to Fowler's Type G penannular brooches (Dickinson 1982) and the western Scottish distribution of this group may also be significant (Newman pers. comm.). The Berie brooch is two-dimensional in design, unlike the rounded Type G forms, and comparisons can also be cited with the wafer-thin Irish disc-pendants suspended from looped pin-heads (Newman pers. comm.). The Type G brooches are generally now dated to the C5th and C6th AD and they perhaps provide the main recognisable cultural and decorative context for the Berie brooch.

From the same deposits came a small bronze penannular brooch of Fowler's Type H. This has a broad chronological currency in the second half of the 1st millennium AD and parallels in the conventionally Pictish assemblages of the north.

A further significant bronze find, in this case from the floor deposits of Structure 1, was a set of tweezers finely incised with lines following the outline, and with a row of punched dots. The tweezers were found complete with fragments of a small ring attached. An almost identical set was found in the excavations of Whitby Abbey (Peers and Radford 1943, 61). The Whitby example forms part of a wider Northumbrian series and is dated (although without precise site context) to the period of c. 650 - 875 AD, on the basis of coins from the same assemblage, which supports the historical dating of the site. The very close similarity in size, form and decoration would seem to indicate a similar date of c. 650 - c. 800 AD for the Berie tweezers (the latter date being imposed by the absence of recognisably Norse or Norse-related material at Berie). This accords well with the ceramic evidence.

Also from Structure 1, or from the final phase of Structure 2, are two partly vitrified crucibles of Laing's Type 8 (1975, 252). These have parallels at a number of sites in Early Christian contexts, including Ballinderry 2 crannog in Ireland (Laing 1975, 251), and further support a dating in the second half of the 1st millennium AD. Fragments of composite bone combs also support this broad dating.

The large ceramic assemblage from Berie still awaits analysis but its broad characteristics are fairly well established. The pottery from Structure 1 is entirely without decoration apart from very few small sherds which are likely to have been redeposited during the disturbance of the recurrent building phases. The vessels have characteristically flaring or upright rims and short everted rim vessels appear to be absent. The pottery is generally very coarse and poorly fired. Overall the assemblage belongs to the final pre-Norse typological group (App. 2) found at a number of sites including the Udal and Dun Cuier, exclusively in association with structures of cellular type.

The ceramic assemblage from Structure 2 is similar although a number of sherds indicate the occasional use of applied cordon decoration. Forms are similar to those from Structure 1 and decoration is very rare. The closest parallel for the assemblage is that from Eilean Olabhat (see below). The assemblages from both of these cellular structures are entirely dissimilar from those of the round-house galleries which have produced a much wider variety of forms and decoration and a much higher proportion of decorated sherds.

A combination of all the material evidence suggests a date for these two structures in the period from the mid-1st millennium AD to the immediately pre-Norse period. It is presently impossible to estimate the duration of the occupation, but it may well have covered several centuries. Structure 1 is likely, on the basis of the metalwork, to date to the period when Northumbrian influences were available on the west of Scotland and therefore possibly after the Northumbrian conquest of Galloway in the late C7th or early C8th AD. A C8th century date may be most probable but the occupation of the structure could have encompassed a much wider period. The brooch from Structure 2 may indicate a date in the C5th or C6th AD, but the pottery has decorative features which may place the start of occupation somewhat earlier. The complete absence of any Norse or Norse-related material appears to indicate abandonment of the site prior to the Norse incursions and therefore probably prior to c. 800AD.

C.10 The Udal, North Uist NF 824 783 (Crawford 1967/78, 1975, 1977, 1985)

Introduction - The excavations at the Udal in North Uist have never been fully published and the following information is derived from a series of interim reports. Further artefactual information is derived from Alan Lane's doctoral thesis on pottery from parts of the site (Lane 1983). The excavator has declined to provide further information or answer questions on stratigraphy and construction and this restricts interpretation. No archaeological plans or photographs have been either published or made available.

Site Structure - The cellular structures appear to have been the first structures built on the UN area of the site and have no stratigraphic link with any earlier material despite claims by the excavator that the Udal contains a complete sequence from 3000 BC - 1700 AD (Crawford 1985, 7). These cellular structures were succeeded directly by Norse structures in the early part of the C9th AD at the end of the period under consideration.

The interim reports are generally unspecific but some broad conclusions can be reached. Crawford recognised seven main structural *foci* (Crawford 1973, 2), consisting of spatially separate sand-revetted cellular structures, each of which was frequently rebuilt over a lengthy period. The spatial separation would seem to suggest that some at least may have occupied contemporaneously.

Crawford proposed a typological and chronological progression from simple oval cells with single 'satellite' cells, to larger oval cells (c. 6m in length) with 'symmetrically' sited satellite cells on their ends. This second phase is claimed to be succeeded by a "basic figure of eight heavily embellished with minor satellites" (Crawford 1973, 3). No evidence is cited for this sequence. It

is difficult to accept that the structures on Crawford's sketch (1973, 9) fall into any such groups. All five illustrated (a further one disappears into the section) appear to have different arrangements of cells and entrances which defy such simple grouping.

No information is given as to the nature of the construction other than that they are sunk into the sand. In the absence of such information it is impossible to compare detailed architectural traits with other sites such as Berie, Cnip and Dun Cuier.

An unspecified number of 'minor house structures' were also noted (Crawford 1973, 3), some 2.4m square with central hearths but with no evidence of walling. Crawford also reports the occurrence of palisaded areas associated with the cellular structures.

Overall the cellular layout and slight, revetted construction has parallels in the structures at Berie and Dun Cuier. The number of structures, if contemporary, indicates that this site contained a larger settlement unit than either of these two sites.

Internal Structure - Each of the structures has a central rectangular hearth and most appear to have kerbed areas flanking these hearths, as was the case at Berie Structures 1 and 2. No further information can be reliably adduced from the sketch plan.

Material Culture and Chronology - Several C-14 dates were obtained from unspecified contexts associated with the cellular structures. These are listed in Appendix 1. In sum they indicate occupation between the late C3rd and early C9th AD. This accords well with the dating of the cellular structures at Berie and Dun Cuier and is later than the Eilean Olabhat dates. The pottery from the site supports both this absolute and relative dating.

The information on the ceramic assemblage from the cellular structures comes primarily from Alan Lane's doctoral thesis (Lane 1983) which deals with the material from the UN site. Lane identified the characteristics of the assemblage from the 'Dark Age' contexts as comprising straight-sided or shouldered jars with upright and flaring rims. All were flat-based, relatively coarse and poorly-fired, and the assemblage was entirely undecorated. The assemblage was succeeded on the site by Norse pottery of entirely different manufacture and with a distinct repertoire of forms. The closest parallel for the pre-Norse assemblage is the Structure 1 assemblage from Berie. The Udal provides a date range for this pottery from c. 400 - 800AD on the basis of the spread of C-14 dates and historical evidence for the date of Norse incursions (App. 2).

Other finds included a penannular silver ring and a gold pin. Composite combs were also found, supporting the C-14 evidence for a date in the second half of the 1st millennium AD.

There appears from the ceramic evidence to be a gap of occupation on the Udal from the immediately post-wheelhouse period until the mid-1st millennium AD, when the cellular structures of the UN site were occupied and the plain ceramic assemblage was in use. This gap appears to account for Crawford's belief that the Dark Age material and structural assemblages were so radically different from those of the preceding period that an invasion must have taken place (Crawford and Switsur 1977). The question of invasion or continuity will be discussed in Chapter 13.

C.11 Foshigarry, North Uist NF 7430 7636 (Beveridge 1930)

Introduction - The cellular structures at Foshigarry comprise D, E and F on Beveridge's plan. The complexity of this part of the site is evident from the excavation report and the plan and descriptions must be treated with caution.

Site Structure - Structures F and E were two adjoining sand-revetted cells. Structure F was some 5 x 3m in size while E was 4 x 2m (Ill. 6.3). The two were apparently entered through the linear structure (H) described in Chapter Eight. Structure D was spatially distinct but possibly connected by a passage to E, and was 4 x 2.5m in size. This latter cell contained the remains of collapsed corbelling.

Internal Structure - All three structures contained a number of wall shelves or aumbreys and all were partially paved. No hearths were recorded.

Material Culture and Chronology - No material is specifically attributed to these structures. In terms of relative chronology they appear to be later than the wheelhouses and contemporary with part of the use of the linear structure.

C.12 Sithean an Altair, North Uist NF 77 76 (Beveridge 1911)

Introduction - Sithean an Altair was partially excavated by Erskine Beveridge prior to 1911. The work was conducted on a small scale and is briefly reported in his book, North Uist. The site lies on the island of Vallay in the machair behind the present sand dunes.

Site Structure - The cellular structure, described as an 'earth-house' by Beveridge (1911, 118), lay beneath two small cists in a machair mound. Beveridge excavated three small chambers and a short passage or gallery. The plan makes little structural sense and the various elements within it may not belong to the same structure. Overall the complex of cells was c. 6m by 4m at its maximum dimensions (Ill. 7.6).

Internal Structure - The likelihood that Beveridge confused elements of different structures or only partially excavated a larger complex makes the interpretation of internal structure unhelpful. No hearths or other internal features were found.

Material Culture and Chronology - The assemblage of material from the excavation is not described in detail but Beveridge does mention the presence of 'raised' decoration on the pottery (1911, 120). This may suggest applied motifs characteristic of the later prehistoric period.

C.14 Dun a Ghallain, Griminish, North Uist NF 7479 7598 (Beveridge 1911)

Introduction - The cellular structure at Dun a Ghallain was constructed inside the roundhouse described in Chapter Five. The re-occupied roundhouse lay on an islet in Loch an Eilean near Griminish.

Site Structure - Details of the structure were poorly recorded and no plan was published. The cellular structure was apparently revetted into the ruined roundhouse in a similar fashion to the cellular structures in Dun Cuier and Loch na Berie. It was irregular in shape and c. 12m in internal diameter.

Internal Structure - The only internal feature recorded was a drain running under a paved floor.

Material Culture and Chronology - No finds are specifically attributed to the cellular structure but it seems probable the recorded finds derive principally from its floor levels. None of the finds are helpful in dating the structure and the relationship with the roundhouse is the only chronological indicator.

C.15 Eilean a Ghallain, Griminish, North Uist NF 7483 7589 (Beveridge 1911)

Introduction - The cellular structure on Eilean a Ghallain again seems to have been constructed inside a roundhouse (Chapter Five). The re-occupied roundhouse lay on an islet in Loch an Eilean near Griminish and adjacent to Dun a Ghallain.

Site Structure - No structural details are recorded except that several 'minor erections' occupied the interior of the roundhouse (Beveridge 1911, 197).

Internal Structure - No details of internal structure were recorded.

Material Culture and Chronology - The finds from the site were not reported in any detail. As with Dun a Ghallain, the secondary relationship of the cellular structure to the roundhouse is the only chronological indicator.

C.16 Dun Thomaidh, North Uist NF 7483 7598 (Beveridge 1930)

Introduction - The series of cellular structures at Dun Thomaidh were constructed in the roundhouse described in Chapter Five.

Site Structure - A series of cellular structures on the islet occupy two spatial concentrations. The first lies inside the atlantic roundhouse and consists of a maze of passages and cells which Beveridge did not understand and which cannot be disentangled from his plan (Ill. 5.7). The second concentration lies on the eastern exterior of the roundhouse and consists of a cluster of five cells in three groups, each with separate access.

Internal Structure - Cells 'd' and 'e' may have been the domestic focus with 'd', the largest in the complex,

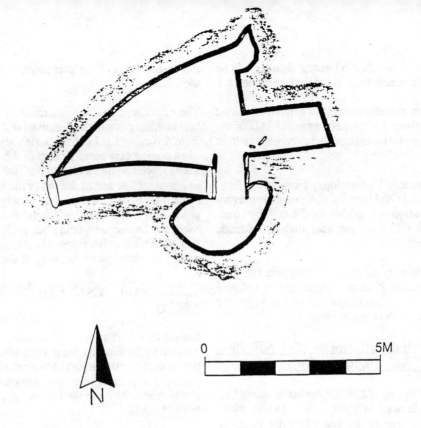

Ill. 7.6 Sithean an Altair (after Beveridge 1911)

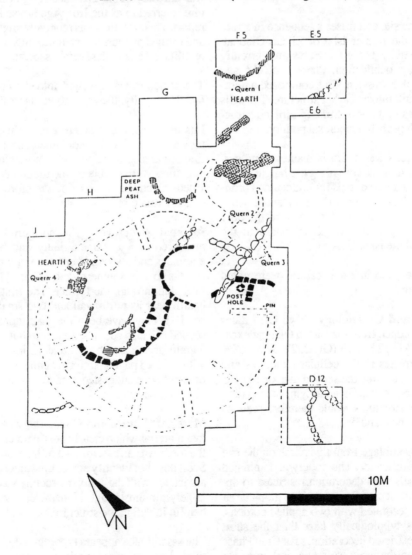

Ill. 7.7 A Cheardach Mhor Cellular Structures (after Young and Richardson 1959)

containing a central hearth. No internal features can be associated with the remaining cells on the east of the islet.

The cells inside the roundhouse appear to have contained drystone pier divisions irregularly arranged. All of the cells in both complexes appear to have been at least partially paved.

Material Culture and Chronology - None of the finds from Dun Thomaidh had specific contexts and no chronological information is available for the cellular structures other than that they are later than the atlantic roundhouse on this site.

Two saddle querns may indicate activity on the site prior to the local quern transition, though this seems unlikely to be associated with the cellular structures which are demonstrably late in the site sequence.

C.19 Eilean Olabhat, North Uist NF 7500 7530 (Armit 1986; 1988b; 1990b)

Introduction - The site of Eilean Olabhat in North Uist was partially excavated in 1986 - 1990 (Armit 1986; 1988b; 1990b) as part of the Loch Olabhat Research Project. The site lies on a promontory which was originally an islet in Loch Olabhat.

Site Structure - The site comprises a sequence of structures surmounting the former islet of Eilean Olabhat, some 80 x 60m in size. These structures are currently being written up for publication. Phase 3 on the site relates to the present discussion. This comprised a number of small cells built into an earlier structure. The cells were sealed by two structures of turf and earth construction associated with probable medieval pottery.

The largest of the cells was c. 2m in diameter and survived sufficiently to indicate corbelling to a height of just over 1m. The cells acted as dumps for midden and bronzeworking debris. They also provided substantial quantities of charcoal which have so far produced the only C-14 date for an important transitional phase in the ceramic typology of the islands (App. 2).

Internal Structure - No internal features were noted within the small cells.

Material Culture and Chronology - Two C-14 dates have so far been obtained from the Eilean Olabhat excavations. A date of AD 124 - 273 (GU 2327, at the 68% confidence level) relates to the cellular structures and metalworking deposits while the second date of 101 BC - 33 AD (GU 2326) relates to underlying occupation levels. The cellular structures would therefore seem to have been in use in the C2nd or C3rd AD.

A small ceramic assemblage from this phase on the site is of typological significance. The pottery is dominated by flaring rim vessels with decoration restricted to applied cordons. The most complete vessel is a globular jar with a flaring rim, decorated with two applied cordons. This assemblage is typologically later than the short everted rims with restricted decoration, as at Cnip Phase 2, and later still than the more varied decoration of the later centuries BC (App. 3). It precedes the plain flaring

rim assemblages of the later phase at Loch na Berie and the Udal.

The cells also contained quantities of metalworking debris including triangular crucibles (earlier than the types from Structure 1 at Loch na Berie), tuyere and a number of two-piece clay moulds. One of these moulds was for a developed handpin with four bar-like 'fingers' arranged in a straight line across the top of the solid semi-circular plate. This is the first C-14 date clearly linked to handpin production and the date is several centuries earlier than expected. Stevenson would place such a pin in the second half of the 1st millennium AD. More dates will be required to clarify the chronology of the type.

C.22 Unival, North Uist NF 800 668 (Scott 1947a)

Introduction - The cellular structure at Unival was excavated by Sir Lindsay Scott as an adjunct to his excavation of the Unival chambered tomb in 1935 and 1939. The structure was built over and among the remains of a chambered tomb on a slight terrace at c. 80m O.D. on the hill of Unival.

Site Structure - Only one post-tomb phase of occupation was noted by Scott, this consisting of the cellular structure referred to as the Iron Age house in his excavation report. This structure was relatively slight in construction and formed of coursed drystone walls. It consisted of two rectilinear cells with several associated recesses.

The structure was revetted into the cairn material and faced internally. Its walls stood to less than 1m in height.

Pits in the cairn contained later prehistoric pottery and the de-roofed chamber contained burnt material suggesting use as a cooking pit. Other possible later prehistoric structures were visible on the mound but were not excavated. Occupation was not therefore confined to the cellular structure.

Internal Structure - The northern of the two cells measured c. 3 x 2m internally and had two external entrances and a separate entrance into the southern cell. Access to this southern cell, of similar size, was only available through the former. The first cell contained a hearth near its north wall and two small recesses to the south. It may have been the main domestic focus. The second cell also contained a hearth but was interpreted as a grain-drying area by Scott as its internal arrangement, with a raised paved platform at one end, and the absence of burnt bone suggested parallels with similar structures in the Faroes.

Material Culture and Chronology - The only artefactual material which clearly post-dated the primary use of the tomb was an assemblage of later prehistoric pottery. Scott does not identify any of this material as definitively associated with the cellular structure so the association is largely circumstantial. Nonetheless only the pottery is helpful in dating the structure.

The assemblage appears typologically uniform and relatively late in the later prehistoric sequence. Flaring and upright rims are characteristic and only one small everted rim is present (Scott 1947a, Fig. 3). Incised decoration is entirely absent. Decoration is confined to applied wavy cordons except for two sherds with rough fingernail impressions on their rims. This latter form of decoration cannot be readily paralleled from the 1st millennium BC pottery and the general vessel forms and decoration suggest a mid-1st millennium AD, date possibly typologically parallel to the assemblage from Eilean Olabhat (App. 2).

C.23 Dun Ban, Grimsay, North Uist NF 8699 5695 (Thomas 1890)

Introduction - The cellular structures at Dun Ban were excavated by Capt. Thomas in the belief that they represented the primary roundhouse occupation. The details of phasing are therefore very difficult to extract from his brief report. The atlantic roundhouse of Dun Ban, within which the cellular constructions are located, is discussed in Chapter Five.

Site Structure - From Thomas's plan it appears that the cellular structures were dominated by a central cell some 4 x 4m in size and irregular in shape. This gave access to two peripheral cells ('d' and 'e') and to the re-used galleries of the roundhouse. Little structural information was recorded but Thomas noted that the walls of some cells indicated possible corbelling of the roofs.

Internal Structure - The nature of the excavation precludes any interpretation of the internal arrangements of the cellular structures. These may well be related to a long period of occupation.

Thomas does note that the interior of the cells often contained intruding peaks of outcrop rock which must have been a feature of the primary floors. This situation is paralleled at Dun Cuier (A.B4) and Dun Carloway (A.L12).

Material Culture and Chronology - No details are given of the material from the excavation. All that is known of the chronology of the cellular structures is that they were post-roundhouse.

C.24 A' Cheardach Mhor, South Uist NF 7571 4128 (Young and Richardson 1959

Introduction - The wheelhouse of A' Cheardach Mhor has been described in Chapter Six. This section discusses the later reoccupation of the site involving the construction of cellular structures.

Site Structure - Three phases were isolated by the excavator as representing this reoccupation (II, III and IV). Phase II and III have only fragmentary walling and no recognisable structure was preserved. Phase IV involved the insertion of a small cell (possibly c. 3m in original diameter) with a slab-revetted wall surmounted by coursing (Ill. 7.7). The cell has its closest parallels in size and construction with the small Phase 2 cells at Cnip. Other fragmentary walling around and within the abandoned wheelhouse may represent unrecognised associated cells.

Internal Structure - No internal features were recorded.

Material Culture and Chronology - Only one sherd of pottery was associated with Phase IV. This was originally identified as a Mediterranean import. This attribution was disputed by Alcock and is not now widely accepted (Alcock 1984, 17). The Phase III pottery is represented by one vessel which has an applied wavy cordon and short everted rim of a form similar to the Phase 2 pottery from Cnip. This latter pottery also derived from the cellular reoccupation of a wheelhouse site.

A cast bronze pin with a bronze wire free-ring head was possibly associated with the Phase IV cell. It is dated, on the basis of a parallel at Lagore, to the C5th or C6th AD (Topping 1985).

Overall the cellular phase can only be broadly dated to the post-wheelhouse period on this site and possibly to the C5th - 6th AD by the association of the bronze pin.

C.28 Dun Cuier, Barra NF 6708 0345 (Young 1955)

Introduction - The site of Dun Cuier has already been discussed in Chapter Five and a reinterpretation of the sequence proposed. The new interpretation isolates the structure defined by Young's inner wall as a cellular structure revetted into the remains of an atlantic roundhouse. The following discussion is based on this reinterpretation.

Site Structure - The cellular structure was dominated by a large central subcircular cell some 8m in internal diameter, occupying almost the whole of the roundhouse interior (Ill. 5.11). Its entrance, as at Berie, re-used the roundhouse entrance. A second doorway appears to have led out towards the north, possibly to a small peripheral cell, but this is not clear from the plan. The wall of the cell was of conventional coursing.

The galleries of the earlier roundhouse appear not to have been used in this phase. MacKie's objection to the early dating of the site, based on the presence of early pottery at a high level in the gallery, misunderstands the nature of the reoccupation (1989, 117). As at Loch na Berie, the galleries were used only as dumps for material derived from refuse, cleaning and construction activities.

Outcrop in the floor appears to have led the excavator to believe that the primary levels had been reached. The presence of outcrop at sites like Dun Carloway (A.L12) up to 1m above floor level show that this need not have been the case. It is possible that further cellular structures existed prior to this structure's occupation.

Internal Structure - Several internal features are recorded which all appear to be associated with the cellular structure. A large central hearth dominates the interior. Several stone settings in its vicinity may indicate rebuilds. In the western arc across the hearth from the entrance are two niches or shelves built into the wall as at Loch na Berie Structure 1 (although these are more widely spaced). Again as at Berie an alignment of stones flanking the hearth on the south may be the remains of kerbing.

The cellular structure occupation material was deposited over a layer of machair sand, which had been laid as a deliberate levelling deposit over the collapse of the atlantic roundhouse. Young, and subsequently MacKie (1989), believed that this material represented a boulder foundation, but this assumes that the cellular structure was a primary construction. The low level of the scarcement suggests that the primary atlantic roundhouse material lies substantially below this sand and below the rubble from the collapse of the primary structure. This misunderstanding accounts for MacKie's other principal objection to the reinterpretation of Dun Cuier i.e. the lack of a post-hole ring, which he saw as being indicative of *broch* interiors (1989, 117). The reinterpretation of Dun Cuier proposed in Chapter Five sees the excavated floor deposits as entirely post-roundhouse.

Material Culture and Chronology - The material from the site was a mixed assemblage from all phases. The presence of many plain flaring rim vessels indicates a termination date in the late pre-Norse period (App. 2) and Lane identified vessels with form and decoration indicating the presence of typologically earlier assemblages (Lane 1983, 255).

Other finds from the site support the dating of the latest occupation to a late stage of the pre-Norse period. A high-backed composite comb has Irish parallels in the second half of the 1st millennium AD, e.g. at Lagore (Young 1955, 316). Two double-edged composite combs are of broadly similar date.

Survey Evidence

Thirteen unexcavated cellular structures are recorded, mostly by Beveridge and the RCAHMS on the basis of reports from local people. Some general points can be made regarding distribution and site structure but little additional evidence is available from these sites.

Distribution - The heavy concentration of cellular structures in North Uist appears to reflect the work of Erskine Beveridge. The remainder are evenly spread throughout the islands (Ill. 7.1). The slight construction of the walling of these structures and their tendency to be subterranean or revetted has made discovery an almost random occurrence dependant on erosion, excavation or other accidental discovery (as at Scolpaig where the cellular structure was discovered when a horse fell through its roof).

The structures are found in most of the available environments, machair, moorland, hilltop and islet, although the moorland examples are difficult to distinguish from medieval and post-medieval shielings.

Site Structure - The unexcavated sites have very little recorded information on site structure. Most are groups of up to three circular or oval cells, often corbelled and always small in size, linked by passages. All appear to have been subterranean in construction. Some, e.g. Tigh nan Leachach (C.27), Usinish 2 (C.25) and Vallaquie 2 (C.18), have evidence of corbelling.

In the absence of properly recorded structural detail it is possible that a number of these structures may be unrelated in chronology or function to the excavated cellular sites. Elements of later medieval and post-medieval landscapes may well be confused in some instances with the cellular structures.

The association of many of the cellular structures with passages of various dimensions indicates a connection with the linear passages. This connection will be explored in Chapter Eight.

Discussion

Construction Method

All of the structures apart from Eilean Olabhat appear to have been constructed by revetting: many were revetted into abandoned wheelhouses or roundhouses while others, e.g. the Udal and Galson, were revetted into sand-hills. Two basic walling techniques were employed; slab-revetting and conventional coursing. In most early excavations the walling method was not recorded.

The conventionally coursed cellular structures comprise Dun Cuier, Dun Bharabhat and Unival (the walling technique at the Udal is not published). These structures were all revetted into pre-existing stone structures; the first two into atlantic roundhouses and the third into a chambered tomb. The walls at Dun Cuier and Unival appear to have been only one stone in width. A central floor area was cleared of rubble and the wall used as a revettment to hold back the debris. At Dun Bharabhat the circuit of the central cell simply reused the existing roundhouse wall.

The slab-revetted cellular structures comprise Cnip Phase 2, Berie Structures 1 and 2 and A' Cheardach Mhor Phase 4. The technique does not appear to have chronological significance within the period under study as Cnip Phase 2 and Berie Structure 1 may be separated by up to 800 years in construction. The basic construction was identical to that of the coursed walled structures except that the bottom course of walling was formed of large flat vertical slabs surmounted by coursing. It is not clear if any functional advantage was gained by this and the effect may have been purely stylistic. This is best demonstrated in Structure 4 at Cnip where the bottom course slabs are graded in height to the area across the hearth from the entrance.

The larger of these structures would have been roofed in timber and the extent of lintelling or corbelling is unclear. Structure 3 at Cnip was found with lintels *in situ* but no trace of lintels or collapsed corbelling was found in any of the other small cells on the site. The rafters of the timber roofs of the large revetted structures such as at Berie and the Udal would have rested on the ground surface behind the revetment wall and water would have drained from the roof into the surrounding material (the packing and previous occupation debris at Berie and the sand at the Udal).

The cellular design of the structures entailed that no spans greater than c. 6m ever had to be roofed, and the requirements of timber conservation may well have been a major consideration in construction. Preserved walls at Cnip and Berie indicate an original height of 6m for the walls and this presumably was designed to give adequate headroom around the walls under the pitched roof whilst minimising the height of the roof above the external ground surface. These three structural traits combine to indicate a non-monumental form of architecture built with regard to three important environmental concerns: the lack of easily available timber; the cold; and the wind.

Chronology

The chronology of the excavated cellular structures is well defined in comparison to other site types by the pottery typology, which becomes more closely datable in the 1st millennium AD (App. 3). C-14 dates are restricted to three sites, Dun Bharabhat, Eilean Olabhat and the Udal. Quern evidence is rare but there is no evidence of cellular structures being in use prior to the local quern transition. Non-ceramic artefactual evidence, principally in the form of metalwork, provides further evidence to amplify the C-14 and pottery dating.

The earliest dating for the cellular structures comes from the C-14 dates from Dun Bharabhat, discussed above, which indicate occupation in the C1st BC and possibly earlier. The pottery from this site is of the undifferentiated decorated everted-rim dominated forms characteristic of the later centuries BC in the Western Isles. Of the other structures only Phase 2 at Cnip has definite ceramic associations of this early type, which is more characteristic of wheelhouse and atlantic roundhouse occupation. One sherd of classic 'Clettraval Ware' (App. 2) from the structures at Galson however may indicate a similarly early date at that site. The plan of the cellular phase at Bharabhat is very similar to the Figure-of-Eight structures at the Udal which date from the C3rd AD onwards at the earliest. This would seem to support the case against premature subdivision of the class on structural grounds at this stage.

Dun Bharabhat, Cnip Phase 2 and Galson may have been occupied as cellular structures from the C1st BC and are unlikely to post-date the C1st AD. Dun Bharabhat and Cnip Phase 2 clearly post-date an atlantic roundhouse and wheelhouse respectively. Further cellular structures post-date wheelhouses at the Udal, Foshigarry and A' Cheardach Mhor, and atlantic roundhouses at Dun Cuier, Berie, Dun Ban, Dun Thomaidh, Dun a Ghallain and Eilean a Ghallain: in no case is the chronological relationship reversed.

The C-14 dates from Eilean Olabhat show the continued occupation of cellular structures through the early centuries AD ,and the pottery from Unival and A' Cheardach Mhor phases II and III indicate broadly similar periods of occupation.

Evidence of later dating comes from three sites: Berie, the Udal and Dun Cuier. C-14 dates from the Udal indicate continuous occupation throughout the period of c. 400 - 800 AD terminating with the Norse incursions. The artefactual evidence for Structures 1 and 2 at Berie indicates occupation over the same period, possibly starting somewhat earlier from the presence of typologically earlier pottery in Structure 2 contexts. The Northumbrian influenced tweezers may indicate an abandonment of Berie as late as the end of the cellular structures at the Udal. The pottery from Dun Cuier shares its range of forms and decoration with the Berie assemblage, and the presence of the high-backed comb indicates a late abandonment. All three of these sites appear to have had continuous occupation from c. 400AD or earlier until the Norse incursions c. 800AD.

Function

The majority of these structures appear to have functioned as domestic structures, often with small outbuildings or lined pits. Substantial central hearths are characteristic of the excavated examples and peripheral kerbing, interpreted as demarcating areas of bedding, is recorded at Berie, Structures 1 and 2, the Udal and Dun Cuier. The material from all of the excavated structures indicates routine domestic use. Assemblages are dominated by fragmentary pottery vessels, large bone assemblages (unless in acidic soils) and a matrix of sand and hearth debris.

Subdivision

None of the discussion above suggests the need to subdivide the cellular structures at this stage. Chronologically they occupy a single span of some 8 or 9 centuries, while structurally they appear all to share basic traits. Architectural features, such as the building and positioning of niches, occur over the whole period and in structures of both basic wall construction types. The plans tend to conform to the same basic design and no functional distinctions can be drawn.

Parallels Outwith the Western Isles

A number of parallels can be cited for the 1st millenium AD occurrence of cellular structures of this type from both Scotland and Ireland. The clearest parallel to the Hebridean group is House 4 at Buckquoy in Orkney (Ritchie 1976), dated to the C8th AD, which has the Figure-of Eight shape and vertical slab revetted wall characteristic of the Hebridean structures. This site has been described as Pictish, and appears to represent the typical Northern Isles house form of the Orkneys during the period of historically documented Pictish influence, if not control. Similar house forms appear to be present at Birsay in Orkney (Hunter 1986). Earlier house types of similar form exist in the clustered villages around some of the Orcadian broch towers e.g. Gurness (Hedges 1987) and Howe (Carter et al 1984), where construction involving slab revetting combines with cellular house plans. At Jarlshof in Shetland (Hamilton 1956) the 'passage-houses' and their outbuildings of the mid-1st millennium AD appear to have incorporated slab-revetting.

The cellular plan of these 1st millennium AD structures cannot, however, be described as a Pictish trait. At Deer Park Farms in Ulster a sequence of timber-built Figure-of-Eight structures occupied the centre of a waterlogged ring-fort (Lynn 1987) in the traditional homeland of the Scots. This structure parallels the plan, scale and internal arrangements of the cellular structures at the Udal and Berie and dates to the same period in the second half of the 1st millennium AD. The main cell is dominated by a central hearth and flanked by kerbed beds; the entrance to a smaller subsidiary cell leads out from the opposite side of the hearth from the main entrance.

Summary

The cellular structures appear to have been constructed and occupied from the C1st BC until the beginning of the C9th AD. No typological progression is indicated by the examination of structure and dating in this chapter. Even very specific architectural traits such as the construction of wall niches opposite the main entrance, the use of vertical slab revetting and the basic Figure-of-Eight plan recur from the earliest cellular structures at Dun Bharabhat and Cnip, to the latest at Berie and Dun Cuier.

The structures appear to represent the standard house forms of the period successive to that dominated by the monumental roundhouses (the atlantic roundhouses and wheelhouses). The house type is non-monumental and appears to be built with practical concerns in mind. Similar structures in both the Northern Isles and in Ireland indicate that we should be wary of attributing the structures to historically documented peoples or cultural groups, and the application of the label Pictish to the northern examples should be treated with caution.

In the architecture and the artefactual material of the cellular structures, connections can be found with the historical Pictish areas, with Ireland and with Northumbria (the Berie tweezers). Part Four will return to the integration of the cellular structures both with the wider Hebridean settlement development and with the archaeological and historical picture developed in other areas.

Chapter Eight - Linear Structures

The linear structures of the Western Isles have been previously classed as 'souterrains' and 'earth-houses' (Ill. 8.1). The terms were used almost interchangeably in early accounts and never fully defined. The criteria for the definition of linear structures has been set out in Chapter Four. Fifteen sites are recorded in the Western Isles, of which two are linear house structures and thirteen are linear passages.

Seven linear structures have been excavated, although only at Drimore (L.13) and Vallay (L.9) was the linear structure the principal or original object of the excavation. In these cases excavation was extremely limited in extent and few details are available. No deliberate attempt has been made to evaluate this structural type through research excavation.

Excavated Sites

a. Linear House Structures

L.1 Cnip, Lewis NB 0980 3665 (Armit 1988a)

Introduction - The linear house structure (Structure 8) at Cnip represents the final structural element in the site sequence prior to abandonment. It overlies and seals the cellular structures of Phase 2 (Chapter Seven) and the wheelhouses of Phase 1 (Chapter Six).

Site Structure - This structure utilised the existing Structure 1 entrance passage and much of the earlier walling for its foundations. In essence it represents the final period of *ad hoc* rebuilding of the original wheelhouse (Structure 1). The new walling was conventional coursing, replacing the slab revetting of the cellular structures. Structure 8 was some 7m in length by 2.2m wide with a paved approach and a small cobbled path providing alternative access from the south (Ill. 8.2).

After abandonment the structure was deliberately deroofed and filled almost immediately with sterile, windblown, machair sand. The walls survived, apparently intact, to c. 2m in height. Roofing would have necessarily been of timber since the width was too great to be bridged by lintels.

Internal Structure - The interior of Structure 8 was divided into three sections. The section nearest the entrance was some 1.5m EW by 2.2m and contained a stone bench built into the north wall. It lacked occupation debris and appears to have served a separate function from the main central chamber. This latter chamber was defined on the west by a stone alignment which may have supported a timber or wattle partition. In the chamber were large quantities of occupation debris including much peat ash, although no formal hearth was apparent.

The innermost division of the structure was formed by the two surviving wheelhouse bays of Structure 1 which were still roofed when excavated. The deposits in these bays were continuous with the central chamber.

Material Culture and Chronology - The pottery from Phase 3 at Cnip is typologically transitional between the decorated everted rim pottery of the 1st millennium BC and the plain later pottery (App. 2). Short everted rims remain characteristic but decoration is restricted to applied wavy cordons and, as at Eilean Olabhat, double cordons predominate (Ill. 8.3). The vessels are generally coarser than those of the preceding phases. The absence of incised decoration, the restriction of motifs and overall small amount of decoration indicate a transitional period, typologically earlier than the Eilean Olabhat assemblage.

The ceramic assemblage indicates a date in the early centuries AD for this structure. In relative chronological terms the structure is later than both the wheelhouses and the cellular structures at Cnip.

Aside from the ceramic assemblage, the deposits associated with Phase 3 contained quantities of cetacean bone and antler-working debris, a large terrestrial bone assemblage and quantities of slag.

b. Linear Passages

L.3 Gress Lodge, Stornoway, Lewis NB 4938 4185 (Liddle 1872, MacRitchie 1916)

Introduction - The complex passage-like structure at Gress Lodge was first reported in the late C19th. By 1969 all trace of it had disappeared. The site lay under the lawn of Gress Lodge near Stornoway on the east coast of Lewis. Its entrance was c. 1m above high water mark when originally reported, c. 40m from the modern house.

Site Structure - The 'earth-house' containing three chambers was the only structure reported on the site. The structure appears to have been subterranean, 1m in width and roofed with lintels. The plan, although incomplete, shows the approximate shape and dimensions of the passage (Ill. 8.4).

Internal Structure - No internal features are recorded except for a central pillar, seemingly structural, in the central chamber.

Material Culture and Chronology - Few finds were reported from Gress Lodge. In 1969, after the structure had become inaccessible, the NMR reports a find of 30 'iron age' sherds from the vicinity. The original finds include bones, shell and querns of unspecified type. The site seems likely to be later prehistoric, on the basis of the pottery, but no greater precision is possible. Lane records that the assemblage also included fragments of late medieval pottery (Lane 1983, 263).

L.7 The Udal, North Uist NF 824 783 (Crawford 1967/78, 1975, 1977, 1985)

Introduction - The linear structure on the US site at the Udal was first excavated by Beveridge (1911) and latterly by Crawford. Neither excavation was published in detail.

Site Structure - The linear structure appears to have run from the side of the US site at the Udal towards the wheelhouse (Chapter Six) which it entered through one

Ill. 8.1 Distribution of Linear Structures in the Western Isles

Ill. 8.2 Cnip, Lewis, Phase Three Structures

of the latter's south-eastern bays. The structure was a passage some 20m long by 0.6m wide. Crawford reports that it was associated with the cellular constructions inside the abandoned wheelhouse (Crawford 1978).

Internal Structure - No internal features were recorded.

Material Culture and Chronology - No material was recorded. In terms of relative dating the structure post-dated the wheelhouse and is likely to have preceded the construction of the cellular structures on the nearby UN machair mound (Crawford 1978).

L.8 Foshigarry, North Uist NF 7430 7636 (Beveridge 1930)

Introduction - The site of Foshigarry has already been discussed in Chapters Six and Seven with reference to its three wheelhouses and its cellular structures. The linear structure is Structure H on Beveridge's plan (Ill. 6.3).

Site Structure - Structure H was a long passage-like building revetted into the debris of Structure C as described in Chapter Six. Its chronological relationship with other structures on the site is unclear, although it shared an entrance with Structure F (see Chapter Seven) with which it may have been contemporary (Ill. 6.3).

Structure H was c. 15m long by 0.6 - 0.7m wide and ran NW/SE with a slight curve to the east. At its south-eastern end it turned sharply northwards for c. 2m. It appears to have been wholly roofed with lintels and paved for part of its length. One entrance into the structure was from the NW end and another side entrance was accessible from the middle of the NE side wall. When roofed the structure would have been c. 1m high

Internal Structure - No evidence exists of any internal divisions or features and the structure appears to have been a simple passage. It did not serve simply as an entrance to the cellular complex of structures, F, E and D, since it continued for more than half its length beyond the entrance to these structures.

The kiln described by Beveridge as belonging to this structure appears likely to belong instead to the intrusive post-medieval structures which lie above (Scott 1948, 74).

Material Culture and Chronology - In the absence of any attributable finds the structure can only be dated by a crude relative chronology. Arguments were presented in Chapter Six to suggest that Structure H was later than Structure C, the wheelhouse (though not necessarily later than all of the wheelhouses on the site): its shared access with Structure F suggests that it was in use at the same time as the cellular complex, or at least that their use overlapped.

L.9 Vallay Earth-House, North Uist NF 77 76 (Beveridge 1911)

Introduction - This structure, on the island of Vallay off North Uist, was investigated by Beveridge prior to 1911. The structure is only provisionally classed as a linear

structure: it may have formed part of a different type of settlement altogether as the structural evidence is so slight. The site lies on a slight knoll in the machair behind the beach on Vallay.

Site Structure - Beveridge reported finding one wall of a curving subterranean passage, revetted into the sand. The wall ran for some 10m and survived to 0.5m in depth. Two short transverse walls were reported.

Internal Structure - No details of internal structure are known.

Material Culture and Chronology - Beveridge reported finding decorated pottery but no details are available. No information exists on the chronology of the site.

L.12 Bruthach a Tuath, Benbecula NF 787 566 (compiled from excavator's notes)

Introduction - The location and circumstances of excavation are described in Chapter Six.

Site Structure - The linear structure, the 'souterrain' in Wallace's notes, was constructed over the abandoned wheelhouse described in Chapter Six. It was entered from the interior of this ruined structure and the later hearths in two of the wheelhouse bays may relate to this linear structure s occupation.

The linear structure was entered by six steps, 0.6 - 0.7m wide, and ran SW for 4.2m at least. No further details were recorded.

Internal Structure - No internal features were recognised.

Material Culture and Chronology - The surviving excavation records do not specify what material was found in the linear structure apart from a bronze projecting ring-headed pin of wide chronological currency. Wallace did note, however, that all of the decorated pottery was found in the wheelhouse deposits.

The absence of a detailed ceramic assemblage and the unspecific dating of the bronze pin prevent any attempt at absolute chronology. The linear structure was clearly, however, post-wheelhouse on the site.

L.13 Drimore, South Uist NF 75 41 (Feachem 1956)

Introduction - This site was reported by Feachem in 1956 as part of the excavation programme associated with the construction of the Drimore Rocket Range in South Uist. The site lies on the Drimore machair in the vicinity of several wheelhouse sites such as A' Cheardach Mhor (W.15) and A' Cheardach Bheag (W.16; Chapter Six). The excavations appear to have been very brief and were never fully published.

Site Structure - The linear structure, reported as a 'souterrain' (Feachem 1956), was not associated with any other visible structure. It consisted of a sand-revetted

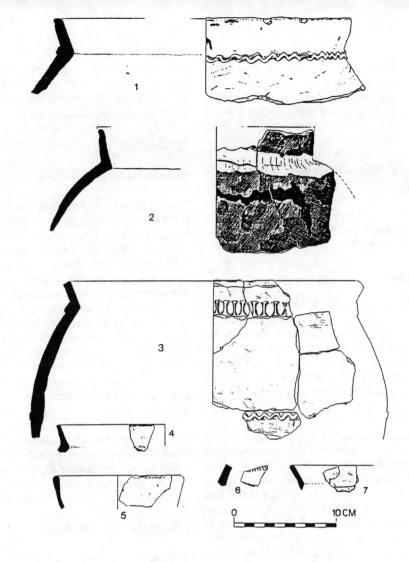

Ill. 8.3 Cnip, Lewis, Phase Three Pottery

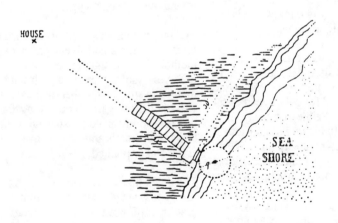

HOUSE
×

SEA SHORE

NO SCALE ON ORIGINAL DRAWING

N

Ill. 8.4 Gress Lodge (after MacRitchie 1916)

passage, 8m long by 1m wide and 1m deep, which was entered by steps leading down from the surface and Feachem reported that small chambers led off these steps. It may be that the linear structure was associated with a cellular complex which went unnoted or which had not survived.

Internal Structure - No internal features of the structure were recorded.

Material Culture and Chronology - No details of the material from the structure were reported, although pottery and bone were recovered.

Survey Evidence

Eight linear structures can be added to the excavated sites from the evidence of field survey. Most were recorded by the RCAHMS on the basis of local reports and the fieldwork of Erskine Beveridge. Some general points of distribution and site structure can be made, but no evidence is available to supplement the excavated data for internal structure, material culture or chronology.

Distribution - The subterranean nature of the linear structures has made their discovery very difficult and consequently few are recorded. Their distribution is spread throughout the islands and reflects the activities of past fieldworkers: Thomas in the Usinish area of South Uist; Beveridge in the northern part of North Uist; and the Rocket Range survey in South Uist and Benbecula. Others were reported by local people when periods of sand deflation or erosion exposed the passages. The known distribution is in no way a reliable indicator of the original distribution of the class.

The linear passages occur in both machair and moorland environments and are found at altitudes of up to 100m at Scalavat (L.14). The linear house structures are confined to the machair although, with only two known, it is not clear whether this has any real significance.

Site Structure - Little structural information can be added to that from the excavated sites. All appear to have been subterranean, either sand-revetted or excavated into hillsides. Dimensions are recorded for only two unexcavated sites; the linear passage at Paible, Taransay (L.5) was recorded as being over 7m in length but its width is unknown; the linear house structure at Vallaquie, North Uist (L.2) was some 7m by 2m. This latter structure is comparable in size with the linear house structure at Cnip.

External structures which may be contemporary have been noted at three linear passage sites; above-ground structures including a possible 'hut-circle' were recorded near the linear structure at Valtos, Lewis (RCAHMS 1928, no. 96; L.2); similarly, stone-built structures of uncertain form are visible adjacent to the linear structure at Scalavat 1, South Uist (L.14; pers. obs. 1988) and the linear structure at Paible, Taransay (L.5), was said to have had an adjoining side-cell prior to its destruction.

These instances suggest that the association of linear passages with other structural elements may be more common than previously thought. As was noted in Chapter Seven, a number of cellular structures incorporate elements which, if found singly, could be classed as linear passages. It may be the case that a number of the linear structures represent the sole surviving or the only visible elements of such cellular complexes.

Discussion

Subdivision

The excavated evidence suggests that a distinction exists in size, internal divisions and evidence for function between the linear house structure at Cnip and the linear passages. The survey evidence shows that the site of Vallaquie in North Uist (L.2) appears to be related to the Cnip structure. The main structural difference from the linear passages is their width and, by implication, their roofing method and function. While the other sites for which dimensions are recorded tend to be c. 0.6 - 0.8m in width, the structures at Cnip and Vallaquie are 2.2m and c. 2m in width respectively. At Cnip the linear structure appears to have been the domestic focus of the Phase Three occupation while the excavated linear passages appear to have been elements in larger, cellular, settlement units.

The linear structures have therefore been divided, on the basis of dimensions (i.e. width), into two sub-classes: the linear house structures (Cnip Structure 8 and Vallaquie) and the linear passages (the remainder of the structures for which dimensions are recorded).

Construction Method

The linear structures are all subterranean, being sand-revetted, as are all the excavated sites, or dug into hillsides, as at Scalavat 1 and 2 (L.14 and 15), Portain (L.10) and possibly Valtos (L.4). All appear to have been built of conventional coursed walling and no indication of slab-revetting has been recorded.

The major constructional divergence between the linear house structures and linear passages is in their roofing method. The passages appear all to have been lintelled at or below the contemporary ground level. Lintels remained *in situ* at a number of sites, e.g. Gress Lodge, the Udal and Foshigarry, confirming the use of this technique. The linear house structures were too wide to be bridged by lintels and would have required timber roofs, either flat or pitched.

The linear house structures were non-monumental structures constructed with the requirements of insulation and ease of roofing in mind. The relatively narrow central span would have made roofing with short timbers possible.

Chronology

The dating of Structure 8 at Cnip has been discussed above. The pottery from the structure suggests a date in the early centuries AD. No dating evidence is available from Vallaquie. In relative terms the Cnip structure post-dates the wheelhouses and cellular structures on that site but its pottery clearly pre-dates the assemblages at other cellular structures such as Berie and the Udal. The linear house structure therefore should be seen as contemporary with part of the development of cellular structures in the Western Isles.

In several cases the linear passages (the Udal, Foshigarry and Bruthach a Tuath) can be seen to be later than the wheelhouses on the same sites. In no instance do they appear to pre-date or be contemporary with the occupation of wheelhouses. Association with cellular structures and with the reoccupation of wheelhouses appears to be common and the majority of the linear passages seem to form elements in larger units. A date range in the same period as the cellular structures, the 1st millennium AD prior to the Norse incursions, can be suggested.

Function

The linear house structure at Cnip has been interpreted as a domestic structure and a similar function can be suggested for Vallaquie on the basis of structural parallels. The function of the linear passages is more difficult to assess. Domestic occupation can be ruled out due the prohibitively small size of the passages, all less than 1m in width. This supports the view that these structures are generally, if not always, elements in a larger settlement.

Several of the linear passages may be entrance passages or connecting passages between elements of cellular structures. This may be the case, for example, at Foshigarry where the linear passage appears to have been utilised as the entrance to cellular structures E and F. The Foshigarry linear passage, however, extends past this entrance and arrives at a butt end several metres beyond these cells. Other linear passages such as those at Bruthach a Tuath and the Udal are entered from reoccupied wheelhouses and have only one entrance.

Storage is a possible function of these structures and one which has been suggested for the larger souterrains of south and east Scotland. The underground nature of the structures may have provided a stable environment to store grain. The suitability of sand for this is, however, open to question. None of the finds from the excavated sites gives any indication as to function.

Parallels outwith the Western Isles

Linear structures have been recorded in several parts of Scotland in the later prehistoric period. The closest parallel, both geographically and structurally, for the Hebridean structures is the site of Tungadal in Skye (Miket pers. comm.) excavated by Roger Miket in 1988. This site comprised a linear house structure associated with a linear passage, entered from its interior. Pottery from the site was similar to that of the early centuries AD in the Western Isles. The excavations there may help in the interpretation of the Western Isles data. The structures at Tungadal highlight the different functions of the two types of structure: the linear house structure is clearly domestic and has a segmented internal structure, as at Cnip, while the linear passage or 'souterrain' leads off this and appears to serve a storage function (although interpretation still presents unresolved difficulties at Tungadal due to the problem of flooding in the linear passage). The linear passage here is a subsidiary domestic structure forming part of a larger settlement unit as appears to be the case for the Hebridean linear passages.

The souterrains of southern and eastern Scotland appear to be similar in scale and construction to the linear house structures of the Western Isles. Excavation, however, has not produced evidence for their use as domestic settlement structures and has suggested a storage function. No real evidence exists for a functional or cultural link with the Hebridean examples. The 'wags' of Caithness provide another possible parallel for the linear house structures, but their function and chronology are as ill-established as those of the Hebridean linear structures.

Summary

The linear passages of the Western Isles are poorly understood in both their function and chronology, although their construction methods and association with larger settlement units are relatively well established. They appear to be a phenomenon associated with the appearance and occupation of cellular settlements and probably served a specialised function within those settlements. Their date range seems to equate with that of the cellular structures and they are structurally difficult to disentangle from this latter group, which often contain rectilinear or linear cellular elements. It is tempting to equate them with the galleries of the complex atlantic roundhouses in function. Their spatial relationship with the domestic *foci* of the cellular structures as peripheral linear extensions, too constricted and elongated for routine domestic occupation, suggests a similar role within the settlement to the roundhouse galleries. While useful in stressing spatial and organisational continuity across chronological periods and structural forms, this does not get us closer to the function of these structures. A combination of archaeological experiment (with storage etc.) and future excavation will be required to advance our knowledge.

The linear house structures are easier to interpret as *foci* of domestic occupation. With only two sites known and only Cnip Structure 8 excavated, it is difficult to interpret the relationship between this group and other Hebridean settlement forms. The Cnip structure dates to a period when cellular structures were the dominant settlement type and forms the final phase of continuous occupation on a settlement which had been laid out in cellular form. The possibility of a close relationship in structure and function with the Tungadal structure in Skye (which appears from survey work to be representative of the Skye souterrains - Miket pers. comm.) further complicates the issue. It is clear, however, that the material culture of Cnip Structure 8 lies in the mainstream of the Western Isles and the settlement develops from conventional Western Isles structural precursors. There appears to be no question that the linear house structure is an externally imposed form.

With so few sites known it is currently only possible to note the existence of a parallel house-building tradition of linear or rectilinear revetted structures during the period of development of the cellular structures. The far greater number of cellular structures documented, despite similar circumstances of preservation and similar lack of targeted research, argues for a dominance of the cellular settlement form.

Chapter Nine - Promontory Forts

None of the promontory forts of the Western Isles has yet been excavated and information is therefore very sparse. Some observations can be made on the basis of the surface evidence regarding patterns of distribution and site structure.

Survey Evidence

Distribution - Twenty sites are known from the field survey evidence and these are heavily concentrated in Lewis, where thirteen sites are recorded (Ill. 9.1). One is known from Harris, two from North Uist and four from Barra. The Lewis concentration is likely to be the direct result of Trevor Cowie's unpublished coastal erosion survey of the late 1970s rather than any original locational factors.

The structures tend to occupy steep-sided promontories where access is easily controlled. The active erosion of many such promontories, which made them suitable locations, makes their archaeological visibility very limited. In most cases only landward walls can be expected to survive. This, combined with the tendency of early workers to focus their attentions on the more monumental settlement forms, has led to a probable under-representation of promontory forts in the archaeological record.

Site Structure - The Hebridean promontory forts are characteristically univallate with encircling or landward walls sealing off the promontory from landward approach. Only Rudha na Berie (P.7) and Dun Mara (Ill. 5.20; P.2), both in Lewis, were clearly multivallate. The three walls which cut off the promontory of Rudha na Berie appear to be part of one design and form a strong defensive barrier. Dun Mara, an atlantic roundhouse with external promontory walls, has two parallel walls which suggests a similar defensive capacity.

The promontory forts often enclose or seal off large areas, e.g. an irregular 240 x 100m at Rudha na Berie. The present enclosed dimensions are minimum figures for the original size of these enclosures.

Several sites appear to have been reoccupied at various periods and for various purposes, e.g. Dun Mara contains intrusive rectilinear structures, Rudha Shilldinish contains lazy-beds and rectilinear houses (P.12) and Casteil Odair (P.15) has evidence of post-medieval shielings.

Discussion

Construction Method

In the absence of excavation it is generally impossible to describe the construction method of these structures. The structure at Barra Head Lighthouse (P.20) is of drystone construction and incorporates a number of features characteristic of broch architecture (see below). A number of other sites, e.g. Casteil Odair, North Uist (P.15), indicate that drystone construction was often employed. Most of the structures are represented on the surface, however, by grassed-over banks.

Chronology

Almost nothing is known of the chronology of the Western Isles promontory forts. No C-14 dates are available and no artefactual material can be linked to their use. The only chronological indicator is structural typology.

The Barra Head Lighthouse site (RCAHMS 1928, no. 450) displays the characteristic traits of broch architecture in the context of a promontory fort rather than a roundhouse (Ill. 9.2). This structure is represented by a 20m long arc of walling sealing off a promontory on the island of Berneray, one of several small islands to the south of Barra. The wall is up to 5m wide and contains 2 super-imposed intra-mural galleries along its southern arc, as well as the low entrance passage with bar-holes characteristic of complex roundhouse entrances. The structure is clearly linked to the architectural tradition of the atlantic roundhouses and would be tentatively dated to the period when complex roundhouses were constructed, c. 400BC - 0 (Armit 1991). The absence of an atlantic roundhouse on the island suggests that this structure may have served a similar function to the Barra roundhouses.

Of the remaining promontory forts only Dun Bhilascleiter in Lewis (RCAHMS 1928, no. 34; P.3) has any indications of sharing elements of broch architecture with the atlantic roundhouses. Reports here suggest the former presence of an intra-mural guard cell. One further site, Dun Mara (P.2), an atlantic roundhouse sited on a promontory, has external banks which are similar to those of the promontory forts and which may suggest a functional or chronological link. The very simple morphology of the promontory forts, however, means that they may well represent several different chronological periods.

These three sites provide the only evidence from the Western Isles of a later prehistoric date for the promontory forts. This very slender evidence is somewhat amplified by work in other areas, discussed below.

Function

There is no unambiguous evidence for the function of these sites. Their location is immediately suggestive of defense, and in this they are more efficient in design and economy of labour than the atlantic roundhouses. Promontory forts could accommodate livestock, provide storage space and give the inhabitants alternative routes of access (i.e. to sea) not available to defenders in a roundhouse. Defense of a large area could be concentrated and access easily controlled.

Few of the sites have evidence for internal contemporary buildings which may have supported permanent settlement. If these were of lean-to type they would have been obscured by the collapse of the walls and in any case they may have been relatively slight and not readily visible to the archaeologist. Some sites, e.g. Casteil Odair, have internal structures but there is no way to assess contemporaneity from field survey alone.

Ill. 9.1 Distribution of Promontory Forts in the Western Isles

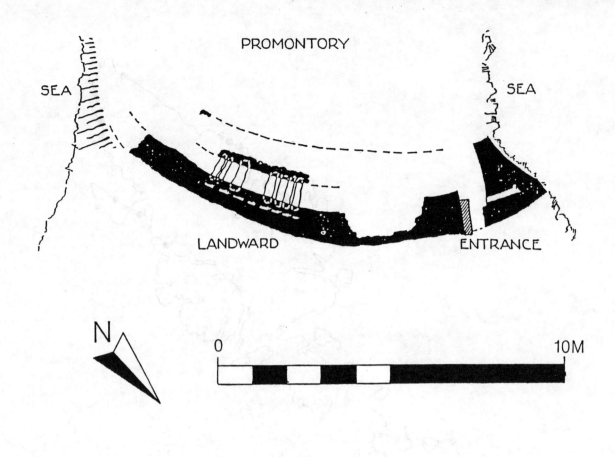

Ill. 9.2 Barra Head Lighthouse (after RCAHMS 1928)

Subdivision

The structures can be divided into two groups on the basis of surface morphology. The first comprise structures where the wall surrounds, or shows signs of having surrounded, the entire promontory, and the second where only the landward side is walled. Encircling walls will be prone to erosion however, and the landward walls will often be all that survives so it is not clear that this subdivision is of real significance. It may also be related to factors of topography and the presence or absence of naturally defensive locations. The evidence at present is too slight to sustain the subdivision of the Western isles promontory forts on this basis.

The conventional division between the univallate and multivallate forts is derived from areas outside the Western Isles (e.g. Lamb 1980). With only two known multivallate examples it seems premature to divide the Hebridean examples on this basis.

Parallels Outwith the Western Isles

Promontory forts occur widely in Atlantic Europe and elsewhere and may have a wide chronological currency and a variety of functions. The closest parallels to the Hebridean promontory forts appear to be those of the Northern Isles, interpreted by Lamb as predominantly of Iron Age date (1980). These include multivallate examples, paralleling Dun Mara (P.2) and Rudha na Berie (P.7), and a range of univallate examples. The northern sites also demonstrate links with the broch architecture of the atlantic roundhouses and Shetland blockhouses. Lamb's study placed the northern multivallate promontory forts in the wider traditions of Atlantic European sites but undermined the Venetic connections which had fixed their chronology to the Caesarian period (Lamb 1980). These northern structures therefore provide some slight support for a dating of the Hebridean promontory forts broadly to the later prehistoric period.

Chapter Ten - Related Structures

Introduction

There are several groups of structures which may form part of the later prehistoric settlement patterns of the Western Isles but which do not fit into the categories defined in Chapter Four, or for which there is no dating evidence. The principal forms are the walled islets and the miscellaneous structures (principally causewayed natural islets and crannogs).

Walled Islets

The walled islets comprise a group of 22 structures which have conventionally been classed with the *island duns* but which, by their size, irregularity or slight walling, could never have been roofed structures (Ill. 10.1). These structures were recognised as a distinct group in the field survey of Lewis and Harris carried out in 1984, where 4 examples were recorded, all with an eastern distribution which they share with the causewayed islets (Armit 1985). The walled islets are linked to the shore by causeways in the same way as the islet-sited atlantic roundhouses and the causewayed islets.

These structures are islet enclosures and share their surface morphology with the promontory forts, some wholly enclosing the islet and some restricted to walling on the closest side to the shore, e.g. Dun Hermidale, South Uist (WA.18). Like the promontory forts they tend to be irregular, following the edge of the islet. The size of these structures varies considerably and examples are recorded from 274 x 70m, at Dun Loch an Duin, Scalpay (WA.4), to only 21 x 19m at Dun Loch an Duna, Leurbost (WA.2). At some sites, e.g. Dun Scor in North Uist (WA.13), several islets may be connected by stone-built causeways.

Dun Loch an Duin, Aird, in Lewis (WA.1), is one of the few walled islets with recorded evidence for structural complexity. This site is now entirely destroyed but a plan survives from the late C19th (Thomas 1890, Ill. 10.2) which is sufficiently detailed, with measurements supplied, to suggest the former presence of a complex entrance. At the entrance the wall thickened from 1.5m to 4m and survived to 3m in height. This wall appears to have contained an oval guard-cell.

At Dun Loch an Duna, Leurbost (Ill. 10.3; WA.2), also in Lewis, a small corbelled cell survives built into the circuit of the wall. This structure has suffered through medieval re-use which has left traces in the substantial, intrusive rectilinear structure and the boat noost smashed through the original wall. A hut-circle, 5m in diameter, may be linked to earlier occupation but its date is entirely unknown.

These structures have never been examined through excavation and their chronology is entirely unknown. Many have evidence for internal structures, often very slight and clearly intrusive, but no evidence for contemporary internal occupation. These structures will be examined in Chapter Twelve, with the miscellaneous structures, with reference to their spatial relationships with known later prehistoric settlement forms.

Miscellaneous Structures

Large numbers of sites have been recorded as *island duns* on the basis of their location and surface morphology but in the absence of any indication of a drystone roundhouse. In some cases these featureless islets have been classed as crannogs, where they are obviously artificial, but normally they were thought to be poorly preserved examples of the island dun class.

A major reassessment of these structures was necessitated by the excavations at Eilean Domhnuill, Loch Olabhat, North Uist (M.13), which began in 1986 (Armit 1986; 1987; 1988b; 1990b). This site is an artificial islet, linked to the shore by a stone causeway in the manner of many atlantic roundhouse sites. The structures on the islet comprise a long sequence of neolithic house structures, built variously with turf and earth, timber and boulder-footed walls. The implications of this site are significant for interpretations of the settlement patterns of all periods in the Western Isles. It is now clear that the occupation of these causewayed islets, whether natural or artificial, can date back to the Early Neolithic and may cover the entire prehistoric period.

The islet sites which lack any traces of substantial drystone constructions have been classed as a separate group from those with evidence for atlantic roundhouse construction. There are 52 examples recorded; 9 from Lewis, 1 from Harris, 3 from Benbecula, 7 from South Uist and 32 from North Uist. None are known from Barra.

Apart from Eilean Domhnuill, only the North Tolsta crannog in Lewis (M.3) has been examined. Both of these sites confirm the potential for early dating of islets which lack evidence of monumental architecture. The North Tolsta crannog was exposed in loch drainage operations in the late C19th and was described by Blundell (1913). The structure was an artificial timber islet containing evidence of internal structures. No dating evidence is available but its timber construction would seem to argue for a relatively early date given the scarcity of timber in later prehistory.

Eilean an Tighe, excavated by Scott (1950) and not included in the catalogue here, was a neolithic settlement site (interpreted in the original report as a pottery manufacturing site) although the absence of a causeway and the small and narrow dimensions of the islet meant that this excavation was not previously regarded as jeopardising the unity of the later prehistoric 'island dun' class.

The importance of the distribution of these sites, in North Uist in particular, to interpretations of prehistoric settlement development will be assessed in Chapter Twelve.

Summary

The occurrence of walled islets and causewayed islets raises a series of problems in the context of the preceding examination of atlantic roundhouses. The recognition that many atlantic roundhouses were the archaeologically most visible elements in much longer settlement sequences means that we are faced with a range of islet

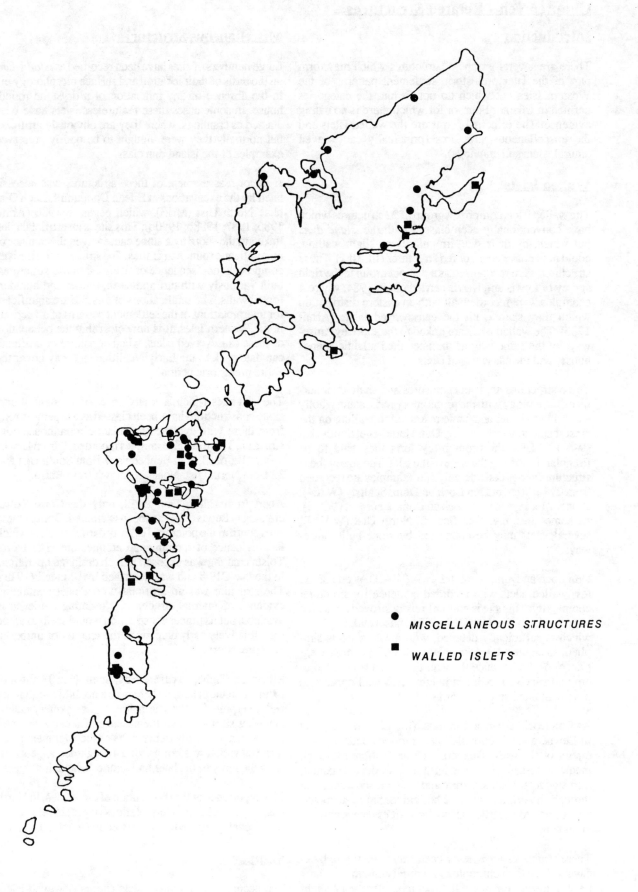

Ill. 10.1 Distribution of Miscellaneous Structures and Walled Islets in the Western Isles

MISCELLANEOUS STRUCTURES

WALLED ISLETS

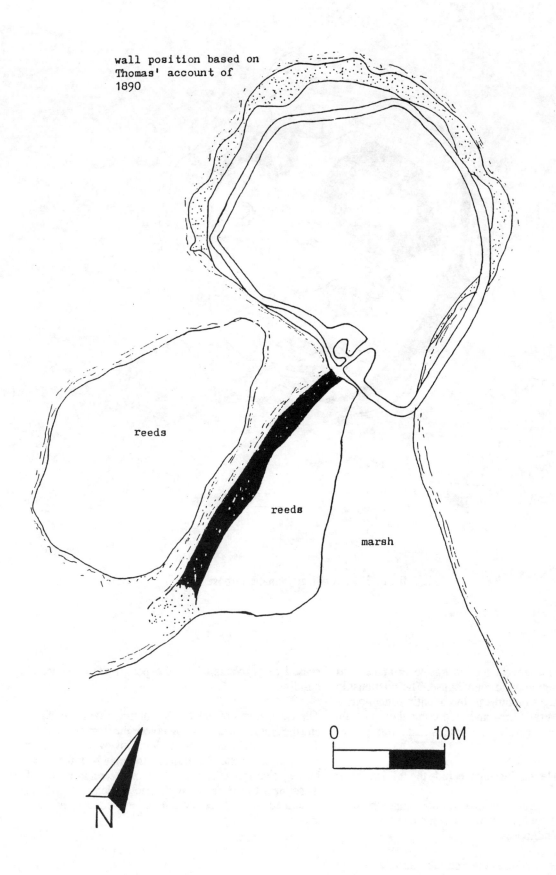

wall position based on
Thomas' account of
1890

reeds

reeds

marsh

0   10M

N

Ill. 10.2 Dun Loch an Duin, Aird (after Thomas 1890)

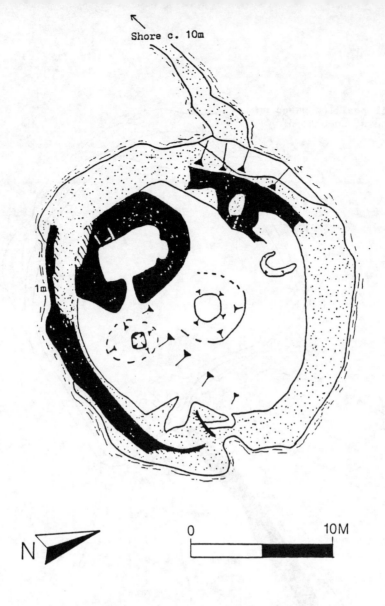

Shore c. 10m

1m

N

0   10M

Ill. 10.3 Dun Loch an Duna, Leurbost

settlement sites where occupation was never in the form
of a monumental atlantic roundhouse. The relationship
of these slighter structures to the atlantic roundhouses
could take several forms and at present there is little
justification for regarding these sites as a unitary phenomenon.

Various possible relationships include the following;

1. The slighter structures may be contemporary non-
monumental elements of the same settlement patterns as
the atlantic roundhouses. ·

2. The slighter structures may be later structures built
after the abandonment of the atlantic roundhouse form.

3. They may be earlier structures, representing sites of
similar function to the atlantic roundhouses, which had

ceased to be occupied by the period of monumental
building.

The excavations of Eilean Domhnuill, Eilean an Tighe
and the North Tolsta crannog favour the third possibility.
The walled and causewayed islets, however, may cover
a very wide chronological range and may be linked only
by negative traits. The question of the relationship of
these sites to the later prehistoric settlements will be
examined in Chapter Twelve in the context of their
spatial distribution.

Chapter Eleven - Structural Analysis

The purpose of this chapter is to explore the relationships within and between the structural forms defined in Chapter Four, on the basis of their observed structure. The quantity of available information which can be used for this sort of analysis is greatest for the atlantic roundhouses and wheelhouses and the analysis of these forms will form the basis of this chapter. Cellular and linear house structures are limited to a very few variables of use in this type of analysis and they will be discussed briefly towards the end of the chapter. The promontory forts and walled islets, as unroofed enclosures, cannot be assessed on a comparable basis to other classes.

Much of the negative data from the original structural analysis has been omitted from this chapter. This material can be found in the thesis on which the present study is based (Armit 1990f).

Atlantic Roundhouses

Analyses of atlantic roundhouse structure in the past has been based on the prior division of sites into architecturally defined classes. In particular it has been the sites defined as *brochs* which have been subject to detailed analysis while the *duns* have generally been avoided.

The first major work on the structural aspects of atlantic roundhouses was Angus Graham's study of *broch* architecture and structure, published in 1947. Graham's paper included discussions of the patterning of traits such as guard cells, scarcement ledges and intra-mural cells and galleries, from *brochs* throughout Scotland where observations had proved possible. Graham distinguished two broad 'strains' in the overall *broch* population, corresponding with the western and northern parts of the Atlantic province. Sir Lindsay Scott introduced height as a further factor in the classification of the *brochs* (1947). The shortcomings of his classification were pointed out by his contemporaries (Scott 1947, 35-6) and summarised by Martlew (1982). The unquantifiable and widespread occurrence of stone-robbing means that we can never hope to estimate original height from surviving structures and their surrounding rubble. Scott included no formal numerical or statistical analysis of structure in his work.

MacKie's work developed Graham's ideas and methods and included some study of *broch* dimensions (MacKie 1965). MacKie developed his numerical methods beyond those of Graham by working with two basic variables, wall thickness and diameter, and with wall proportion or wall base percentage, which was a product of these two basic variables. MacKie's results (presented in MacKie 1965, fig. 3) were used to infer regional groupings within the plotted relationships of wall proportion to external diameter. Like Graham and Scott, MacKie was concerned with *brochs*, as he defined them, on a national level. Consideration of structures outwith his strictly defined *broch* category was largely avoided. The pre-selection of sites for separate consideration on the criteria of surviving architectural features has already been argued to be misleading. In the context of the Western Isles sites it is important to consider the range of atlantic roundhouses and to examine the unity or possible divisions within the class.

The most recently published work on the structural analysis of *brochs* was that by Martlew (1982). This study used a number of techniques, most notably cluster analysis, to explore the typology of the structures classified as *brochs*. This study, however, did not tackle the basic problem of the integration of these structures with the mass of unclassified but related structures in their regional contexts. MacKie's classification was taken as the basis for the selection of sites and indeed MacKie's sample of sites from his earlier work was re-used in Martlew's analysis. It is difficult to see how real progress can be made if the underlying assumptions of this classification scheme remain unchallenged. Nonetheless, Martlew did recognise some regional variants within the sites studied. The Western Isles *brochs*, for example, seemed to constitute a reasonably coherent group of relatively thin-walled structures (Martlew 1982, 265).

The variables which are available from the majority of atlantic roundhouse sites comprise only diameter and wall thickness. For the reasons described in previous chapters, the specific architectural features of broch architecture are not preserved or visible on the vast majority of sites, but the cumulative evidence of excavation suggests that they were originally very widespread. It would not be a particularly meaningful exercise to restrict analysis to the few known broch towers or to the complex roundhouses alone.

The purpose of this section is to assess the validity of the atlantic roundhouse class as a device to embrace the range of structures divided by previous typologies. A range of simple analyses on the basis of surface morphology and excavated evidence can provide an indication as to whether the previous architectural typological groupings can be observed within the atlantic roundhouse class. The tests have been selected to provide information on the size range and available living space of the structures and to indicate the degree of monumentality insofar as this can be interpreted from field evidence. Cluster analysis, such as that employed by Martlew, has been avoided since both the variables involved and the number of sites are relatively few and easily assessed in univariate analysis. It is potentially misleading to combine variables when the problems and inadequacies of each set of data on individual variables demand cautious treatment.

The sites selected for study are the atlantic roundhouses of North Uist and Barra. These islands are the only two where sufficient fieldwork has been carried out to give reasonable confidence that the great majority of sites have been located. The database for these islands is less open to distortion than those of other islands, such as South Uist, Benbecula and Lewis, where data gathering has been sporadic and restricted. The use of North Uist and Barra will also allow easier comparison of the results with the locational and spatial analysis of Chapter Twelve which, for the same reasons, is restricted to these two islands.

Atlantic Roundhouses (N.Uist and Barra)
External Diameter

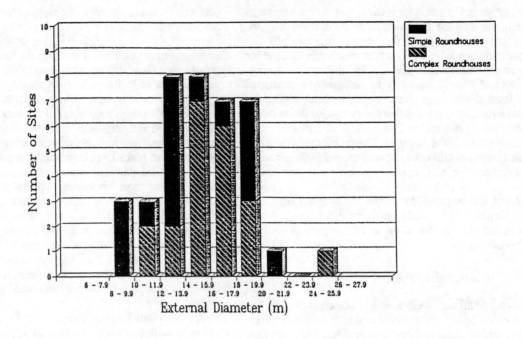

Ill. 11.1 Atlantic Roundhouses (North Uist and Barra): External Diameter

Atlantic Roundhouses (N.Uist and Barra)
Internal Area

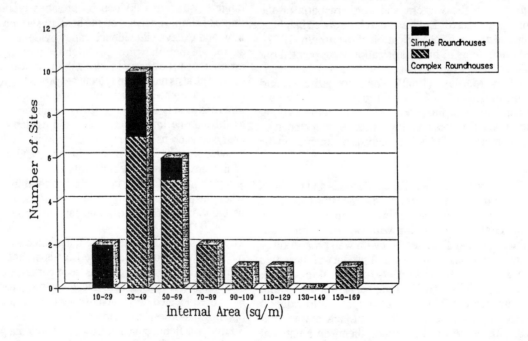

Ill. 11.2 Atlantic Roundhouses (North Uist and Barra): Internal Area

The unity of atlantic roundhouses can be assessed through the analysis of the following variables:

1. external diameter
2. internal diameter and area
3. wall base % (percentage of the overall diameter constituted by the walls)

Other variables could be suggested. A basic one, as mentioned above, is height, which would clearly relate to function and degree of monumentality. Unfortunately, as has been indicated in previous chapters, there is insufficient evidence from either field survey or excavation to make this possible. Other variables would comprise the presence or absence of particular architectural features but again these are not generally observable in the field.

The measurements used below are based on the main central cells of the structures and do not include the size of galleries and cells in calculations of internal area. In many cases, where structures are not completely circular, the mean diameter has been taken. Martlew stresses the potential importance of circularity as a defining characteristic of *brochs* although acknowledging the constraints of location (1982, 272). In the Western Isles, where so many atlantic roundhouses are built on islets, the constraints on shape are very great. It would be difficult to argue that absolute circularity is a particularly helpful guide to classification. It would, however, affect the structural stability of the roundhouses and their potential degree of monumentality through height, so any great divergence from circularity should be noted. Of the 38 atlantic roundhouses in North Uist and Barra, for which measurements are possible, the maximum divergence of the major and minor external axes is 6m at Dun na Dise, North Uist (A.NU41) (although this figure may be distorted - see below).

The following sections will firstly discuss the selected variables before examining the overall implications of the analysis for the atlantic roundhouse class in the Western Isles. In many cases the measurements of certain variables are somewhat approximate due to the distortions imposed by partial collapse and the variable quality of recording.

External Diameter

External diameter is in many cases the only structural variable which can be measured from the field evidence. It has been used here to demonstrate broad size range for a relatively large sample of sites from North Uist and Barra. Illustration 11.1 shows the external diameters of the atlantic roundhouses from these two islands in the form of a stacked bar graph. Where structures diverge from true circularity the mean external diameter has been taken. The question of divergence from circularity is considered separately below. An immediately striking feature is the very wide absolute range of the diameters from 9m, at Eilean Scalaster (A.NU44) and Dun Ban Hacklett (A.NU45), to 24m at Rudh an Duin (A.NU3), all in North Uist. The distribution is a normal one with a mean of 15.6m for Barra and 14.6m for North Uist (14.9m overall mean).

The simple roundhouses show a distribution of external diameter which appears to diverge from the normal distribution of the overall atlantic roundhouse population. There appear to be concentrations of simple structures between 8 - 9.9m, 12 - 13.9m and 18 - 19.9m. The small absolute number of sites for which external diameters can be recorded, however, prevents any very secure conclusions being drawn on the significance of this feature. A further complication is that all the simple roundhouse sites are unexcavated and their measurements are often based on early descriptions expressed in imperial units. The conversion of imperial to metric measurements may lend a spurious sense of precision to approximations in the original data and cause clusters around certain measurements. Cnoc a Comhdhalach (A.NU14) and Dun Loch Hunder (A.NU35) are both complex roundhouses, possibly broch towers, and both also fall into the 10 - 11.9m range, as does the excavated complex roundhouse of Dun Bharabhat in Lewis (A.L18) (not included in Ill. 11.1). There is no indication of a size range difference between the complex roundhouses and the other roundhouses in these islands on the basis of external diameter. Instead the most striking impression is of the great range within the class of atlantic roundhouses as a whole, whether complex roundhouses alone, or the whole class together, are considered.

Internal Area

Only 23 sites have available measurements of internal diameter, enabling the calculation of approximate internal areas, compared to 38 sites for which external diameters are available. Of these 23 sites 17 are definitely complex roundhouses, for it is mainly the excavated or very well preserved sites for which measurements are available, i.e. precisely those sites where there is also good preservation of architectural detail. The comparisons here between complex and simple roundhouses mean very little due to this basic problem of data recovery.

Internal area was calculated by the use of mean internal diameter and an assumption of general circularity (Ill. 11.2). Clearly this is a somewhat crude index of actual internal area but it does give the approximate order of size range and available internal space. On the basis of this calculation, a mean internal area of $58.2m^2$ was derived for the atlantic roundhouses of North Uist and Barra.

The comparison of complex and simple roundhouses is of very limited value: the apparent concentration of simple roundhouses at the lower end of the scale of internal area, although overlapping the complex roundhouse range, cannot be used to support a division of the two classes. The larger structures were more likely to attract excavation until recent years, being more visually impressive and more immediately of interest to the early antiquarian workers. The larger sites, therefore, have produced a greater degree of architectural information. There will thus be a tendency for the larger sites to exhibit a greater degree of architectural complexity, even if all of the sites were originally of similar construction.

The measurements are useful in highlighting the differences in scale within the complex roundhouse class. This difference in available space within the structures is of a different order to that of external diameter and reinforces the range and variety within a class united by common architectural traits. While, in terms of external diameter, the largest atlantic roundhouse is some 2.6 times as large as the smallest, this compares to a difference of c. 154m^2 for Rudh an Duin (A.NU3), to c. 15m^2 for Eilean Scalaster (A.NU44), both in North Uist. The smallest complex roundhouse, in terms of internal area, is Dun Loch Hunder, North Uist (A.NU35), at c. 33m^2. This means that even between two complex roundhouses in North Uist, both of which may well have been broch towers, there is a difference of the order of 466% in internal floor space. This presents a strong argument against interpretations of origins and function of broch architecture which depend on the uniformity of the class. It suggests that the interpretation of the function of broch architecture, as one element in the settlement, must recognise great differences in scale between the sites on which it is used.

One major difficulty in the interpretation of internal area variability is the question of multiple floor levels. It is quite clear from many of the excavated sites, from the Western Isles and elsewhere, that a large proportion, if not all, complex roundhouses would have been multi-storey structures. The whole architectural design of the type lends itself to the creation of super-imposed floors. Specialised architectural features, such as scarcements and upper gallery entrances, allow the positions of upper floors occasionally to be observed (as at Loch na Berie, see Chapter Five). What is entirely unknown is the function of these upper levels since, being necessarily of timber construction, none survives. The only possibility for survival lies in the waterlogged sites where collapsed upper floors may be preserved. Such circumstances are rare, with Loch na Berie being currently the most likely candidate. Even if such survival occurs, however, the chances of finding secure indications of function remain remote. At present it is impossible to determine whether these upper floor levels were used for domestic habitation, storage or any other of a range of possible functions. Without this information comparisons of internal diameter must be treated with caution. The vertical division of living areas, however, would represent a significant difference in the disposition of domestic space within a structure and does not undermine the range and variety within the complex roundhouse class which these comparisons suggest. Even if Dun Loch Hunder had had five storeys of domestic habitation, and Rudh an Duin only one, the latter site would still have contained a larger available area of living space (assuming a wall batter on upper storeys which would progressively reduce available space in upper floors). The larger sites, and especially Rudh an Duin and Dun an Sticer, may well be exceptional within their local contexts and this possibility and its implications will be considered further in subsequent chapters.

Wall Base Percentage

The wall base percentage represents the proportion of overall mean diameter formed by the walls at their base (Ill. 11.3). Measurements are again only approximate since it is seldom possible to measure walls at the base due to rubble accumulations and, since the walls tend to narrow as they rise, only limited accuracy will be possible. Nonetheless crude comparisons are possible between the complex and simple roundhouses, and between the Western Isles roundhouses and those of other areas.

The use of this variable is taken to provide a crude index of 'massiveness' or potential for height and monumentality. The greater the wall base percentage the greater would be the potential stable height of the structure, assuming overall circularity. The non-circular atlantic roundhouses, where divergence from the maximum to minimum diameters exceeds 1m, are particularly important in this context. To achieve a similar degree of monumentality these structures would require particularly massive wall bases to counteract the instability generated by an irregular base.

In absolute terms the wall base percentage, for atlantic roundhouses as a whole, ranges from 34%, at Dun Nighean Righ Lochlain (A.NU21), Dun an Sticer (A.NU1) and Dun Torcuill (A.NU19), to 62.4% at Dun na Mairbhe (A.NU15), the latter lacking visible evidence of galleries. The complex roundhouses range from 34% at Dun Torcuill (A.NU19) to 56.3% at Bal na Craig (A.B11).

The range of wall base percentage shows no apparent difference between the complex and simple roundhouses, reaffirming the picture derived from external diameter, and more cautiously inferred from the internal areas.

The fact that measurements are possible from some of the simple roundhouses may suggest that they are preserved sufficiently well to indicate that they were genuine solid-walled structures. Six sites come under consideration here, all in North Uist; Eilean a Ghallain (A.NU6), Dun Grogarry (A.NU24), Dun Mhic Rhaouill (A.NU26), Eilean Scalaster (A.NU44), Dun Nighean Righ Lochlainn (A.NU21) and Dun na Mairbhe (A.NU15). Of these only one, Dun Nighean Righ Lochlainn, can be reasonably cited as evidence of the existence of simple solid-walled roundhouses in the sample. Of the others, Eilean a Ghallain was excavated by means of a central pit, as described in Chapter Five, and the nature of the walls remains entirely unknown; Dun Grogarry and Dun na Mairbhe are represented only by grassy, robbed-out mounds with occasional facing stones of the inner and outer wall faces; the remaining sites, Eilean Scalaster and Dun Mhic Rhaouill, were originally described by Beveridge, who did not describe or investigate the nature of the walls, and they cannot now be independently examined. Dun Nighean Righ Lochlainn was described in some detail by the Royal Commission, and it does appear to have been solid walled, although the much-disturbed interior could obscure an inner wall.

Further analyses have been carried out on the relationships of wall base % to mean external diameter and internal area (Armit 1990f, Chapter 11). These again showed no difference between the complex roundhouses and those where no complexity has been recorded.

Circularity

The three structures in the sample with the greatest divergence from circularity are all demonstrably galleried structures and therefore complex roundhouses. The greatest divergence from circularity occurs at Dun na Dise, North Uist (A.NU41) where the major and minor axes are 20m and 14m respectively. These measurements may, however, be distorted by the collapse around the eroding edge of the islet on which the structure sits. The problems at this site highlight the dangers of placing too much weight on circularity as a definitive characteristic of architectural complexity and of placing too much reliance on structural data from sites in widely varying states of preservation.

Dun Chlif (A.B3) and Dun Scurrival (A.B2), both in Barra, have major and minor axes diverging by 4m in each case. Dun Chlif appears to have been built to a non-circular plan because of the restrictions imposed by a cramped outcrop island location. In the case of Dun Scurrival the irregularity may relate to secondary modification or the desire to maximise the occupied area of the flat hill-top on which it is located. The reasons for non-circularity may vary from site to site and it appears that all of these sites have more in common, structurally, with the circular complex roundhouses than they do with each other.

Atlantic Roundhouse Function and Variation

The simple analyses carried out above have a number of implications for our interpretation of the function of atlantic roundhouses in the Western Isles. The wide range of variation reflects differences in the scale of construction of these structures. The capacity for accommodation of people was highly variable within both the complex and simple atlantic roundhouses. Whether this indicates that accommodation was intended for varying population sizes, or whether space was used differently and involved a different range of functions on different sites, will be considered in subsequent chapters. Theories based on the unity of scale and construction of the *brochs* as a class cannot be maintained in view of the wide variability in scale in the Western Isles.

Attempts to isolate the complex roundhouse class by structural features have proved impossible. The variable most likely to differentiate a *broch* class would initially appear to be wall base percentage, since this most directly reflects potential height and is thus an index of the degree of monumentality. Instead this variable demonstrates almost exact correspondence between the simple and complex roundhouses. The external diameter of the two sub-groups covers a similar range, again indicating a correspondence in scale of construction. Only internal area seems to differentiate the two sub-groups, with the simple roundhouses clustering at the lower end of the scale. The sampling problems discussed above, however, negate this result, as does the inferential evidence of scale from the external diameters of sites where the internal area is currently unknown.

Overall the analyses indicate a wide variation in the scale of construction but give no evidence for a differentiation between the structures where complex architectural features are visible and those where they are not. This supports the arguments advanced in previous chapters for the artificiality of the *broch/dun* division in the Western

Isles and supports the atlantic roundhouse classification.

The analyses conducted here have some effects on the interpretation of regional variation proposed by MacKie (1965). The Western Isles wall base percentage range overlaps with the Shetland site range with the inclusion of Dun na Mairbhe. The Western Isles complex roundhouse wall base percentage mean is also boosted by the inclusion of Bal na Craig (A.B11), data which was unavailable to MacKie. The inclusion of the greater number of sites brought about by the abandonment of the very strict *broch* definition tends to mask some of MacKie's distinctions. Dun Torcuill (A.NU19), however, has the lowest wall base percentage for the Western Isles in both MacKie's and the present analyses.

Wall base percentage remains low overall for the Western Isles: 13 sites are below 50%, compared to only 2 over 50%, for Western Isles complex roundhouses. This compares to 5 below 50% and 12 greater than 50% for the Shetland *brochs*, on the basis of MacKie's figures (1965, 105). Even allowing for the different criteria applied to site selection this appears to imply distinctly local concentrations of structural traits.

Wheelhouses

No detailed structural analysis has been carried out on the wheelhouses of the Western Isles or elsewhere. Several variables can be usefully considered to identify consistency and variability in the class and to compare aspects of their structure with the atlantic roundhouses. The relationship of sand-revetted to free-standing wheelhouses can be considered in terms of some of these variables. The relationship of wheelhouses with bonded piers to those with unbonded piers cannot be assessed, since only Bac Mhic Connain and Foshigarry A have bonded piers and the latter has insufficient structural data for incorporation into most of the analyses below.

The variables for consideration are:

1. internal diameter and area
2. central area diameter
3. number of piers

External diameter is not generally applicable for this class which are, in almost all cases, revetted into sand hills or earlier structures. As in the case of the atlantic roundhouses the measurements are taken on the basis of the central domestic unit in cases where galleries, souterrains or cells are attached to main structure.

Internal Area

Illustration 11.4 shows the range of internal areas of 18 of the Western Isles wheelhouses, where internal diameter is known. The mean internal area of this group is $63.0m^2$ compared to $58.2m^2$ for the atlantic roundhouses of North Uist and Barra. This represents a considerable measure of correspondence in scale, although one should not overlook the great range of variation, particularly within the atlantic roundhouse class. The wheelhouses have a lesser range of variation in internal area than the atlantic roundhouses. Their closer correspondence in scale mirrors the very regular architecture of the

Atlantic Roundhouses (N.Uist and Barra)
Wall Base %

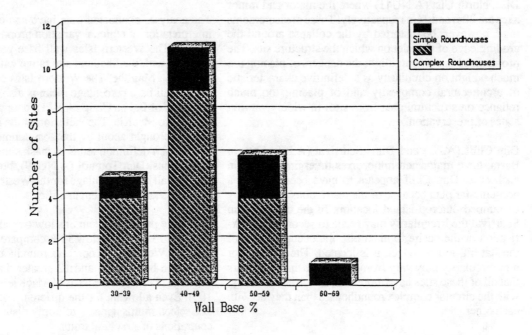

Ill. 11.3 Atlantic Roundhouses (North Uist and Barra): Wall Base %

Wheelhouses (Western Isles)
Internal Area

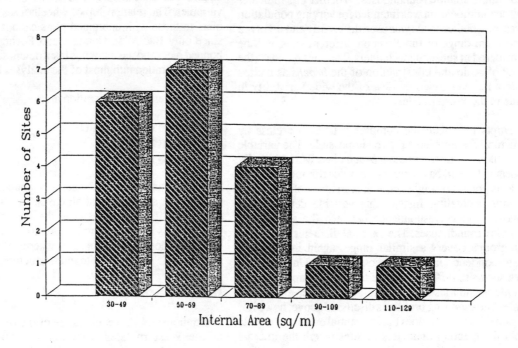

Ill. 11.4 Wheelhouses (Western Isles): Internal Area

class. Sollas is the largest example, with an internal area of 113m^2 compared to Cnip 1 and Cnoc a Comhdhalach with internal areas of approximately 38.5m^2. This is an order of difference of approximately 295% compared to c. 466% for the atlantic roundhouses.

Comparison of internal areas of the wheelhouses and the atlantic roundhouses is clearly very hazardous. As well as the presence of additional floors in the atlantic round-houses, a further problem in comparability comes from our lack of knowledge of the function of the main cells relative to the settlement as a whole, in either class of structure. The recurrence of a dominant central cell in both classes, with peripheral galleries or cells, suggests that the main cells may have played a similar domestic role, but this is still far from proven. All that can be said is that if the focal cells of the two types played this similar role as domestic focus, then the two types of structure are directly comparable in scale and share a wide range of variation from the mean internal area.

Number of Piers

In absolute terms the number of piers ranges from seven to twelve and seems to be related principally to the requirements of roof support. The larger wheelhouses required more piers for increased stability of the stone corbelled cells. The size of cells therefore, and spacing of piers, stayed relatively constant with increased size of the wheelhouse internal area.

Analysis conducted in the original study (Armit 1990f, Ill. 11.9) shows that the number of piers rises with increasing internal area. This is entirely as one would expect from a structural point of view, in order to preserve stability with increasing size. There is no difference in this trend between the sand-revetted and free-standing examples, although the free-standing wheelhouses, as a group, tend to be smaller and therefore have fewer piers than the sand-revetted examples. This may indicate that the sand-dune environment was more conducive to the development of this form of architecture than the non-machair areas, with the free-standing, non-machair wheelhouses being outliers of the group in at least a geographical sense.

Central Area Diameter

The generally smaller size of the free-standing relative to sand-revetted wheelhouses was demonstrated by analysis of the central area diameters (Armit 1990f, Ill. 11.10).

Wheelhouse Function and Variation

Overall the wheelhouses are remarkably constant in proportion and design. This is presumably because, as discussed in Chapter Six, so much of wheelhouse structure is determined by the necessarily strict imposition of a rigidly prescribed architectural form.

One notable feature of the original analyses is the clustering of the free-standing wheelhouses at the lower end of the size range (Armit 1990f). There are two alternative explanations for this if we assume it to be a genuine reflection of the original range of sites. Free-standing wheelhouses may be smaller because they are in less

amenable areas for construction, the absence of the sand-hill environment affecting the potential for stability of a large structure. It may alternatively be the case that the free-standing sites, situated principally on the inland areas of the islands, are in areas marginal to the economies of the wheelhouse-builders and thus are smaller as a reflection of smaller population group, less access to labour and/or lower status.

The other principal feature to emerge from the analyses was the correspondence in scale, of available internal space, between the wheelhouses and the atlantic round-houses. The interpretation of this close correspondence must be accompanied by qualifications based on the potential lack of comparability of the two forms, especially in the potential of the atlantic roundhouses to have additional floor levels. Nonetheless the similarity, in the size of what presumably was the principal domestic space, is striking.

Cellular Structures and Linear House Structures

The irregularity of the cellular structures prevents meaningful comparison with the wheelhouses and atlantic roundhouses in most of the forms of analysis above. This limitation in itself highlights the distinctiveness of the type from the foregoing forms. In very few cases is there sufficiently detailed information available to reconstruct internal area. Other variables comparable with those above are not available.

The internal area of the cellular structures is presented for the principal cells of certain sites where measurements can be made (Ill. 11.5). This is obviously somewhat unsatisfactory given that the very nature of cellular structures will tend to give less emphasis to the central area which is much more clearly defined by the architecture of an atlantic roundhouse or wheelhouse. The poor quality of the database restricts the calculation of internal area to only three sites: Dun Cuier (A.B4), Berie Structure 1 (A.L19) and Dun Bharabhat (A.L18). Other sites are excluded from this discussion through the incomplete available plans (e.g. A' Cheardach Mhor), the lack of accurately drawn published plans (e.g. the Udal) or the lack of evidence to suggest that the principal cell, or cells, of a cellular complex had been excavated. The two linear house structures are included for comparison with the cellular structures in terms of their internal area.

The very small sample prevents any meaningful conclusions being drawn from this exercise except to note that the scale of the structures is generally very small compared to the atlantic roundhouses and wheelhouses. The cellular structures cluster at the low end of the internal size range for these other two forms. The two linear house structures have two of the lowest three internal areas for any structures considered in this chapter (the other being the North Uist atlantic roundhouse, Eilean Scalaster (A.NU44)).

Summary

The principal features to emerge from the structural analysis of the atlantic roundhouses and wheelhouses of the Western Isles can be summarised as follows:

Cellular and Linear House Structures
Internal Area

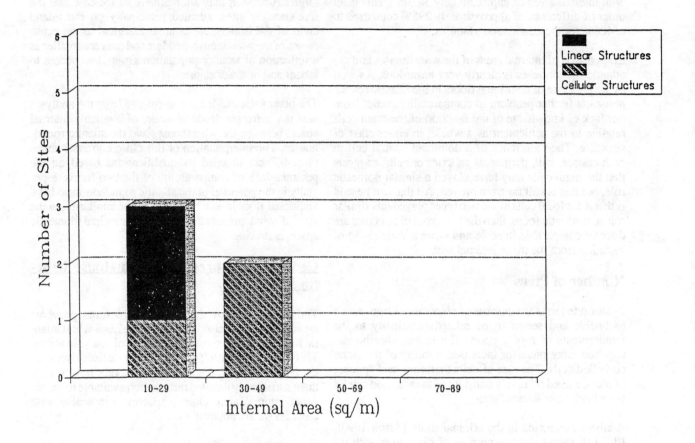

Ill. 11.5 Cellular Structures and Linear House Structures: Internal Area

1. The structural analysis of the atlantic roundhouses gives no support to the subdivision of the class into separate *broch* and *dun* classes with its consequent implications for function and date. Instead an overall unity is implied albeit encompassing a very wide range of scale.

2. The structural analysis does lend support to the unity of the Western Isles atlantic roundhouse class as a group, distinct from other regional groups, in particular those of the Northern Isles. It should be remembered however that the methods of site selection differ in each case and this will affect the reliability of the comparison. In addition to this it should be stressed that the introduction of sites other than MacKie's *brochs* tends to erode the differences rather than strengthen them.

3. Close structural relationships are demonstrated within the wheelhouse class for the Western Isles. This is to be expected from the rigid architectural conformity dictated by the construction method.

4. Within the wheelhouse class the free-standing examples, essentially those outwith the machair environment, tend to be the smallest in the group. This implies a distinction which may be based either on simple factors of construction difficulty or on more complex social and economic factors.

5. The wheelhouses and atlantic roundhouses demonstrate a close correspondence in terms of the scale of living space they provide, if the fundamental assumption is made that the ground floor central cells provide the principal living space in each case.

6. The cellular and linear house structures are significantly smaller, as a group, in terms of the internal space they provide for domestic purposes. This may be the result of the fragmentation of the settlement at these sites into cells which take on functions combined in one cell on the atlantic roundhouse and wheelhouse sites. In any case it implies a different orgainsation of settlement space and one which may represent a smaller population group on the level of the individual site.

Chapter Twelve - Locational and Spatial Analysis

Introduction: Previous Applications in Atlantic Scotland

The stone-built structures of Atlantic Scotland have attracted several researchers in the field of locational and spatial analysis. Martlew went so far as to claim that the *brochs* may be the 'only prehistoric settlement distribution suitable for detailed spatial analysis' (1981, 16). The neolithic funerary monuments of the area have also witnessed similar study in recent years involving similar methods and assumptions. The principal feature which has led to a concentration of spatial studies in this area is the excellent survival of the massive stone structures. These combine an original massive scale of construction with a relative absence of destructive later land-use. The completeness of distribution relative to much of the rest of British prehistoric archaeology makes the monuments of the area particularly suitable for work of this kind.

The first of the recent analyses of the Atlantic Scottish sites relevant to this discussion was a study of the social organisation of Iron Age Caithness through the assessment of land carrying capacity relative to site distributions (Heisler 1977). This approach will be assessed below in the light of the data from North Uist and Barra. Martlew, in 1981, used the Caithness *brochs* as a case study in the evaluation of a series of locational and spatial techniques. Noel Fojut's study of the 'geography' of the Shetland *brochs* applied a similar range of techniques in an attempt to elucidate the decisions made by their builders in the process of site location (Fojut 1982).

Recently published research on the Atlantic Scottish Iron Age has tended to move away from inter-site spatial and locational analysis to focus on the intra-site level. Reid (1989) and Foster (1989) have both focused on the spatial configurations of sites in an attempt to derive information on social organisation and change. These approaches have been examined elsewhere (Armit 1990f).

Applicability in the Western Isles

The Western Isles, at first glance, seem a promising area for locational and spatial analysis. The advantages of island groups in spatial studies, as self-defining bounded landscape units, has long been recognised (e.g. Fojut 1982, 38). This boundedness, however, brings problems with particular spatial techniques, e.g. nearest neighbour analysis (used in the original study, Armit 1990f). The quality of site survival in the Western Isles also suggests that the results may be more meaningful in terms of the later prehistoric settlement patterns than in other areas.

The completeness of distribution in the Western Isles is most prone to attrition through the following factors;

1. Subsequent Settlement

2. Stone-Robbing

3. Peat Growth

4. Machair Movement

5. Coastal Erosion

6. Misidentification

Each of these potential causes of bias in the site distributions will be assessed below where relevant to the specific cases examined. On the whole, however, the quality of site survival is very good. This quality of survival is a necessary precondition if detailed analysis of site/landscape and inter-site relationships is to be attempted.

A series of questions can be addressed through locational and spatial analysis in the Western Isles. One is the relationship between monumental and non-monumental structures. The distributional factors which distinguish the atlantic roundhouses from the miscellaneous structures and walled islets on the one hand and the wheelhouses on the other, are potentially significant for the interpretation of the phenomenon of monumental construction in the later prehistoric period. The relationship between the complex and simple atlantic roundhouses can also be addressed by these means.

Overall there are two principal underlying aims in the present chapter;

1. the definition of environmental factors affecting the siting of settlement.

2. the definition of differential locational and spatial factors between different site types which may shed light on the different relationships of sites to their environment and to each other.

The atlantic roundhouses of North Uist and Barra are the best preserved populations of later prehistoric monuments in the Western Isles for reasons outlined in Chapter Eleven. These structures have, therefore, been used in the analysis of the atlantic roundhouses. The distribution and survival of monuments on North Uist also enables the analysis of the relationship between the atlantic roundhouses and the miscellaneous structures and walled islets on the island.

The wheelhouses of Vallay constitute a sample of sites from an almost uniquely intensively studied area. Although unsatisfactory in not including any upland wheelhouses, this area is the only one in which locational and spatial analysis of a wheelhouse distribution is possible. There is no equivalent group of cellular or linear house structures or promontory forts with which to conduct such analyses, so this chapter is principally restricted to the groups of sites mentioned above.

It is necessary to assume for the purposes of the present chapter, that the sites within a given class (with the exception of the miscellaneous structures) were in occupation contemporaneously. The durability of the structures concerned, and the labour investment in their construction, argues for prolonged usage. The dating evidence, albeit principally from outwith the Western Isles (Armit 1991), also suggests that we may be justified in seeing the majority of sites within a class, as overlapping in their periods of occupation. The degree of landscape organisation demonstrated below, and the evidence cited in previous chapters for the long duration of settlement foci, combine to support the validity of this assumption.

Site/Landscape Relationships

General Distribution - North Uist

The distribution of atlantic roundhouses in North Uist is shown in Ill. 12.1. The open circles represent sites which are either imprecisely located or which cannot be positively identified as atlantic roundhouses rather than other forms of massive stone structure. The present inter-tidal sands are indicated as shaded areas which would probably have been dry machair in the later prehistoric period. The 60m contour is indicated.

Of the factors which may be expected to distort the original distribution pattern of the atlantic roundhouses in North Uist, the most significant are likely to have been stone-robbing and coastal change (both machair redeposition and tidal erosion). The first of these has been discussed above and is not considered to constitute a serious problem. The massive construction of the structures makes total removal difficult, while the common location on knolls and islets makes the identification of even very robbed-out structures possible. In addition, the preservation of local memory through place-name evidence can provide clues to 'missing' sites. Coastal change is a more serious problem. The redeposition of the machair sands may conceal atlantic roundhouses sites but, if so, it is very surprising that none has been found in an eroding machair context as is the case with the majority of wheelhouse sites. This constitutes strong circumstantial evidence for the lack of impact of sand movement on the atlantic roundhouse distribution. Overall, there appears to be a strong case to suggest that the atlantic roundhouse distribution is a relatively good representation of the original later prehistoric distribution.

A number of features of site location are observable from initial examination of the distribution of sites in North Uist. The atlantic roundhouses show a series of locational tendencies, some of which will be examined further below. There is a clear coastal distribution with almost no sites on the central spine of the island, and a total avoidance of the eastern low-lying interior with its maze of lochs. The high ground of the island is avoided, with only one site lying above the 60m contour (this site being a dubious example, South Clettraval (A.NU25)).

The roundhouses show a general linear spread of distribution along the north coast from Portain to the Valley Strand. A cluster of sites occupies the Hougharry/Tigharry area, north of a gap in the distribution, in the area around Kirkibost. From Baleshare to Eaval in the east is a further string of coastally located sites. The atlantic roundhouses occupy the majority of the historically inhabited areas of North Uist with the notable exception of Lochmaddy. This east coast township occupies an area where there is little evidence of any later prehistoric settlement, on a rocky coastline fringing areas of blanket peat-bog.

The distribution of complex roundhouses in North Uist is an instructive one and sheds some further light on the relationship between simple and complex roundhouses discussed in Chapters Five and Eleven. The greatest density of complex sites lies on the Valley Strand and all five were excavated by Beveridge. Of the remaining five sites, three are the best three preserved atlantic roundhouses in the island (Dun an Sticer (A.NU1), Dun Torcuill (A.NU19) and Dun Loch Hunder (A.NU35)): only two sites of the general, unexcavated, poorly preserved atlantic roundhouse distribution have evidence of intramural galleries. The implication is that complex architectural features are found where circumstances allow, and it would be unwise to assume that these circumstances have fortuitously produced the original distribution of complex roundhouse sites. Had Beveridge built his house on Baleshare instead of Vallay, our picture of North Uist complex roundhouse (and for that matter wheelhouse) distribution might be very different.

The comparison of the distributions of the miscellaneous structures, walled islets and promontory forts with that of the atlantic roundhouses reveals an interesting series of dissimilarities (Ill. 12.2). For large areas of the island the distributions of the miscellaneous structures and walled islets on the one hand, and the atlantic roundhouses on the other, appear to be complementary. There is a general spread of the former sites along the north coast, but these appear to be further from the coast than the atlantic roundhouses. The area around Hougharry and Tigharry, where the atlantic roundhouses have a dense distribution, has only one miscellaneous structure. A cluster of both miscellaneous structures and walled islets on Baleshare is in an area of roundhouse settlement, but from there eastwards the distribution is again in non-roundhouse, inland areas. The most noticeable difference is the density of both miscellaneous structures and walled islets in the eastern low-lying area around and to the west of Lochmaddy, in an area totally avoided by the atlantic roundhouses.

There are two major implications of these distributional differences. The first is that the absence of atlantic roundhouses in the inland and eastern areas does not appear to be the result of a lack of fieldwork and there does seem to be a genuine avoidance of these areas: this gives more weight to the use of the observed distribution pattern of the atlantic roundhouses. The second is that the miscellaneous structures and walled islets appear to avoid the best land in the island, that inhabited and intensively exploited in the historical period. This could be due to either an original genuine avoidance of these areas, if for example they were occupied at that period by the atlantic roundhouses, or to a lack of survival in these areas.

With only two promontory forts in North Uist it is difficult to comment meaningfully on distribution patterns. Both are coastal and lie within the atlantic roundhouse occupied areas. This adds little, however, to our knowledge of the relationship between the classes.

Ill. 12.3 shows the distribution of wheelhouses in the Valley Strand hydrological catchment area. The approximate boundary of the catchment is indicated on the distribution map. The site of Sithean Mor has been included on the map as it comprises a substantial machair

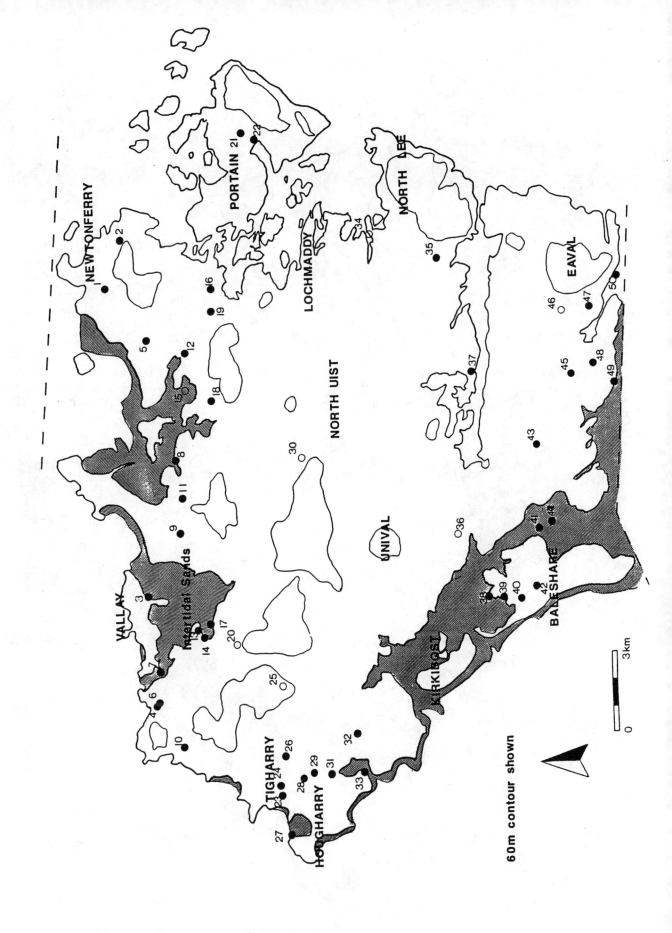

Ill. 12.1 Distribution of Atlantic Roundhouses in North Uist

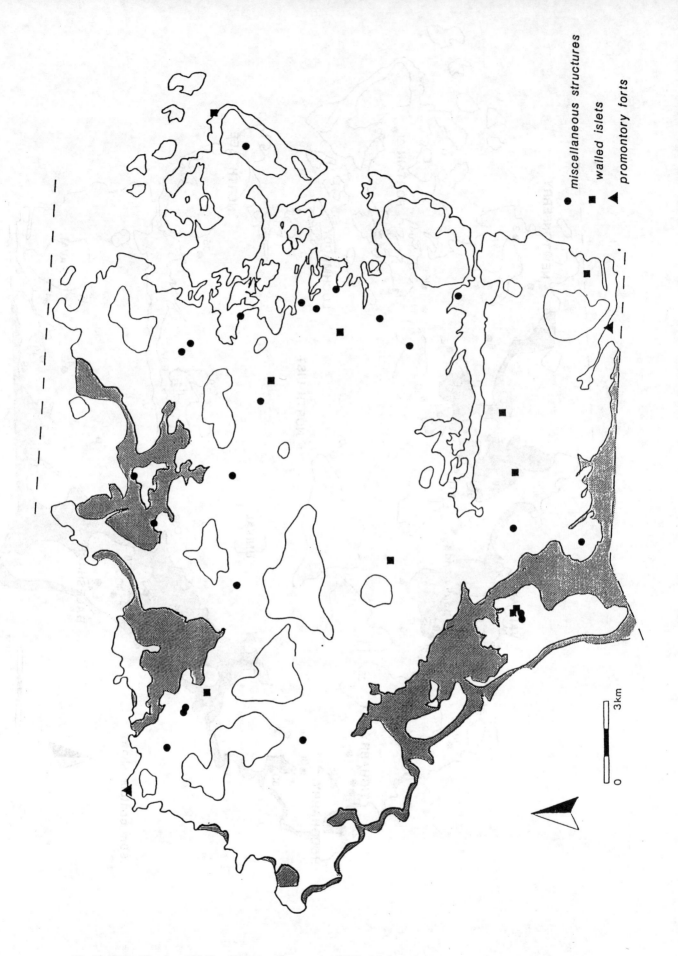

Ill. 12.2 Distribution of Miscellaneous Structures, Walled Islets and Promontory Forts in North Uist

mound with some stonework and may well be a wheelhouse site: its structural remains were not sufficiently diagnostic for inclusion in the catalogue. With only seven definite sites and one possible example it is dangerous to draw too many conclusions from the observed distribution, especially since the inland wheelhouses (such as Clettraval (W.11) and Tigh Talhamanta, Allasdale (W.25)) are not known to occur in the catchment. Nonetheless some general points can be made.

There is a tendency for siting on the modern high water mark, which is likely to have equated to the periphery of the later prehistoric machair plain. Beveridge's thorough exploration of the archaeology of this catchment has meant that there is a reasonable probability that all of the wheelhouse sites are known and represented on the map: it is therefore a distribution comparable to that of the atlantic roundhouses in terms of completeness. In Ill. 12.4 the wheelhouse distribution is overlain by that of the atlantic roundhouses present in the same hydrological catchment. The numbers and siting of the two types of monument are strikingly similar. Four of the atlantic roundhouse sites, including one dubious example, lie further inland than the wheelhouse distribution but the difference is marginal. The implications of the distributions within the Valley catchment will be discussed in subsequent sections of this chapter.

The factors liable to distort settlement distributions are more serious in relation to the wheelhouses than to the atlantic roundhouses. As well as stone-robbing, there is the problem of sand cover wholly obscuring the sites. This is very clearly the case in a number of excavated sites revealed only by subsequent erosion (e.g. Cnip (W.1)). Misidentification is also a serious problem since the diagnostic traits of wheelhouse architecture are rarely visible without excavation. It is only the uniquely thoroughly excavated nature of the Valley sites which permits locational and spatial analysis of any sort. The problems of submersion and coastal erosion, too, introduce difficulties: the wheelhouses at Foshigarry, for example, have entirely disappeared through coastal erosion since 1900. Other sites may have been similarly destroyed. Only the coherence of the distribution can be advanced as a reassuring feature but this may be misleading. These problems should be borne in mind in subsequent analyses.

General Distribution - Barra

The distribution of atlantic roundhouses in Barra (with the adjacent islands of Fuday and Vatersay) is shown in Ill. 12.5. The completeness of distribution and the effect of the various potential sources of distortion are much the same for the Barra roundhouses as for those of North Uist. With the exception of the Eoligarry area there is little sign of substantial coastal change in Barra, or its nearby islands, and the coastline appears substantially as it would have been in the later prehistoric period.

The distribution of atlantic roundhouses appears to be relatively well-preserved and largely unaffected by the most destructive forms of natural distortion of the pattern. The principal problems relate to the site of Dun a Sleibh (A.B10) which is a site of dubious identification: the place-name on which the identification has been based in

previous sources may relate to the relatively recently located Dun a Kille (A.B9) in the same general locality.

The general distribution pattern is somewhat different from that of North Uist. There is less obvious coastal dominance in siting: instead, those sites which are near the coast tend to be actually on the coast while other sites may be well inland, insofar as this is possible on an island of Barra's size. The whole of the western side and centre of Barra are occupied by a spread of atlantic roundhouse sites. There is, as in North Uist, an avoidance of the east coast, which is significantly rockier and less hospitable than the west, and the settlement occupies broadly those areas inhabited in historical periods (with the exception of the later fishing centre of Castlebay). The higher ground, as in North Uist, tends to be avoided although the hillier nature of the island makes this less pronounced; Bal na Craig (A.B11), for example, lies above the 60m contour.

Nature of Site

The locations of the structures are markedly different in the two islands. 75% of the North Uist roundhouses are located on islets, with 25% on a variety of other locational types (data in Armit 1990f, Ill. 12.8). In Barra there is greater variety, with coastal and hilltop locations as common as islets. It is important, however, that every loch of any size in Barra does contain an atlantic roundhouse and so the concentrations on other locations may simply reflect availability. The implication is that islet locations were favoured for atlantic roundhouse settlements but that other locations where access could be controlled (e.g. hilltops and coastal promontories) were used as necessary. The avoidance of the machair is striking (5% in North Uist, 0% in Barra), especially in North Uist, with its great area of machair. This avoidance is probably to be explained in simple structural terms, i.e. that the sand environment did not provide any suitable foundation for a massive free-standing stone structure; it need not indicate a lack of exploitation of the machair by the inhabitants of these settlements.

The known wheelhouses of the Western Isles have an overwhelming concentration on machair locations (80%). Only a small number of moorland examples and one islet site are recorded and the latter is an islet in a machair area. This locational range presents a stark contrast with the atlantic roundhouses of both North Uist and Barra. In Barra the relative lack of machair makes the contrast less significant, but in North Uist it is very marked. The revetted nature of wheelhouse architecture is well-suited to the machair environment which provides sand-hills into which the structures can be set. By contrast, the massively constructed atlantic roundhouses require a relatively firm base of outcrop rock, found most easily on islets, knolls, hilltops or coastal promontories. This contrast highlights the differences between the two structural forms which appear to have developed to fill two distinct niches within the Hebridean environment.

Solid Geology

The homogeneity of the Western Isles precludes the use of this variable to assess environmental influence on site

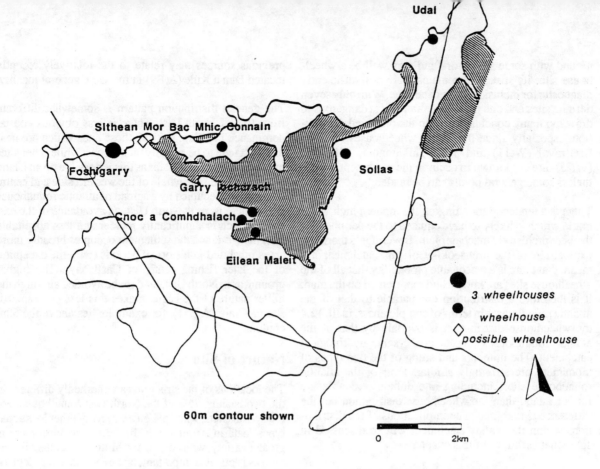

Ill. 12.3 Distribution of Wheelhouses in the Vallay Catchment, North Uist

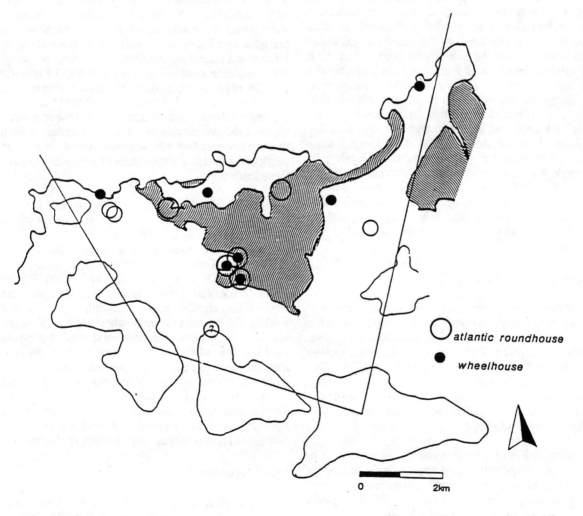

Ill. 12.4 Distribution of Wheelhouses and Atlantic Roundhouses in the Vallay Catchment, North Uist

location. The islands are formed largely of Lewisian gneiss, a stone of no particular constructional utility, with relatively insignificant occurrences of metamorphic rocks. Both Barra and North Uist are formed of this rock type with no significant areas of other formations.

Slope/Drainage

The islets and knolls upon which the atlantic roundhouses were preferentially sited render this variable largely irrelevant. Similarly the wheelhouses under consideration, being situated in the relatively flat machair environment, were all situated in well-drained sand-hills where the degree of slope was largely irrelevant.

Land Quality

The drastic changes in the soil formations of the Western Isles, in both their nature and distribution, since the later prehistoric period have been discussed in Chapter Two. Peat growth, the leaching of soils, machair development and the effects of climatic change have all contributed to the creation of a wholly distinct character for the modern Hebridean landscape. In addition to natural deterioration, which may have had anthropogenic involvement, there is extensive evidence for the reclamation of peat-covered areas in historical and early modern periods. Given this background it would be highly misleading to attempt to assess the later prehistoric settlement distributions for their relationship to land of varying quality in the area today. In the present state of knowledge there is no way to allow for the tracts of agricultural land which will have been covered over by the retreating machair, drowned by peat growth or otherwise obscured.

This discussion of general site distributions has already mentioned the broadly coastal distribution of atlantic roundhouses and wheelhouses in North Uist. It would seem likely that this would have been related to the concentration of better quality land in the coastal belt, although not necessarily the machair itself, where the high alkalinity of the soil may have made this an unfavourable choice for agriculture. Prior to the onset of peat growth on the coastal belt, the non-machair coastal fringe may have been the preferred agricultural land. Gradually, as the factors mentioned above became ever more deleterious to the farming of the inland areas, the relative importance of the machair may have increased. The miscellaneous structures and walled islets, by contrast, occur also in areas where the land quality must always have been relatively poor, on the eastern lowland areas around present-day Lochmaddy. This landscape is fragmented by hundreds of small lochs and would have suffered first from the onslaught of peatland expansion.

In Barra the high-quality land is likely to have been concentrated in the major valleys, but atlantic roundhouses also extend in their distribution into less hospitable areas around the west coast. The agricultural value of these areas in prehistory is unknown, but evidence of later cultivation is common, in the form of lazy beds.

Distance to Coast

This section follows Fojut (1982, 45) in plotting the distance to the coast of the Western Isles sites against a near-random sample of the Ordnance Survey grid intersection points for each island. Although not strictly random, these points are clearly unrelated to archaeological features and the landscape of the islands under consideration, and they form a convenient comparison with the archaeological sites.

The atlantic roundhouses of North Uist show a clear tendency to be located close to the coast. 93% of the structures lie less than 1km from the coast compared to only 56% of the random sample of points. None of the roundhouses in North Uist is more than 2km from the sea, although 24% of the random sample exceed this distance. In Barra most of the available land lies very close to the coast but still the atlantic roundhouses lie much closer on average than the random sample points (data in Armit 1990f, Ill. 12.12).

Both the miscellaneous structures and walled islets of North Uist exhibit a pattern of coastal distribution distinct from that of the roundhouses, which amplifies the initial observations made on the basis of general distributions. The walled islets have 63% at 0-1km from the coast, 27% at 1-2 and 10% at greater than 2km. The miscellaneous structures have 55% at 0-1km, 27% at 1-2 and 18% at greater than 2km. The Vallay wheelhouses are, without exception, within 1km of the coast.

Distance to Water

The growth of peat and the deposition and movement of the machair have disrupted prehistoric drainage across huge tracts of the Western Isles to such an extent that no reconstruction of distance to fresh water can realistically be attempted for the later prehistoric sites. The tendency for atlantic roundhouse sites to be situated in lochs would again seriously prejudice the study if it were possible to reconstruct the later prehistoric drainage. This siting is likely to be based on a range of factors, defensive, symbolic and psychological, and only perhaps incidentally related to the need for a convenient fresh water supply. The correlation between atlantic roundhouse sites and fresh water would therefore be likely to be significantly greater than for other types of site, without this having any necessary implication for the reasons for siting the structures.

Altitude

The original study conducted an analysis of the altitudes of the known sites against near random OS grid intersections (Armit 1990f, Ill. 12.15). There is a concentration of 75% at under 10 OD compared to only 28% of the random points in this band. Only 5% lie above 30m OD and all of these are dubious sites; this compares with 26% of the land area above 30m. In Barra the situation is less marked although there is still a concentration at the lower end of the range and few roundhouses above 70m OD relative to the random points. This appears to reflect the hilltop locations of many of the Barra sites and the general spread of sites across a greater proportion of the interior of the island than in North Uist. It suggests that altitude may be a less important factor in siting than distance to the coast, which would inevitably produce a preponderance of low-lying sites in North Uist but not

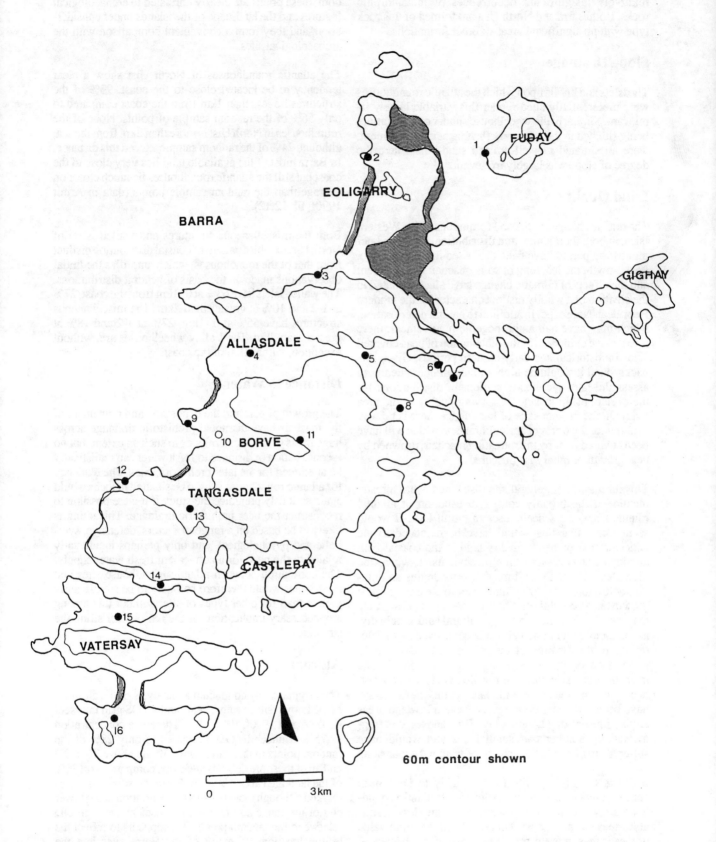

Ill. 12.5 Distribution of Atlantic Roundhouses in Barra

necessarily in Barra, where the high land is close to the coast.

The wheelhouse altitude range presents an interesting pattern of two seemingly distinct concentrations; a dominant low-lying cluster at below 20m OD and almost entirely below 10m OD, with a smaller concentration above 70m OD. It is not clear, however, that this is a representative distribution since it includes all of the known Western Isles wheelhouses which, as has been discussed, do not necessarily form a coherent sample of the original population. If we can take it as representative it would indicate a sharp division in land use between sites occupying the low-lying land, principally the machair coast, and a band of upland sites, principally on the central spines of the islands. This might indicate a division of land and resources between two contemporary groups of sites exploiting distinct aspects of the Hebridean environment.

Definition of Site Catchments

In the discussions which follow, the term site catchment will be used somewhat loosely to describe the area over which the occupants of an individual site exerted influence. The meaning of the term and its social and economic implications remain necessarily vague in the present context and the term is used primarily for convenience.

Thiessen Polygons

Thiessen polygons have been used in the past in attempts to define territories associated with individual sites. The sites are seen to act as central places with control over the surrounding area and resources based on distance, dictating ease of transport and movement. The limitations of Thiessen polygons in archaeological applications have been examined elsewhere (e.g. Martlew 1981) and will not be rehearsed in detail here. The assumption of a uniform flat plain as the setting for analysis is a particularly relevant constraint in the Highland context, however. The implication that the sites are single central places within a definable 'territory', and relate to a strata of society on a one site to one group level, is similarly dangerous in a prehistoric context. As Martlew points out (1981, 33), Thiessen polygons merely separate areas which are closer to one site than another. To progress beyond this limited piece of information we have to apply assumptions regarding the relevance of these areas to the societies under study. If we consider that distance was the principal limiting factor on the exploitation of resources then we may attribute a broad economic reality to the polygons. Similarly, ease of movement for defence rather than economic exploitation may be interpreted as a means of giving meaning to the defined area. The reintroduction and acknowledgement of a degree of subjectivity is required if Thiessen polygons are to have any validity at all in the present context.

Thiessen polygons have been plotted for the atlantic roundhouses of North Uist and Barra and for the wheelhouses of the Valley catchment. Uncertain sites have been omitted. The technique is used here essentially as a heuristic device to enable the formulation of models of site catchment.

The atlantic roundhouses of North Uist show interesting patterns when Thiessen polygons are plotted around them (Ill. 12.6). The area along the north coast from Portain to the Vallay Strand hints at a possible pattern of land organisation. Portain itself is divided into two near-equal halves by the polygons, each of the site catchments containing equivalent stretches of coast and a similar division of upland and lowland. Following the coast west from Portain the sites appear to form a linear band, all with coastal access and with the polygons defining strips of land running inland to the hills. In the Newtonferry peninsula the site catchment boundaries trace the central spine of the hills and allow broadly equivalent access to coast, machair and pasture for each site. This pattern of narrow strips of land from coast to hills is more pronounced along the middle of the north coast until it reaches the Vallay Strand, where the island of Vallay disrupts the pattern. Here sites focus on the strand itself rather than open coast, until the pattern resumes to the west.

The Hougharry/Tigharry group of sites has a less clear pattern but may represent a similar land division, as may the sites on Baleshare. The gap between these groups again appears very pronounced. The sites to the east of Baleshare appear to have larger catchments conforming less to the strip pattern and may imply a different land holding pattern in this poorer area of the island, with its irregular coast and fragmented landscape.

Overall there appears to be a pattern of relatively evenly spaced sites on the north coast, possibly reflecting a well-organised land division system with evenly divided catchments, both in size and resources. The pattern implies a use of varied resources by each settlement: coast, machair, coastal lowland and the hills to the south. The evenness of the catchments implies a broadly equal land holding for each structure and a similar economic base. Relative to other sites on the island the size of site catchments implies that this was an area under less pressure for land than elsewhere. On both Baleshare and the Hougharry/Tigharry area, site catchments are significantly smaller, although under the distortions of the polygons, a similar pattern may be hinted at (the requirement to draw the boundaries as perpendicular to the bisectors of the lines between sites will naturally distort any landscape pattern based on long, narrow strips of land).

Used heuristically, the polygon method can suggest a specific landscape division for North Uist and one which springs naturally from the resources available in the islands, which are varied but not individually rich. Historically, Hebridean populations have tended to be nonspecialist in their economic patterns, and have exploited the whole range of available resources on a seasonal basis. Although the climate and soils may have been significantly better in later prehistory there is no reason to suspect that similar wide-ranging economic systems may not have been practised. The atlantic roundhouse settlement pattern, both from general observations and with the aid of the polygons, suggests that these were sites of broadly equivalent territorial control, exploiting a wide range of resources and with minimal specialisation. Considerable variation appears even within North Uist itself, however: the eastern sites, outwith the north coastal belt, occupy larger areas but without the availability of ma-

Ill. 12.6 Thiessen Polygons: Atlantic Roundhouses in North Uist

Ill. 12.7 Thiessen Polygons: Atlantic Roundhouses in Barra

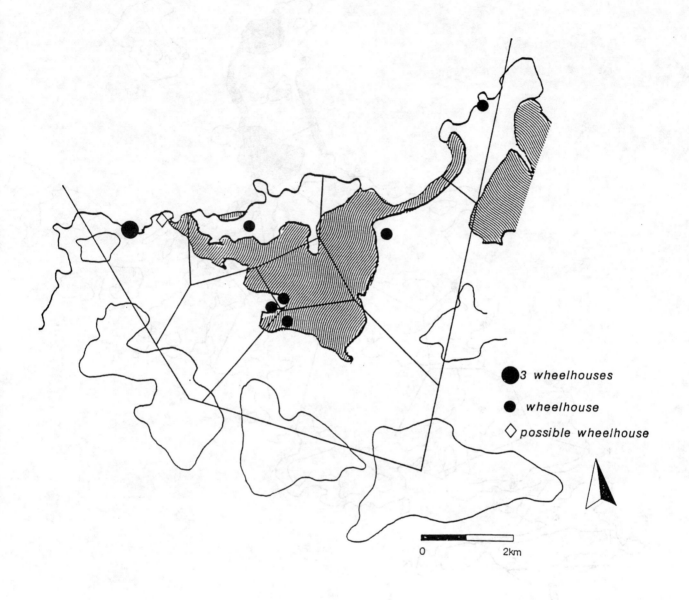

3 wheelhouses

wheelhouse

possible wheelhouse

Ill. 12.8 Thiessen Polygons: Wheelhouses in the Vallay Catchment

chair. The Baleshare/Tigharry groups are more crowded than those of the north although similar catchment types may be postulated.

In Barra the atlantic roundhouses present a somewhat different picture with the application of Thiessen polygons (Ill. 12.7). The site catchments are of broadly equivalent size to those of the north coast North Uist sites, but the landscape organisation which the distribution and polygons imply is different and related to the topography of the island. Barra is divided into a number of valleys and distinct landscape units and is more fragmented topographically than North Uist. The atlantic roundhouses appear to each occupy one of those landscape niches. The polygon centred on Dun Cuier (A.B4), for example, corresponds almost exactly with the Allasdale valley. Dun na Kille (A.B9) and Bal na Craig (A.B11) occupy equal portions of the Borve valley (although interestingly Bal na Craig is the sole site without obvious coastal access). The sites are remarkably evenly distributed and appear central to each of these landscape units. Outside this pattern are three sites, Dun Ban (A.B12), Dun Chlif (A.B3) and Beinn Tangavat (A.B14), all of which are coastal and occupy marginal areas with stretches of rocky coast backing onto steep hillsides. Medieval or post-medieval cultivation rigs on each of these areas, however, demonstrate that they were not without agricultural potential, though not as rich as the valleys.

The relative lack of machair in Barra makes this a much less important resource than in North Uist. It is concentrated in specific areas (most notably Eoligarry) which would have made any organised attempt to divide it formally between settlements difficult. There is thus more scope for differences in emphasis in site economies here than in North Uist.

In Barra the atlantic roundhouse catchments appear to be dictated by natural land divisions and the settlement pattern gives the appearance of having evolved to occupy naturally provisioned niches. In North Uist, by contrast, the continuous machair plains of the north and west coasts provide no such naturally defined territories. The land divisions there, insofar as they can be postulated from the distribution of sites and overlaying of polygons, suggest a more formal division of land, with a regularity which suggests cooperative action at some stage in its establishment, rather than gradual and natural evolution.

The site catchments of the Vallay wheelhouses are noticeably similar in size and type to those of the roundhouses (Ill. 12.8), although the distribution appears to be focused more definitely on the machair (Ill. 12.4 shows the wheelhouses with the atlantic roundhouses of the same area indicated). There is a close correspondence in the pattern of polygons, which is to a large extent caused by the reuse of Garry Iochdrach, Eilean Maleit and Cnoc a Comhdhalach as wheelhouse sites. The Udal appears to inherit the catchment of Dun Skellor if one takes the polygons at face value. Sollas bears a similar relationship to Dun Toloman, Sithean Mor to Dun Thomaidh, Bac Mhic Connain to Rudh an Duin and Foshigarry to Dun and Eilean a Ghallain. Clearly such sweeping equations are unsupportable on the basis of the Thiessen polygons

alone, but they do indicate a broad continuity in the scale and resource range of the areas around these sites.

Visibility - A separate method of assessing site catchment, at least where intervisibility is relatively minimal, is the plotting of areas of visibility from the sites themselves. In the context of monumental structures, which appear to have been constructed deliberately to be visually impressive, it might be expected that settlements will be sited to be visible from as much of their catchment as possible, as well as to enable a constant watch over their land holdings.

The visibility ranges of the atlantic roundhouses of Barra has been plotted in Ill. 12.9. Boundaries of visible areas are shown as accurately as can be gauged from the Ordnance survey maps of the area, using a 10m height for the structures (this height is an absolute maximum and provides a maximising view of visibility); shaded areas represent areas outwith the view of known atlantic roundhouse sites. In the cases of Dun na Kille and Bal na Craig, and of Baigh Hirivagh 1 and 2, the visibility areas of the pairs of sites are virtually identical and are shown each as one area. Areas which are visible but not accessible from individual sites, e.g. where separated by sea channels, have not been included within that site's visibility area. The North Uist sites have not been plotted because of the problems of intervisibility clusters which would make the pattern unintelligible; in addition the movement of machair in the occupied areas will have obscured contemporary visibility patterns. The latter problem applies with even more force to the Vallay wheelhouses.

In Barra, the patterns of site visibility show a pattern which, when combined with the information derived from the Thiessen polygons (Ill. 12.7), may shed some light on land divisions. There is a close correspondence for some of the sites in the more fertile valley areas: the visibility area of Dun Cuier (A.B4) corresponds almost exactly with the Thiessen polygon around the site and with the Allasdale valley; Dun Scurrival (A.B2) seems to have a slightly larger catchment (at the expense of Dun Chlif (A.B3)) if the visibility data is preferred; Dun na Kille (A.B9), Bal na Craig (A.B11), Dun Mhic Leoid (A.B13) and the two Vatersay roundhouses (A.B15 and A.B16), all have closely similar visibility areas and polygon-defined catchments; Dun Loch an Duin (A.B5) and Loch nic Ruaidhe (A.B8) in the east have a similar correspondence. This recurrence of site catchments defined by different methods suggests that we may be approaching some understanding of the actual 'territories' of these settlements.

The sites which 'lose' areas of their site catchments on the basis of visibility areas are those situated in marginal coastal locations; Dun Ban (A.B12), Dun Chlif (A.B3) and Beinn Tangavat (A.B14). These three sites appear to lie outwith the prime land of the island and occupy small catchments of poorer quality than the other mainland Barra sites. Similarly the islands around Barra, with the exception of Vatersay, might be seen as equally marginal. There appears to be a core of substantial and naturally defined territories concentrated on Barra and Vatersay, each occupied by an atlantic roundhouse, with a periphery of settlement areas occupying smaller, marginal catchments around the rocky coast of Barra and on the

Ill. 12.9 Visibility Areas of Atlantic Roundhouses in Barra

surrounding islands. The construction of atlantic round-houses was not restricted to groups in the larger site catchments.

Few substantial areas of Barra are outwith the view of the atlantic roundhouses. In this context the absence of visibility areas covering the south-eastern part of the island is interesting. It is possible that other atlantic roundhouse sites lie undiscovered in these areas: perhaps a more likely possibility, however, is that they primarily represent rough grazing associated with individual sites (especially perhaps Beinn Tangavat (A.B14), Loch nic Ruaidhe (A.B8) and Bal na Craig (A.B11)), or alternatively were used as a communal facility.

On Fuday and south Vatersay, areas lying outwith the immediate view of the respective roundhouses on these islands appear likely to have been grazing land associated with the settlements. It may be that visibility over agricultural land was considered as a prime locational factor while grazing lands were less important.

Carrying Capacity

There have been a number of attempts to assess land carrying capacity relative to site distributions in Atlantic Scotland. These have been carried out principally in Caithness (Heisler 1977, Martlew 1981) and the Shetlands (Fojut 1982). Heisler's work has been criticised as being founded on unreliable assumptions; the most basic of these is perhaps the assumption that absolute population size has a direct relationship to social complexity (Martlew 1981, 26). The weaknesses of Heisler's work also derive from the very large number of arbitrary figures required to formulate his calculations. In calculating the maximum energy yield from the potential crop and domestic animal resources within a given area he used the C19th production figures with a purely arbitrary estimate of the contribution of marine and riverine resources. Clearly this latter assumption highlights an important problem for Atlantic Scotland as a whole, but especially in the attempt to apply similar methods of analysis to island groups with an even greater historical reliance on these resources. Further assumptions are involved the calculation of population structure and the resulting calorific requirements of a reconstructed population (Heisler 1977, 130). The final division of potential energy yield by the energy requirements of the population gives a maximum population figure which can be used to estimate a number of individuals associated with an average roundhouse site. The assumptions, however, are so many, so interdependent and so poorly founded that there seems to be little value in the application of this degree of detail which results in a spurious semblance of accuracy, as when the figure of 203 people per *broch* is quoted (Heisler 1977, 131). Heisler's final conclusions, that "each broch could not have been an independent chiefdom" (Heisler 1977, 134 (his emphasis)) hardly seem to require his preceding analysis to adduce.

Fojut's system of calculating carrying capacity was more geared to the site specific resource base of the Shetland *broch* sites (Fojut 1982, 53). The potential of each site was assessed and then potential population figures for sites arrived at. Fojut's analysis perhaps gets closer to the original potential of the sites but there are still major problems in the assumptions of land usage, the spatial relationship of used land to the settlement, the maximisation of resources and the problem of marine resources.

For Barra and North Uist it is impossible to assess the available resources for site catchments in later prehistory. The changes in land quality and soil formations and distributions have been discussed in Chapter Two and mentioned above. Neither Heisler's nor Fojut's methods can be used for these areas. It may, however, be possible to arrive at a scale order figure for population potential by a comparison with historically recorded figures. Since any assessment of land productivity would be almost pure assumption the only defensible approach at present is simply to compare minimum and maximum figures with the distribution of sites.

In 1755 North Uist had a recorded population of 1909 people (Sinclair 1791-99, xxxviii). The economy of this population was a transitional one between a purely subsistence agricultural, pastoral and fishing economy and the growth in importance of the kelp industry. The population is therefore somewhat higher than the medieval population would have been. The areas occupied by this medieval population appear to correspond closely to the area occupied by the atlantic roundhouse catchments, perhaps with a more clearly coastal distribution (Crawford 1965), the one significant difference being the complete absence of medieval settlement in the eastern low-lying areas. These factors of kelp, contraction of settlement area, together with climatic deterioration and coastal change, combine to make comparison of prehistoric and C18th populations difficult, with some factors boosting population and others reducing it. Nonetheless it is useful to consider the implications of this scale of population for the atlantic roundhouse distribution. The benefits of this form of analysis are that the assumptions are explicit and the limitations of comparability are kept to the fore: no assumptions are made about environmental change.

A later prehistoric population of 1500 - 2500 might be a reasonable estimate on the basis of the 1909 figure for 1755. 51 atlantic roundhouses occupy the area where this 1755 population was recorded and thus a figure of 29 - 49 is arrived at for the mean population of a roundhouse catchment. While this is clearly a very approximate figure it does indicate the scale of population associated with the atlantic roundhouse sites. It would require a very substantial later 1st millennium BC population indeed, and one far in excess of even the kelp-boosted early C19th figures, to justify the suggestion that atlantic roundhouses were some form of tribal centres, for example.

In Barra the relationship of historic to prehistoric population figures has similar problems. Instead of kelp, which was less important in Barra than North Uist in 1755, an equivalent problem is commercial fishing based on Castlebay, which has no indication of any prehistoric occupation. Unfortunately the figures are not sufficiently subdivided to remove the Castlebay population from the calculations. The figure of 1150 for the population of Barra in 1755 is therefore likely to be a high estimate of its subsistence agricultural and marine carrying capacity. A range of 600 - 1500 may be suggested as possible for the later prehistoric population. The figures include all of the islands around and to the south of Barra itself. These figures would give a range of 33 - 83 for the population of an average atlantic roundhouse catchment, with the upper figure likely to be an over-estimate of the absolute maximum. The lower figure is close to the low figure of 29 for North Uist and, on balance, these lower figures may perhaps be more realistic for the later prehistoric period. Even at the top end of the scale however we are dealing with relatively small population groups of probably 7-10 families or less (average family size being 7 for the recorded figures from 1799). It would appear that relatively small population groups were able to participate in the construction and maintenance of the monumental stone roundhouses.

The occurrence of atlantic roundhouses on a number of the smaller islands around Barra is particularly useful in helping to define minimum areas, and approaching a minimum population and resource base required to justify, construct, and maintain these structures (Ill. 5.1 and 12.5). The distribution shows that, for example, Vatersay could support two such sites, Fuday, Pabbay, Sandray, and Mingulay, one each, while Berneray housed a galleried promontory fort (P.20). Very few of the islands south of Barra were without such structures and it seems reasonable to assume that these sites controlled territories comprising only the islands on which they were situated. The smallest of these, Pabbay and Fuday, are of a similar size to the average catchments defined by Thiessen polygons on Barra itself (see below). The larger islands contain significant proportions of upland, which would have reduced the value of resources relative to land area. Islands less than 3km^2 are without roundhouse sites. Pabbay has probably the minimum resource base of any roundhouse island catchment. The island is approximately 3km^2 in size and has no access to other land, being between Sandray and Mingulay with their respective sites. The island has a rocky coast with no machair resource and no obvious available agricultural land. Clearly the territorial requirements of the roundhouse builders were highly variable and potentially minimal.

Vatersay, with its two atlantic roundhouses, emerges in the records of 1799 as housing two farms of uncertain population. The remaining southern islands have between 3 and 9 families each, i.e. c. 21 - 63 people. Unless the productivity of these small islands has changed beyond all recognition in the past two millennia, this would appear to be the scale order of population which was able to support roundhouse construction and use, and again it agrees well with the overall figures for North Uist and Barra.

Overall, then, we appear to have arrived at population figures for the atlantic roundhouse catchments which, despite all the uncertainties involved, indicate a scale order for average populations. All the variations in site catchment type and size, and the range of structural form and size, indicate that considerable variation in actual population between sites is to be expected.

In terms of the historic populations of the medieval and post-medieval periods, the population size and variation associated with the site catchments of the atlantic roundhouses would be lower even than the levels of population controlled by the tacksmen. These were members of the very lowest levels of clan elite, who operated as administrators in return for land grants and privileges. Crawford records that there were some 20 tacksmen in North Uist in 1718, a figure which reduced to 16 by 1764 (Crawford 1965, 62). This compares to some 43 known atlantic roundhouses occupying essentially the same parts of the island in the later prehistoric period.

It would require extreme levels of population in the 1st millennium BC to sustain the idea that atlantic roundhouses could all represent the dwellings of a social group of equivalent status to the medieval tacksmen, far less any higher strata of a ruling elite. This is not to suggest that atlantic roundhouses were occupied by prehistoric tacksmen operating as their medieval successors did, but on a smaller scale, but rather to indicate the sorts of population levels we are dealing with in a broadly comparable tribally organised society in the medieval period. The question of what proportion of the population actually inhabited the roundhouse itself is not so easily resolved as the question of population scale for the site catchment.

Discussion

It appears that the various classes of settlement show different locational biases. The atlantic roundhouses and wheelhouses have a strikingly coastal distribution and indeed proximity to the sea seems to be a major consideration in siting in the later prehistoric period. The same does not apply to the miscellaneous structures and walled islets which are more widely spread across the interior of North Uist. This coastal distribution is likely to reflect the wide range of resources exploited by the later prehistoric inhabitants of the islands. Coastal siting gives access to the machair and the sea as well as the low-lying land inland from the coast, whilst still being within range of upland pasture.

The fundamental difference in distribution between the atlantic roundhouses and wheelhouses and the miscellaneous structures and walled islets is of some significance. In Chapter Ten evidence was cited for a potentially early range of dates for many of the miscellaneous structures and walled islets. Eilean Domhnuill in North Uist (M.13), for example, has been shown to be Neolithic (Armit 1988b; 1990b), while further evidence exists for non-monumental occupation underlying atlantic roundhouse sites (Chapter Five). In this context the locational evidence suggests a possible model for the development of settlement and economy from the earlier to later prehistoric periods, at least in North Uist.

The widespread distribution of the miscellaneous structures and walled islets across areas of the island not inhabited in the later prehistoric period suggests that a contraction had occurred in the overall area of the island being exploited for settlement. It is possible that in the 2nd millennium BC and earlier, virtually the entire land mass of North Uist, below approximately 20m OD, was settled and presumably farmed. This would have been in the period before the widespread development of blanket peats and before the formation of the present machair. As peat encroached throughout the 1st millennium BC, much of the interior of the island would have become economically unviable and settlement would have come to focus much more on the coastal belt. One would expect in these circumstances, a broadening of the resource base, with increasing emphasis on marine resources. It may have been at this stage that the machair first came to be regarded as prime agricultural land.

This model would suggest that settlement on the coastal belt would become increasingly dense, leading to population pressure and the possibility of conflict between communities. Territorial consciousness and the need to display control over resources would be expected to become more significant factors in settlement location and design. It may be in this context that we see the appearance of monumental architecture in the mid-late 1st millennium BC. With competition for increasingly limited resources and the need to display territorial authority, there would have been openness to the adoption of the monumental atlantic roundhouse form. Atlantic roundhouse building may have begun in the Western Isles after the complex architectural traits of broch architecture had begun to develop elsewhere (Armit 1991), but its adoption was within the context of a continuous development process in Hebridean settlement patterns. This would help to explain why monumental architecture does not appear to have developed on the settlements of the interior of the island. The earlier prehistoric coastal settlements would often survive to develop into monumental later prehistoric settlements, and new settlements would also be established in these areas. In effect, the contraction of settlement left a 'tidemark' of older, obsolete settlement locations in the interior and eastern areas of North Uist. The same pattern may be observed on the east coast of Lewis, where the non-monumental structures are concentrated, with later prehistoric settlement largely confined to the west coast with its wider range of resources.

It may be that with the increasing concentration of population on the coastal belt there would have been episodes of formal land division in these areas. Possible indications of such land divisions were noted in North Uist. Whether such land division was initiated by a central authority or whether it reflects cooperative behaviour among communities of broadly equal status is a question for future research. The large number of sites relative to the probable size of the population demonstrates that we cannot see the existence of an atlantic roundhouse as indicating a settlement of a necessarily high social status. Some of these sites presumably must represent the settlements of high status families but it is not yet clear how this could be demonstrated archaeologically.

The displacement of population from the interior would presumably have been a slow process, and they may have been easily absorbed into the settlements of the coastal belt, but it is possible that these groups came to fall low in the social system and formed a bottom tier of the social hierarchy in the later prehistoric period. The roots of the development of a system of clientage may lie here, if land on the coastal belt was granted to displaced groups by the inhabitants of the coastal settlements. In this context monumental architecture may have acted as a focus for the display of control over people as well as land. The construction and maintenance of these settlements may have formed part of the clientage system, being carried out by the lower, dependent strata of society.

The pattern seems to continue into the last centuries of the 1st millennium BC and early 1st millennium AD with the development of the wheelhouses. These tend to be even more coastal in location than the atlantic roundhouses. This may indicate the total abandonment of the non-machair areas for agricultural purposes, although it may simply reflect the construction methods of the new architectural form. The density of sites may have remained substantially the same as for the atlantic roundhouses, although land pressure probably intensified as the environment generally worsened. Again, the possibility of widespread unrecognised wheelhouse settlement away from the coastal belt should be stressed. Sites such as Clettraval (W.11) and Allasdale (W.25) show that the inland areas were not entirely abandoned and some specialised economic activity associated with stock-rearing may have been carried out there. The relationship of such settlements to the main coastal distribution remains unclear. The greatest visible difference in the transition from atlantic roundhouse to wheelhouse settlement is the abandonment of architectural display (at least outward architectural display) as a means of establishing territorial control.

The settlement patterns of the cellular and linear structures are unclear, but with the emergence of identifiable medieval and post-medieval settlement in North Uist, similar processes can be seen as in the later prehistoric period (Crawford 1965). Settlement was exclusively coastal and based on the exploitation of the whole range of available resources. Until the opening up of consumer markets from the seventeenth century onwards, principally for commercial fishing and kelp, the settlement development processes which are discernible in the prehistoric period appear to have continued.

The picture is somewhat different in Barra, where environmental deterioration would have been less marked. Peat growth was less severe than in North Uist and the better-drained valleys would have provided land of reasonable quality throughout the later prehistoric period. There is no sign of the abandonment of areas of land: by contrast, settlement may have expanded into marginal areas, with the settlement of the surrounding islands and the marginal rocky coasts. It is possible that a worsening climatic regime caused a concentration on pastoral rather than agricultural elements in the economy and made the land less able to support the same levels of population: alternatively population growth may have prompted the movement. Local topographical and environmental factors, then, may have led to differing local responses to the worsening environmental situation in later prehistory. In both North Uist and Barra, however, the indications are that the period from the early 1st millennium BC, at latest, through the rest of prehistory was a period of environmental stress and economic adaptation, all of which left its mark on the settlement patterns of the period.

It is possible to trace a broad picture of long-term settlement development which can provide a context in which the development of the distinctive architecture of the islands can be understood. In the next chapter this picture will be expanded and reviewed in the light of the whole range of evidence examined in previous chapters, and in the wider Atlantic Scottish context.

Chapter Thirteen - Conclusions

Introduction

This final chapter falls into two parts. Firstly the main results of the preceding chapters will be discussed in terms of their implications for settlement development. In the second part some possible factors affecting settlement development will be discussed and a number of approaches will be considered in the construction of interpretative models for the data.

Settlement Types and Settlement Development

A series of distinct types of settlement have been defined for the later prehistoric period in the Western Isles. The classification of these structures, detailed in Chapter Four, has been shown to define relatively unitary groups in architectural, functional and chronological terms. These groups cross-cut previous classifications which have often been based on classificatory schemes imported from outwith the local context. In particular, the atlantic roundhouses have been argued to be an essentially unitary group. The many divisions imposed on these structures in previous classificatory schemes do not find support in the Western Isles material.

The following discussion summarises the available evidence for the nature of the settlement which these various defined types represent.

Atlantic Roundhouses

The evidence from the Western Isles suggests that the atlantic roundhouses form a unitary settlement tradition dating to the second half of the 1st millennium BC. The problems of dating the sites have been stressed in Chapter Five, but essentially the available dating suggests a period corresponding to the complex roundhouse construction period throughout Atlantic Scotland, with an absence of recognised simple roundhouse settlement. Although broch towers occur, possibly in considerable numbers, there is no indication of the development of nucleated villages focused on these structures as one finds in the Orkneys. No evidence can be adduced at present to suggest the construction of atlantic roundhouses in the Hebrides in the 1st millennium AD.

The structural unity of the type has been demonstrated by a consideration of the range of architectural features on the excavated sites. It has been shown that wherever atlantic roundhouse sites have been excavated, traces of broch architecture have been found and the lack of any simple roundhouses in this near-random sample appears significant. There is no evidence among the excavated sites for a mid-1st millennium AD *dun* class of sites as was suggested in earlier interpretative schemes.

The examination of site location and site structure among the surveyed sites similarly supports the concept of a unitary atlantic roundhouse class. The sites appear to occupy the landscapes of the islands in an organised manner suggestive of contemporaneity. The range of associated structural traits, such as annexes, cross-cause-way walls etc, suggests similar functions and concerns. The range of locational types occupied similarly suggests a high degree of unity in the atlantic roundhouse class. The division into *brochs* and the various forms of *dun*, with the consequent implications for dating, does not find a reflection in chronology, site structure, location or function.

The central site in the definition of a late *dun* class, Dun Cuier, has been shown to be a misinterpreted complex roundhouse, probably dating to the mid-late 1st millennium BC (on the basis of unstratified early ceramics, a saddle quern, detailed parallels with Loch na Berie and the architectural affiliations of the roundhouse). Many of the apparent multiplicity of monument classes, now embraced in the atlantic roundhouse class, appear to derive from the problems of field interpretation. Varying preservation and the pre-existing qualitative division of sites on the basis of architectural worth have led to the creation of artificial monument classes.

The application of the classification scheme proposed in this study enables the recognition of a widespread class of monumental domestic settlements of the mid-late 1st millennium BC. The architecture of these sites indicates the importance of display and of prestige within the communities of the islands. The location and site structure of the settlements implies that they were the homes of farming communities exploiting a range of economic resources. Their numbers, relative to the inferred carrying capacity of the islands, suggest that they were not directly representative of a ruling elite. The implication from the evidence discussed in Chapter Twelve is that they could be constructed and inhabited by groups of varying social status extending significantly below a level analogous to medieval tacksmen, i.e. the lowest level of the island's medieval aristocracy.

There is no reason why *a priori* we should expect an architectural form to relate solely to one social class. The evidence from the Western Isles suggests the contrary. An examination of the economic potentials of the areas of atlantic roundhouses settlement, together with the overall density of this settlement, suggests that atlantic roundhouses would have been occupied by groups of a wide range of social status. A medieval analogy, assuming broadly comparable population sizes, would suggest that atlantic roundhouses were constructed by social groups equivalent in status to clan chiefs, minor chiefs, tacksmen and some tenant farmers.

The study of atlantic roundhouses within the Hebridean context should not obscure the fact that this is a widespread monument form with close architectural affiliation with sites throughout Atlantic Scotland. The nature of these connections will be explored below.

Wheelhouses

The wheelhouses form a class united by a specific architectural tradition. The construction method described in Chapter Six dictates ground plan and to a large extent, spatial organisation. This distinctive architecture makes the class relatively easy to define. The wheelhouses appear to date from the later centuries BC to the C1st AD. The conventional dating of the type to the mid-1st millennium AD appears to have been based on the misinterpretation of excavated sequences and the context of artefactual material on the excavated sites. The concepts of diffusion and time-lag of portable artefacts, have also contributed to the persistent late dating of the type. The C-14 evidence from Hornish Point indicates the possibility of an origin as early as the C3rd BC, while artefactual material from a number of sites and C-14 evidence from the Udal indicates occupation into the C1st AD. The type appears to persist later than the atlantic roundhouses but our chronologies are currently too poorly defined to establish the nature or duration of the overlap period when both forms were constructed.

The wheelhouses have a machair-based distribution (though with outliers discussed in Chapter Twelve) and may reflect the increased importance of the machair as a resource in their period. The evidence for their distribution, although slight, suggests a scale of site catchment control and population similar to that of the atlantic roundhouses. The division between the two forms does not necessarily appear to be related to the scale or social position of the population who constructed and inhabited them.

The wheelhouses were monumental structures, although their monumentality found different expression from that of the atlantic roundhouses. The wheelhouses were built with the practical requirements of their environment in mind: scarce timber, cold and wind. The atlantic roundhouses are so conspicuous in the Hebridean landscapes today, as in prehistory, precisely because of their non-adaptive characteristics: their height, free-standing nature and overall size. The wheelhouses were sited on the machair for their proximity to agricultural land: the atlantic roundhouses combined a siting near to their most important resources with a control over access, whether by construction on islets or on hilltops or knolls. The distinction between atlantic roundhouses and wheelhouses in structural terms is the distinction between practical and well-adapted monumental architecture and conspicuous, impractical and ill-adapted display.

Like the atlantic roundhouses the wheelhouses display links with areas outwith the Western Isles. In this case, however, only the Shetlands have structures of the same architectural form (see Chapter Six for discussion). The highly specific architectural technique demonstrates the strength of the cultural links which we must envisage between these two areas. The total absence of recognised wheelhouses in the Orkneys and Caithness becomes all the more striking in the face of these parallels.

Cellular Structures

The cellular structures appear to occupy the period from the C1st BC until the immediately pre-Norse period, conventionally c. 800 AD. The unity of this class is initially less obvious than that of the wheelhouses and atlantic roundhouses. Their unifying characteristics include an absence of monumentality, revetted construction and a series of recurring architectural and spatial traits. Recurring architectural traits include the use of slab-revetting, while spatial characteristics include the

dominance of a principal central cell, the focusing on the area across the central hearth from the entrance and the provision of paired wall-niches. Nonetheless there is less uniformity within this class than in those previously considered, at least in architectural terms. This may be due in part to the longer time-span occupied by the type.

The lack of recognition of the cellular structures as a specific class of monument until recently has hampered their study and there is as yet no reliable information on their distribution. Consequently inferences on population levels and social significance are not currently possible.

The cellular structures, whilst non-monumental, share several structural characteristics with the wheelhouses. Their revetted construction and minimisation of roofing spans demonstrate similar concerns with insulation and timber conservation. They represent a practical architecture designed with regard to the Hebridean environment.

Like the wheelhouses and atlantic roundhouses the cellular structures demonstrate links with areas outwith the Western Isles. These links are clearest with the Orcadian sites such as Buckquoy and Birsay (discussed in Chapter Seven) but extend to non-Pictish areas such as Ulster. In the latter context, the site of Deer Park Farms contained 1st millennium AD structures of strikingly similar form and spatial organisation (Lynn 1988). Artefactual material suggests links with areas as diverse as Ireland, Pictland and Northumbria.

Linear House Structures

The majority of the linear structures of the Western Isles have been shown to be simple passages which probably formed parts of larger structural complexes: it is likely that these were often unrecognised wheelhouse or cellular complexes. Only two linear structures appear to represent genuine settlement structures and these have been discussed in Chapter Eight as linear house structures.

Like the cellular structures the linear house structures are a settlement form of the 1st millennium AD. With only two sites known and only one excavated it is impossible to generalise on questions of date or function. The linear house structures share traits with the cellular structures. They appear to have been revetted and built with minimal roofing spans for timber conservation. They were non-monumental structures but Cnip, like several cellular structures, was built on the site of a monumental settlement with no break in occupation.

The wider connections of these structures are not well understood. Parallels in Skye have been cited in Chapter Eight but further parallels place too great a strain on our very limited understanding of the structures in the Western Isles.

Promontory Forts

The absence of any secure dating for the promontory forts restricts any conclusions as to their relationships with other settlement forms. They appear to be related to the atlantic roundhouses in a number of instances, e.g. the use of broch architecture at Barra Head Lighthouse, the importance of access control in both monument forms, and the combination of atlantic roundhouse and promontory defences at Dun Mara in Lewis. There is little indication, however, that we have recovered a coherent sample of the original distribution of these sites or that they all belong to one identifiable period. In this context they can play little part in wider interpretations of developing Hebridean settlement patterns at this stage. They do however remain a key area for future fieldwork and integration into the regional settlement framework.

Miscellaneous Structures and Walled Islets

These two classes of site may encompass an enormous range of variability in structure and dating. At present it is possible only to separate them from the clearly later prehistoric settlement types with which they have been confused in the past. In Chapter Twelve it was demonstrated that the distribution patterns of these types of site are fundamentally distinct from those of the later prehistoric forms, and the contrast between the two groups is potentially significant for the interpretation of long-term settlement pattern change in the islands. These sites occupied much wider areas of the islands than the later prehistoric structures and appear to have exploited areas which had become economically unviable by the mid-late 1st millennium AD.

The evidence currently favours the hypothesis that the majority of these structures are earlier in date than the later prehistoric period. The structures are all non-monumental and encompass a wide variety of structural forms. The disentangling of these sites from the later prehistoric settlement types has opened up new possibilities for understanding the settlement patterns of both groups of sites.

Summary

The settlement forms defined in Chapter Four appear to relate to a series of sequential chronological periods, although in each case the nature and duration of overlaps is unclear. Most of our evidence for settlement distributions and settlement pattern change derives from North Uist and Barra. North Uist is more likely to be representative of the wider Western Isles situation given its topographical nature and its size. Most of this summary generalises on the basis of the observed situation in North Uist. Nonetheless it is recognised that an increase in the evidence from other islands in the chain might show variations from the observed patterns.

From a pattern of widespread, non-monumental settlement in the earlier prehistoric period, the atlantic roundhouses emerged in the mid-1st millennium BC. These monumental structures occupy more restricted economic niches than their predecessors, restricted largely to the coastal belt in North Uist for example. From the last centuries BC into the C1st AD (by which time the atlantic roundhouses were likely to have been out of primary use) the wheelhouses were constructed, applying principles of local environmental adaptation to the concept of monumental architecture. They appear even more concentrated on the coastal belt, especially on the machair, although sporadic inland sites complicate the picture. From the C1st AD monumental architecture disappeared and was replaced by a more practical tradition of cellular

structures and linear house structures, the former predominating numerically. This cellular architectural tradition persisted until the settlement patterns of the islands were disrupted by the Norse incursions in the C9th AD.

The two principal trends observable from the structures and their distributions are:

a. the appearance, transformation and subsequent demise of monumental architecture.

b. the increasing emphasis on the coastal belt as a settlement focus, reflecting a wider resource base and the abandonment of inland areas in the face of environmental deterioration.

Throughout, the scale of the settlement unit and the range and degree of variation within defined types show no sign of significant change. Domestic ceramics, too, indicate continuity of cultural traditions.

The atlantic roundhouses have been the focus of most previous study. The chronological and typological division of these sites has prevented analysis of the settlement patterns of which they were all an integral part. The realisation of the unity of the atlantic roundhouse tradition and the placing of that architectural tradition in its local context provide an opportunity to examine the phenomenon of monumentality in the developing settlement patterns of the area. To explain settlement pattern change one must begin the process of integration of the evidence of the monumental structures with that of the less imposing monuments: one must also integrate the architectural and structural evidence with the whole range of available data including artefactual material and the evidence of site distributions.

Causes of Change

This section examines a range of factors which may have had a bearing on settlement development in the Western Isles. Population change was until recently the principal explanatory mechanism invoked for the appearance of the atlantic roundhouses and other structural forms. Environmental change has been a major concern of archaeologists for over twenty years but has made little impact on the interpretation of Atlantic Scottish prehistoric settlement. Finally, the importance of social change within and outside the Western Isles will be considered in terms of its effects on the observed settlement patterns.

Population Change

Three periods of population incursion have been proposed at various times during this period in the Western Isles. These comprise the alleged migration of the broch-builders from southern England in the C1st BC, Crawford's 'Scotto-Picts' in the early 1st millennium AD and the Norse in the early C9th AD.

The Broch-Builders - The diffusionist approach to Atlantic Scottish studies has been referred to at various points throughout the text. This discussion will not, therefore, rehearse the arguments against the diffusionist interpretations at length. The belief that broch architecture was created by incomers from the south of England has its roots in the diffusionist schemes of the 1930s and '40s and has found enthusiastic proponents in Atlantic Scottish studies since that time. After Childe's initial formulation of the diffusionist hypothesis for the area (1935), Scott (1947) and subsequently Hamilton (1956) and MacKie (1965) proposed further refinements. In essence, the detailed arguments in favour of the hypothesis depended on parallels in selected traits from the material culture of Atlantic Scottish Iron Age with similar traits in the south. The parallels of certain forms of ceramics and in particular, ceramic decoration, combined with a number of items of bonework all appeared convincing to workers operating within the diffusionist paradigm (e.g. MacKie 1965). Objections to these schemes have concentrated on several different aspects of the supposed parallels and on the overall theoretical basis of the diffusionist hypothesis (e.g. Clarke 1971; Harding 1984; Lane 1989; Armit 1990).

The background of stone architectural traditions, the duration of the development of broch architecture and the continuity of landscape utilisation and domestic material culture all argue for continuity of population throughout the 1st millennium BC in Atlantic Scotland. There is no evidence for a break in the settlement record in Atlantic Scotland at any point in this period, and the development of broch architecture manifestly takes place over a protracted period prior to the period of supposed immigration. Although the material culture parallels require explanation, the theory of migration from southern England no longer appears convincing and is certainly inadequate to explain the nature of the Atlantic Scottish Iron Age.

The Scotto-Picts - In his paper of 1977 Iain Crawford proposed that the break in settlement and changes in material culture at the Udal (C.10), in the period prior to 400AD, "marks one of the rare total and precise watersheds in the archaeological record that are so complete as to compel an invasion interpretation" (Crawford and Switsur 1977, 129). Crawford proposed that an invasion by a 'Scotto-Pictish' people could account for the changes. This was a new concept at the time and one which was not taken up elsewhere.

It appears from subsequent work that the break in continuity observed at the Udal was a feature of the incomplete nature of the Udal sequence. The excavations at Cnip (W.1) and Eilean Olabhat (C.19) have demonstrated that the ceramic sequence is continuous from the period of the atlantic roundhouses and wheelhouses through to the immediately pre-Norse period (App. 2). The development of the cellular structures at Cnip, with no break in occupation, from their wheelhouse predecessors also shows that the structural change is a gradual one. The invocation of a Scotto-Pictish invasion appears to derive from a misplaced belief in the continuity of the Udal sequence.

The Norse - The archaeology of the Norse period for the Western Isles is still under-developed. Only at the Udal is there evidence for the succession of pre-Norse and Norse settlement (Crawford 1977). Aside from the Udal, only Drimore has clear evidence of a Norse settlement (Maclaren 1974). Against this absence of identified settlement must be set several other forms of evidence;

a. the ubiquity of Norse stray finds, particularly on the machair.

b. the relatively widespread occurrence of Norse burials.

c. the overwhelming number of Norse place-names throughout the Western Isles.

The last of these factors confirms that, without doubt, the Norse influence over the islands was immense and presumably linguistically Norse people inhabited the whole of the Western Isles at the end of the 1st millennium AD.

In the context of this study it is the relationship of the Norse to the pre-Norse populations which is the main subject of interest. Lane has identified a ceramic assemblage which is characteristically Norse in its range of forms and fabrics, at the Udal (1983). This assemblage is not found in association with the later prehistoric settlement structures under study here. Similarly, the longhouses and the metalwork artefacts characteristic of Norse settlement are absent from the later prehistoric structures.

None of the cellular structures has evidence for continuity beyond the C8th AD. Only the Udal, Loch na Berie and possibly Dun Cuier can be convincingly interpreted as dating so late. At the Udal, Crawford saw the Norse incursions as violent and destructive involving a complete replacement of pre-existing power structures and the imposition of Norse control (Crawford and Switsur 1977, 131). This may well be the case, but it is difficult to accept some of the evidence from the Udal which Crawford uses to make the point: the Norse 'fort' which is held to be the symbol of subjugation was only 7m across and survived to 3-4 courses high (Crawford and Switsur 1977, 131). It is difficult to see in advance of full publication how this can be interpreted as a fort.

At Loch na Berie the final pre-Norse structures were abandoned and decayed naturally, with no sign of deliberate destruction. There were no artefacts from this site to suggest any Norse contacts, despite the chronological proximity of the site to the conventional Norse period. The absence of definite Norse settlement on the later prehistoric sites, other than the Udal, must suggest that there was a degree of dislocation in what had been, until this time, a continuous process of settlement development.

The nature of the Norse takeover of the islands lies outwith the immediate scope of this study but its effects appear to have included the dislocation of the settlement processes described here. Whether violent invasion or gradual absorption was involved, the results were complete cultural transformation and the realigning of contacts outwith the islands.

Summary - There is strong evidence to support the idea of a Norse population movement into the islands from the early C9th AD onwards. Linguistic, place-name and other documentary evidence combine with major changes in other aspects of material culture and the apparent dislocation of settlement patterns. There is no convincing evidence of this nature for the earlier inferred population incursions. The southern-English migration has been weakened by the extended chronology while the 'Scotto-Pictish' invasion rests on a misunderstanding of the completeness of the Udal sequence.

Wholesale invasion or migration need not be the only form of population movement capable of affecting material culture and social relations. The demonstrable contacts over wide and changing areas throughout later prehistory argue for the possibility of small-scale population movement. This could take the form of the movement of individuals or small groups through marriage networks, as specialist craftsmen, through economic failure or through inheritance or kinship networks. Some individuals and small population groups may well have been relatively mobile in the period and may have contributed to the adoption and spread of material culture, but the evidence for wholesale migration or invasion in later prehistoric Atlantic Scotland is unconvincing.

Environmental Change

The effects of environmental change on human populations have been a major focus of archaeological work since the 1960s. Processual approaches have often centred on the study of environmental adaptation of human societies, and the post-processual disdain for such approaches has not yet fundamentally affected archaeological practice. In Atlantic Scotland, however, processual archaeology did not have a significant impact on studies of the later prehistoric period until the early 1980s with the work of Noel Fojut (1982). Instead, diffusionist models, formulated in the cultural historical tradition, prevailed throughout the 1970s and into the early '80s. There is still a need to integrate the architectural and structural evidence for settlement with its environmental background for much of the Atlantic Province, and the Western Isles are no exception.

The radical nature of environmental change in the Western Isles over the prehistoric period has been stressed in Chapter Two. The twin processes of peat expansion on the one hand and coastal change and machair development on the other combined to give a dynamic environmental framework in which later prehistoric populations were compelled to operate. It is likely that anthropogenic factors helped to initiate and hasten the eradication of the potential of inland soils: over-grazing and over-intensive agricultural activity together with deforestation may all have contributed to the general environmental decline of the islands. A prime objective in future research must be to establish the rate and chronology of the environmental changes wrought by these processes and to assess this in terms of settlement pattern change.

From the perspective of human economic potentials the combined result of these processes would have been a lessening of the value of inland areas and a proportional increase in the value of the coastal belt with its access to a combination of resources. The environmental processes would have appeared imperceptibly slow to the human populations of the islands and could not have formed a conscious impetus to action.

A number of general settlement and economic developments might be predicted from this broad pattern of environmental change:

a. a change from widespread inland settlement to a more intensive settlement of the coastal belt.

b. an increased exploitation of the machair for agriculture.

c. the need to exploit a wider range of resources with possibly increased emphasis on pastoralism, hunting, fishing, wildfowl and shellfish.

d. population pressure on the reduced area of settlement and/or movement into marginal land.

e. social dislocation and the renegotiation of power structures as relative resource values change. The social effects of these processes will be dependent on the timescale of settlement pattern change.

f. scarcity of timber as a construction material.

These anticipated outcomes do seem to be generally applicable to the first later prehistoric settlement pattern shift from the miscellaneous structures and walled islets to the atlantic roundhouses. The economic base of the settlements is not directly witnessed through excavation due to the nature of early recording methods and the lack of survival of economic indicators such as bone and shell on many atlantic roundhouse sites. Intensification of coastal, relative to inland settlement, is demonstrated however, and economic patterns inferred from site distribution would fit the anticipated outcomes of environmental change.

Interestingly the last two anticipated factors, social reorganisation and timber scarcity, may have had unpredicted effects. The pressure on resources appears to have resulted in an increased stress on territoriality and display in settlement design and construction: the adoption of atlantic roundhouses suggests that the importance of prestige and display of command on resources resulted in an architecture in which scarce timber was wantonly and conspicuously employed. This provides one indication that human action in the Hebridean context was not environmentally conditioned, and not predictable from a knowledge of the environmental processes in isolation.

In the subsequent period with the development first of wheelhouses and then of cellular structures, architecture adapts to the environmental constraints described above, gradually abandoning monumentality. This later period sees a further concentration of coastal settlement and evidence for the development of a wide resource base (Finlay 1985). It also demonstrates the long-term convergence of observed settlement patterns with environmentally-based predictions. In the long-term then, broad settlement pattern shifts may relate closely to environmental dictates and constraints, but short-term settlement change, and the specific cultural responses employed, are not predictable from environmental considerations alone.

Ill. 13.1 shows a simplified model of the environmental influences acting upon settlement. Environmental constraints exert a powerful influence but their interplay with social factors creates responses from the human communities which cannot be described as environmentally determined. The phenomenon of monumental architec-

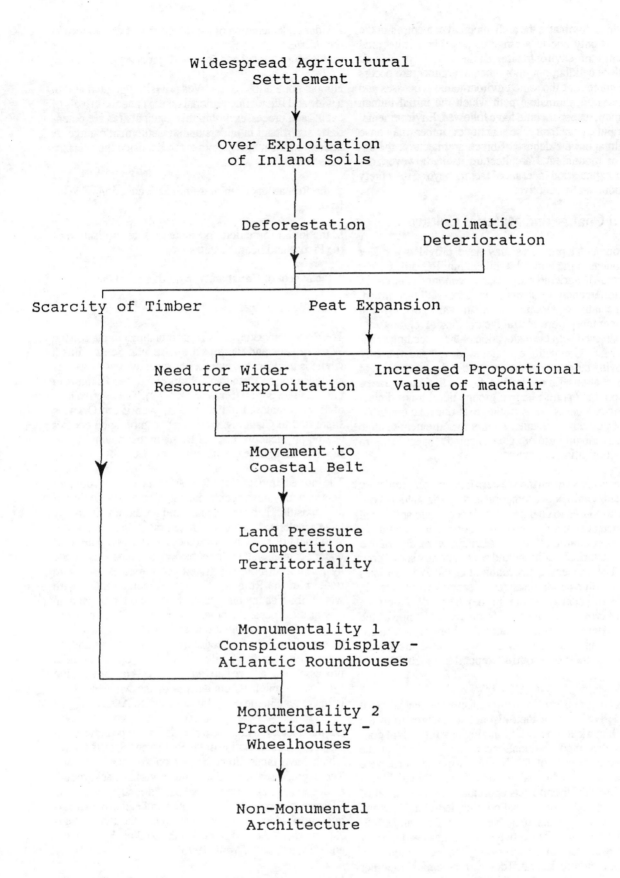

Ill. 13.1 Environmental Influences on Later Prehistoric Settlement

ture which dominates the archeological perception of the period is only one of a range of possible architectural outcomes of environmental decline. The subsequent growth of cellular, non-monumental architecture occurs in the context of the same environmental processes and illustrates an alternative path which the initial human settlement response could have followed. Environmental constraints, principally the scarcity of timber, may have brought about the demise of broch architecture: the demise of monumental architecture itself, however, demands explanation in terms of factors beyond the purely environmentally adaptive.

Social Change and Material Culture

Environmental processes may have provided a major component in the initial 1st millennium BC shift from a widespread, agriculturally based economy centred on non-monumental settlements to a coastally confined, non-specialist economic system in which display and monumentality were central factors. Social relations became stressed with the dislocation of the preceding economic base. Competitive societies developed, initially employing monumental architecture in the negotiation of power relations. Environmental factors limited the range of responses open to human groups but did not dictate specific responses. This section examines the contribution of non-environmental factors to settlement change and the changing use of material culture, specifically in the legitimisation of power.

Human groups within the Western Isles in later prehistory operated within both a temporal and a geographical context. Responses to changes in their economic and social circumstances and the deployment of material culture in the renegotiation of social relations were all framed within historical traditions and contemporary social contacts. The worsening environment of the Western Isles could enforce certain changes in economy, reflected in settlement patterns, and these may be predicted on the basis of cross-cultural parallels: an understanding of the specific developments in material culture cannot be approached in this cross-cultural way and demands the analysis of context in both its temporal and spatial dimensions.

The later prehistoric settlement forms of the Western Isles derive many of their distinctive features from the local 'historical' context. Changing environmental conditions disrupted traditional economic patterns but the specific responses of the Hebridean populations were framed within traditional practice. The preferential location of settlement on islets continued into the period of atlantic roundhouse occupation: this traditional location pattern, with its roots in the Neolithic (cf Eilean Domhnuill (M.13)) persisted until the inland areas were superseded by the machair as the primary focus of settlements. The use of highly decorated domestic ceramics is another feature of Western Isles prehistory which persisted until the mid-1st millennium AD.

The Hebridean context has been stressed throughout this study as essential to the understanding of settlement development in the area. This is especially significant at the level of the construction of a local chronological sequence and at the stage of site classification. To obtain a wider understanding of the development of societies in the Western Isles we must integrate the local sequence with wider regional and 'national' processes.

Human populations of the Western Isles operated within a wide and fluctuating regional context and the effects of events and processes within this regional area are potentially significant in understanding settlement change. A number of the major factors centred outside the Western Isles were:

a. the Roman invasion and limited occupation of Scotland.

b. the initial formation and increasing centralisation of the Pictish and Scottish states.

c. the advent of Christianity in northern Britain.

d. the advent of literacy.

The Roman invasion has no apparent direct impact on the Western Isles and its impact on Atlantic Scotland as a whole is unclear. Fitzpatrick has recently reassessed the evidence for an Orcadian submission to the Romans in the Claudian period (Fitzpatrick 1989). The relative lack of Roman material indicates that, even if the Orkneys submitted to Claudius, there was no prolonged contact and no physical presence of Rome in the Atlantic Province sufficient to leave material remains.

The indirect impact of the Roman occupation of southern Scotland may have been more significant. The setting of an opposition between Roman and northern Briton may have accelerated processes of centralisation and the development of an ethnic awareness. For the communities under occupation there may have been gains to be made by forming a more integrated centralised economy to trade with the Romans. For all the communities with whom they came into contact, the model of Roman organisation became a potential influence. The impact of Roman military installations and roads must have fundamentally affected perceptions of the landscape and the possibilities for the manifestation of power. All of these processes would have had indirect effects on the Atlantic Province through its contacts with the wider northern British scene in the early 1st millennium AD.

Of the factors listed above it is the appearance and increasing centralisation of the Pictish and Scottish states which have most direct impact on Atlantic Scotland. These processes form the wider regional background, analogous to the environmental background, in which the Western Isles populations operated. Indicators of increasing centralisation have been observed in the archaeological record of the Orkneys which parallel those of the wider Pictish state (Armit 1990).

In the Orkneys, complex roundhouses developed from a background of simple roundhouse construction in the mid-1st millennium BC (Armit 1990). The early roundhouses were isolated farmsteads without any indications of settlement nucleation. In the last centuries BC recognisable broch towers were constructed and some of these became the focus for nucleated settlement. The process of increasing architectural complexity was accompanied in the Orkneys by the progressive nucleation of settlement. Architecture appears to have played an active role in the development of increasing centralisation of power which paralleled the wider processes of incipient state formation throughout Scotland from the last centuries BC through the 1st millennium AD. By the mid-1st millennium AD Orcadian rulers appear to have functioned as sub-kings within an wider Pictish state (Armit 1990).

The part played by monumental architecture in legitimising and naturalising power structures has been discussed elsewhere (Barrett 1981, Armit 1990). Naturalisation of power, however, can find expression in the manipulation of many forms of material culture and need not be restricted to monumental architecture. Where power requires demonstration at a local level, monumental domestic architecture of the kind found in Atlantic Scotland can be effective. It presents a clear display of permanence, control over resources and forms a potential focus for the practice of clientship or other forms of subjugation. The broch towers of the Orkneys with their clustered villages appear to represent the culmination of monumental domestic architecture in the region. The spatial relationships of village to broch tower naturalise the position of the structure and its inhabitants as central, permanent and dominant, within the settlement and within society.

Widespread, 'low-status' monumentality in the Western Isles appears to be representative of power exercised at a highly localised level. Although broch architecture had the potential to display command over people and their labour, many of the atlantic roundhouses may simply have reflected power over the limited resources of the locality. The Western Isles atlantic roundhouses were symbols of power, but not of the degree or extent of power which was to be increasingly centred on elite groups during the 1st millennium AD.

Where power requires legitimisation over wider areas monumental domestic architecture is less effective. Its dominance and centrality in the lives of the Gurness community, for example, derives from its strong visual dominance over all of the activities of their everyday lives. This effect can only ever be local in a society in which movement of the population is limited. In a market economy or in any form of emerging state where central places were visited and observed by a substantial proportion of the population, the use of monumental domestic architecture could be extended. In a spatially fragmented society of limited mobility, the power of monumental architecture is not extensive: to extend power over larger areas and spatially diffuse populations the deployment of material culture had to change.

It has been customary to see the disappearance of monumental architecture in Atlantic Scotland as part of a process of cultural decline and representative of the demise of power networks in the area. In the context described above, with monumental architecture seen as a part of a wider process of power centralisation, this need not be the case. Monumental architecture can be viewed as one of a range of material cultural items through which power can be demonstrated. It can also be seen as applicable to one stage in the development of centralisation and potentially as redundant beyond that stage. With the disappearance of monumental domestic architecture in Atlantic Scotland we see the appearance of fine personal ornament, particularly metalwork and bonework, which was not a feature of the preceding period. This may be traced as early as the C2nd or C3rd AD at Eilean Olabhat (C.19) where fine metalwork was produced.

If control could be exerted over the raw materials for metal-working and provision made for the subsistence of craftsmen, control over the production and dissemination of metalwork could be concentrated in the hands of a restricted group of the population. By this means, membership of, kinship to, or subservience to particular authorities could be demonstrated by the ownership and display of material symbols of that authority: items of fine metalwork could function as badges of authority or of designated authority. The symbols of power became portable and were not restricted in impact to the vicinity of their source. Control over the production and ownership of fine metalwork would have enabled a much wider but less intensive display of power. In this context, local power-bases incorporating architectural display may have come to be regarded as potentially subversive and their abandonment and demolition may have been actively encouraged, if not enforced. The relationship between extensive power, exerted over widening areas, and intensive, local power in Mann's sense (1986), is one of the key areas for understanding the emergence of the early Scottish states from the later prehistoric background.

The disappearance of broch architecture then, does not seem to represent a cultural decline but rather a progression to a more centralised society where the use of material culture as symbols of power has transferred its emphasis from monumental architecture to portable items. The power which could be represented by portable artefacts in the 1st millennium AD was considerably more extensive than that represented by monumental domestic architecture in the previous centuries.

It may be in this context that the wheelhouses came to be built. They represent domestic monumental architecture but of a most unprepossessing external appearance. They do not provide a means of access control as the atlantic roundhouses did and they do not visibly reinforce territorial or resource control. It could be suggested that they represent the last fading remnants of monumental domestic architecture in a situation where its original purpose had all but disappeared. Wheelhouses were not defensive or outwardly monumental and they appear to have functioned in a period when land claims were sufficiently stable to obviate the need for territorial display. It may be that the establishment of centralised control, perhaps from the Orkneys, provided an alternative, non-local means of regulating such claims and discouraged the active display of territoriality. The monumentality of wheelhouse interiors may reflect the local historical context with local groups continuing to practice the demonstration of prestige through architecture, even after the atlantic roundhouses had become economically and socially redundant. With the dominance of the cellular structures this form of prestige display appears to have almost entirely disappeared.

It is possible that the new system of power symbolism derived from and was centred on the Orkneys, and that this is the reason for the absence of wheelhouses there: the establishment of realigned means of power display may have eclipsed monumental architecture more quickly and more completely than in the Western Isles and Shetlands, at the periphery of the emerging power structures.

The advent of Christianity in northern Britain and the closely associated advent of literacy were of fundamental significance to the developing states of the mid-1st millennium AD. Initially the Scots and subsequently the Picts seem to have employed religious symbolism and writing further to naturalise their authority. The alliance of the Church and secular authorities has been explored elsewhere (e.g. Nieke and Duncan 1989) for northern Britain. From the explicit combination of religion and secular power in Scottic kingly inauguration rites (e.g. Columba's involvement in the succession of Aedan to the throne of Dalriada) to the widespread use of Christian symbolism on stone monuments and portable artefacts (e.g. Henderson 1987), it is apparent that secular authority attempted its own legitimisation through its association with divine powers. This process almost certainly predates Christianity: pre-Christian religion, myths, stories, songs etc may well have portrayed the existing secular authorities as firmly embedded in a divine or pre-ordained pattern. With the advent of literacy this process is documented for us.

There is no visible impact of Christianity or literacy in the later prehistoric settlement sites of the Western Isles. Nonetheless, the part these factors played in strengthening and legitimising centralising authorities outwith the islands should not be overlooked as part of the contextual background in the 1st millennium AD.

Settlement Change in Context

The changing settlement patterns in the Western Isles have been examined in relation to factors of population, environmental and social change. Each of these appears to have had a substantial impact on settlement patterns, although the impact of the first appears to be restricted to the Norse incursions at the end of the period under study. The broad shifts in settlement pattern and resource exploitation appear to have been constrained and heavily influenced by the major environmental processes in progress throughout the 1st millennia BC and AD. These processes however, could not dictate the specific responses of the human populations of the Western Isles. The appearance of monumental domestic architecture and other, less visually impressive, aspects of material culture cannot be predicted from the study of environmental processes in isolation.

The evidence from the Western Isles suggests that social factors relating to the historical traditions of settlement in the islands, and to the impact of socio-political contacts outwith the islands, played a major part in the development of Western Isles societies. The place of the Western Isles in a wider Atlantic Province, and ultimately in a north British and north European context, provided a set of constraints and possibilities for the expression of social relations through material culture, analogous to those imposed by the processes of environmental change. Items of material culture were absorbed where there was a perceived or unconscious social, symbolic or economic use. The adoption of material culture forms need not indicate a common perceived function or symbolism between groups and still less, a common ethnic or political affiliation.

The importance of context, in all of the forms discussed above, is central to developing an understanding of settlement development and the use of material culture. It is to be hoped that the accumulating data-base will continue to provide additional information at a range of contextual levels, of a quality which will enable us to improve upon present knowledge. With a qualitative and quantitative increase in data, new areas of material culture can be analysed (e.g. wood from waterlogged and underwater sites) and existing areas expanded. The Western Isles are one of very few areas where there is the hope of ultimately accumulating detailed and reliable information on a very wide range of areas of cultural development over a continuous period from the Neolithic to the post-Medieval. The analysis and interpretation of this material in its Hebridean context and its articulation with wider regional and national processes should be a central aim of Hebridean archaeology.

Bibliography

List of Abbreviations

Arch. Scot. - Archaeologia Scotica
BAR - British Archaeological Reports
DES - Discovery and Excavation in Scotland
GAJ - Glasgow Archaeological Journal
PPS - Proceedings of the Prehistoric Society
PRSE - Proceedings of the Royal Society of Edinburgh
PSAS - Proceedings of the Society of Antiquaries of Scotland
SAR - Scottish Archaeological Review
SAF - Scottish Archaeological Forum
Scott. Jour. Geol. - Scottish Journal of Geology
Trans.Inst.Br.Geog. - Transactions of the Institute of British Geographers
World Arch. - World Archaeology

Alcock, L 1963 Dinas Powys (Cardiff)

Alcock, L 1984 *A Survey of Pictish Settlement Archaeology* in Friell and Watson (eds) Pictish Studies (Oxford)

Anderson, J 1883 Scotland in Pagan times: Vol 2 the Iron Age (Edinburgh)

Armit, I 1985 Later Prehistoric Defensive Structures of Lewis and Harris unpublished MA Dissertation, University of Edinburgh

Armit, I 1986 Excavations at Loch Olabhat, North Uist, 1986 Department of Archaeology, Edinburgh University, Project Paper No.5

Armit, I 1986a *Kneep* DES 1986 47

Armit, I 1987 Excavation of a Neolithic Island Settlement at Loch Olabhat, North Uist 1987 Department of Archaeology, Edinburgh University, Project Paper No.8

Armit, I 1988 *Broch Landscapes in the Western Isles* SAR 5 78-86

Armit, I 1988a Excavations At Cnip, West Lewis 1988 Department of Archaeology, Edinburgh University, Project Paper No.9

Armit, I 1988b Excavations at Loch Olabhat, North Uist, 1988 Department of Archaeology, Edinburgh University, Project Paper No.10

Armit, I 1990 *Broch-building in Atlantic Scotland; the Context of Innovation* World Arch. 21 435-45

Armit, I (ed) 1990a Beyond the Brochs: Changing Perspectives on the Atlantic Scottish Iron Age (Edinburgh)

Armit, I 1990b Excavations at Loch Olabhat, North Uist, 1989 Department of Archaeology, Edinburgh University, Project Paper No.12

Armit, I 1990c *Brochs and Beyond in the Western Isles* in Beyond the Brochs: Changing Perspectives on the Atlantic Scottish Iron Age 41-70, (Edinburgh)

Armit, I 1990d *Epilogue* in Beyond the Brochs: Changing Perspectives on the Atlantic Scottish Iron Age 194-210, (Edinburgh)

Armit, I 1990e *Monumentality and Elaboration* SAR 7, 84-95 (1990)

Armit, I 1990f The Later Prehistoric Settlement of the Western Isles of Scotland unpublished Ph.D. thesis, University of Edinburgh

Armit, I 1991 *The Atlantic Scottish Iron Age: five levels of chronology* PSAS 121

Armit, I 1992 *The Hebridean Neolithic* in Sharples, N and Sheridan, A (eds) Vessels for the Ancestors (Edinburgh)

Barber, J 1985 Innsegall (Edinburgh)

Barber, J forthcoming Western Isles Excavations

Barber, J, Halstead, P, James, H and Lee, F 1989 *An Unusual Iron Age Burial at Hornish Point South Uist* Antiquity 63 773-8

Barclay, GJ 1985 *Excavations at Upper Suisgill, Sutherland* PSAS 115 159-98

Barrett, J 1981 *Aspects of the Iron Age in Atlantic Scotland. A Case Study in the Problems of Archaeological Interpretation* PSAS 111 205-219

Beveridge, E 1905 Coll and Tiree (Edinburgh)

Beveridge, E 1911 North Uist (Edinburgh)

Beveridge, E 1930 *Excavation of an Earth House at Foshigarry and a Fort, Dun Thomaidh, in North Uist* PSAS 65 299-357

Beveridge, E 1931 *Earth Houses at Garry Iochdrach and Bac Mhic Connain in North Uist* PSAS 66 32-67

Birks, HJB and Madsen BJ 1979 *Flandrian Vegetational History of Little Loch Roag, Isle of Lewis, Scotland* Journal of Ecology 67 825-842

Blundell, FO 1913 *Further Notes on the Artificial Islands in the Highland Area* PSAS 47 267-302

Bohncke, SJP 1988 *Vegetation and Habitation History of the Callanish Area, Isle of Lewis, Scotland* in Birks, HH, Birks, HJB, Kaland, PE and Moe, D (eds) The Cultural Landscape - Past, Present, Future (Cambridge) 445-61

Bohncke, SJP and Cowie, TG forthcoming Excavation and Paleoenvironmental Survey of a Site near Tob nan Leobag, Callanish, Isle of Lewis Callanish Project Paper No.1

Bradley, R 1978 The Prehistoric Settlement of Britain (Cambridge)

Breeze, D 1984 *A Potsherd of Castor Ware from Cross-kirk* in Fairhurst, H Excavations at Crosskirk, Caithness (Edinburgh)

Calder, C 1937 *A Neolithic Double Chambered Cairn on the Calf of Eday, Orkney* PSAS 71 115-154

Calder, C 1938 *Excavations of Iron Age Dwellings on the Calf of Eday, Orkney* PSAS 73 167-185

Carter, SP, Haigh *et al* 1984 *Interim Report on the Structures at Howe, Stromness, Orkney* GAJ 11 61-73

Caulfield, S 1977 *Quern Replacement and the Origin of Brochs* PSAS 109 129-139

Childe, VG 1935 The Prehistory of Scotland (Edinburgh)

Close-Brooks, J 1976 *Small Finds* in Tabraham, C *Excavations at Dun Carloway Broch, Isle of Lewis* PSAS 108 161

Collingwood, RG 1953 Roman Britain (London)

Crawford, IA 1965 *Contributions to a History of Domestic Settlement in North Uist* Scottish Studies 10:2 34-63

Crawford, IA 1966 *Bosta, Bernera Mhor* DES 1966 41

Crawford, IA 1967/78 Excavations at the Udal, North Uist (Interim Reports) typescripts

Crawford, IA 1975 *Scot (?), Norseman and Gael* SAF 6 1-16

Crawford, IA 1985 The West Highlands and Islands: A View of 50 Centuries (Cambridge)

Crawford, IA and Switsur, R 1977 *Sandscaping and C-14; the Udal, North Uist* Antiquity 51 124-136

Curwen, C 1938 *An Iron Age Site at Aignish, near Stornoway* PSAS 73 45

Dickinson, T 1982 *Fowler's Type G Penannular Brooches Reconsidered* Medieval Archaeology 26 41-88

Driscoll, ST and Nieke, MR (eds) Politics and Power in Early Medieval Britain and Ireland (Edinburgh)

Dryden, H 1857 *An Account of a Circular Building and Other Ancient Remains Discovered in South Uist* PSAS 3 124-127

Edwards, AJH 1923 *Report on the Excavation of an Earth House at Galson, Borve, Lewis* PSAS 58 185-203

Evans, JG 1971 *Habitat Change on the Calcareous Soils of Britain; the Impact of Neolithic Man* in Simpson, D (ed) Economy and Settlement (London)

Fairhurst, H 1971 *The Wheelhouse Site at A Cheardhach Bheag on Drimore Machair, South Uist* GAJ 2 72-106

Fairhurst, H 1984 Excavations at Crosskirk Broch, Caithness (Edinburgh)

Fairhurst, H and Taylor, DB 1971 *A Hut-Circle Settlement at Kilphedir, Sutherland* PSAS 103 65-99

Feachem, RW 1956 *Earthhouse at Drimore* DES 1956 38

Finlay, J 1985 Faunal Evidence for Prehistoric Economy and Settlement in the Outer Hebrides unpublished Ph.D. thesis, University of Edinburgh

Fitzpatrick, AP 1989 *The Submission of the Orkney Islands to Claudius: New Evidence?* SAR 6 24-33

Fojut, N 1982 *Towards a Geography of the Shetland Brochs* GAJ 9 38-59

Fojut, N 1982a *Is Mousa a Broch?* PSAS 112 220-228

Foster, SM 1989 *Analysis of Spatial Patterns (Access Analysis) as an insight into Social Structure: examples from the Scottish Iron Age* Antiquity 63, 40-50

Foster, SM 1989a *Transformation in Social Space: the Iron Age in Orkney and Caithness* sar 6 34-54

Fraser, D 1983 Land and Society in Neolithic Orkney BAR 117 2 vols. (Oxford)

Friell, JCP and Watson, WG (eds) Pictish Studies BAR 125 (Oxford)

Gelling, P 1985 *Excavations at Skaill, Deerness* in Renfrew, AC (ed) The Prehistory of Orkney (Edinburgh)

Glentworth, R 1979 *Observations on the Soils of the Outer Hebrides* PRSE 1979 123-137

Graham, A 1947 *Some Observations on the Brochs* PSAS 81 48-99

Green, D, Haselgrove, C and Spriggs, C 1978 Social Organisation and Settlement: Contributions from Anthropology BAR 471 (Oxford)

Guido, CM 1978 The Glass Beads of the Prehistoric and Roman Period in Great Britain and Ireland (London)

Hamilton, JRC 1956 Excavations at Jarlshof (Edinburgh)

Hamilton, JRC 1968 Excavations at Clickhimin (Edinburgh)

Harding, DW (ed) 1976 Hillforts (London)

Harding, DW 1984 *The Function and Classification of Brochs and Duns* in Miket, R *et al* (eds) Between and Beyond the Walls (Edinburgh)

Harding, DW and Armit, I 1987 *Loch na Berie* DES 1987 60-61

Harding, DW and Armit, I 1988 *Loch na Berie* DES 1987 31-32

Harding, DW and Armit, I 1990 *Survey and Excavation in West Lewis* in Armit, I (ed) 1990 Beyond the Brochs:

Changing Perspectives on the Atlantic Scottish Iron Age 41-70 (Edinburgh)

Harding, DW and Topping, PG 1986 Callanish Archaeological Research Centre 1st Annual Report (Edinburgh)

Henderson, I 1987 *Early Christian Monuments of Scotland Displaying Crosses but No Other Ornament* in Small, A (ed) The Picts: A New Look at Old Problems (Dundee) 45-58

Henshall, AS 1963 and '72 The Chambered Tombs of Scotland Vols 1 and 2 (Edinburgh)

Hedges, JW 1985 *The Broch Period* in Renfrew, AC ed. The Prehistory of Orkney (Edinburgh)

Hedges, JW 1987 Bu, Gurness and the Broch of Orkney Vol 1-3 BAR 163-5 (Oxford)

Hedges, JW and Bell, B 1980 *That Tower of Scottish Prehistory, the Broch* Antiquity 54 87-94

Heisler, DM 1977 Carrying Capacity and Social Organization in the Atlantic Iron Age of Scotland unpublished Ph.D. dissertation, University of Missouri-Columbia

Hill, P 1988 Whithorn 2: Interim Report

Hillier, B and Hanson, J 1984 The Social Logic of Space (Cambridge)

Hirons, K 1986 Preliminary Investigation of Lake Sediments from the Machairs of the Uists and Benbecula, Outer Hebrides typescript

Hodder, I 1986 Reading the Past (Cambridge)

Hunter, JR 1986 Rescue Excavations at the Brough of Birsay 1974-82 (Edinburgh)

Lacaille, AD 1937 *A Stone Industry, Potsherds and a Bronze Pin from Valtos, Uig, Lewis* PSAS 71 279-296

Laing, L 1975 The Archaeology of Late Celtic Britain and Ireland (London)

Lamb, R 1980 Iron Age Promontory Forts in the Northern Isles BAR 79 (Oxford)

Lane, A 1983 Dark Age and Viking Age Pottery from the Hebrides with Special Reference to the Udal, North Uist unpublished Ph.D. thesis, University of Glasgow

Lane, A 1987 *English Migrants in the Hebrides:' Atlantic Second B' Revisited* PSAS 117 47-66

Lane, A 1990 *Hebridean Pottery: Problems of Definition, Chronology, Presence and Absence* in Armit, I (ed) 1990 Beyond the Brochs: Changing Perspectives on the Atlantic Scottish Iron Age 108-130 (Edinburgh)

Leach, E 1978 *Does Space Syntax really 'Constitute the Social'?* in Green, D, Haselgrove, C and Spriggs, C Social Organisation and Settlement: Contributions from Anthropology BAR 471, 385-401

Lethbridge, TC 1952 *Excavations at Kilpheder, South Uist, and the Problem of Brochs and Wheelhouses* PPS XVIII 176-193

Liddle, P 1872 *Note of an Underground Structure at Gress near Stornoway and Other Ancient Remains in the Island of Lewis* PSAS 10 741-744

Lynn, C 1987 *Deer Park Farms* Archaeology Ireland Vol.1:1 11-15

Macartney, E 1984 *Analysis of Faunal Material* in Fairhurst, H Excavations at Crosskirk, Caithness (Edinburgh)

Macaulay Institute for Soil Research 1982 Soil Survey of Scotland - Outer Hebrides (Aberdeen)

MacDonald, D 1978 Lewis: a History of the Island (Edinburgh)

MacGregor, M 1976 Early Celtic Art in North Britain (Leicester)

Macinnes, L 1984 *Brochs and the Roman Occupation of Lowland Scotland* PSAS 114 235-50

Maclaren, A 1974 *A Norse House on Drimore Machair, South Uist* GAJ 3 9-18

MacKenzie, JB 1905 *Antiquities and Old Customs in St Kilda* PSAS 39 397

MacKie, EW 1965 *The Origin and Development of the Broch and Wheelhouse Building Cultures of the Scottish Iron Age* PPS XXX 93-146

MacKie, EW 1971 *English Migrants and Scottish Brochs* GAJ 2 39-71

MacKie, EW 1972 *Some New Quernstones from Brochs and Duns* PSAS 104 137-146

MacKie, EW 1974 Dun Mor Vaul: an Iron Age Broch on Tiree (Glasgow)

MacKie, EW 1974a The Origin and Development of the Broch and Wheelhouse Building Cultures of the Scottish Iron Age unpublished Ph.D. thesis, University of Glasgow

MacKie, EW 1975a *The Brochs of Scotland* in Fowler, PJ (ed) Rural Archaeology (London)

MacKie, EW 1975b *The Vitrified Forts of Scotland* in Harding, DW (ed) Hillforts (London)

MacKie, EW 1981 *Dun an Ruaigh Ruaidh, Loch Broom, Ross and Cromarty* GAJ 7 32-79

MacKie, EW 1984 *Testing Hypotheses About Brochs* SAR 2 117-128

MacKie, EW 1985 *Review of Fairhurst 1984* in Ant.Jour.65 500-1

MacKie, EW 1989 *Dun Cuier Again* SAR 6 116-8

MacRitchie, D 1916 *Earth Houses and their Occupation* PSAS 51 178-199

MacSween, A 1982 A Study of Iron Age Settlement on the Isle of Skye unpublished MA Dissertation, University of Edinburgh

Mann, M 1986 The Sources of Social Power, Vol.1: A History of Power from the Beginning to A.D. 1760 (Cambridge)

Martlew, R 1981 The Analysis of Prehistoric Settlement Location Dept. of Geography, University of Leicester, Occ. Paper 4

Martlew, R 1982 *The Typological Study of the Structures of the Scottish Brochs* PSAS 112 254-276

Mathieson, J 1928 *Antiquities on the St Kilda Group of Islands* PSAS 62 127

Morrison, D 1975 Traditions of the Western Isles (Stornoway)

Newell, PJ 1988 *A Buried Wall in Peatland by Sheshader, Isle of Lewis* PSAS 118 79-93

Nieke, MR 1984 Settlement Patterns in the Atlantic Province of Scotland in the 1st Millennium AD: a Study of Argyll unpublished Ph.D. thesis, University of Glasgow

Nieke, MR and Duncan, HB 1989 *Dalriada: The Establishment and Maintenance of an Early Historic Kingdom in Northern Britain* in Driscoll, ST and Nieke, MR (eds) Politics and Power in Early Medieval Britain and Ireland (Edinburgh) 6-21

Pearson, GW and Stuiver M 1986 *High-Precision Calibration of the Radiocarbon Time-Scale 500 - 2500 BC* Radiocarbon 28 no.2b 839-62

Peers, C and Radford CAR 1943 *The Saxon Monastery at Whitby* Archaeologia 89 27-88

Raftery, B 1984 La Tene in Ireland (Marburg)

Ralston, IBM 1986 Radiocarbon Dates (Scotland) typescript

Reid, ML 1989 *A Room with a View: an Examination of Round-houses with Particular Reference to Northern Britain* Oxford Journal of Archaeology 8(1) 1-39

Renfrew, AC 1979 Investigations in Orkney (London)

Renfrew, AC (ed) 1985 The Prehistory of Orkney (Edinburgh)

RCAHMS 1928 The Outer Hebrides, Skye and the Small Isles (Edinburgh)

RCAHMS 1946 Orkney and Shetland (Edinburgh)

Ritchie, A 1976 *Excavation of Pictish and Viking-Age Farms at Buckquoy, Orkney* PSAS 108 174-227

Ritchie, A 1985 *Orkney in the Pictish Kingdom* in Renfrew (ed) The Prehistory of Orkney (Edinburgh) 183-204

Ritchie, A and Ritchie, JNG 1981 Scotland: Archaeology and Early History (Edinburgh)

Ritchie, W 1966 *Sea Level and Coastal Changes in the Uists* Trans.Inst.Br.Geog. 39 79-86

Ritchie, W 1967 *The Machair of South Uist* Scott.Geog.Mag. 83 161-173

Ritchie, W 1979 *Machair Development and Chronology in the Uists and Adjacent Islands* PRSE 1979 107-122

Ritchie, W 1985 *Inter-tidal and Sub-tidal Organic Deposits and Sea-Level Change in the Uists, Outer Hebrides* Scott.Jour.Geol. 21 (2) 161-176

Robinson, SW 1986 A Computational Procedure for the Utilization of High-Precision Radiocarbon Calibration Curves Open-File Report, U.S. Dept. of the Interior Geological Survey

Sands, J 1876 *Notes on the Antiquities of St Kilda* PSAS 12 188

Sands, J 1878 Life on St Kilda (Edinburgh)

Scott, JG 1956 *Drimore* DES 1956 32

Scott, L 1947 *The Problem of the Brochs* PPS XIII 1-37

Scott, L 1947a *The Chambered Tomb of Unival, North Uist* PSAS 82 1-48

Scott, L 1948 *Gallo-British Colonies; The Aisled Roundhouse Culture in the North* PPS XIV 46-125

Scott, L 1950 *Eilean an Tighe; a Pottery Workshop of the 2nd Millennium BC* PSAS 85 1-37

Sharples, NM 1984 *Excavations at Pierowall Quarry, Westray, Orkney* PSAS 114 75-126

Simpson, DDA 1965 *Toe Peninsula, Northton, Isle of Harris* DES 1965 22

Simpson, DDA 1966 *A Neolithic Settlement in the Outer Hebrides* Antiquity 40 137-139

Sinclair, J (ed) 1791-99 The Statistical Account of Scotland Vol. XX The Western Isles (Edinburgh)

Small, A (ed) The Picts: A New Look at Old Problems (Dundee)

Stevenson, RBK 1955 *Pins and the Chronology of Brochs* PPS 21 282-294

Stuiver, M and Pearson, GW 1986 *High-Precision Calibration of the Radiocarbon Time-Scale AD 1950 - 500 BC* Radiocarbon 28 no.2b 805-39

Tabraham, C 1976 *Excavations at Dun Carloway Broch, Isle of Lewis* PSAS 108 156-167

Thomas, FWL 1857 *Notice of Beehive Houses in Harris and Lewis* PSAS 3 127-170

Thomas, FWL 1870 *On the Primitive Dwellings and Hypogea of the Outer Hebrides* PSAS 7 153-195

Thomas, FWL 1890 *On the Duns of the Outer Hebrides* Arch.Scot. 5 365-415

Topping, PG 1985 Later Prehistoric Pottery of the Western Isles unpublished Ph.D. thesis, University of Edinburgh

Topping, PG 1986 *Neutron Activation Analysis of Later Prehistoric Pottery from the Western Isles of Scotland* PPS 52 105-129

Topping, PG 1987 *Typology and Chronology in the Later Prehistoric Pottery Assemblages of the Western Isles* PSAS 117 67-84

Warner, R 1983 *Ireland, Ulster and Scotland in the Earlier Iron Age* in O'Connor, A and Clarke, DV (ed) From the Stone Age to the '45 (Edinburgh)

Wilkins, DA 1984 *The Flandrian Woods of Lewis (Scotland)* Journal of Ecology 72 251-258

Young, A 1952 *An Aisled Farmhouse at the Allasdale, Isle of Barra* PSAS 87 80-106

Young, A 1955 *Excavations at Dun Cuier, Isle of Barra, Outer Hebrides* PSAS 89 290-328

Young, A 1961 *Brochs and Duns* PSAS 95 171-199

Young, A 1966 *A Sequence of Hebridean Pottery* in Rivet, ALF (ed) The Iron Age in Northern Britain 45-58

Young, A and Richardson, KM 1959 *A Cheardhach Mhor, Drimore, South Uist* PSAS 93 135-173

Appendix One - C14 dates from the Western Isles

The following tables list the dates from each site in the Western Isles, first in their uncalibrated form with laboratory reference number and a note on site context. The dates are then calibrated using the micro-computer package CALND which uses the high precision dendrochronological data of Stuiver and Pearson (1986) and the calibration procedure of Robinson (1984). Each calibrated date is presented here as a Weighted Average, or centroid, of the calibrated distribution (the range of possible dates) with a note of the upper and lower 68% confidence limits. Illustration A1.1 presents the dates in graphic form, with the exception of those from Dun Carloway and the Udal where they are poorly contexted or do not relate to the later prehistoric occupation of the sites.

Lab Ref. - Laboratory Reference Number
Context - Sample context within site
Uncal.   - Uncalibrated date with standard deviation
WA   - Weighted average (centroid) after calibration
68% H   - 68% confidence upper (oldest) limit
68% L   - 68% confidence lower (youngest) limit

Dun Carloway (Tabraham 1976)

Lab Ref	Context	UnCal	WA	68%H	68%L
GX-3428	Final Phase	1300+/-150 bp	1321AD	1230AD	1412AD

Dun Bharabhat, Lewis (Harding and Armit 1990)

Lab Ref	Context	UnCal.	WA	68% H	68% L
GU 2434	Secondary Occupation	60+\-50 bc	31BC	101BC	AD33
GU 2435	Secondary Occupation	150+\-50 bc	143BC	214BC	83BC
GU 2436	Material under foundation	600+\-50 bc	733BC	807BC	671BC

These dates derive from the interior occupation of the complex roundhouse on Dun Bharabhat, with GU 2436 providing a *terminus post quem* for construction and the remaining two dates providing a *terminus ante quem* for the primary occupation and partial collapse of the structure.

The Udal, North Uist (Crawford nd)
(Data taken from Ralston 1986).

Lab Ref	Context	UnCal.	WA	68% H	68% L
Q-1139	Layer XI ('Scotto-Pictish')	675+/-115 ad	745AD	638AD	872AD
Q-1132	Layer XII ('Scotto-Pictish')	595+/-115 ad	673AD	581AD	762AD
Q-1137	Layer XIII ('Scotto-Pictish')	450+/-80 ad	555AD	439AD	631AD
Q-1131	Layer XIV (post-wheelhouse)	340+/-120 ad	435AD	276AD	557AD

It is impossible to comment fully on these dates without access to the appropriate contextual information.

Eilean Olabhat, North Uist (Armit 1986 and 1988 b.)

Lab Ref	Context	UnCal.	WA	68% H	68% L
GU 2326	Primary occupation	60+\-50 bc	31BC	101BC	AD33
GU 2327	Metalworking debris	ad 150+\-50	AD214	AD124	AD273

GU 2326 derives from primary occupation of a slightly built, possibly cellular, structure while GU 2327 is from charcoal associated with a deposit of metalworking debris which includes a handpin mould.

Baleshare, North Uist (Barber forthcoming)

Lab Ref	Context	UnCal.	WA	68% H	68% L
GU-1960	Midden under quern/walls	290+\-55 bc	321BC	403BC	238BC
GU-1974	Cultivated Deposit	260+\-50 bc	288BC	393BC	219BC
GU-1970	Midden	315+\-50 bc	348BC	407BC	274BC
GU-1961	Cultivated deposit	440+\-55 bc	455BC	526BC	409BC
GU-1963	Midden	425+\-55 bc	438BC	486BC	403BC
GU-1962	Burial- prob contaminated	205+\-50 bc	222BC	342BC	142BC
GU-1964	Sand after structures	160+\-80 bc	159BC	303BC	75BC
GU-1972	Dumped material	135+\-50 bc	122BC	189BC	75BC
GU-1968	Sand sealing quern	95+\-50 bc	72BC	140BC	11BC
GU-1975	Dumped deposits	107+\-50 bc	86BC	181BC	28BC

+ 6 LBA Dates

The extensive Hebridean machair site at Baleshare was partially excavated in 1984 by the Scottish Central Excavation Unit as part of a wider programme of rescue excavation which also included work at Hornish Point (Barber forthcoming). The excavation revealed a number of fragmentary structures none of which can be conclusively linked with specific structural forms.

Hornish Point, South Uist (Barber forthcoming)

Lab Ref	Context	UnCal.	WA	68% H	68% L
GU-2015	Midden above structures	230+\-50 bc	253BC	358BC	181BC
GU-2024	Dumped deposits over Wh.	220+\-50 bc	241BC	352BC	170BC
GU-2025	,, ,, ,,	335+\-50 bc	367BC	410BC	295BC
GU-2028	Structure 7- contemp. Wh.?	320+\-50 bc	353BC	407BC	274BC
GU-2026	,, ,,	235+\-50 bc	259BC	362BC	187BC
GU-2017	Sand- Structures contemp?	385+\-50 bc	402BC	426BC	395BC
GU-2022	Rev wall- ,, ,,	360+\-50 bc	386BC	420BC	391BC
GU-2021	Cultivation- ,, ,,	375+\-50 bc	395BC	424BC	393BC
GU-2027	Cultivation under Wh.	420+\-50 bc	429BC	474BC	402BC
GU-2020	Cultivation under site	550+\-50 bc	650BC	792BC	521BC

Hornish Point is another Hebridean machair site excavated in the Central Excavation Unit's rescue programme in 1984 (Barber forthcoming). The dates form a coherent series and are all from reliable contexts linked to a series of structures which include at least one certain and two probable wheelhouses. The last two dates, GU 2027 and 2020, indicate that the structural sequence commenced after use of the area for cultivation in the late C5th BC.

The preliminary stratigraphic matrix for the site shows that the very tight cluster of dates GU 2017, 2021 and 2022, are likely to be contemporary with the occupation of Structures 1 and 2, both of which have the characteristic radial piers associated with wheelhouses (Barber pers. comm.). This would date the structures with a high degree of probability to between 430 and 390BC. The best preserved wheelhouse, Structure 5, is not dated directly but is post-dated by GU 2014, 2024 and 2025 which together suggest abandonment by around 300BC. The dates for the fragmentary Structure 7, which is stratigraphically parallel to Structure 5, are not inconsistent with this dating.

141

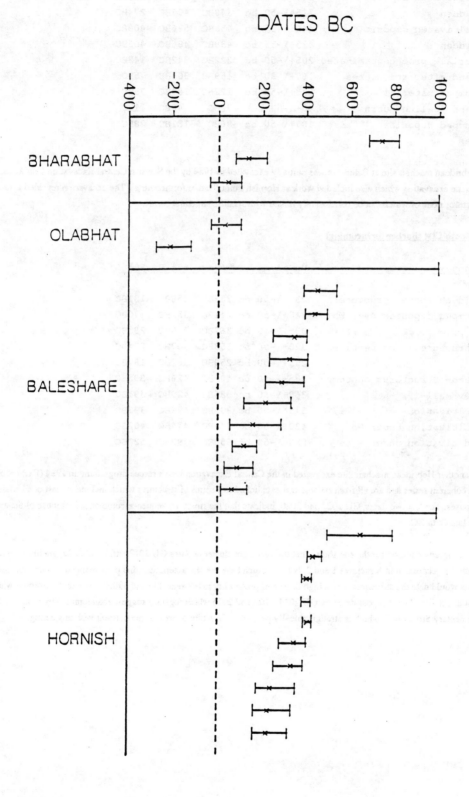

Ill. A1.1 C-14 Dates for the Western Isles

Appendix Two - Later Prehistoric Pottery in the Western Isles

The early pottery typologies constructed firstly by Lindsay Scott (1948) and later modified by Alison Young (1966) have been reassessed in Patrick Topping's doctoral thesis (1985). Scott's pottery typology was based on the excavated sequence at Clettraval. This started with the premise that the whole ceramic tradition of the Atlantic Scottish Iron Age derived from Wessex after the C1st BC 'Belgic invasions', and defined broad phases on the basis of a numerical analysis. Scott concluded that incised decoration was the predominant early form which then disappeared as relief decoration became more common. Curvilinear grooved decoration was believed to be restricted to the early period as were stamped decoration and applied bosses. Topping demonstrated that the assertions underlying Scott's typology were based on too few sherds and unclear stratigraphy (Topping 1985, 218-221).

Young's pottery typology was based on the Clettraval sequence and attempted to trace the ancestry of the early incised forms from local neolithic ceramics. Young saw the incised lattice, herringbone and chevron motifs as of neolithic descent, along with the applied rondels, while pin-stamping and finger-channelling were thought to be purely Iron Age inventions. Everted rims and applied cordons, skeuomorphs perhaps of leather thongs, were also seen as Iron Age introductions (Young 1966, 48). Again the basic problems of the Clettraval database hampered proper study and Mackie's excavations at Dun Mor Vaul (MacKie 1974) showed that the decorated forms co-existed in the record as far back as the mid-1st millennium BC. None of the attempts to apply typologies to the characteristic decorated assemblages of the Hebridean Iron Age have had any demonstrable utility or chronological significance.

A number of typological stages can be identified in the pottery of the 1st millennium AD in the Western Isles and the emergence of these forms from the preceding highly decorated assemblages can be traced. The recognition of the mid-late 1st millennium AD forms came initially from Young's work at Dun Cuier (C.28) and A' Cheardach Mhor (1955, 1959 and 1966; W.15) and was developed by Alan Lane on the basis of his work on the Udal pottery from North Uist (Lane 1983). This late stage has now been traced back to its development from the decorated forms at Cnip (W.1) with an intermediate assemblage at Eilean Olabhat (Armit 1988a and 1988b; C.19). The decorated early assemblages have not been subdivided in this thesis. Four stages of development can be traced: these are in no way definitive and are simple reflections of the excavation of particular sites with assemblages relating to particular parts of the sequence. Nonetheless it is useful to define and describe the types and summarise the dating evidence for each.

1. Mid-late 1st millennium BC decorated assemblages

The characteristic Atlantic Iron Age pottery forms have been recorded at a range of sites encompassing principally the monumental types of structure, the atlantic roundhouses and wheelhouses.

A wide range of form and a high percentage of decorated vessels with a wide variety of motifs are present. Decoration can be incised, applied, channelled or stamped. Rims are characteristically short and everted or inturned; flaring rims appear to be absent. No convincing typology has been formulated to subdivide these assemblages and many forms and motifs appear to be current from the mid-1st millennium BC through to the C1st BC or later.

The earliest dating of the type is the mid-1st millennium BC at Dun Mor Vaul (MacKie 1974) and it persists on a number of wheelhouse sites, e.g. Kilpheder (W.22) and A' Cheardach Mhor (W.15), after the local quern replacement horizon. At Dun Bharabhat (A.L18) this type of assemblage is associated with the final occupation in the last two centuries BC. At Cnip (W.1) it is succeeded directly, with no break in occupation, by the next assemblage type.

2. Cnip Phase 3 assemblage

This is a unique assemblage at present and dated only by its typological precedence over the C-14 dated assemblage at Eilean Olabhat (C.19). The large jars and decoration restricted to applied wavy cordons are similar to the Eilean Olabhat assemblage but the rims are short and everted as with the typologically preceding assemblage.

The full analysis of the Cnip ceramic assemblage should clarify the period when the pottery forms were changing. It is important to note that this type of form and motif were also present in the earlier assemblages and the development involves the reduction of variety rather than actual transformation.

3. Eilean Olabhat assemblage

The assemblage from Eilean Olabhat, North Uist, contemporary with the metalworking phase on that site, occupies a typologically intermediate position between the Iron Age and immediately pre-Norse forms. This type of assemblage has not been found in quantity but is present at A' Cheardach Mhor, in the post-wheelhouse levels, at Berie Structure 2 (C.5) and at Dun Cuier. All of these occurrences would support the C-14 dating at Eilean Olabhat (Appendix One), which places the material in the C2nd or C3rd AD. This also fits with the C-14 and artefactual dating for the succeeding forms.

These vessels have decoration restricted to applied wavy cordons, characteristically two (one below the rim and one at the widest part of the body). Vessels are relatively large jars and flaring rims are characteristic.

4. Pre-Norse assemblages

The ceramic assemblages of the immediately pre-Norse period in the Western Isles, dating from approximately 400 - 800AD, are relatively well established. This type of assemblage is known from the Udal (C.10) and Berie, Structures 1 and 2. Its chronology is therefore fixed by C-14 and by a range of diagnostic metalwork. Pottery of this form is also present, mixed with elements of the earlier assemblages, at Dun Cuier (A.B4) and Dun Carloway (A.L12).

These assemblages have a number of characteristics;

a. Total absence of decoration.

b. Rims are upright or flaring; no short everted rims.

c. Vessels tend to be large jars, with barrel and bucket shapes predominant.

d. Vessels are coarser than in preceding stages and coils are often clearly visible in section ('tongue-in-groove' style at the Udal). They are competently made but not as well-fired or as well-finished as earlier forms.

This pre-Norse assemblage type is easily distinguished from the succeeding Norse pottery by the total absence of characteristically Norse grass-marking and the absence of platter forms; forms and fabrics of the Norse period tend to be distinct from all preceding native developments (Lane 1983, 243).

Summary

A development can be traced in the ceramic assemblages of the Western Isles through the 1st millennium AD from the preceding 1st millennium BC assemblages. The early styles with their variety of form and decoration, through a gradual restriction in the range of decoration, give way to the development of plain flaring rims assemblages. The main trends can be summarised as follows:

a. Decoration: the reduction in the variety and quantity of decoration, and finally its abandonment.

b. Quality of Manufacture: the reduction in the numbers of small and fine vessels, until assemblages become entirely constituted of large coarse pots.

c. Rim Form: the lengthening of everted rims into the later flaring rim form.

This may be interpreted as signifying a change in the role played by ceramics in the domestic context. The assemblages become less elaborate, less differentiated and more purely utilitarian. The reduction in the elaboration of ceramics coincides with the abandonment of monumental architecture, and with the emergence of fine metalwork as an arena for elaboration. As yet there is insufficient information to establish whether the decline of decorated assemblages was sudden or gradual: it is clear however that the later assemblages have their roots in the early styles.

Introduction

The following catalogue lists all the known settlement sites in the Western Isles for which a later prehistoric date is known or suspected. The catalogue is divided by the classification system set out in Chapter Four. In the case of the atlantic roundhouses, for manageability's sake, the list has been subdivided by to island.

Within each division of the catalogue, sites are listed from north to south, firstly by island and then by grid reference. The heading 'Ref' denotes the specific reference for each site which encodes the class of the site (e.g. 'A' for atlantic roundhouse, 'W' for wheelhouse etc.) and its sequential catalogue number. Sites on which evidence for more than one settlement form is present are listed independently under each separate class: Ill. 4.2 provides a cross-referenced tabulation for excavated sites in this category. An entry 'Y' for 'Galleries' indicates that intramural galleries or cells have been detected.

The 'comments' section provides a brief summary of points relevant to the present work but does not seek to set out a comprehensive synthesis of all previous sources of information. The 'references' section provides the key references to fuller descriptions for individual monuments. Sites discussed at length in the text of the present work are not further described in the catalogue but instead are cross-referenced to the relevant chapter. All measurements, under 'altitude' and 'dimensions' are given in metres. Dimensions for atlantic roundhouses, promontory forts, walled islets and miscellaneous structures refer to external dimensions, except where stated, but refer to internal dimensions for wheelhouses, cellular and linear structures. Altitude is given to the nearest 5m.

Atlantic Roundhouses - Lewis

Ref: A.L1
Name: DUN SMIRVIG
Island: Lewis
NGR: NB 52 64
Location: Islet
Altitude:
Dimensions:
Shape: Circular
Galleries?:
Additional Features:

Comments: This site is now preserved as a mound in a loch but local tradition, recorded in 1867, suggests the former presence of a circular tower.

References: RCAHMS no.31.

Ref: A.L2
Name: DUN MARA
Island: Lewis
NGR: NB 4947 6313
Location: Promontory
Altitude: 5
Dimensions: 28 x 22
Shape: Oval

Galleries?:
Additional Features: Later Rectilinear Structures, Outer Walls

Comments: This roundhouse is situated on a strongly defended promontory with two external walls (Ill. 5.20).

References: RCAHMS no.13.

Ref: A.L3
Name: DUN SLEIBHE
Island: Lewis
NGR: NB 5050 6267
Location: Islet
Altitude: 40
Dimensions:
Shape: Circular
Galleries?:
Additional Features:

Comments: This site is now preserved as a mound in a drained loch but local tradition suggests the former presence of a circular tower.

References: RCAHMS no.30.

Ref: A.L4
Name: DUN AIRNESTEAN
Island: Lewis
NGR: NB 4886 6266
Location: Islet
Altitude: 5
Dimensions:
Shape: Circular
Galleries?:
Additional Features:

Comments: This site is an inaccessible tidal islet but clear vegetation marks indicate a circular building. Finds of iron age pottery have been recorded from the site.

References: RCAHMS no.33.

Ref: A.L5
Name: DUN BHARABHAT, GALSON
Island: Lewis
NGR: NB 4617 5965
Location: Islet
Altitude: 50
Dimensions: 19 x 16
Shape: Oval
Galleries?:
Additional Features: Causeway 14m, Cross-Causeway Wall, Three Additional 'Causeways'

Comments: This structure has walls preserved c. 2.5m wide and lies on a low islet. It has three stone 'causeways' radiating out into the loch, for which no explanation is readily forthcoming.

References: RCAHMS no.36.

Ref: A.L6
Name: DUN SOBHUILL
Island: Lewis
NGR: NB 4430 5950

Location: Promontory
Altitude: 5
Dimensions:
Shape: Circular
Galleries?: Y
Additional Features:

Comments: An 8m arc of a wall 4.5m wide, with a mural cell, is preserved on an eroding promontory.

References: RCAHMS no.29.

Ref: A.L7
Name: DUN SHIAVAT
Island: Lewis
NGR: NB 4759 5925
Location: Islet
Altitude: 65
Dimensions:
Shape: Circular
Galleries?:
Additional Features:

Comments: This site has substantial preserved walling but is wholly inaccessible due to its location and lack of a causeway.

References: RCAHMS no.14.

Ref: A.L8
Name: DUN BORVE
Island: Lewis
NGR: NB 4185 5803
Location: Moorland
Altitude: 40
Dimensions: 16
Shape: Circular
Galleries?: Y
Additional Features: Scarcement, Staircase

Comments: This site has walls c. 3.5m wide and lies buried in peat up to its second storey level (Ill. 5.15).

References: RCAHMS no.11.

Ref: A.L9
Name: DUN LOCH AN DUIN, SHADER
Island: Lewis
NGR: NB 3928 5435
Location: Islet
Altitude: 35
Dimensions: 17.5 x 16
Shape: Oval
Galleries?: Y
Additional Features: Later Rectilinear Occupation, Causeway 40m, Outer Wall, Harbour

Comments: This is a well-preserved galleried structure with walls some 3m wide. The galleries were observed on a subsequent visit to that on which the plan was made (Ill. 5.21).

References: RCAHMS no.28

Ref: A.L10
Name: DUN ARNOL
Island: Lewis
NGR: NB 3013 4901
Location: Islet
Altitude: 5
Dimensions: 15
Shape: Circular
Galleries?:
Additional Features: Causeway 20m, Later Circular Structure

Comments: This structure was unrecorded prior to 1984 but retains walls up to 4 courses high.

References: Armit 1985.

Ref: A.L11
Name: DUN LOCH AN DUNA, BRAGAR
Island: Lewis
NGR: NB 2854 4740
Location: Islet
Altitude: 25
Dimensions: 16.5
Shape: Circular
Galleries?: Y
Additional Features: Causeway, Outer Wall, Cross-Causeway Walls, External Rectilinear Structures, Scarcement, Annexe

Comments: This massive structure survives with walls c. 3.5m wide up to first floor level (Ill. 5.16).

References: RCAHMS no.10.

Ref: A.L12
Name: DUN CARLOWAY
Island: Lewis
NGR: NB 1901 4122
Location: Knoll
Altitude: 90
Dimensions: 15
Shape: Circular
Galleries?: Y
Additional Features: Stairs, Scarcement

Comments: This site was excavated by Tabraham and is discussed in Chapter Five (Ill. 5.2).

References: Tabraham 1976.

Ref: A.L13
Name: DUN BOROSDALE
Island: Lewis
NGR: NB 2125 4101
Location: Islet
Altitude: 17
Dimensions:
Shape: Circular
Galleries?:
Additional Features: Causeway

Comments: This site was located from the air in 1984 by DW Harding. It is not accessible to surface survey.

References: Armit 1985.

Ref: A.L14
Name: DUN STUAIGH
Island: Lewis
NGR: NB 1540 4025
Location: Islet
Altitude: 5
Dimensions: 14 x 13
Shape: Circular
Galleries?: Y
Additional Features:

Comments: This structure has walls 3m wide and lies on a tidal islet.

References: RCAHMS no.70.

Ref: A.L15
Name: DUN LOCH AN DUIN, CARLOWAY
Island: Lewis
NGR: NB 1975 3990
Location: Islet
Altitude: 0
Dimensions: 9 x 7.5
Shape: Circular
Galleries?:
Additional Features: Later Occupation, Abrupt-Ending Causeway, Cross-Causeway Wall, Annexe

Comments: This dilapidated and overgrown site has had the landward end of its causeway destroyed by a modern road (Ill. 5.17).

References: RCAHMS no.76.

Ref: A.L16
Name: DUN CAMUS NA CLIBHE
Island: Lewis
NGR: NB 085 364
Location: Moorland
Altitude:
Dimensions:
Shape:
Galleries?:
Additional Features:

Comments: This site is known only through a strong place-name tradition.

References: RCAHMS no.101.

Ref: A.L17
Name: DUN BHARABHAT, G.BERNERA
Island: Lewis
NGR: NB 1558 3555
Location: Islet
Altitude: 5
Dimensions: 15.5 x 14
Shape: Circular?
Galleries?: Y
Additional Features: Later Circular Structure, Causeway 33m, Stairs, Scarcement

Comments: This structure survives to first floor level and has complex architectural features preserved (Ill. 5.13).

References: RCAHMS no.71.

Ref: A.L18
Name: DUN BHARABHAT, CNIP
Island: Lewis
NGR: NB 0988 3531
Location: Islet
Altitude: 40
Dimensions: 11
Shape: Circular
Galleries?: Y
Additional Features: Causeway, Annexe

Comments: This site was excavated by Harding and is discussed in Chapter Five (Ill. 5.3).

References: RCAHMS no.72.

Ref: A.L19
Name: LOCH NA BERIE
Island: Lewis
NGR: NB 1035 3525
Location: Islet
Altitude: 5
Dimensions: 20
Shape: Circular
Galleries?: Y
Additional Features: Stairs, Scarcement, Causeway

Comments: This site was excavated by Harding and Armit and is discussed in Chapter Five (Ills. 5.4 and 5.5)

References: RCAHMS no.69.

Ref: A.L20
Name: DUN BHARABHAT CROULISTA 2
Island: Lewis
NGR: NB 0386 3487
Location: Islet
Altitude: 20
Dimensions: 10 x 8
Shape: Subcircular
Galleries?:
Additional Features: Later Structures, Harbour

Comments: This is a partly artificial islet with walls c. 2m wide and no trace of a causeway.

References: RCAHMS no.75.

Ref: A.L21
Name: DUN BARRAGLOM
Island: Lewis
NGR: NB 1677 3435
Location: Coastal
Altitude: 5
Dimensions: 15
Shape: Circular
Galleries?:
Additional Features: Later Baile, Possible Outer Wall

Comments: This site is set on an eroding cliff edge and is built over by a later baile.

References: RCAHMS no.77.

Ref: A.L22
Name: DUN BHARABHAT, BREASCLETE
Island: Lewis
NGR: NB 223 343
Location: Islet
Altitude: 5
Dimensions:
Shape:
Galleries?:
Additional Features: Causeway

Comments: This site is preserved as a very substantial stone mound, submerged in a dammed loch.

References: No references, located 1985.

Ref: A.L23
Name: DUN TIDDABORRAGH
Island: Lewis
NGR: NB 1829 3399
Location: Knoll
Altitude: 5
Dimensions: 18.3
Shape: Circular
Galleries?:
Additional Features: Possible Outer Wall

Comments: Very little now remains of this eroding massive stone roundhouse.

References: RCAHMS no.73.

Ref: A.L24
Name: DUN BORRANISH
Island: Lewis
NGR: NB 0502 3322
Location: Islet
Altitude: 5
Dimensions: 15 x 14
Shape: Subcircular
Galleries?: Y
Additional Features: Causeway 16m, Outer Wall, Earlier Causeway

Comments: This site is a massive subcircular roundhouse with walls c. 3.5 - 4m wide. The causeway appears to be of two-phase construction.

References: RCAHMS no.74.

Ref: A.L25
Name: DUN LOCH AN DUIN, BAYBLE
Island: Lewis
NGR: NB 516 305
Location: Islet
Altitude: 50
Dimensions: 16.5 x 15
Shape: Oval
Galleries?: Y
Additional Features: Later Rectilinear Structure, Causeway

Comments: This site survives as a stone mound robbed to provide stone for a later rectilinear house.

References: RCAHMS no.49.

Ref: A.L26
Name: DUN CROMORE
Island: Lewis
NGR: NB 4011 2068
Location: Islet
Altitude: 5
Dimensions: 13
Shape: Circular
Galleries?: Y
Additional Features: Later Rectilinear Structures, Submerged Causeway, Annexe, Stairs

Comments: This is a well-preserved roundhouse with walls varying from 1 - 2m wide and with a possible earlier roundhouse preserved as a courtyard (Ill. 5.14).

References: RCAHMS no.38, Armit 1985.

Atlantic Roundhouses - Harris

Ref: A.H1
Name: DUN LOCH AN DUIN TARANSAY
Island: Harris
NGR: NB 0216 0127
Location: Islet
Altitude: 70
Dimensions: 12 x 11
Shape: Oval
Galleries?:
Additional Features: Causeway 35m

Comments: The site is now truncated by erosion or robbing but appears to have been oval or circular. The walls are c. 3m wide.

References: RCAHMS no.117.

Ref: A.H2
Name: DUN CHLACH, TARANSAY
Island: Harris
NGR: NB 0411 0044
Location: Moorland
Altitude: 5
Dimensions:
Shape:
Galleries?:
Additional Features:

Comments: No trace remains of this structure which has been robbed out and covered by blown sand.

References: RCAHMS no.142.

Ref: A.H3
Name: DUN RHATHA, TARANSAY
Island: Harris
NGR: NF 0358 9961
Location: Knoll
Altitude: 15
Dimensions: 18.5 x 18
Shape: Oval
Galleries?:
Additional Features: Later Internal Modifications

Comments: The walls of this site are c. 3.5m wide and appear to have originally formed an oval structure.

References: RCAHMS no.118.

Ref: A.H4
Name: DUN BHUIRGH, BORVE
Island: Harris
NGR: NF 0325 9400
Location: Knoll
Altitude: 70
Dimensions: 13.5
Shape: Circular
Galleries?:
Additional Features: Later Circular Structure, Outer Wall, Annexe

Comments: The walls of this site are c. 2.5m wide and have a retaining wall 1.7m high for one third of the circuit (Ill. 5.19). The site occupies a commanding location and its entrance is on the north-east, away from the shallowest approach to the summit.

References: RCAHMS no.123.

Ref: A.H5
Name: DUN LOCH LANGAVAT
Island: Harris
NGR: NG 0432 9161
Location: Islet
Altitude: 35
Dimensions: 12.5
Shape: Circular
Galleries?:
Additional Features: Causeway 20m

Comments: This roundhouse, with walls c. 1.5m wide is connected to the shore by a partly submerged causeway. The structure is now very dilapidated.

References: RCAHMS no.124.

Ref: A.H6
Name: TOE HEAD
Island: Harris
NGR: NF 9700 9134
Location: Coastal
Altitude: 10
Dimensions: 16.6
Shape: Circular
Galleries?:
Additional Features: Later Chapel

Comments: The site was partly excavated by Simpson in 1965, revealing the dimensions of the structure under a relatively recent chapel.

References: DES 1965.

Ref: A.H7
Name: DUN SEANA CHAISTEAL
Island: Harris
NGR: NF 9017 8717
Location: Knoll
Altitude: 40
Dimensions: 17.6
Shape: Circular
Galleries?:
Additional Features: External Enclosure

Comments: This structure is preserved with walls up to 2m in height and 3.3m wide.

References: RCAHMS no.119.

Ref: A.H8
Name: PABBAY
Island: Harris
NGR: NF 8852 8659
Location: Knoll
Altitude: 25
Dimensions: 26 x 24
Shape:
Galleries?:
Additional Features: External Rectilinear Structure

Comments: The site is preserved as a substantial stone mound.

References: RCAHMS no.44.

Ref: A.H9
Name: DUN INNSEGALL
Island: Harris
NGR: NF 0194 8521
Location: Islet
Altitude: 3
Dimensions: 16.3 x 16
Shape: Oval
Galleries?:
Additional Features: Causeway 26m

Comments: This structure is connected *via* a causeway to another islet but not to the shore. Its walls are c. 3m wide.

References: RCAHMS no.144.

Ref: A.H10
Name: ST. CLEMENTS DUN, RODEL
Island: Harris
NGR: NF 0502 8321
Location: Knoll
Altitude: 50
Dimensions: 13.5
Shape: Circular
Galleries?: Y
Additional Features: External Structures, Internal Modification, Outer Wall, Annexe, External Structures

Comments: The main roundhouse has walls c. 3m wide and has a series of possibly contemporary structures, of uncertain form, clustered between it and its outer wall. It is approached by an artificial path (Ill. 5.18).

References: RCAHMS no.121.

Ref: A.H11
Name: DUNAN RUADH
Island: Harris
NGR: NF 9747 8312
Location: Islet
Altitude: 5
Dimensions: 14
Shape: Circular
Galleries?:
Additional Features:

Comments: The structure has walls c. 3.3m wide and lies on an overgrown islet.

References: RCAHMS no.123.

Atlantic Roundhouses - North Uist

Ref: A.NU1
Name: DUN AN STICER
Island: North Uist
NGR: NF 8972 7768
Location: Islet
Altitude: 5
Dimensions: 18.5
Shape: Circular
Galleries?: Y
Additional Features: Later Rectilinear Structure Inside, External Rectilinear Structure, Complex of Causeways, Outer Wall

Comments: This massive well-preserved structure is occupied by substantial medieval occupation, attributed to a son of Archibald the Clerk c. 1600 AD. The roundhouse has well preserved galleries and west entrance and survives to c. 3.6m high. It is approached via two substantial causeways which converge on a small rocky islet with one further causeway leading from here to the main islet. These causeways seem designed for wheeled traffic and are likely to be medieval in their present form.

References: RCAHMS no.171, Beveridge 1911, 138/144.

Ref: A.NU2
Name: DUN IOSAL AN DUIN
Island: North Uist
NGR: NF 9171 7699
Location: Islet
Altitude: 5
Dimensions:
Shape: Oval
Galleries?:
Additional Features: Causeway 35m, Outer Wall

Comments: The site is inaccessible and overgrown and has not been inspected other than from the shore of the loch. No dimensions have been recorded.

References: RCAHMS no.196, Beveridge 1911, 144.

Ref: A.NU3
Name: RUDH AN DUIN
Island: North Uist
NGR: NF 7857 7617
Location: Islet
Altitude: 5
Dimensions: 24
Shape: Circular
Galleries?: Y
Additional Features: Causeway

Comments: Excavated by Beveridge (Ill. 5.6). Discussion in Chapter Five.

References: RCAHMS no.184, Beveridge 1911, 214/8.

Ref: A.NU4
Name: DUN A GHALLAIN
Island: North Uist
NGR: NF 7479 7598
Location: Islet
Altitude: 5
Dimensions:
Shape:
Galleries?:
Additional Features: Causeway, Later Occupation

Comments: Excavated by Beveridge prior to 1911. Discussed in Chapter Five. Located in an inaccessible marshy loch.

References: RCAHMS no.191, Beveridge 1911, 196/7.

Ref: A.NU5
Name: DUN ROSAIL
Island: North Uist
NGR: NF 8781 7597
Location: Knoll
Altitude: 5
Dimensions:
Shape:
Galleries?:
Additional Features:

Comments: The site survives as a substantial mound with no measurable original dimensions. The mound is c. 2.5m high.

References: RCAHMS no.325, Beveridge 1911, 226.

Ref: A.NU6
Name: EILEAN A GHALLAIN
Island: North Uist
NGR: NF 7483 7589
Location: Islet
Altitude: 5
Dimensions: 12.75
Shape: Circular
Galleries?:
Additional Features: Causeway, Secondary Internal Occupation

Comments: Excavated by Beveridge prior to 1911. Discussed in Chapter Five. Walls 2.1 - 3m wide. Located in an inaccessible marshy loch.

References: RCAHMS no.192, Beveridge 1911, 197.

Ref: A.NU7
Name: DUN THOMAIDH
Island: North Uist
NGR: NF 7564 7562
Location: Islet
Altitude: 5
Dimensions: 14.6
Shape: Circular
Galleries?: Y
Additional Features: Later Occupation, Causeway 80m, Causeway Gap, External Occupation and Enclosure, Harbour

Comments: Excavated by Beveridge (Ill. 5.7); discussed in Chapters Five and Seven.

References: RCAHMS no.212, Beveridge 1930.

Ref: A.NU8
Name: OBAN SKIBINISH 1
Island: North Uist
NGR: NF 8348 7518
Location: Islet
Altitude: 5
Dimensions:
Shape: Oval
Galleries?:
Additional Features: Causeway 40m, External Structure, Outer Wall

Comments: This site lies on a tidal islet and is represented by a mound some 1.5m high and a small ruined external structure to its east.

References: RCAHMS no.182, Beveridge 1911, 220/1.

Ref: A.NU9
Name: DUN SKELLOR
Island: North Uist
NGR: NF 8075 7509
Location: Moorland
Altitude: 20
Dimensions: 17-20?
Shape: Circular
Galleries?:
Additional Features:

Comments: The structure is now a substantial grassy mound. The dimensions have been based on visible facing stones around the base of the mound.

References: RCAHMS no.293, Beveridge 1911, 219.

Ref: A.NU10
Name: DUN SCOLPAIG
Island: North Uist
NGR: NF 7310 7503
Location: Islet
Altitude: 20
Dimensions:
Shape:
Galleries?:
Additional Features: Causeway, C19th Tower

Comments: Built over by a tower in 1830. A local tradition relates to C15th AD occupation by Donald Herroch.

References: RCAHMS no.322, Beveridge 1911, 193/4.

Ref: A.NU11
Name: DUN TOLOMAN
Island: North Uist
NGR: NF 8207 7492
Location: Islet
Altitude: 10
Dimensions:
Shape: Oval
Galleries?:

Additional Features: Causeway (Probable), East and West Annexes, Outer Wall

Comments: The site is a substantial marsh islet with no wall dimensions measurable. The mound is c. 25 x 20m.

References: RCAHMS no.294, Beveridge 1911, 219/20.

Ref: A.NU12
Name: OBAN TRUMISGARRY
Island: North Uist
NGR: NF 8726 7470
Location: Islet
Altitude: 5
Dimensions:
Shape: Circular
Galleries?:
Additional Features: Causeway 30m

Comments: This site survives only as a overgrown stony mound on an islet in a tidal loch.

References: RCAHMS no.324, Beveridge 1911, 225.

Ref: A.NU13
Name: GARRY IOCHDRACH
Island: North Uist
NGR: NF 7724 7427
Location: Machair
Altitude: 5
Dimensions: 14.6
Shape: Circular
Galleries?: Y
Additional Features: Secondary Wheelhouse

Comments: Excavated by Beveridge (Ill. 5.8). Discussed in Chapter Five. Wheelhouse discussed in Chapter Six. The diameter is taken on the north-west/south-east axis where both opposing external wall-faces appear to be intact.

References: Beveridge 1931.

Ref: A.NU14
Name: CNOC A COMHDHALACH
Island: North Uist
NGR: NF 7708 7413
Location: Machair
Altitude: 5
Dimensions: 11.6
Shape: Circular
Galleries?: Y
Additional Features: Secondary Internal Structures

Comments: Excavated by Beveridge prior to 1911 (Ill. 5.9). Discussed in Chapter Five. Internal wheelhouse discussed in Chapter Six.

References: RCAHMS no.269, Beveridge 1911, 200/6.

Ref: A.NU15
Name: DUN NA MAIRBHE
Island: North Uist
NGR: NF 86 74
Location: Islet

Altitude: 5
Dimensions: 18.6
Shape: Circular
Galleries?:
Additional Features: Annexe

Comments: This tidal islet site has preserved walls 5.8m wide and 0.3m high.

References: RCAHMS no.183, Beveridge 1911, 224/5.

Ref: A.NU16
Name: DUN BRU
Island: North Uist
NGR: NF 8956 7390
Location: Islet
Altitude: 5
Dimensions: 10
Shape: Oval
Galleries?:
Additional Features: Causeway 18m, Possible Outer Wall

Comments: A stony mound, 3m high, occupies this rocky islet. Dimensions were recorded by the RCAHMS.

References: RCAHMS no.296, Beveridge 1911, 152.

Ref: A.NU17
Name: EILEAN MALEIT
Island: North Uist
NGR: NF 7748 7388
Location: Islet
Altitude: 5
Dimensions: 16
Shape: Circular
Galleries?: Y
Additional Features: Causeway, Secondary Internal Structures

Comments: Excavated by Beveridge prior to 1911 (Ill. 5.10). Discussed in Chapter Five. Internal wheelhouse discussed in Chapter Six.

References: RCAHMS no.270, Beveridge 1911, 207/9.

Ref: A.NU18
Name: DUN AONGHUIS
Island: North Uist
NGR: NF 8560 7381
Location: Islet
Altitude: 5
Dimensions:
Shape:
Galleries?:
Additional Features: Later Occupation, Causeway, Outer Wall, Harbour

Comments: A small medieval fort, or 'late dun' surmounts this islet and is described by Beveridge and the RCAHMS (traditional occupation by Angus Fhionn c. 1500 AD). There are traces of an earlier roundhouse in the form of massive foundations for a circular structure under the internal rectilinear medieval buildings. A submerged and partially dismantled causeway may relate to this phase. The outer wall and boat noost or harbour may relate to any phase of the site's use.

References: RCAHMS no.213, Beveridge 1911, 223/4.

Ref: A.NU19
Name: DUN TORCUILL
Island: North Uist
NGR: NF 8887 7373
Location: Islet
Altitude: 5
Dimensions: 18.6 x 16
Shape: Oval
Galleries?: Y
Additional Features: Later Internal Occupation, Causeway 35m

Comments: This is an exceptionally well-preserved site with walls 2.3 - 3.8m wide and up to 3m high. Later structures occupy the interior and the area to the front of the roundhouse opposite the causeway.

References: RCAHMS no.172, Beveridge 1911, 149, Thomas 1890, 365

Ref: A.NU20
Name: BUAILE RISARY
Island: North Uist
NGR: NF 7665 7278
Location: Moorland
Altitude: 50
Dimensions:
Shape:
Galleries?:
Additional Features: Later Baile Settlement

Comments: Excavated by Beveridge prior to 1911. Discussed in Chapter Five.

References: Beveridge, 210, RCAHMS no.193.

Ref: A.NU21
Name: DUN NIGHEAN RIGH LOCHLAIN
Island: North Uist
NGR: NF 9528 7239
Location: Islet
Altitude: 5
Dimensions: 10
Shape: Circular
Galleries?:
Additional Features: Causeway, Internal Secondary Occupation

Comments: This structure rises directly from the loch and has a submerged causeway.

References: RCAHMS no.199, Beveridge 1911, 146.

Ref: A.NU22
Name: DUN LOCH NA CAIGINN
Island: North Uist
NGR: NF 9510 7199
Location: Islet
Altitude: 5
Dimensions: 12
Shape: Circular

Galleries?: Y
Additional Features: Later Rectilinear Structures, Causeway 30m, Cross-Causeway Wall, Harbour, Outer Wall

Comments: The structure survives to a height of 1.2m on an overgrown defended islet.

References: RCAHMS no.189, Beveridge 1911, 148.

Ref: A.NU23
Name: DUN LOCH CNOC NAN UAN
Island: North Uist
NGR: NF 7184 7146
Location: Islet
Altitude: 20
Dimensions:
Shape:
Galleries?:
Additional Features: Causeway 36m

Comments: This site is represented by a 20m diameter mound in a drained loch.

References: RCAHMS no.320, Beveridge 1911, 192.

Ref: A.NU24
Name: DUN GROGARRY
Island: North Uist
NGR: NF 7125 7146
Location: Islet
Altitude: 5
Dimensions: 18
Shape: Circular
Galleries?:
Additional Features: Causeway 20m, Outer Wall

Comments: The site occupies an islet in a partially drained loch. It retains evidence of walls 5m thick and up to c. 1.5m high.

References: RCAHMS no.179, Beveridge 1911, 191.

Ref: A.NU25
Name: SOUTH CLETTRAVAL
Island: North Uist
NGR: NF 749 714
Location: Moorland
Altitude: 110
Dimensions: 13
Shape: Circular
Galleries?:
Additional Features:

Comments: The massive stone roundhouse is constructed over the remains of a chambered tomb.

References: RCAHMS no.178, Beveridge 1911, 189.

Ref: A.NU26
Name: DUN MHIC RHAOUILL
Island: North Uist
NGR: NF 7263 7128
Location: Islet
Altitude: 20
Dimensions: 12.75
Shape: Circular

Galleries?:
Additional Features: Later Occupation, Causeway 45m, External Occupation, Harbour

Comments: The sole description of this site comes from Beveridge's work. His description of the diameter is ambiguous, not specifying internal or external diameter; it has been assumed that he referred to external diameter, the opposite view implying an internal diameter of less than 2m which seems unlikely to have gone without specific comment.

References: RCAHMS no.205, Beveridge 1911, 192.

Ref: A.NU27
Name: AN CHAISTEIL
Island: North Uist
NGR: NF 6970 7119
Location: Coastal
Altitude: 5
Dimensions:
Shape:
Galleries?:
Additional Features: Later Occupation

Comments: Only isolated facing slabs survive.

References: RCAHMS no.319, Beveridge 1911, 191.

Ref: A.NU28
Name: DUN SCARIE
Island: North Uist
NGR: NF 7178 7055
Location: Islet
Altitude: 5
Dimensions:
Shape:
Galleries?:
Additional Features: Later Rectlinear Structures, Causeway 34m

Comments: Only a turf covered stony mound, 1.2m high, remains on this site.

References: RCAHMS no.318, Beveridge 1911, 190.

Ref: A.NU29
Name: SITHEAN TUATH
Island: North Uist
NGR: NF 7193 7017
Location: Islet
Altitude: 10
Dimensions: 18
Shape: Circular
Galleries?:
Additional Features:

Comments: This site is a 3m high stony mound on an islet in a drained loch. There are insufficient lengths of walling to give dimensions.

References: Beveridge 1911, 190.

Ref: A.NU30
Name: SRATH BEAG AN DUIN

Island: North Uist
NGR: NF 82 70
Location: Moorland
Altitude: c. 50
Dimensions: 12
Shape:
Galleries?:
Additional Features:

Comments: Confirmation of the place-name is given by the remains of a stony mound with facing stones.

References: RCAHMS no.295.

Ref: A.NU31
Name: EILEAN DUBH
Island: North Uist
NGR: NF 7173 6958
Location: Islet
Altitude: 5
Dimensions: 13
Shape: Circular
Galleries?:
Additional Features:

Comments: All that remains of this site is a mound in a drained loch. The external diameter measurement must be regarded as approximate.

References: Beveridge 1911, 188.

Ref: A.NU32
Name: DUN LOCH SHANNDAIDH
Island: North Uist
NGR: NF 7325 6858
Location: Islet
Altitude: 10
Dimensions:
Shape:
Galleries?:
Additional Features:

Comments: This islet retains some evidence of having been the site of a massive stone structure.

References: Beveridge 1911, 189, Thomas 1890, 403.

Ref: A.NU33
Name: DUN STEINGARRY
Island: North Uist
NGR: NF 7198 6838
Location: Islet
Altitude: 5
Dimensions:
Shape: Circular
Galleries?:
Additional Features:

Comments: This site is a mound in a loch drained prior to 1793.

References: RCAHMS no.316, Beveridge 1911, 188.

Ref: A.NU34
Name: DUN LEIRARAY
Island: North Uist

NGR: NF 9126 6778
Location: Islet
Altitude: 5
Dimensions:
Shape: Circular
Galleries?:
Additional Features:

Comments: No trace of structure now survives on this rocky outcrop islet.

References: RCAHMS no.302, Beveridge 1911, 158.

Ref: A.NU35
Name: DUN LOCH HUNDER
Island: North Uist
NGR: NF 9048 6526
Location: Islet
Altitude: 5
Dimensions: 12.5 x 10.5
Shape: Circular
Galleries?: Y
Additional Features: Causeways 40 and 50m, Additional islet, Cross-Causeway Wall

Comments: The roundhouse is reached over two causeways with an intervening islet. The walls survive to 2m high and contain two super-imposed intra-mural galleries.

References: RCAHMS no.173, Beveridge 1911, 161.

Ref: A.NU36
Name: DUN LOCH NAN STRUBHAN
Island: North Uist
NGR: NF 80 64
Location: Islet
Altitude: 5
Dimensions:
Shape: Oval
Galleries?:
Additional Features: Causeway 32m

Comments: The structure survives as a stony mound c. 2m high.

References: RCAHMS no.177, Beveridge 1911, 185.

Ref: A.NU37
Name: DUN NIGHEAN RIGH LOCHLAIN
Island: North Uist
NGR: NF 8636 6398
Location: Islet
Altitude: 5
Dimensions: 10
Shape: Oval
Galleries?:
Additional Features: Causeway 25m, Internal Structure?

Comments: The structure rises straight from the loch and has a south-east entrance. The interior is too overgrown to enable the character of secondary occupation to be assessed. The site is also known as Dun Breinish or Dun Eidann.

References: RCAHMS no.214, Beveridge 1911, 165.

Ref: A.NU38
Name: DUNAN MOR
Island: North Uist
NGR: NF 7815 6339
Location: Machair
Altitude: 5
Dimensions:
Shape:
Galleries?:
Additional Features:

Comments: The place name suggests the former presence of a roundhouse, now represented by a substantial mound.

References: RCAHMS no.314, Beveridge 1911, 185.

Ref: A.NU39
Name: DUN BAILLERAY
Island: North Uist
NGR: NF 7817 6282
Location: Moorland
Altitude: 5
Dimensions:
Shape: Circular
Galleries?:
Additional Features: Later Cottages

Comments: This structure comprises a stony mound surmounted by relatively recent structures.

References: RCAHMS no.315, Beveridge 1911, 184.

Ref: A.NU40
Name: DUN MOR
Island: North Uist
NGR: NF 7808 6218
Location: Islet
Altitude: 5
Dimensions:
Shape: Circular
Galleries?:
Additional Features: Causeway

Comments: This site is represented by a stony mound in a drained loch.

References: RCAHMS no.313, Beveridge 1911, 184.

Ref: A.NU41
Name: DUN NA DISE
Island: North Uist
NGR: NF 8072 6172
Location: Islet
Altitude: 5
Dimensions: 20 x 14
Shape: Oval
Galleries?: Y
Additional Features:

Comments: The structure lies on a tidal islet and is now suffering greatly from erosion. The galleries are visible in section. To some extent the dimensions may be distorted by collapse and displacement.

References: RCAHMS no.175, Beveridge 1911, 181.

Ref: A.NU42
Name: DUN NA H-OLA
Island: North Uist
NGR: NF 7854 6161
Location: Islet
Altitude: 5
Dimensions:
Shape:
Galleries?:
Additional Features:

Comments: The site is preserved as a mound, 0.3m high and c. 20m in diameter, in an machair loch drained in 1911.

References: RCAHMS no.312, Beveridge 1911, 183.

Ref: A.NU43
Name: BEINN NA COILLE
Island: North Uist
NGR: NF 8363 6151
Location: Moorland
Altitude: 20
Dimensions: 21 x 18.5
Shape: Oval
Galleries?:
Additional Features: Later Shielings

Comments: This structure is surmounted by extensive later buildings, rectilinear structures and 'boat-shaped' shielings, which prevent detailed measurements.

References: RCAHMS no.311.

Ref: A.NU44
Name: EILEAN SCALASTER
Island: North Uist
NGR: NF 8094 6113
Location: Islet
Altitude: 5
Dimensions: 10 x 8
Shape: D-shaped
Galleries?:
Additional Features:

Comments: The structure has walls 2.3m wide and 1.3m high. An entrance is traceable on the east side.

References: RCAHMS no.203, Beveridge 1911, 181.

Ref: A.NU45
Name: DUN BAN HACKLETT
Island: North Uist
NGR: NF 8605 6012
Location: Islet
Altitude: 5
Dimensions: 9
Shape: Circular
Galleries?:
Additional Features: Causeway 25m, External 'Hut Circle', Outer Wall

Comments: The site is surrounded by an outer wall of approximately 20m diameter. The structure inside is c. 2m high with a probable 9m diameter.

References: RCAHMS no.186.

Ref: A.NU46
Name: LOCH OBISARY C
Island: North Uist
NGR: NF 88 60
Location: Islet
Altitude: 5
Dimensions: 20
Shape: Circular
Galleries?:
Additional Features:

Comments: The wall of this structure projects above the surface of the loch but the interior is entirely flooded.

References: RCAHMS no.298, Beveridge 1911, 167/9.

Ref: A.NU47
Name: DUN AN T-SIAMAIN
Island: North Uist
NGR: NF 8857 5947
Location: Islet
Altitude: 5
Dimensions: 14 x 12.75
Shape: Oval
Galleries?:
Additional Features: Later Shielings, Zigzag Causeway 25m, Cross-Causeway Wall, Harbour

Comments: The structure is full of collapsed rubble which prevents accurate measurement of the internal diameter.

References: RCAHMS no.211, Beveridge 1911, 169/70.

Ref: A.NU48
Name: DUN LOCH NAN GEALAG
Island: North Uist
NGR: NF 8650 5939
Location: Islet
Altitude: 5
Dimensions:
Shape: Oval
Galleries?:
Additional Features: Causeway 30m, Causeway Gap

Comments: The site survives as a mass of tumbled stone with fragments of a stone wall on its south side.

References: RCAHMS no.174, Beveridge 1911, 176.

Ref: A.NU49
Name: DUN CHEIREIN
Island: North Uist
NGR: NF 8578 5855
Location: Knoll
Altitude: 10
Dimensions:
Shape:
Galleries?:
Additional Features:

Comments: This site is now occupied by a crofter's cottage.

References: RCAHMS no.310, Beveridge 1911, 176.

Ref: A.NU50
Name: RUADH AN DUIN, EAVAL
Island: North Uist
NGR: NF 8973 5850
Location: Islet
Altitude: 5
Dimensions:
Shape:
Galleries?:
Additional Features: Later Shielings

Comments: A curved fragment of massive stone walling, 14m long, 1.2m wide and 0.6m high. The RCAHMS report appears to be describing later rough walling on the islet.

References: RCAHMS no.188.

Ref: A.NU51
Name: DUN BAN, GRIMSAY 1
Island: North Uist
NGR: NF 8699 5695
Location: Islet
Altitude: 10
Dimensions: 15
Shape: Circular
Galleries?: Y
Additional Features: Later Cellular Occupation, Causeway 30m

Comments: Excavated by Thomas (Ill. 5.11). The roundhouse is discussed in Chapter Five and the cellular structures in Chapter Seven.

References: RCAHMS no.299, Beveridge 1911, 172, Thomas 1890, 399.

Atlantic Roundhouses - Benbecula

Ref: A.BE1
Name: DUN UACHDAR
Island: Benbecula
NGR: NF 8003 5538
Location: Islet
Altitude: 5
Dimensions: 16 x 15
Shape: Oval
Galleries?:
Additional Features: Later Walling, Causeway 42m

Comments: The site has a submerged causeway and has been modified with the addition of a recent irregular wall.

References: RCAHMS no.359.

Ref: A.BE2
Name: DUN BHUIDHE MHURCHDAIDH
Island: Benbecula
NGR: NF 7942 5452
Location: Islet
Altitude: 5
Dimensions: 18
Shape: Circular
Galleries?: Y

Additional Features: Later Baile, Causeway 70m, 2nd Causeway 150m) Cross-Causeway Wall, Internal Square Structure, Outer Wall

Comments: The site lies in a drained loch and has a substantial baile settlement over the original features. It is approached by two causeways with a large intervening islet.

References: RCAHMS no.349.

Ref: A.BE3
Name: DUN LOCH NA BEIRE
Island: Benbecula
NGR: NF 8323 5421
Location: Islet
Altitude: 10
Dimensions:
Shape:
Galleries?:
Additional Features: Harbour

Comments: The site is an overgrown islet with place-name evidence and local tradition to suggest the former presence of a substantial roundhouse.

References: RCAHMS no.365.

Ref: A.BE4
Name: DUN EILEAN IAIN
Island: Benbecula
NGR: NF 7889 5351
Location: Islet
Altitude: 5
Dimensions: 35
Shape: Circular
Galleries?:
Additional Features: Later Structures, Causeway 80m, Harbour

Comments: The site contains three substantial boat-shaped buildings secondary to the main structure. The nature of the original structure is unclear but a round-house is suggested by the quantity of stone.

References: RCAHMS no.348.

Ref: A.BE5
Name: DUN TORCUSAY
Island: Benbecula
NGR: NF 7618 5313
Location: Islet
Altitude: 5
Dimensions: 13 x 11
Shape: Oval
Galleries?: Y
Additional Features: Causeway

Comments: This is an islet entirely obscured by reeds which cover internal stonework. The causeway is of unusual construction being represented by two parallel lines of stone which presumably supported a timber superstructure.

References: RCAHMS no.347.

Ref: A.BE6
Name: DUN LOCH AN DUNAIN
Island: Benbecula
NGR: NF 7786 5129
Location: Islet
Altitude: 5
Dimensions: 25 x 17
Shape: Oval
Galleries?:
Additional Features: Later Occupation, Causeway 45m

Comments: This site is a robbed out stone structure on an islet in a drained loch.

References: RCAHMS no.362.

Ref: A.BE7
Name: DUN AONGHAIS
Island: Benbecula
NGR: NF 7968 5125
Location: Islet
Altitude: 5
Dimensions: 10
Shape: Circular
Galleries?:
Additional Features: Later Occupation, Causeway 75m

Comments: The site is an overgrown rubble covered islet.

References: RCAHMS no.345.

Ref: A.BE8
Name: DUN RUADH
Island: Benbecula
NGR: NF 7986 5105
Location: Islet
Altitude: 5
Dimensions:
Shape: Oval
Galleries?:
Additional Features: Later Circular Structure, Causeway 75m

Comments: The site is an overgrown islet with natural outcrop forming part of the circuit of the walls.

References: RCAHMS no.344.

Ref: A.BE9
Name: DUN SHUNISH
Island: Benbecula
NGR: NF 7807 5086
Location: Islet
Altitude: 5
Dimensions: 11
Shape: Circular
Galleries?:
Additional Features:

Comments: The site is a former islet in a drained loch.

References: RCAHMS no.361.

Ref: A.BE10
Name: DUN MHIC UISDEIN
Island: Benbecula

NGR: NF 8001 5065
Location: Islet
Altitude: 5
Dimensions: 17 x 15
Shape: D-shaped
Galleries?:
Additional Features:

Comments: The wall of this structure is formed of very large stones and is almost straight on its west side.

References: RCAHMS no.343.

Ref: A.BE11
Name: DUN GUNISARY BAY
Island: Benbecula
NGR: NF 7985 4916
Location: Islet
Altitude: 5
Dimensions: 17 x 13
Shape: Oval
Galleries?:
Additional Features: Causeway 15m

Comments: The site projects c. 1m above the water level in a small loch. The structure has been substantially robbed.

References: RCAHMS no.346.

Ref: A.BE12
Name: DUN FHEARCHAIR
Island: Benbecula
NGR: NF 8010 4890
Location: Islet
Altitude: 10
Dimensions: 15
Shape:
Galleries?:
Additional Features:

Comments: This site is a shapeless stony mound now occupying a promontory into a loch.

References: RCAHMS no.360.

Ref: A.BE13
Name: DUN OB SAILE
Island: Benbecula
NGR: NF 8115 4874
Location: Islet
Altitude: 5
Dimensions:
Shape: Circular
Galleries?:
Additional Features:

Comments: The site is in poor condition and occupies a small tidal islet.

References: Located 1985, no references.

Atlantic Roundhouses - South Uist

Ref: A.S1
Name: DUN BUIDHE, ARDNAMONIE

Island: South Uist
NGR: NF 7735 4629
Location: Islet
Altitude: 5
Dimensions: 18
Shape: Circular
Galleries?: Y
Additional Features: Causeway, External Structures

Comments: The walls of this structure are c. 3.5m wide and the mound stands some 3m high. There are traces of a gallery within the walls, c. 0.8m wide.

References: RCAHMS no.373.

Ref: A.S2
Name: ARDNAMONIE
Island: South Uist
NGR: NF 7723 4624
Location: Islet
Altitude: 5
Dimensions:
Shape:
Galleries?:
Additional Features: Later Baile

Comments: The site survives as a very substantial stone mound under a later baile.

References: RCAHMS no.433.

Ref: A.S3
Name: DUN NA BUAIL-UACHDRAICH
Island: South Uist
NGR: NF 7777 4606
Location: Islet
Altitude: 5
Dimensions: 17
Shape: Circular
Galleries?:
Additional Features: Outer Wall

Comments: The walls of this structure are c. 4.5m wide and c. 1.2m high. An outer wall flanks the south part of the islet

References: RCAHMS no.374.

Ref: A.S4
Name: DUN LOCH AN DAILL
Island: South Uist
NGR: NF 7969 4592
Location: Islet
Altitude: 5
Dimensions:
Shape:
Galleries?:
Additional Features: Causeway 30m

Comments: No details are available on this site which appears never to have been visited. Access is prevented by the deeply submerged causeway and nesting birds. Quantities of stone indicate the presence of a roundhouse.

References: RCAHMS no.417.

Ref: A.S5
Name: DUN UISELAN
Island: South Uist
NGR: NF 7776 4536
Location: Islet
Altitude: 5
Dimensions: 23 x 17
Shape: Oval
Galleries?: Y
Additional Features: Two Later Rectilinear Structures, Causeway 60m

Comments: This site is an overgrown islet with a substantial causeway which bends midway along its course. The roundhouse entrance lies around the islet from the causeway.

References: RCAHMS no.376.

Ref: A.S6
Name: DUN MOR
Island: South Uist
NGR: NF 7744 4152
Location: Islet
Altitude: 5
Dimensions: 11 x 9
Shape: Oval
Galleries?:
Additional Features: Later Structures, Causeway, Outer Wall

Comments: The structure was robbed out in the early part of this century and is very dilapidated. Late rectilinear and oval structures occupy part of the structure.

References: RCAHMS no.383.

Ref: A.S7
Name: DUN CILLE BHANAIN
Island: South Uist
NGR: NF 7685 4138
Location: Promontory
Altitude: 5
Dimensions: 18 x 15
Shape: Oval
Galleries?:
Additional Features:

Comments: The mound of this structure survives to c. 0.8m in height and is overlain by a chapel.

References: RCAHMS no.416.

Ref: A.S8
Name: DUN ALIGARRY
Island: South Uist
NGR: NF 7655 3917
Location: Islet
Altitude: 2
Dimensions: 18
Shape: Circular
Galleries?:
Additional Features: Possible Causeway

Comments: The structure survives with walls c. 4m wide on an islet in a drained loch. A modern shooting butt obscures the interior.

References: RCAHMS no.427.

Ref: A.S9
Name: DUN BUIDHE, DRUIDIBEG
Island: South Uist
NGR: NF 7744 3883
Location: Islet
Altitude: 5
Dimensions:
Shape: Circular
Galleries?:
Additional Features: Causeway 62m, Outer Wall

Comments: The structure survives as a stone mound c. 2.5m high and is surrounded by an outer wall of c. 31m diameter.

References: RCAHMS no.430, Blundell 1913, 295.

Ref: A.S10
Name: DUN ALTABRUG
Island: South Uist
NGR: NF 7490 3439
Location: Islet
Altitude: 5
Dimensions: 10 x 9
Shape: Oval
Galleries?:
Additional Features: Causeway 33m, Outer Wall

Comments: The structure survives to c. 1.3m high with walls 3 - 4m wide and a north-east entrance.

References: RCAHMS no.378, Blundell 1913, 295.

Ref: A.S11
Name: DUN GRO GHOT
Island: South Uist
NGR: NF 8579 3436
Location: Moorland
Altitude: 45
Dimensions:
Shape:
Galleries?:
Additional Features:

Comments: A substantial stone mound and the placename suggest the existence of an atlantic roundhouse on this site.

References: RCAHMS no.418.

Ref: A.S12
Name: STONEYBRIDGE
Island: South Uist
NGR: NF 7386 3357
Location: Islet
Altitude: 5
Dimensions:
Shape:
Galleries?:
Additional Features:

Comments: The substantial walling of a roundhouse was located while trenching around a modern house in 1963. The site occupies a former islet in a drained loch.

References: RCAHMS no.426.

Ref: A.S13
Name: DUN VULAN
Island: South Uist
NGR: NF 7140 2980
Location: Islet
Altitude: 3
Dimensions: 18
Shape: Circular
Galleries?: Y
Additional Features: Later Circular Structure

Comments: This site is an eroding roundhouse by a modern road which has obscured the original locational setting and drainage of the area. The walls are 4 - 5m wide and contain a gallery on the north-east. An internal secondary structure occupies the roundhouse.

References: RCAHMS no.375.

Ref: A.S14
Name: LOCH ERISORT
Island: South Uist
NGR: NF 7776 2967
Location: Moorland
Altitude: 15
Dimensions: 14
Shape: Circular
Galleries?:
Additional Features: Later Shieling

Comments: This appears to be a stone roundhouse with concentric walls and a north-west entrance.

References: NMR.

Ref: A.S15
Name: DUN LOCH AN DUIN, BORNISH
Island: South Uist
NGR: NF 7414 2907
Location: Islet
Altitude: 5
Dimensions: 15
Shape: Circular
Galleries?:
Additional Features: Causeway 30m, Outer Wall

Comments: This structure had walls of c. 5m wide. It was largely obliterated to build two sheepfolds prior to 1914. the outer wall is unlikely to be contemporary with the the original structure of which only a short arc remains visible.

References: RCAHMS no.377.

Ref: A.S16
Name: DUN LOCH GREANABRECK
Island: South Uist
NGR: NF 7445 2724
Location: Islet
Altitude: 5

Dimensions: 15 x 10
Shape: Oval
Galleries?:
Additional Features: Causeway 43m

Comments: The structure surmounts an oval artificial islet. The walls are up to 5m wide.

References: RCAHMS no.425, Blundell 1913, 294.

Ref: A.S17
Name: DUN LOCH CNOC A BUIDHE
Island: South Uist
NGR: NF 7483 2587
Location: Islet
Altitude: 5
Dimensions: 14.5
Shape: Circular
Galleries?:
Additional Features: Later Rectilinear Structure, Causeway 80m

Comments: The structure has a south entrance and walls up to c. 2m wide and 1m high, with an intrusive rectilinear structure. A well-built S-shaped causeway connects it to the shore of the loch.

References: RCAHMS no.382.

Ref: A.S18
Name: DUN EILEAN AN STAOIR
Island: South Uist
NGR: NF 7328 2579
Location: Islet
Altitude: 5
Dimensions: 17 x 14
Shape: Oval
Galleries?:
Additional Features: Harbour, External Circular Structure

Comments: The walls are set back from the present edge of the islet and the structure has a well-built and paved boat harbour. The site was classed as a late dun by the RCAHMS but the reasons for this are not clear.

References: RCAHMS no.379.

Ref: A.S19
Name: DUN LOCH AN DUIN
Island: South Uist
NGR: NF 7449 2265
Location: Islet
Altitude: 5
Dimensions:
Shape:
Galleries?:
Additional Features:

Comments: The site is now represented by a substantial, though much robbed, stone mound.

References: RCAHMS no.423.

Ref: A.S20
Name: OROSAY

Island: South Uist
NGR: NF 7302 1734
Location: Islet
Altitude: 30
Dimensions: 11
Shape: Circular
Galleries?:
Additional Features: 2 External Circular Structures, Causeway 120m,

Comments: The site occupies the summit of a very large tidal islet connected to the mainland by a very long causeway, some 3 - 4m wide. The remainder of the island is occupied by traces of cultivation but no evidence of recent structures. The islet described as Orasay by the RCAHMS is in fact an intervening islet crossed by the causeway.

References: RCAHMS no.435.

Ref: A.S21
Name: DUN SMERCLETT
Island: South Uist
NGR: NF 7464 1522
Location: Islet
Altitude: 5
Dimensions:
Shape:
Galleries?:
Additional Features:

Comments: The site is a small tidal islet from which traces of the stone structure have been largely removed.

References: RCAHMS no.420.

Atlantic Roundhouses - Barra

Ref: A.B1
Name: DUNAN RUADH
Island: Barra
NGR: NF 726 082
Location: Promontory
Altitude: 10
Dimensions:
Shape: Circular
Galleries?: Y
Additional Features:

Comments: This site lies on the island of Fuday off Barra. It was inaccessible at the time of survey and all data derives from the RCAHMS inventory. A 5m arc of walling was visible suggesting a circular structure.

References: RCAHMS no.443.

Ref: A.B2
Name: DUN SCURRIVAL
Island: Barra
NGR: NF 6954 0810
Location: Hilltop
Altitude: 60
Dimensions: 17 x 13
Shape: Oval
Galleries?: Y

Additional Features: Secondary Internal Occupation, External Structures, Scarcement (noted in early sources)

Comments: This massive galleried structure has internal and external secondary occupation in the form of rectilinear stone structures. There is also evidence of possible secondary modification to the course of wall with its northern part being a secondary extension. An external wall may be contemporary and may have served to control access to the main structure; this uses outcrop and survives up to 0.8m high by 26m long.

References: RCAHMS no.449, Scott 1947, 3, Young 1955, 291, Armit 1988a.

Ref: A.B3
Name: DUN CHLIF
Island: Barra
NGR: NF 6819 0528
Location: Promontory
Altitude: 5
Dimensions: 16 x 12
Shape: Oval
Galleries?: Y
Additional Features:

Comments: The structure is situated on a tidally isolated promontory. Midden deposits are visible around the site which is suffering greatly through tidal erosion. The structure survives to 1.2m in external height and c. 0.6m internally. The interior is approximately circular with a diameter of 7.5m. The site is also known locally as Dunan Ruadh na Chlif and Sorn Coir Fhinn (the fire-place of the kettle of Fhinn)

References: RCAHMS no.448, Scott 1947, 4, Armit 1988a, Young 1955, 291.

Ref: A.B4
Name: DUN CUIER
Island: Barra
NGR: NF 6708 0345
Location: Hilltop
Altitude: 40
Dimensions: 21 x 22.5
Shape: Circular
Galleries?: Y
Additional Features: Later Internal Cellular Structure, Scarcement

Comments: Excavated by Young (Ill. 5.12). There is a detailed discussion of the atlantic roundhouse in Chapter Five; the internal cellular structure discussed in Chapter Seven.

References: RCAHMS no.441, Young 1955, Armit 1988a.

Ref: A.B5
Name: DUN LOCH AN DUIN
Island: Barra
NGR: NF 694 032
Location: Islet
Altitude: 40
Dimensions: 14.9
Shape: Circular

Galleries?: Y
Additional Features: Causeway

Comments: Since the RCAHMS visit, the site has been submerged by the construction of a dam. All measurements used in structural analysis derive from the RCAHMS.

References: RCAHMS no.445, Scott 1947, 4, Young 1955, 193, Armit 1988a.

Ref: A.B6
Name: BAIGH HIRIVAGH 1
Island: Barra
NGR: NF 7113 0297
Location: Islet
Altitude: 5
Dimensions:
Shape:
Galleries?:
Additional Features: Causeway 35m

Comments: The detailed description in RCAHMS suggests that this site existed but no trace was visible by 1965. The measurements given by the RCAHMS appear to refer to the mound rather than the external wall as they also report that the outer face had been removed. Consequently the dimensions have not been used in structural analysis.

References: RCAHMS no.455.

Ref: A.B7
Name: BAIGH HIRIVAGH 2
Island: Barra
NGR: NF 7153 0263
Location: Islet
Altitude: 5
Dimensions: 12
Shape: Circular
Galleries?: Y
Additional Features: Causeway 40m

Comments: This dilapidated site lies on an exposed tidal Islet. Its walls have now substantially fallen away but galleries are visible in the eroding edges.

References: RCAHMS no.456, Young 1955, 293, Armit 1988a.

Ref: A.B8
Name: DUN LOCH NIC RUAIDHE
Island: Barra
NGR: NF 7025 0188
Location: Islet
Altitude: 60
Dimensions:
Shape:
Galleries?:
Additional Features: Causeway 30m, Annexe

Comments: The site occupies an inaccessible inland loch location; possible occupation was noted on other islets in loch in 1985 but the islets were inaccessible for close inspection.

References: RCAHMS no.454, Young 1955, 292, Armit 1988a.

Ref: A.B9
Name: DUN NA KILLE
Island: Barra
NGR: NF 6477 0167
Location: Coast
Altitude: 5
Dimensions: 16
Shape: Circular
Galleries?:
Additional Features:

Comments: The structure is incorporated within a recent graveyard wall corner on the coastal plain. The visible arc enables an estimate of external diameter at c. 16m. The entrance is visible on the east, 0.9m high by 0.55m wide. Five courses of walling survive to a height of c. 1.7m.

References: RCAHMS no.469, Young 1955, 293, Armit 1988a.

Ref: A.B10
Name: DUN AN T'SLEIBH
Island: Barra
NGR: NF 66   01
Location: Knoll
Altitude: 15
Dimensions:
Shape:
Galleries?:
Additional Features:

Comments: Traces of this site were noted by Scott, with walls 3m wide enclosing an internal diameter of c. 6.5m. Absolutely no trace of this site has been noted by previous or subsequent sources and the identification of the structure as a roundhouse must remain doubtful.

References: RCAHMS no.471, Scott 1947, 4, Armit 1988a.

Ref: A.B11
Name: BAL NA CRAIG
Island: Barra
NGR: NF 6765 0121
Location: Moorland
Altitude: 100
Dimensions: 16
Shape: Circular
Galleries?: Y
Additional Features: Later Baile Settlement

Comments: This site was recorded by the RCAHMS as a chambered cairn. Survey in 1985 located a complex roundhouse over the chambered cairn amid the ruins of numerous later structures including a post-medieval baile. This identification was later found to correlate to the 1st edition Ordnance Survey maps where the site is referred to as a dun.

References: RCAHMS no.458, Armit 1988a.

Ref: A.B12
Name: DUN BAN
Island: Barra
NGR: NF 6311 0037
Location: Promontory
Altitude: 10
Dimensions: 18
Shape: Subcircular
Galleries?: Y
Additional Features: External Structures

Comments: This is a galleried structure with walls 4m wide, 1.2m high. Outcrop appears in the centre at a level c. 2.5m above the outer foundations. An entrance to the east was noted in the NMR from 1965 field visit. The structure survives up to 1.2m in height to the east.

References: RCAHMS no.446, Young 1955, 293, Armit 1988a.

Ref:13
Name: DUN MHIC LEOID
Island: Barra
NGR: NF 6311 0037
Location: Islet
Altitude: 10
Dimensions:
Shape: Subcircular
Galleries?:
Additional Features: Later Tower

Comments: The subcircular remains of a substantial stone roundhouse underlie and form the foundation and quarry for a later medieval tower in Loch St. Clair. The site is too overgrown to enable dimensions to be measured.

References: Armit 1988a.

Ref: A.B14
Name: BEINN TANGAVAT
Island: Barra
NGR: NF 640 968
Location: Moorland
Altitude: 50
Dimensions: 16.5
Shape: Circular
Galleries?: Y
Additional Features: Later Rectilinear structures inside and around.

Comments: This site was located during field survey in 1985. It comprises a complex roundhouse in overgrown condition, occupied by the remains of later settlement.

References: Armit 1988a

Ref: A.B15
Name: DUN A CHAOLAIS
Island: Barra
NGR: NF 6280 9704
Location: Hilltop
Altitude: 40
Dimensions: 16
Shape: Circular
Galleries?: Y

Additional Features: Later Baile Settlement, External Structures, Scarcement, Intra-Mural Stairs

Comments: This is a well-preserved structure with walls c. 2.5m high by 4m wide overall. A later baile settlement occupies the site and the area around the structure. A circular mound, with facing stones suggesting a 16m diameter, is situated on a terrace below Dun a Chaolais.

References: RCAHMS no.442, Armit 1988a.

Ref: A.B16
Name: DUN VATERSAY TOWNSHIP
Island: Barra
NGR: NF 6266 9454
Location: Hilltop
Altitude: 50
Dimensions: 15
Shape: Circular
Galleries?:
Additional Features: External Structures, Enclosure

Comments: This structure is best preserved to the south and east where the outer face suggests a diameter of c. 15m. An outer courtyard or enclosure is visible in sporadic facing stones to the east of the main structure.

References: RCAHMS no.472, Armit 1988a.

Ref: A.B17
Name: DUN SANDRAY
Island: Barra
NGR: NF 6374 9137
Location: Hilltop
Altitude: 170
Dimensions: 15.5 x 12.75
Shape: Oval
Galleries?: Y
Additional Features: Enclosure

Comments: Dun Sandray lies on the island of Sandray off Barra. It was inaccessible at the time of survey and all data derives from the RCAHMS inventory. The walls of the structure survive to 2m high and a lintelled ground gallery survives substantially intact. The structure has an entrance to the west-north-west. Traces of an outer wall indicate a former enclosure.

References: RCAHMS no.444, Armit 1988a.

Ref: A.B18
Name: DUNAN RUADH PABBAY
Island: Barra
NGR: NF 6129 8764
Location: Promontory
Altitude: 5
Dimensions:
Shape:
Galleries?: Y
Additional Features:

Comments: This site lies on the island of Pabbay off Barra. It was inaccessible at the time of survey and all data derives from the RCAHMS inventory. Parts of the walls were visible on the south-west arc showing a width of c. 4m containing a gallery.

References: RCAHMS no.447, Armit 1988a.

Wheelhouses

Ref: W.1
Name: CNIP
Island: Lewis
NGR: NB 0980 3665
Location: Machair
Altitude: 0
Dimensions: 7
Shape: Circular
Additional Features: Later Occupation

Comments: Excavated by Armit. Discussed in Chapter Six (Ill. 6.2). Later cellular and linear house structures discussed in Chapters Seven and Eight respectively.

References: Armit 1988.

Ref: W.2
Name: CALUM MACLEODS WHEELHOUSE
Island: Lewis
NGR: NB 1021 3564
Location: Machair
Altitude: 10
Dimensions:
Shape: Circular
Additional Features:

Comments: Excavated by Calum Macleod of Reef in the 1950s, when walling and indications of piers were noted. The site is now an eroding machair knoll.

References: NMR.

Ref: W.3
Name: THE UDAL
Island: North Uist
NGR: NF 824 783
Location: Machair
Altitude: 5
Dimensions: 9.8
Shape: Circular
Additional Features: Later Cellular Structures

Comments: Excavated by Iain Crawford. Discussed in Chapter Six. Later cellular structures dicussed in Chapter Seven.

References: Crawford 1967/78, 1975, 1977, 1985.

Ref: W.4
Name: FOSHIGARRY
Island: North Uist
NGR: NF 7430 7636
Location: Machair
Altitude: 0
Dimensions: 10.5, 10.5, ?
Shape: Circular
Additional Features: Later Cellular Structures

Comments: Excavated by Beveridge. Discussed in Chapter Six (Ill. 6.3). Cellular structures discussed in Chapter Seven.

References: Beveridge 1930.

Ref: W.5
Name: BAC MHIC CONNAIN
Island: North Uist
NGR: NF 7695 7620
Location: Machair
Altitude: 5
Dimensions: 9
Shape: Circular
Additional Features:

Comments: Excavated by Beveridge. Discussed in Chapter Six (Ill. 6.4).

References: RCAHMS no.271, Beveridge 1931.

Ref: W.6
Name: SOLLAS (MACHAIR LEATHANN)
Island: North Uist
NGR: NF 8035 7577
Location: Machair
Altitude: 5
Dimensions: 12
Shape: Circular
Additional Features:

Comments: Excavated by Beveridge. Discussed in Chapter Six (Ill. 6.5). The site was re-excavated by Atkinson but this latter project remains unpublished.

References: RCAHMS no.272, Beveridge 1911.

Ref: W.7
Name: GARRY IOCHDRACH
Island: North Uist
NGR: NF 7724 7427
Location: Machair
Altitude: 5
Dimensions: 7.9
Shape: Circular
Additional Features: Earlier and Later Occupation

Comments: Excavated by Beveridge. Discussed in Chapter Six (Ill. 5.8). Earlier occupation discussed in Chapter Five.

References: Beveridge 1931.

Ref: W.8
Name: CNOC A COMHDHALACH
Island: North Uist
NGR: NF 7708 7413
Location: Machair
Altitude: 5
Dimensions: 7
Shape: Circular
Additional Features: Earlier Occupation

Comments: Excavated by Beveridge. Discussed in Chapter Six (Ill. 5.9). Earlier occupation discussed in Chapter Five.

References: RCAHMS no.269, Beveridge 1911

Ref: W.9
Name: BALELONE
Island: North Uist
NGR: NF 719 741
Location: Machair
Altitude: 0
Dimensions:
Shape:
Additional Features:

Comments: Excavated by Barber. Discussed in Chapter Six.

References: Barber forthcoming.

Ref: W.10
Name: EILEAN MALEIT
Island: North Uist
NGR: NF 7748 7388
Location: Machair
Altitude: 5
Dimensions: 9
Shape: Circular
Additional Features: Causeway, Earlier Occupation

Comments: Excavated by Beveridge. Discussed in Chapter Six (Ill. 5.10). Earlier occupation discussed in Chapter Five.

References: RCAHMS no.270, Beveridge 1911.

Ref: W.11
Name: CLETTRAVAL
Island: North Uist
NGR: NF 7489 7136
Location: Moorland
Altitude: 95
Dimensions: 8
Shape: Circular
Additional Features: Later Re-occupation

Comments: Excavated by Scott. Discussed in Chapter Six (Ill. 6.6 and 6.7).

References: Scott 1948.

Ref: W.12
Name: A CHEARDACH RUADH
Island: North Uist
NGR: NF 7763 6157
Location: Machair
Altitude: 5
Dimensions:
Shape:
Additional Features:

Comments: Excavated partially by Scott but details remain unpublished.

References: RCAHMS no.286, Beveridge 1911, 229, Scott 1956.

Ref: W.12
Name: BRUACH BAN
Island: Benbecula
NGR: NF 787 567

Location: Machair
Altitude: 5
Dimensions: 10
Shape: Circular
Additional Features:

Comments: Excavated by Scott. Discussed in Chapter Six.

References: NMR.

Ref: W.13
Name: BRUTHACH A TUATH
Island: Benbecula
NGR: NF 787 566
Location: Machair
Altitude: 5
Dimensions: 8.8
Shape: Circular
Additional Features:

Comments: Excavated by Wallace. Discussed in Chapter Six.

References: RCAHMS no.354.

Ref: W.14
Name: HORNISH POINT
Island: South Uist
NGR: NF 758 470
Location: Machair
Altitude: 5
Dimensions: 7.5
Shape: Circular
Additional Features:

Comments: Excavated by Barber. Discussed in Chapter Six.

References: Barber forthcoming.

Ref: W.15
Name: A CHEARDACH MHOR
Island: South Uist
NGR: NF 7571 4128
Location: Machair
Altitude: 5
Dimensions: 10.8
Shape: Circular
Additional Features: Later Cellular Occupation

Comments: Excavated by Young and Richardson. Discussed in Chapter Six (Ill. 6.8). Cellular structures discussed in Chapter Seven.

References: Young and Richardson 1959.

Ref: W.16
Name: A CHEARDACH BHEAG
Island: South Uist
NGR: NF 7577 4037
Location: Machair
Altitude: 5
Dimensions: 9
Shape: Circular
Additional Features:

Comments: Excavated by Fairhurst. Discussed in Chapter Six (Ill. 6.9).

References: Fairhurst 1971.

Ref: W.17
Name: GEIRNISH
Island: South Uist
NGR: NF 8425 3998
Location: Machair
Altitude: 15
Dimensions:
Shape: Circular
Additional Features: Later Shielings

Comments: Structural remains described by the RCAHMS suggest the former presence of a wheelhouse on this site.

References: RCAHMS no.393.

Ref: W.18
Name: A CHEARDACH MHOR 2
Island: South Uist
NGR: NF 7557 3924
Location: Machair
Altitude: 5
Dimensions:
Shape:
Additional Features:

Comments: A substantial midden, pottery of broadly later prehistoric type and a mound with stones, all suggest the presence of a wheelhouse on this site.

References: NMR.

Ref: W.19
Name: USINISH
Island: South Uist
NGR: NF 8433 3326
Location: Moorland
Altitude: 80
Dimensions: 9
Shape: Circular
Additional Features:

Comments: Described by Thomas. Discussed in Chapter Six (Ill. 6.10).

References: RCAHMS no.395, Thomas 1870.

Ref: W.20
Name: SITHEAN A PHIOBAIRE
Island: South Uist
NGR: NF 732 204
Location: Machair
Altitude: 5
Dimensions:
Shape:
Additional Features:

Comments: This mound site is recorded as a wheelhouse by Lethbridge but without supporting information.

References: Lethbridge 1952.

Ref: W.21
Name: BRUTHACH A TIGH TALLAN
Island: South Uist
NGR: NF 732 203
Location: Machair
Altitude: 5
Dimensions:
Shape:
Additional Features:

Comments: This mound site is recorded as a wheelhouse by Lethbridge but without supporting information.

References: Lethbridge 1952.

Ref: W.22
Name: KILPHEDER
Island: South Uist
NGR: NF 7327 2026
Location: Machair
Altitude: 5
Dimensions: 8.8
Shape: Circular
Additional Features:

Comments: Excavated by Lethbridge. Discussed in Chapter Six (Ill. 6.11).

References: Lethbridge 1952.

Ref: W.23
Name: SOUTH UIST
Island: South Uist
NGR: not known
Location: Moorland
Altitude:
Dimensions:
Shape:
Additional Features:

Comments: The site is described in some detail by Dryden and appears to have been a wheelhouse. Its location on South Uist is unknown.

References: Dryden 1857.

Ref: W.24
Name: NORTH BORVE
Island: Barra
NGR: NF 6563 0285
Location: Machair
Altitude: 8
Dimensions: 16 x 13
Shape: Oval
Additional Features:

Comments: Traces of an arc of walling with a radial pier were noted by RCAHMS surveyors in 1965.

References: NMR.

Ref: W.25
Name: TIGH TALAMHANTA ALLASDALE
Island: Barra
NGR: NF 6768 0220
Location: Moorland

Altitude: 115
Dimensions: 8
Shape: Circular
Additional Features:

Comments: Excavated by Young. Discussed in Chapter Six. (Ill. 6.12).

References: RCAHMS no.459, Young 1952.

Ref: W.26
Name: BORVE POINT 2
Island: Barra
NGR: NF 6519 0167
Location: Machair
Altitude: 8
Dimensions:
Shape: Circular
Additional Features:

Comments: An arc of walling, 1.5m long by 0.8m wide, was recorded, with a possible pier on its south-east.

References: NMR.

Cellular Structures

Ref: C.1
Name: EUROPIE
Island: Lewis
NGR: NB 5116 6396
Location: Machair
Altitude: 35
Dimensions:
Shape: Cellular
Additional Features:

Comments: A passage c. 10m long leads to a circular cobrbelled cell at this site, recorded by RCAHMS surveyors in 1965.

References: NMR

Ref: C.2
Name: GALSON
Island: Lewis
NGR: NB 44 59
Location: Machair
Altitude: 5
Dimensions:
Shape: Cellular
Additional Features:

Comments: Excavated by Edwards. Discussed in Chapter Seven (Ill. 7.2).

References: RCAHMS no.20, Edwards 1923.

Ref: C.3
Name: CNIP
Island: Lewis
NGR: NB 0980 3665
Location: Machair
Altitude: 0
Dimensions:
Shape: Cellular

Additional Features: Earlier and Later Occupation

Comments: Excavated by Armit. Discussed in Chapter Seven (Ill. 7.3). The earlier wheelhouses are discussed in Chapter Six and the linear house structure is discussed in Chapter Eight.

References: Armit 1988a.

Ref: C.4
Name: DUN BHARABHAT
Island: Lewis
NGR: NB 0988 3531
Location: Islet
Altitude: 40
Dimensions: 5
Shape: Cellular
Additional Features: Earlier Occupation

Comments: Excavated by Harding. Discussed in Chapter Seven (Ill. 5.3). Earlier atlantic roundhouse is discussed in Chapter Five.

References: Harding and Topping 1986.

Ref: C.5
Name: LOCH NA BERIE
Island: Lewis
NGR: NB 1035 3525
Location: Islet
Altitude: 5
Dimensions:
Shape: Cellular
Additional Features: Earlier Occupation

Comments: Excavated by Harding and Armit. Discussed in Chapter Seven (Ill. 7.4 and 7.5). Earlier atlantic round-house discussed in Chapter Five.

References: Harding and Armit 1987, 1988.

Ref: C.6
Name: MEALISTA
Island: Lewis
NGR: NA 991 242
Location: Moorland
Altitude:
Dimensions:
Shape: Cellular
Additional Features:

Comments: This cellular structure appears to have been dismantled for building stone.

References: Thomas 1867.

Ref: C.7
Name: NISABOST
Island: Harris
NGR: NF 0419 9679
Location: Moorland
Altitude: 20
Dimensions:
Shape: Cellular
Additional Features:

Comments: The site comprises three irregular corbelled cells.

References: RCAHMS no.149.

Ref: C.8
Name: NORTHTON 3
Island: Harris
NGR: NF 9873 9027
Location: Machair
Altitude: 5
Dimensions:
Shape: Cellular
Additional Features:

Comments: A passage and corbelled cell were reported of which no trace is now visible.

References: RCAHMS no.154.

Ref: C.9
Name: SCREVAN
Island: North Uist
NGR: NF 9007 7862
Location: Machair
Altitude: 15
Dimensions:
Shape: Cellular
Additional Features:

Comments: A passage leading to a circular cell was recorded.

References: RCAHMS no.266, Beveridge 1911, 114.

Ref: C.10
Name: THE UDAL
Island: North Uist
NGR: NF 824 783
Location: Machair
Altitude: 5
Dimensions:
Shape: Cellular
Additional Features: Earlier and Later Occupation

Comments: Excavated by Crawford and Beveridge. Discussed in Chapter Seven. The earlier wheelhouse occupation is discussed in Chapter Six and the linear structure in Chapter Eight.

References: Beveridge 1911, 129/30, Crawford 1967/78.

Ref: C.11
Name: FOSHIGARRY
Island: North Uist
NGR: NF 7430 7636
Location: Machair
Altitude: 0
Dimensions:
Shape: Cellular
Additional Features: Earlier and Later Occupation

Comments: Excavated by Beveridge. Discussed in Chapter Seven. Earlier wheelhouse occupation discussed in Chapter Six and linear structure discussed in Chapter Eight.

References: Beveridge 1931.

Ref: C.12
Name: SITHEAN AN ALTAIR
Island: North Uist
NGR: NF 77 76
Location: Machair
Altitude: 5
Dimensions:
Shape: Cellular
Additional Features:

Comments: Excavated by Beveridge. Discussed in Chapter Seven (Ill. 7.6).

References: Beveridge 1911, 118/121.

Ref: C.13
Name: TOTA DUNAIG
Island: North Uist
NGR: NF 77 76
Location: Machair
Altitude:
Dimensions:
Shape: Cellular
Additional Features:

Comments: Slight remains of a cellular structural complex were described by Beveridge.

References: Beveridge 1911, 232/3.

Ref: C.14
Name: DUN A GHALLAIN
Island: North Uist
NGR: NF 7479 7598
Location: Islet
Altitude: 5
Dimensions:
Shape: Cellular
Additional Features: Earlier Occupation

Comments: Excavated by Beveridge. Discussed in Chapter Seven. Atlantic roundhouse discussed in Chapter Five.

References: RCAHMS no.191, Beveridge 1911.

Ref: C.15
Name: EILEAN A GHALLAIN
Island: North Uist
NGR: NF 7483 7589
Location: Islet
Altitude: 5
Dimensions:
Shape: Cellular
Additional Features: Earlier Occupation

Comments: Excavated by Beveridge. Discussed in Chapter Seven. Atlantic roundhouse discussed in Chapter Five.

References: RCAHMS no.192, Beveridge 1911.

Ref: C.16
Name: DUN THOMAIDH
Island: North Uist
NGR: NF 7564 7562
Location: Islet
Altitude: 5
Dimensions:
Shape: Cellular
Additional Features: Earlier Occupation

Comments: Excavated by Beveridge. Discussed in Chapter Seven (Ill. 5.7). Atlantic roundhouse discussed in Chapter Five.

References: RCAHMS no.212, Beveridge 1930.

Ref: C.17
Name: SCOLPAIG
Island: North Uist
NGR: NF 7282 7535
Location: Machair
Altitude: 5
Dimensions:
Shape: Cellular
Additional Features:

Comments: Beveridge reported an underground structure being found here during ploughing.

References: Beveridge 1911, 117.

Ref: C.18
Name: VALLAQUIE 2
Island: North Uist
NGR: NF 8627 7532
Location: Machair
Altitude: 5
Dimensions:
Shape: Cellular
Additional Features:

Comments: A passage and corbelled cell are recorded in the NMR on this site.

References: NMR

Ref: C.19
Name: EILEAN OLABHAT
Island: North Uist
NGR: NF 7500 7530
Location: Islet
Altitude: 5
Dimensions:
Shape: Cellular
Additional Features: Outer Wall, Later Occupation

Comments: Excavated by Armit. Discussed in Chapter Seven.

References: Armit 1986, 1988b.

Ref: C.20
Name: TIGH TALAMHANTA
Island: North Uist
NGR: NF 9490 7122
Location: Moorland

Altitude: 20
Dimensions:
Shape: Cellular
Additional Features:

Comments: A complex of cells and passages were reported on this site.

References: RCAHMS no.267, Beveridge 1911, 115.

Ref: C.21
Name: DRUIM NA H-UAMHA
Island: North Uist
NGR: NF 729 697
Location: Moorland
Altitude: 10
Dimensions:
Shape: Cellular
Additional Features:

Comments: A cellular structure reported in 1896 on this site, subsequently filled up and is no longer visible.

References: RCAHMS no.268, Beveridge 1911, 116.

Ref: C.22
Name: UNIVAL
Island: North Uist
NGR: NF 800 668
Location: Moorland
Altitude: 80
Dimensions:
Shape: Cellular
Additional Features: Earlier Chambered Tomb

Comments: Excavated by Scott. Discussed in Chapter Seven (Ill. 7.11).

References: Scott 1947a.

Ref: C.23
Name: DUN BAN
Island: North Uist
NGR: NF 8699 5695
Location: Islet
Altitude: 5
Dimensions:
Shape:
Additional Features: Earlier Occupation

Comments: Excavated by Thomas. Discussed in Chapter Seven (Ill. 5.11). Earlier atlantic roundhouse discussed in Chapter Five.

References: Thomas 1890.

Ref: C.24
Name: A CHEARDACH MHOR
Island: South Uist
NGR: NF 7571 4128
Location: Machair
Altitude: 5
Dimensions:
Shape: Cellular
Additional Features: Earlier Occupation

Comments: Excavated by Young and Richardson. Discussed in Chapter Seven (Ill. 7.7). Earlier wheelhouse discussed in Chapter Six.

References: Young and Richardson 1959.

Ref: C.25
Name: USINISH 2
Island: South Uist
NGR: NF 8431 3330
Location: Moorland
Altitude: 80
Dimensions:
Shape: Cellular
Additional Features:

Comments: A series of inter-connecting cells were recorded by the RCAHMS.

References: RCAHMS no.395.

Ref: C.26
Name: USINISH 4
Island: South Uist
NGR: NF 843 333
Location: Moorland
Altitude: 80
Dimensions:
Shape: Cellular
Additional Features:

Comments: A series of three cells connected by passages were reported at this site.

References: RCAHMS no.396.

Ref: C.27
Name: TIGH NAN LEACACH
Island: South Uist
NGR: NF 8129 2277
Location: Moorland
Altitude: 150
Dimensions:
Shape: Cellular
Additional Features:

Comments: A series of three corbelled cells were reported at this site.

References: RCAHMS no.397.

Ref: C.28
Name: DUN CUIER
Island: Barra
NGR: NF 6708 0345
Location: Hilltop
Altitude: 40
Dimensions:
Shape: Cellular
Additional Features: Earlier Occupation

Comments: Excavated by Young. Discussed in Chapter Seven (Ill. 5.12). Earlier atlantic roundhouse discussed in Chapter Five.

References: RCAHMS no.441, Young 1956, Armit 1988.

Linear House Structures

Ref: L.1
Name: CNIP
Island: Lewis
NGR: NB 0980 3665
Location: Machair
Altitude: 0
Dimensions: 7 x 2.2
Shape: Linear
Additional Features: Earlier Wheelhouse and Cellular Occupation

Comments: Excavated by Armit. Discussed in Chapter Eight (Ill. 8.2). Earlier occupation discussed in Chapters Six and Seven.

References: Armit, 1988a.

Ref: L.2
Name: VALLAQUIE
Island: North Uist
NGR: NF 8646 7547
Location: Machair
Altitude: 5
Dimensions: 7 x 2
Shape: Linear
Additional Features:

Comments: The site was investigated in 1871 when it was revealed as a curved gallery some 6m long by c. 2m wide. It appears to have had a south entrance.

References: RCAHMS no.274, Beveridge 1911, 114/5.

Linear Structures

Ref: L.3
Name: GRESS LODGE
Island: Lewis
NGR: NB 4938 4185
Location: Machair
Altitude: 5
Dimensions:
Shape: Linear
Additional Features:

Comments: Discussed in Chapter Eight (Ill. 8.4).

References: Liddle, 1872, MacRitchie, 1916, RCAHMS no.58.

Ref: L.4
Name: VALTOS 1
Island: Lewis
NGR: NB 088 367
Location: Moorland
Altitude: 70
Dimensions:
Shape: Linear
Additional Features:

Comments: This site was temporarily exposed by wind erosion prior to 1914. It appears to have been a subterranean passage with a slab roof.

References: RCAHMS no.96.

Ref: L.5
Name: PAIBLE, TARANSAY
Island: Harris
NGR: NF 0323 9917
Location: Machair
Altitude: 5
Dimensions: 7.3 Long
Shape: Linear
Additional Features:

Comments: This 'earth-house' was removed to provide stones for construction and road-building.

References: RCAHMS no.153.

Ref: L.6
Name: BERNERAY 2
Island: Harris
NGR: NF 9071 8151
Location: Machair
Altitude: 5
Dimensions: 4 x 0.8
Shape: Linear
Additional Features:

Comments: This structure was dismantled to obtain building stone.

References: RCAHMS no.151.

Ref: L.7
Name: UDAL
Island: North Uist
NGR: NB 824 783
Location: Machair
Altitude: 5
Dimensions: 20 x 0.6
Shape: Linear
Additional Features: Earlier and Later Occupation

Comments: This site was excavated by Crawford and Beveridge. It is discussed in Chapter Eight. Wheelhouse and cellular structures on the site are discussed in Chapters Six and Seven.

References: RCAHMS no.273, Beveridge 1911, Crawford 1967/78.

Ref: L.8
Name: FOSHIGARRY
Island: North Uist
NGR: NB 7430 7636
Location: Machair
Altitude: 0
Dimensions: 15 x 0.6
Shape: Linear
Additional Features: Earlier and Later Occupation.

Comments: This site was excavated by Beveridge and is discussed in Chapter Eight. Wheelhouse and cellular structures on the site are discussed in Chapters Six and Seven.

References: Beveridge 1931.

Ref: L.9
Name: VALLAY EARTH-HOUSE
Island: North Uist
NGR: NF 77 76
Location: Machair
Altitude:
Dimensions:
Shape: Linear
Additional Features:

Comments: This site was excavated by Beveridge and is discussed in Chapter Eight.

References: Beveridge 1911, 117/8.

Ref: L.10
Name: PORTAIN
Island: North Uist
NGR: NF 9529 7241
Location: Moorland
Altitude: 15
Dimensions:
Shape: Linear
Additional Features:

Comments: The site was described as a curving passage built into the bank of a loch.

References: Beveridge 1911, 116.

Ref: L.11
Name: KIRKIBOST
Island: North Uist
NGR: NF 752 655
Location: Machair
Altitude: 5
Dimensions:
Shape: Linear
Additional Features:

Comments: Little information is recorded about this site which appears to have been a subterranean passage.

References: Beveridge 1911, 116.

Ref: L.12
Name: BRUTHACH A TUATH
Island: Benbecula
NGR: NF 787 566
Location: Machair
Altitude: 5
Dimensions: 4 x 0.6
Shape: Linear
Additional Features: Earlier Wheelhouse

Comments: This site was excavated by Wallace and is discussed in Chapter Eight. The wheelhouse on the site is discussed in Chapter Six.

References:

Ref: L.13
Name: DRIMORE
Island: South Uist
NGR: NF 75 41
Location: Machair
Altitude: 5
Dimensions: 8 x 1
Shape: Linear
Additional Features:

Comments: This site was excavated by Feachem and is discussed in Chapter Eight.

References: Feachem 1956.

Ref: L.14
Name: SCALAVAT 1
Island: South Uist
NGR: NF 8482 3398
Location: Moorland
Altitude: 100
Dimensions:
Shape: Linear
Additional Features: Later Occupation

Comments: This site appears to have been a subterranean passage built over by later structures.

References: RCAHMS no.394.

Ref: L.15
Name: SCALAVAT 2
Island: South Uist
NGR: NF 84 33
Location: Moorland
Altitude: 100
Dimensions:
Shape: Linear
Additional Features:

Comments: This site appears to have been a subterranean passage built over by later structures.

References: RCAHMS no.394.

Promontory Forts

Ref: P.1
Name: DUN EISTEAN
Island: Lewis
NGR: NB 535 651
Location: Promontory
Altitude: 20
Dimensions:
Shape: Irregular
Additional Features: Internal Rectilinear Structure

Comments: A wall, 2m wide surrounds the promontory with internal rectilinear structures. Local tradition suggests C12th AD occupation by the Morrisons and it is conceivable that the site may have a late origin.

References: RCAHMS no.15.

Ref: P.2
Name: DUN MARA

Island: Lewis
NGR: NB 4947 6313
Location: Promontory
Altitude: 5
Dimensions:
Shape: Linear
Additional Features:

Comments: Two walls seal off the promontory which contains an atlantic roundhouse with which the walls may be contemporary.

References: RCAHMS no.13.

Ref: P.3
Name: DUN BHILASCLEITER
Island: Lewis
NGR: NB 5602 5762
Location: Promontory
Altitude: 5
Dimensions:
Shape: Linear
Additional Features:

Comments: A wall, 3.3m wide seals off this promontory and extends to 24m in length. Early reports of a guard cell cannot now be confirmed from surface traces.

References: RCAHMS no.34.

Ref: P.4
Name: DUN OTHAIL
Island: Lewis
NGR: NB 5425 5150
Location: Promontory
Altitude: 5
Dimensions:
Shape: Linear
Additional Features: Later Chapel

Comments: The reported site of a promontory fort is no longer traceable.

References: RCAHMS no.35.

Ref: P.5
Name: DUN CASTEIL A MHORAIR
Island: Lewis
NGR: NB 5366 4970
Location: Coastal
Altitude: 5
Dimensions: 20 x 8
Shape: Irregular
Additional Features: Internal Rectilinear Structure

Comments: This site is a walled coastal stack with an internal rectilinear structure. It may have a late foundation date.

References: RCAHMS no.48.

Ref: P.6
Name: SHAWBOST
Island: Lewis
NGR: NB 249 483
Location: Promontory

Altitude: 5
Dimensions:
Shape:
Additional Features:

Comments: This site appears to have been entirely eroded by tidal action.

References: NMR.

Ref: P.7
Name: RUDHA NA BERIE
Island: Lewis
NGR: NB 2367 4733
Location: Promontory
Altitude: 5
Dimensions:
Shape: Linear
Additional Features: Internal Structures

Comments: Three walls seal off the approach to this promontory. Early reports of internal structure could not be verified.

References: RCAHMS no.12.

Ref: P.8
Name: STAC A CHAISTEAL
Island: Lewis
NGR: NB 2024 4540
Location: Promontory
Altitude: 5
Dimensions:
Shape: Linear
Additional Features:

Comments: A wall, 3m long and 4.5m wide survives as a fragment of the original promontory defense. The entrance is central to the surviving fragment.

References: NMR.

Ref: P.9
Name: DUN LAIMISHADER
Island: Lewis
NGR: NB 1746 4313
Location: Promontory
Altitude: 5
Dimensions:
Shape: Linear
Additional Features: Internal Structures

Comments: The wall runs across the neck of the promontory and along the east side. A series of internal circular cells were recorded.

References: NMR.

Ref: P.10
Name: DUN MOR
Island: Lewis
NGR: NB 513 339
Location: Promontory
Altitude: 5
Dimensions:
Shape:

Additional Features:

Comments: The wall runs along the north and east of the promontory.

References: RCAHMS no.47.

Ref: P.11
Name: DUN DUBH
Island: Lewis
NGR: NB 5570 3260
Location: Promontory
Altitude: 5
Dimensions:
Shape: Linear
Additional Features:

Comments: The wall seals off the neck of a very steep-sided easily defended promontory. The wall is 5m wide, 1.2 - 1.5m high, 32m long and has an entrance 1.4m wide.

References: NMR.

Ref: P.12
Name: RUDHA SHILLDINISH
Island: Lewis
NGR: NB 4540 3067
Location: Promontory
Altitude: 10
Dimensions: 90 x 90
Shape: Irregular
Additional Features: Internal Rectilinear Structures and Cultivation

Comments: The walls of this site enclose a complex of multi-phase occupation including later turf and stone structures and cultivation rigs.

References: RCAHMS no.46.

Ref: P.13
Name: DUNAN CROSBOST
Island: Lewis
NGR: NB 4035 2430
Location: Promontory
Altitude: 5
Dimensions:
Shape: Linear
Additional Features:

Comments: The wall across the neck of this promontory has been all but removed for modern structures nearby.

References: RCAHMS no.41.

Ref: P.14
Name: DUN STUAIDH
Island: Harris
NGR: NF 0422 8316
Location: Promontory
Altitude: 5
Dimensions: 30 x 9
Shape:
Additional Features: Internal Structures

Comments: Walls run around the north, west and south of the promontory, 2m wide and up to 1.5m high. Two small oval turf-built enclosures are visible inside.

References: RCAHMS no.122.

Ref: P.15
Name: CAISTEIL ODAIR
Island: North Uist
NGR: NF 7317 7686
Location: Promontory
Altitude: 20
Dimensions: 120
Shape:
Additional Features:

Comments: This is a well-defended promontory with the remains of a very substantial stone wall across its neck, 120m long and up to 5m in spread. Slight structures were recorded internally and externally by Beveridge and the RCAHMS. These are no longer extant.

References: RCAHMS no.190, Beveridge 1911, 195/6.

Ref: P.16
Name: AN DUNAN
Island: North Uist
NGR: NF 8936 5872
Location: Promontory
Altitude: 5
Dimensions: 7m long
Shape: Linear
Additional Features: 2 Later Circular Structures, 1 Later Boat-Shaped Structure

Comments: A wall, 1.1m wide and 0.6m high seals off this promontory and encloses several slight structures.

References: Beveridge 1911, 171.

Ref: P.17
Name: DUN BIRUASLAM
Island: Barra
NGR: NF 607 964
Location: Promontory
Altitude: 60
Dimensions: 100 Long
Shape: Linear
Additional Features: later Internal Occupation

Comments: A wall surrounding parts of this promontory is c. 3m wide and 1m high, utilising outcrop for parts of its course.

References: RCAHMS no.451, Armit 1988.

Ref: P.18
Name: DUN MINGULAY
Island: Barra
NGR: NF 545 822
Location: Promontory
Altitude: 85
Dimensions:
Shape: Linear
Additional Features:

Comments: This site has been entirely eroded.

References: RCAHMS no.452, Armit 1988.

Ref: P.19
Name: DUN BRISTE
Island: Barra
NGR: NF 550 806
Location: Promontory   Altitude: 100
Dimensions: 25m Long   Shape: Linear
Additional Features:

Comments: This wall is some 2 - 3.5m wide and appears to be abutted by traces of circular structures.

References: RCAHMS no.453.

Ref: P.20
Name: BARRA HEAD
Island: Barra
NGR: NF 5480 8025
Location: Promontory
Altitude: 200
Dimensions: 20m arc
Shape: Linear
Additional Features:

Comments: The walls of this structure are up to 5m wide and contain superimposed intra-mural galleries (Ill. 9.2).

References: RCAHMS no.450, Armit 1988.

Walled Islets

Ref: WA.1
Name: DUN LOCH AN DUIN, AIRD
Island: Lewis
NGR: NB 555 358
Location: Islet
Altitude: 40
Dimensions: 30 x 20
Shape: Irregular
Additional Features: Causeway 28m, Internal Structures, Harbour

Comments: This site was recorded as having an elaborate entrance and guard cell but these have now disappeared (Ill. 10.2).

References: RCAHMS no.50, Thomas 1890, Armit 1985.

Ref: WA.2
Name: DUN LOCH AN DUNA LEURBOST
Island: Lewis
NGR: NB 3903 2614
Location: Islet
Altitude: 30
Dimensions: 21 x 19
Shape: Circular
Additional Features: Causeway 35m, Internal Occupation, Harbour

Comments: This site has several internal structures surrounded by walls 1.3 - 1.5m wide (Ill. 10.3).

References: RCAHMS no.39, Armit 1985.

Ref: WA.3
Name: DUN BHARCLIN
Island: Lewis
NGR: NB 3945 2327
Location: Islet
Altitude: 5
Dimensions: 73 x 17
Shape: Irregular
Additional Features: Internal Structures

Comments: This irregular islet is now inaccessible but appears to contain internal structures.

References: RCAHMS no.40.

Ref: WA.4
Name: DUN LOCH AN DUIN, SCALPAY
Island: Harris
NGR: NG 2247 9659
Location: Islet
Altitude: 10
Dimensions: 70 x 27
Shape: Irregular
Additional Features: Possible Causeway

Comments: The site is now visible as a partly submerged wall.

References: RCAHMS no.145.

Ref: WA.5
Name: DUN LOCH NAN CLACHAN
Island: North Uist
NGR: NF 7678 7382
Location: Islet
Altitude: 5
Dimensions: 28 x 23
Shape: Subcircular
Additional Features: Causeway

Comments: This islet has a collapsed enclosing wall but no visible internal structure.

References: RCAHMS no.181, Beveridge 1911, 199, Blundell 1913, 298.

Ref: WA.6
Name: DUN MHIC LAITHINN
Island: North Uist
NGR: NF 9777 7314
Location: Islet
Altitude: 5
Dimensions: 50 x 30
Shape: Oval
Additional Features: Later Shielings

Comments: The wall around this tidal islet utilises the outcrop for parts of its circuit.

References: RCAHMS no.210, Beveridge 1911, 144/6.

Ref: WA.7
Name: DUN LOCH FADA
Island: North Uist

NGR: NF 8796 7121
Location: Islet
Altitude: 10
Dimensions: 120 x 50
Shape: Irregular
Additional Features: 2 Causeways, Possible Internal Structure

Comments: The enclosing wall has entrances at the north and south facing two causeways. The wall utilises outcrop for parts of its circuit.

References: RCAHMS no.202, Beveridge 1911, 154.

Ref: WA.8
Name: EILEAN BUIDHE
Island: North Uist
NGR: NF 8963 6861
Location: Islet
Altitude: 5
Dimensions: 45m long
Shape: Irregular
Additional Features: Causeway 120m, 3 Internal Circular Structures, 2 Harbours

Comments: This irregular wall is 1m wide and survives up to 0.8m high.

References: RCAHMS no.206, Beveridge 1911, 56.

Ref: WA.9
Name: DUN LOCH HUNA
Island: North Uist
NGR: NF 813 669
Location: Islet
Altitude: 10
Dimensions: 70 x ?
Shape: Oval
Additional Features: Later Rectlinear Structure, Causeway 30m, Harbour, Annexe

Comments: Much of the structure is obscured by modern shooting butts but some traces of earlier wall footings can be observed.

References: RCAHMS no.204, Beveridge 1911, 185.

Ref: WA.10
Name: DUN NA CEITHIR-EILEANA
Island: North Uist
NGR: NF 8638 6260
Location: Islet
Altitude: 5
Dimensions:
Shape: Irregular
Additional Features: Possible Causeway, 3 Harbours, Internal Structure

Comments: A small cell abuts the inner side of the wall, c. 2.5m in diameter. The wall survives to 1.8m high and is 1.3m wide.

References: RCAHMS no.304, Beveridge 1911, 166.

Ref: WA.11
Name: LOCH MOR BALESHARE 1
Island: North Uist
NGR: NF 7921 6229
Location: Islet
Altitude: 5
Dimensions: 9m long
Shape: Curved
Additional Features: Causeway 28m

Comments: A massive semi-circular or D-shaped mound occupies part of this islet, surrounded by an outer wall. Three very crudely built cells are built into the outer wall.

References: RCAHMS no.176, Beveridge 1911, 182.

Ref: WA.12
Name: LOCH MOR BALESHARE 2
Island: North Uist
NGR: NF 7928 6222
Location: Islet
Altitude: 5
Dimensions: 19 x 12
Shape:
Additional Features: Causeway 11m

Comments: The wall around this islet is set 3m back from the water's edge.

References: RCAHMS no.176, Beveridge 1911, 183.

Ref: WA.13
Name: DUN SCOR
Island: North Uist
NGR: NF 8439 6209
Location: Islet
Altitude: 5
Dimensions: 60 x 40
Shape: Oval
Additional Features: Causeway 70m

Comments: Two intervening islets are crossed by the causeway to this walled site. The wall itself is 1m wide.

References: RCAHMS no.208, Beveridge 1911, 180.

Ref: WA.14
Name: DUN A GHEADAIS
Island: North Uist
NGR: NF 9136 5938
Location: Islet
Altitude: 5
Dimensions: 26 x 19
Shape: Irregular
Additional Features: Causeway 30m

Comments: The wall on this site utilises natural outcrop.

References: RCAHMS no.185, Beveridge 1911, 170

Ref: WA.15
Name: LOCH OBISARY A
Island: North Uist
NGR: NF
Location: Islet
Altitude: 5

Dimensions:
Shape:
Additional Features:

Comments: This is an overgrown steep-sided natural islet with a wall c. 1.8m wide around parts of its perimeter.

References: RCAHMS no.198, Beveridge 1911, 167/9.

Ref: WA.16
Name: LOCH OBISARY D
Island: North Uist
NGR: NF
Location: Islet
Altitude: 5
Dimensions:
Shape:
Additional Features: Later Rectilinear Structure, Causeway 20m, Harbour

Comments: This is a steep-sided peat-covered natural islet with fragmentary walling.

References: RCAHMS no.198, Beveridge 1911, 167/9.

Ref: WA.17
Name: LOCH SCADAVAY 1
Island: North Uist
NGR: NF
Location: Islet
Altitude: 5
Dimensions:
Shape:
Additional Features: 3 Harbours

Comments: A 1.6m wide wall surrounds this islet.

References: RCAHMS no.207, Beveridge 1911, 159.

Ref: WA.18
Name: DUN HERMIDALE
Island: Benbecula
NGR: NF 8262 5236
Location: Islet
Altitude: 5
Dimensions: 45 Long
Shape: Curved
Additional Features: Causeway 6m, Internal Structures

Comments: The wall appears to have been very substantial although only occupying the landward side of the islet. There appears to have been a cell in the wall at the north-east and possibly a series of structures abutting the inner wall-face.

References: RCAHMS no.363.

Ref: WA.19
Name: DUN LOCH DRUIM AN IASGAIR
Island: South Uist
NGR: NF 8036 4348
Location: Islet
Altitude: 5
Dimensions: 18 x 12
Shape: Irregular
Additional Features: Internal Circular Structures

Comments: The encircling wall is c. 1.8m wide and has two opposing entrances. A series of complex entrance features are described by the RCAHMS who class the structure as a Late Dun.

References: RCAHMS no.381.

Ref: WA.20
Name: DUN MOR 2
Island: South Uist
NGR: NF 7744 4152
Location: Islet
Altitude: 5
Dimensions:
Shape: Irregular
Additional Features: Later Baile Settlement, Causeway

Comments: The original features, if any, are obscured by a late baile settlement over the site.

References: RCAHMS no.383.

Ref: WA.21
Name: DUN EILEAN CHREAMCH
Island: South Uist
NGR: NF 7427 1919
Location: Islet
Altitude: 5
Dimensions: 27
Shape: Circular
Additional Features: Causeway 40m

Comments: This site was converted into a walled garden in 1865 obscuring the original structure.

References: RCAHMS no.421.

Ref: WA.22
Name: DUN NA KILLE
Island: South Uist
NGR: NF 7461 1905
Location: Islet
Altitude: 5
Dimensions: 40 x 30
Shape: Oval
Additional Features: Causeway 200m, 4 Internal rectilinear Structures, 2 Harbours

Comments: The surrounding wall is set slightly back from the water's edge on this overgrown site. No wallface is preserved but the rubble spread extends to c. 3m.

References: RCAHMS no.384.

Miscellaneous Structures

Ref: M.1
Name: LOCH AN DUIN, SHADER 2
Island: Lewis
NGR: NB 392 543
Location: Islet
Altitude: 5
Dimensions:
Shape: Circular
Additional Features: Causeway, 40m

Comments: This artificial islet with causeway lies adjacent to, and is clearly earlier than, an atlantic roundhouse in the same loch.

References: Armit 1985.

Ref: M.2
Name: LOCH CARLOWAY
Island: Lewis
NGR: NB 1927 4217
Location: Islet
Altitude: 0
Dimensions:
Shape:
Additional Features:

Comments: This site was a tidal islet where local memory suggested the presence of a structure which was destroyed in the construction of a pier.

References: RCAHMS no.182.

Ref: M.3
Name: NORTH TOLSTA
Island: Lewis
NGR: NB 5   4
Location: Islet
Altitude:
Dimensions:
Shape: Circular
Additional Features: Causeway, Internal Occupation

Comments: A stone and timber islet was revealed in C19th drainage operations. Few details of its structure are recorded but it appears to have had internal timber buildings.

References: Blundell 1913.

Ref: M.4
Name: BREACLETE, BERNERA
Island: Lewis
NGR: NB 1632 3643
Location: Islet
Altitude: 5
Dimensions:
Shape: Circular
Additional Features: Possible Causeway

Comments: This site is a slight stone spread on a partly natural islet, with no sign of walling or substantial structure.

References: Armit 1985.

Ref: M.5
Name: DUN BHARABHAT CROULISTA 1
Island: Lewis
NGR: NB 0401 3487
Location: Islet
Altitude: 20
Dimensions:
Shape: Irregular
Additional Features: Later Rectilinear Structure, Causeway, 30m

Comments: This is an outcrop islet with a causeway but no sign of structure prior to the rectilinear structure, although prehistoric pottery has been found around the site (Topping pers. comm.).

References: RCAHMS no.75.

Ref: M.6
Name: LOCH AIRIDH NA LIC
Island: Lewis
NGR: NB 3992 3410
Location: Islet
Altitude: 60
Dimensions: 10.5 x 8.5
Shape: Circular
Additional Features: Causeway

Comments: This is a clearly artificial stone islet with no visible structure, although there are local reports of timber structures being exposed during loch drainage operations.

References: RCAHMS no.51.

Ref: M.7
Name: LOCH ORASAY
Island: Lewis
NGR: NB 39 28
Location: Islet
Altitude: 50
Dimensions:
Shape:
Additional Features:

Comments: This artificial islet has not been relocated since originally reported.

References: Blundell 1913, 300/1.

Ref: M.8
Name: LOCHS PARISH
Island: Lewis
NGR: NB 3311 2119
Location: Islet
Altitude: 5
Dimensions:
Shape:
Additional Features: Later Rectilinear Structure, Causeway

Comments: This islet has a causeway but no visible original structure.

References: NMR.

Ref: M.9
Name: LOCH ARNISH
Island: Lewis
NGR: NB
Location: Islet
Altitude:
Dimensions:
Shape:
Additional Features:

Comments: This site was recorded as a stony artificial islet with no visible structure.

References: Blundell 1913.

Ref: M.10
Name: DUN BORAIGEO
Island: Harris
NGR: NF 0307 8372
Location: Coastal
Altitude: 5
Dimensions:
Shape: Curved
Additional Features:

Comments: A 6m long arc of walling is preserved on this coastal outcrop but there is insufficient space for this to have formed part of a roundhouse of any size.

References: RCAHMS no.143.

Ref: M.11
Name: EILEAN AN DUNAIN
Island: North Uist
NGR: NF 8956 7997
Location: Islet
Altitude: 0
Dimensions: 11
Shape: Circular
Additional Features:

Comments: This is a stony mound on a rocky tidal islet some 1.5m in height. There is no visible structure preserved although the RCAHMS did report substantial quantities of stone so the site cannot be discounted as a destroyed roundhouse.

References: RCAHMS no.120.

Ref: M.12
Name: DUNAN RUADH
Island: North Uist
NGR: NF 8463 7657
Location: Islet
Altitude: 5
Dimensions:
Shape:
Additional Features:

Comments: The place name suggests former occupation although there is no visible sign preserved.

References: RCAHMS no.323, Beveridge 1911, 224.

Ref: M.13
Name: EILEAN DOMHNUILL
Island: North Uist
NGR: NF 7468 7532
Location: Islet
Altitude: 5
Dimensions:
Shape:
Additional Features: Causeway 41m

Comments: This site is an artificial stony islet with a causeway. On excavation it has proved to be wholly of Early Neolithic date.

References: Armit 1986/89.

Ref: M.14
Name: LOMBAIDH
Island: North Uist
NGR: NF 7 7
Location: Islet
Altitude: 5
Dimensions:
Shape:
Additional Features: Later Occupation

Comments: This site is a tidal islet with several relatively recent rectilinear structures.

References: Beveridge 1911, 214.

Ref: M.15
Name: EILEAN AN ACAIRE
Island: North Uist
NGR: NF 7 7
Location: Islet
Altitude: 5
Dimensions:
Shape:
Additional Features:

Comments: This tidal islet had traces of former walling which seemed too slight to represent a substantial structure.

References: Beveridge 1911, 214.

Ref: M.16
Name: OBAN SKIBINISH 2
Island: North Uist
NGR: NF 83 75
Location: Islet
Altitude: O
Dimensions:
Shape: Irregular
Additional Features:

Comments: This tidal islet had traces of walling on its south-east side which seemed too slight to represent a substantial structure.

References: RCAHMS no.182, Beveridge 1911, 220/1.

Ref: M.17
Name: DUNAN DUBH
Island: North Uist
NGR: NF 8904 7454
Location: Islet
Altitude: 5
Dimensions:
Shape:
Additional Features: Causeway 40m, Outer Wall

Comments: This site is a mound with fragmentary traces of a surrounding wall.

References: RCAHMS no.200, Beveridge 1911, 149.

Ref: M.18
Name: DUN LOCH NA GEARRACHAN A
Island: North Uist
NGR: NF 7659 7440
Location: Islet
Altitude: 5
Dimensions: 10 x 8
Shape: Oval
Additional Features: Causeway 35m

Comments: This site is a stony mound with no visible structure.

References: RCAHMS no.195, Beveridge 1911, 198, Blundell 1913, 298.

Ref: M.19
Name: DUN LOCH NA GEARRACHAN B
Island: North Uist
NGR: NF 7674 7419
Location: Islet
Altitude: 5
Dimensions: 10 x 7.6
Shape: Oval
Additional Features: Causeway 25m

Comments: This site is a stony mound with no visible structure.

References: RCAHMS no.195, Beveridge 1911, 199, Blundell 1913, 298.

Ref: M.20
Name: DUN LOCH AN DUIN
Island: North Uist
NGR: NF 8927 7416
Location: Islet
Altitude: 5
Dimensions: 14 x 11
Shape: Oval
Additional Features: Causeway 60m

Comments: This site is a partly artificial islet utilising outcrop rock. It is connected to the shore by a zigzag causeway

References: RCAHMS no.201, Beveridge 1911, 152.

Ref: M.21
Name: LOCH NAN GEIRRANN
Island: North Uist
NGR: NF 8465 7278
Location: Islet
Altitude: 5
Dimensions: 5
Shape: Circular
Additional Features: Causeway

Comments: Pottery and hammerstones were found on this site, which lacks visible structure. A probable causeway runs to the shore across a low sandy spit.

References: Beveridge 1911, 222.

Ref: M.22
Name: BAC A STOC
Island: North Uist
NGR: NF 9006 7244
Location: Islet
Altitude: 0
Dimensions: 26 x 12
Shape: Oval
Additional Features:

Comments: This is a rocky tidal islet with no trace of structure, although slight walling was reported by Beveridge.

References: RCAHMS no.303, Beveridge 1911, 153.

Ref: M.23
Name: DUN EASHADER
Island: North Uist
NGR: NF 80 72
Location: Islet
Altitude: 30
Dimensions: 16 x 12
Shape: Oval
Additional Features: Causeway?

Comments: This is an artificial islet for which the causeway is no longer visible.

References: RCAHMS no.194, Beveridge 1911, 218/9.

Ref: M.24
Name: DUN LOCH NA CANLICH
Island: North Uist
NGR: NF 9640 7192
Location: Islet
Altitude: 5
Dimensions:
Shape:
Additional Features:

Comments: Despite a local tradition of a site here there is no visible trace.

References: Beveridge 1911, 149.

Ref: M.25
Name: EILEAN MOSSAM
Island: North Uist
NGR: NF 8723 7154
Location: Islet
Altitude: 10
Dimensions: 23 x 16
Shape: Oval
Additional Features:

Comments: This is a somewhat dubious reference to a possible occupied islet of which no trace has since been relocated.

References: Beveridge 1911, 154.

Ref: M.26
Name: DUN LOCH VAUSARY
Island: North Uist
NGR: NF 7489 7019

Location: Islet
Altitude: 10
Dimensions:
Shape:
Additional Features: Causeway 60m

Comments: This is an overgrown islet some 18m in diameter with no visible trace of structure.

References: RCAHMS no.317, Beveridge 1911, 189.

Ref: M.27
Name: LOCH NA BUAILE
Island: North Uist
NGR: NF 9073 7004
Location: Islet
Altitude: 5
Dimensions: 29 x 10
Shape: Irregular
Additional Features: Causeway 35m

Comments: This is a high, wooded islet with no trace of structure.

References: RCAHMS no.301, Beveridge 1911, 155.

Ref: M.28
Name: OB NAN STEARNAIN
Island: North Uist
NGR: NF 9117 6873
Location: Islet
Altitude: 10
Dimensions:
Shape:
Additional Features:

Comments: Walling was recorded on this rocky outcrop islet but had disappeared by 1965.

References: Beveridge 1911, 156.

Ref: M.29
Name: LOCHMADDY
Island: North Uist
NGR: NF 9042 6864
Location: Islet
Altitude: 5
Dimensions: 10 x 9
Shape: Circular
Additional Features:

Comments: This islet has a stone spread which may be natural and the causeway reported by Beveridge appears very likely to be natural.

References: Beveridge 1911, 157.

Ref: M.30
Name: LOCHMADDY B
Island: North Uist
NGR: NF 9003 6763
Location: Islet
Altitude: 10
Dimensions: 12.8 x 7.3
Shape:
Additional Features: Causeway

Comments: No visible structure is apparent on this islet site.

References: Beveridge 1911, 160.

Ref: M.31
Name: DUN DEORAVAT
Island: North Uist
NGR: NF 8889 6609
Location: Islet
Altitude: 5
Dimensions: 12 x 3.5
Shape:
Additional Features: Causeway?

Comments: The very small size of this islet makes it unlikely that it was ever occupied by a substantial structure unless loch levels have changed greatly.

References: Beveridge 1911, 159.

Ref: M.32
Name: ARD BHEAG
Island: North Uist
NGR: NF 9067 6425
Location: Islet
Altitude: 5
Dimensions:
Shape: Circular
Additional Features:

Comments: This site survives a grassed over, low mound on a tidal islet.

References: Beveridge 1911, 162.

Ref: M.33
Name: LOCH MOR BALESHARE 4
Island: North Uist
NGR: NF 7903 6208
Location: Islet
Altitude: 5
Dimensions:
Shape: Irregular
Additional Features: Causeway 42m

Comments: A massive causeway leads out to an artificial stone islet with no trace of structure.

References: RCAHMS no.176, Beveridge 1911, 183.

Ref: M.34
Name: LOCH MOR BALESHARE 3
Island: North Uist
NGR: NF 7908 6202
Location: Islet
Altitude: 5
Dimensions:
Shape: Irregular
Additional Features: Causeway 17m

Comments: A short causeway leads to an apparently natural islet with no trace of structure.

References: RCAHMS no.176, Beveridge 1911, 183.

Ref: M.35
Name: DUN LOCH AN IASGAICH
Island: North Uist
NGR: NF 82 62
Location: Islet
Altitude: 5
Dimensions:
Shape:
Additional Features: Causeway 20m

Comments: Very little information is available on this site which appears to be a causewayed islet with little evidence for a major stone structure.

References: Beveridge 1911, 181.

Ref: M.36
Name: EILEAN NAN TIGHEAN
Island: North Uist
NGR: NF 8169 5971
Location: Islet
Altitude: 5
Dimensions:
Shape:
Additional Features: Later Occupation, Causeway 30m

Comments: This is a causewayed islet with no evidence for primary prehistoric occupation.

References: Beveridge 1911, 288.

Ref: M.37
Name: DUN LOCH AN FHAING
Island: North Uist
NGR: NF 8450 5757
Location: Islet
Altitude: 5
Dimensions:
Shape:
Additional Features: Causeway?

Comments: This site survives as a low stony mound in the centre of a loch.

References: RCAHMS no.308.

Ref: M.38
Name: DUN LOCH HORNERAY
Island: North Uist
NGR: NF 8653 5720
Location: Islet
Altitude: 10
Dimensions:
Shape:
Additional Features: Causeway?

Comments: This is an islet with a low stony spread.

References: Beveridge 1911, 175.

Ref: M.39
Name: DUN BAN, GRIMSAY 2
Island: North Uist
NGR: NF 8597 5665
Location: Islet
Altitude: 10

Dimensions:
Shape:
Additional Features: Causeway?

Comments: This site is an overgrown rocky islet with slight walling filling gaps in the outcrop.

References: RCAHMS no.307, Beveridge 1911, 175.

Ref: M.40
Name: DUN LOCH A MHUILINN
Island: North Uist
NGR: NF 8737 5553
Location: Islet
Altitude: 15
Dimensions:
Shape: Oval
Additional Features: Causeway

Comments: The causeway to this islet utilises two intervening islets. All of the islets have low stony spreads.

References: RCAHMS no.306, Beveridge 1911, 175.

Ref: M.41
Name: SRUATHAN BEAG, RONAY
Island: North Uist
NGR: NF 8972 5520
Location: Islet
Altitude: 10
Dimensions:
Shape:
Additional Features: Causeway?

Comments: A possible submerged causeway leads out to an islet with no apparent structure.

References: RCAHMS no.305, Beveridge 1911, 177.

Ref: M.42
Name: LOCH OBISARY B
Island: North Uist
NGR: NF
Location: Islet
Altitude: 5
Dimensions:
Shape: Circular
Additional Features:

Comments: This is a partly submerged stony mound with traces of slight walling.

References: RCAHMS no.198, Beveridge 1911, 167/9.

Ref: M.43
Name: GRAMSDALE
Island: Benbecula
NGR: NF 8121 5486
Location: Islet
Altitude: 5
Dimensions:
Shape:
Additional Features: Causeway

Comments: The site is reported as lying near the west shore of Loch Olabhat, Benbecula, connected to the shore by a submerged causeway. No further details are available.

References: NMR.

Ref: M.44
Name: DUN BOROSDALE
Island: Benbecula
NGR: NF 7814 5285
Location: Islet
Altitude: 5
Dimensions:
Shape:
Additional Features:

Comments: This site is a submerged islet, now impossible to verify without underwater survey. It was reported as being vegetation covered and locally known as a dun.

References: RCAHMS no.364.

Ref: M.45
Name: DUN SAIBH
Island: Benbecula
NGR: NF 8638 4978
Location:
Altitude: 5
Dimensions:
Shape:
Additional Features:

Comments: No details are known of this site which may not be an antiquity.

References: NMR

Ref: M.46
Name: DUN LOCH AN DUIN, MHOIR
Island: South Uist
NGR: NF 7593 4671
Location: Islet
Altitude: 5
Dimensions:
Shape:
Additional Features:

Comments: The site of this islet is now occupied by a croft in a drained loch.

References: RCAHMS no.428.

Ref: M.47
Name: DUN LOCHAN NAN CARRANAN
Island: South Uist
NGR: NF 7838 4584
Location: Islet
Altitude: 5
Dimensions: 13 x 12
Shape: Oval
Additional Features:

Comments: This site appears to be a substantially artificial islet with no trace of walling.

References: RCAHMS no.429.

Ref: M.48
Name: LOCH CEANN A BHAIGH
Island: South Uist
NGR: NF 76   30
Location: Islet
Altitude: 5
Dimensions:
Shape:
Additional Features:

Comments: This site was reported as a crannog to Blundell but not visited by him and has not since been relocated.

References: Blundell 1913, 295.

Ref: M.49
Name: DUN LOCH AN EILEAN
Island: South Uist
NGR: NF 7450 2376
Location: Islet
Altitude: 5
Dimensions:
Shape:
Additional Features: Causeway

Comments: This is an overgrown and inaccessible islet with a partly natural submerged causeway.

References: RCAHMS no.419.

Ref: M.50
Name: DUN SGEIR GHLAS
Island: South Uist
NGR: NF 7515 2091
Location: Islet
Altitude: 5
Dimensions: 17
Shape: Circular
Additional Features: Causeway

Comments: This site is an artificial islet, some 1.5m high with no sign of actual structure.

References: RCAHMS no.422, Blundell 1913, 294.

Ref: M.51
Name: DUN AN DUICHAL
Island: South Uist
NGR: NF 7431 1885
Location: Islet
Altitude: 5
Dimensions:
Shape:
Additional Features: Later Rectilinear Structures

Comments: This artificial islet has no visible causeway and no structure other than a secondary small rectilinear structure.

References: RCAHMS no.431.

Ref: M.52
Name: LOCH ARD, BORNISH
Island: South Uist
NGR: NF
Location: Islet
Altitude:
Dimensions:
Shape:
Additional Features:

Comments: This artificial islet was recorded by Blundell but has not since been relocated.

References: Blundell 1913, 294.

Appendix Four - Structural Data used in Chapter Eleven

Atlantic Roundhouses

Mean = Mean external diameter (m)   Wall% = Wall base percentage
Int = Internal diameter (m)   Area = Internal area (m^2)

North Uist

Site Name	Mean	Wall%	Int	Area
Dun an Sticer	18.5	34.1	12.2	116.9
Dun Iosal an Duin				
Rudh an Duin	24	41.7	14	153.94
Dun a Ghallain				
Dun Rosail				
Eilean a Ghallain	12.75	40	7.65	45.96
Dun Thomaidh	14.6			
Oban Skibinish 1				
Dun Skellor	18.5			
Dun Scolpaig				
Dun Toloman				
Oban Trumisgarry				
Garry Iochdrach	14.6	46	7.9	49.02
Cnoc a Comhdhalach	11.6	39.7	7	38.48
Dun na Mairbhe	18.6	62.4	7	38.48
Dun Bru				
Eilean Maleit	16	50	8	50.27
Dun Aonghais				
Dun Torcuill	17.5	34.3	11.5	103.87
Buaile Risary				
Dun Loch na Caiginn	12			
Dun Loch Cnoc nan Uan				
Dun Grogarry	18	55.6	8	50.27
South Clettraval	13			
Dun Mhic Raouill	12.75	42.7	7.3	41.85
An Chaisteil				
Dun Scarie				
Sithean Tuath				
Srath Beag an Duin	12			
Eilean Dubh	13			
Dun Loch Shanndaidh				
Dun Steingarry				
Dun Leiraray				
Dun Loch Hunder	11.5	43.5	6.5	33.18
Dun Loch nan Strubhan				
Dun Nighean R. Lochlainn	10			
Dunan Mor				
Dun Bailleray				
Dun Mor				
Dun na Dise	17	47.1	9	63.62
Dun na h Ola				
Beinn na Coille	19.75			
Eilean Scalaster	9	51.1	4.4	15.21
Dun Ban Hacklett	9			
Loch Obisary C	20			
Dun an t-Siamain	13.4			
Dun Loch nan Gealag				
Dun Cheirein				
Rudh an Duin Eaval				
Dun Ban Grimsay 1	15	53.3	7	38.48

Barra

Site Name	Mean	Wall%	Int	Area
Dunan Ruadh				
Dun Scurrival	15			
Dun Chlif	14	46	7.5	44.18
Dun Cuier	19.5	53.8	9	63.62
Dun Loch an Duin	14.9	49	7.6	45.36
Baigh Hirivagh 1				
Baigh Hirivagh 2	12			
Dun Loch nic Ruaidhe				
Dun na Kille	16			
Dun an t'Sleibh				
Bal na Craig	16	56.3	7	38.48
Dun Ban	18	44.4	10	78.54
Dun Mhic Leoid				
Beinn Tangavat	16.5	36.4	10.5	86.59
Dun a Chaolais	16	45	8.8	60.82
Dun Vatersay	15			
Dun Sandray	14.1	41.1	8.3	54.11
Dunan Ruadh Pabbay				

Wheelhouses

Piers = Number of piers
Diameter = Internal diameter
Cent. = Central area diameter
Area = Internal area

Site Name	Piers	Diameter	Cent.	Area
Cnip 1	8	7	3.2	38.5
Cnip 2		7		38.5
Udal	11	9.8	6	75.4
Foshigarry A	10.5	6		86.6
Foshigarry B	10.5	5.5		86.6
Foshigarry C				
Bac Mhic Connain	8	9	3.5	63.6
Sollas	12	12	7.5	113.1
Garry Iochdrach	7	7.9	4	49
Cnoc a Comhdhalach	7	7	3.5	38.5
Eilean Maleit	9	8	3.6	50.3
Clettraval	8	7.5	4.3	44.2
Bruach Ban	8	10		78.5
Bruthach a Tuath	10	8.8	6	60.8
Hornish Point	7.5			44.2
A Cheardach Mhor	11	10.8	6.8	91.6
A Cheardach Bheag	12	9	5.5	63.6
Usinish	10	9	5	63.6
Kilpheder	11	8.8	5.5	60.8
Allasdale	7	8	4	50.2